ADOBE® ILLUSTRATOR® CS4

CLASSROOM IN A BOOK®

The official training workbook from Adobe Systems

www.adobepress.com

Adobe

WHAT'S ON THE DISC

Here is an overview of the contents of the Classroom in a Book disc

Lesson files … and so much more

The *Adobe Illustrator CS4 Classroom in a Book* disc includes the lesson files that you'll need to complete the exercises in this book, as well as other content to help you learn more about Adobe Illustrator CS4 and use it with greater efficiency and ease. The diagram below represents the contents of the disc, which should help you locate the files you need.

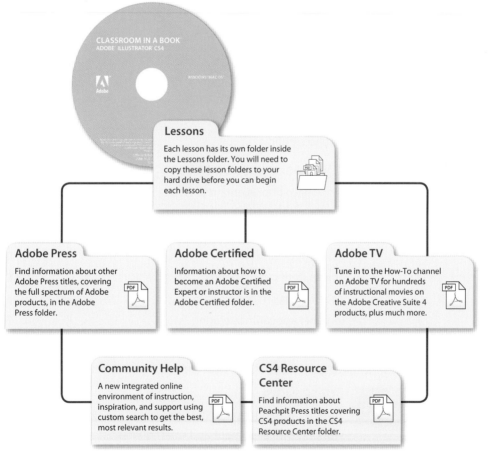

Lessons

Each lesson has its own folder inside the Lessons folder. You will need to copy these lesson folders to your hard drive before you can begin each lesson.

Adobe Press

Find information about other Adobe Press titles, covering the full spectrum of Adobe products, in the Adobe Press folder.

Adobe Certified

Information about how to become an Adobe Certified Expert or instructor is in the Adobe Certified folder.

Adobe TV

Tune in to the How-To channel on Adobe TV for hundreds of instructional movies on the Adobe Creative Suite 4 products, plus much more.

Community Help

A new integrated online environment of instruction, inspiration, and support using custom search to get the best, most relevant results.

CS4 Resource Center

Find information about Peachpit Press titles covering CS4 products in the CS4 Resource Center folder.

CONTENTS

GETTING STARTED

About Classroom in a Book. 1

Prerequisites. 1

Installing the program 2

Fonts used in this book 2

Copying the Classroom in a Book files 2

To install the Classroom in a Book files. 2

Restoring default preferences 3

To save current Illustrator preferences 3

To delete current Illustrator preferences 4

To restore saved preferences after completing the lessons. . . . 4

Additional resources 4

Adobe certification 5

WHAT'S NEW IN ADOBE ILLUSTRATOR CS4

Workspace improvements 6

Multiple artboards 7

Smart guides 7

Gradient enhancements 8

Transparency in gradients. 8

The Blob Brush tool 8

In-panel appearance editing 9

Enriched Graphic Styles panel 9

A QUICK TOUR OF ADOBE ILLUSTRATOR CS4

Getting started 12

Working with multiple artboards 12

Working with alignment and smart guides. 14

Working with the Blob Brush tool. 16

Placing Adobe Photoshop images in Illustrator CS4 17

Using Live Trace 17

Using Live Paint. 18

Working with color groups and Edit Color/Recolor Artwork . 19

Working with type 20

Using the Appearance panel 20

Saving the appearance as a graphic style 21

Applying warp to the text 22

Creating and editing a gradient 22

Working with symbols 24

Creating a clipping mask. 25

1   GETTING TO KNOW THE WORK AREA

Lesson overview 26

Getting started 28

Understanding the workspace 31

Working with the Tools panel. 32

The Control panel. 35

Working with panels 36

Using panel menus 40

Resetting and saving your workspace 41

Changing the view of artwork 42

Viewing artwork 42

Using the view commands 43

Using the Zoom tool 44

Scrolling through a document 45

Navigating multiple artboards 45

Arranging documents. 47

Document groups 50

Using the Navigator panel 52

Finding Resources for using Illustrator 54

Searching for a topic in Help 54

Checking for updates 55

Exploring on your own. 56

2 SELECTING AND ALIGNING

Lesson overview 60

Getting started 62

Using the Selection tool 62

Using the Direct Selection tool 63

Creating selections with a marquee 65

Creating selections with the Magic Wand tool 66

Grouping items 66

Adding to a group 66

Working in isolation mode 68

Selecting similar objects 68

Applying selection techniques 69

Advanced selection techniques 71

Aligning objects 73

Aligning to a key object 73

Aligning points 74

Distributing objects 74

Aligning to the artboard 75

Exploring on your own 76

3 CREATING AND EDITING SHAPES

Lesson overview 78

Getting started 80

Creating a document with multiple artboards 80

Working with basic shapes 83

Accessing the basic shape tools 83

Creating with shapes 84

Outlining strokes 91

Working with line segments 93

Joining paths 94

Using the Eraser tool 96

Combining objects 98

Working with Pathfinder effects 99

Working with shape modes 100

Using Live Trace to create shapes 103

Exploring on your own 106

4   TRANSFORMING OBJECTS

Lesson overview 108

Getting started 110

Working with artboards 111

Adding artboards to the document 111

Editing artboards 112

Transforming content 115

Working with rulers and guides 115

Scaling objects 116

Reflecting objects 118

Rotating objects 119

Distorting objects 120

Shearing objects 123

Positioning objects precisely 124

Changing the perspective 125

Using the Free Distort effect 127

Making multiple transformations 128

Exploring on your own 129

5   DRAWING WITH THE PEN AND PENCIL TOOLS

Lesson overview 132

Getting started 134

Creating straight lines 136

Creating curved paths 137

Building a curve 139

Converting curved points to corner points 140

Creating the apple illustration 143

Creating the arrow 144

Splitting a path 145

Adding arrowheads 146

Drawing curves 147

Selecting a curve 147

Drawing the leaf 147

Drawing different kinds of curves 148

Convert between smooth points and corner points 150

Drawing the apple shape 151

Editing curves 153

Deleting and adding anchor points. 155

Drawing with the Pencil tool 156

Editing with the Pencil tool. 158

Finishing the apple illustration 160

Assembling the parts 160

Painting the artwork 161

Exploring on your own. 162

6   COLOR AND PAINTING

Lesson overview 164

Getting started 166

Understanding color. 167

Color modes. 167

Understanding the color controls 168

Creating color 170

Building and saving a custom color. 170

Editing a swatch 171

Using Illustrator swatch libraries. 172

Creating a spot color. 172

Using the Color Picker. 174

Creating and saving a tint of a color 175

Copying attributes. 175

Creating color groups. 176

Working with the Color Guide panel. 177

Editing a color group. 178

Editing colors in artwork 181

Working with the Kuler panel 182

Assigning colors to your artwork 184

Adjusting colors 188

Painting with gradients and patterns 189

Using patterns. 189

Creating your own pattern 191

Applying a pattern. 192

Editing a pattern. 192

Working with Live Paint 194

Editing Live Paint regions 196

Exploring on your own. 198

7   WORKING WITH TYPE

Lesson overview. 202

Getting started 204

Working with type 205

Creating point type 205

Creating area type 206

Importing a plain text file 207

Creating columns of text. 208

Understanding text flow 209

Working with overflow text and text reflow. 210

Threading text. 211

Resizing type objects 212

Formatting type 214

Changing the font size 216

Changing the font color. 217

Changing additional text attributes 217

Changing paragraph attributes. 219

Saving and using styles 221

Creating and using a paragraph style. 221

Creating and using a character style. 222

Sampling text 223

Reshaping text with an envelope warp 224

Wrapping text around an object. 227

Creating text on paths and shapes. 227

Creating text outlines 230

Exploring on your own. 232

8   WORKING WITH LAYERS

Lesson overview. 234

Getting started 236

Creating layers 237

Moving objects and layers 239

Locking layers 241

Viewing layers 242

Pasting layers...244

Creating clipping masks....................................247

Merging layers...248

Applying appearance attributes to layers 250

Isolating layers..252

Exploring on your own......................................254

9 BLENDING SHAPES AND COLORS

Lesson overview 258

Getting started 260

Working with gradients 261

Creating and applying a linear gradient....................261

Adjusting the direction and angle of a gradient blend......264

Creating a radial gradient 265

Changing colors and adjusting the gradient 266

Applying gradients to multiple objects 269

Adding transparency to gradients 273

Working with blended objects 275

Creating a blend with specified steps......................276

Modifying the blend 277

Creating smooth color blends 279

Exploring on your own......................................281

10 WORKING WITH BRUSHES

Lesson overview 284

Getting started 286

Working with the Blob Brush tool...........................287

Drawing with the Blob Brush tool 287

Editing with the Blob Brush and Eraser tools 288

Merge paths with the Blob Brush tool 290

Working with brushes.......................................292

Using Art brushes..292

Drawing with the Paintbrush tool 293

Editing paths with the Paintbrush tool.....................295

Using Scatter brushes......................................297

Changing brush options 297

Applying a Scatter brush to paths 299

Changing the color attributes of brushes 300

Changing the brush color using Hue Shift colorization 301

Changing the brush color using Tints colorization. 302

Using a fill color with brushes 304

Using Calligraphic brushes 305

Using Pattern brushes. 307

Creating brushes 310

Creating swatches for a Pattern brush 310

Creating a Pattern brush from swatches 311

Painting with the Pattern brush 312

Applying the Scribble effect. 314

Exploring on your own. 316

The Blob Brush tool 316

Applying brushes. 316

Creating brushes 316

11 APPLYING EFFECTS

Lesson overview 320

Getting started 322

Using live effects. 322

Applying an effect 323

Editing an effect 327

Creating a banner logo with the Warp effect 329

Creating the logotype. 329

Stylizing the banner and logotype. 330

Creating the 3D cylinder 333

Using the 3D Extrude & Bevel effect 334

Applying a symbol as mapped artwork 336

Creating a revolved object 338

Changing the lighting. 340

Mapping a Photoshop image. 341

Adjusting the lighting. 342

Exploring on your own. 343

12 APPLYING APPEARANCE ATTRIBUTES AND GRAPHIC STYLES

Lesson overview 346

Getting started 348

Using appearance attributes 349

Editing and adding appearance attributes 349

Reordering appearance attributes 351

Adding an additional stroke and fill 352

Using graphic styles 353

Creating and saving a graphic style 354

Applying a graphic style to an object 355

Applying a graphic style to a layer 355

Applying existing graphic styles 358

Adding to an existing graphic style 360

Applying an appearance to a layer 361

Copying, applying, and removing graphic styles 362

Exploring on your own 364

13 WORKING WITH SYMBOLS

Lesson overview 368

Getting started 370

Working with symbols 371

Using Illustrator symbol libraries 371

Creating symbols 373

Spraying symbol instances 375

Editing symbol sets using the symbolism tools 377

Editing symbols 378

Updating a symbol 380

Breaking a link to a symbol 380

Replacing symbols 382

Storing and retrieving artwork in the Symbols panel 383

Mapping a symbol to 3D artwork 384

Symbols and Flash integration 384

Exploring on your own 388

14 COMBINING ILLUSTRATOR CS4 GRAPHICS WITH OTHER ADOBE APPLICATIONS

Lesson overview 390

Getting started 392

Working with Adobe Bridge 392

Combining artwork 395

Vector versus bitmap graphics 395

Editing the artboard 396

Placing an Adobe Photoshop file 397

About layer comps. 398

Editing and duplicating a placed image. 400

Applying color edits to a placed image 401

Masking an image 402

Applying a clipping mask to an image 403

Creating compound paths and opacity masks 404

Editing an imported mask. 407

Sampling colors in placed images 408

Replacing a placed image 409

Exporting a layered file to Adobe Photoshop 410

Placing Illustrator files in Adobe InDesign. 411

Integrating Illustrator and Adobe Flash 413

Creating Illustrator files for Adobe Flex 415

Exploring on your own. 416

15 OUTPUT

Lesson overview 418

Getting started 420

Understanding the printing process 420

Understanding printing devices 422

Halftone screens. 422

Screen frequency 422

Output device resolution. 423

About color. 423

RGB color model. 424

CMYK color model 424

Spot colors 424

What is color management?..............................424

Setting up color management in Illustrator 427

Soft-proofing colors 428

Color separations 429

Previewing color separations............................429

Printing color separations...............................430

Specifying the bleed area 432

Separating colors 434

Specifying the screen frequency.........................436

Working with two-color illustrations.....................437

Separating spot colors 437

Understanding trapping 439

Overprinting objects 440

Saving and exporting artwork...........................443

Using the Document Info panel 443

Saving a file with transparency 444

Saving in the EPS format 444

Printing transparent artwork 445

Saving as Adobe PDF 446

Index...450

GETTING STARTED

Adobe® Illustrator® CS4 is the industry-standard illustration application for print, multimedia, and online graphics. Whether you are a designer or a technical illustrator producing artwork for print publishing, an artist producing multimedia graphics, or a creator of web pages or online content, Adobe Illustrator offers you the tools you need to get professional-quality results.

About Classroom in a Book

Adobe Illustrator CS4 Classroom in a Book® is part of the official training series for Adobe graphics and publishing software from Adobe Systems, Inc.

The lessons are designed so that you can learn at your own pace. If you're new to Adobe Illustrator, you'll learn the fundamentals you need to master to put the application to work. If you are an experienced user, you'll find that *Classroom in a Book* teaches many advanced features, including tips and techniques for using the latest version of Adobe Illustrator.

Although each lesson provides step-by-step instructions for creating a specific project, there's room for exploration and experimentation. You can follow the book from start to finish, or do only the lessons that correspond to your interests and needs. Each lesson concludes with a review section summarizing what you've covered.

Prerequisites

Before beginning to use *Adobe Illustrator CS4 Classroom in a Book*, you should have working knowledge of your computer and its operating system. Make sure that you know how to use the mouse and standard menus and commands, and also how to open, save, and close files. If you need to review these techniques, see the printed or online documentation for your Windows or Mac OS.

⬤ **Note:** When instructions differ by platform, Windows commands appear first, and then the Mac OS commands, with the platform noted in parentheses. For example, "press Alt (Windows) or Option (Mac OS) and click away from the artwork." In some instances, common commands may be abbreviated with the Windows commands first, followed by a slash and the Mac OS commands, without any parenthetical reference. For example, "press Alt/Option" or "press Ctrl/Command+click."

Installing the program

Before you begin using *Adobe Illustrator CS4 Classroom in a Book*, make sure that your system is set up correctly and that you've installed the required software and hardware.

The Adobe Illustrator CS4 software is not included on the Classroom in a Book CD; you must purchase the software separately. For complete instructions on installing the software, see the Adobe Illustrator Read Me file on the application DVD or on the web at www.adobe.com/support.

Fonts used in this book

The Classroom in a Book lesson files use the fonts that come with Adobe Illustrator CS4 and install with the product for your convenience. These fonts are installed in the following locations:

• Windows: [startup drive]\Windows\Fonts\

• Mac OS X: [startup drive]/Library/Fonts/

For more information about fonts and installation, see the Adobe Illustrator CS4 Read Me file on the application DVD or on the web at www.adobe.com/support.

Copying the Classroom in a Book files

The Classroom in a Book CD includes folders containing all the electronic files for the lessons. Each lesson has its own folder. You must install these folders on your hard disk to use the files for the lessons. To save room on your hard disk, you can install the folder for each lesson as you need it.

To install the Classroom in a Book files

1 Insert the Classroom in a Book CD into your CD-ROM drive.

2 Do one of the following:

• Copy the entire Lessons folder onto your hard disk.

• Copy only the specific lesson folder that you need onto your hard disk.

Restoring default preferences

The preferences file controls how command settings appear on your screen when you open the Adobe Illustrator program. Each time you quit Adobe Illustrator, the position of the panels and certain command settings are recorded in different preference files. If you want to restore the tools and settings to their original default settings, you can delete the current Adobe Illustrator CS4 preferences file. Adobe Illustrator creates a new preferences file, if one doesn't already exist, the next time you start the program and save a file.

You must restore the default preferences for Illustrator before you begin each lesson. This ensures that the tools and panels function as described in this book. When you have finished the book, you can restore your saved settings.

To save current Illustrator preferences

1 Exit Adobe Illustrator CS4.

2 Locate the AIPrefs (Windows) or Adobe Illustrator Prefs (Mac OS) file, as follows.

- (Windows XP) The AIPrefs file is located in the folder [startup drive]\ Documents and Settings\[username]\Application Data\Adobe\Adobe Illustrator CS4 Settings\en_US*.

- (Windows Vista) The AIPrefs file is located in the folder [startup drive]\ Users\[username]\AppData\Roaming\Adobe\Adobe Illustrator CS4 Settings\en_US*.

- (Mac OS X) The Adobe Illustrator Prefs file is located in the folder [startup drive]/Users/[username]/Library/Preferences/Adobe Illustrator CS4 Settings/en_US*.

*Folder name may be different depending on the language version you have installed.

● **Note:** If you cannot locate the preferences file, use your operating system's Find command, and search for AIPrefs (Windows) or Adobe Illustrator Prefs (Mac OS).

If you can't find the file, you either haven't started Adobe Illustrator CS4 yet or you have moved the preferences file. The preferences file is created after you quit the program the first time and is updated thereafter.

3 Copy the file and save it to another folder on your hard disk.

4 Start Adobe Illustrator CS4.

▶ **Tip:** To quickly locate and delete the Adobe Illustrator preferences file each time you begin a new lesson, create a shortcut (Windows) or an alias (Mac OS) to the Illustrator CS4 Settings folder.

To delete current Illustrator preferences

1 Exit Adobe Illustrator CS4.

2 Locate the AIPrefs (Windows) or Adobe Illustrator Prefs (Mac OS) file, as follows.

- (Windows XP) The AIPrefs file is located in the folder [startup drive]\ Documents and Settings\[username]\Application Data\Adobe\Adobe Illustrator CS4 Settings\en_US*.

- (Windows Vista) The AIPrefs file is located in the folder [startup drive]\ Users\[username]\AppData\Roaming\Adobe\Adobe Illustrator CS4 Settings\en_US*.

- (Mac OS X) The Adobe Illustrator Prefs file is located in the folder [startup drive]/Users/[username]/Library/Preferences/Adobe Illustrator CS4 Settings/en_US*.

*Folder name may be different depending on the language version you have installed.

3 Delete the preferences file.

4 Start Adobe Illustrator CS4.

Note: In Windows XP, the Application Data folder is hidden by default. The same is true for the AppData folder in Windows Vista. To make either one visible, open Folder Options in Control Panel and click the View tab. In the Advanced Settings pane, find Hidden Files and folders and select the Show Hidden Files and Folders button.

To restore saved preferences after completing the lessons

1 Exit Adobe Illustrator CS4.

2 Delete the current preferences file. Find the original preferences file that you saved and move it to the Adobe Illustrator CS4 Settings folder.

Note: You can move the original preferences file rather than renaming it.

Additional resources

Adobe Illustrator CS4 Classroom in a Book is not meant to replace documentation that comes with the program or to be a comprehensive reference for every feature in Illustrator CS4. Only the commands and options used in the lessons are explained in this book. For comprehensive information about program features, refer to any of these resources:

- Adobe Illustrator CS4 Community Help, which you can view by choosing Help > Illustrator Help. Community Help is an integrated online environment of instruction, inspiration, and support. It includes custom search of expert-selected, relevant content on and off Adobe.com. Community Help combines content from Adobe Help, Support, Design Center, Developer Connection, and Forums—along with great online community content so that users can easily find the best and most up-to-date resources. Access tutorials, technical support, online product help, videos, articles, tips and techniques, blogs, examples, and much more.

- Adobe Illustrator CS4 Support Center, where you can find and browse support and learning content on Adobe.com. Visit www.adobe.com/support/illustrator/.

- Adobe TV, where you will find programming on Adobe products, including a channel for professional photographers and a How To channel that contains hundreds of movies on Illustrator CS4 and other products across the Adobe Creative Suite 4 lineup. Visit http://tv.adobe.com/.

Also check out these useful links:

- The Illustrator CS4 product home page at www.adobe.com/products/illustrator/.

- Illustrator user forums at www.adobe.com/support/forums/ for peer-to-peer discussions of Adobe products.

- Illustrator Exchange at www.adobe.com/cfusion/exchange/ for extensions, functions, code, and more.

- Illustrator plug-ins at www.adobe.com/products/plugins/illustrator/.

Adobe certification

The Adobe Certified program is designed to help Adobe customers and trainers improve and promote their product-proficiency skills. There are four levels of certification:

- Adobe Certified Associate (ACA)

- Adobe Certified Expert (ACE)

- Adobe Certified Instructor (ACI)

- Adobe Authorized Training Center (AATC)

The Adobe Certified Associate (ACA) credential certifies that individuals have the entry-level skills to plan, design, build, and maintain effective communications using different forms of digital media.

The Adobe Certified Expert program is a way for expert users to upgrade their credentials. You can use Adobe certification as a catalyst for getting a raise, finding a job, or promoting your expertise.

If you are an ACE-level instructor, the Adobe Certified Instructor program takes your skills to the next level and gives you access to a wide range of Adobe resources.

Adobe Authorized Training Centers offer instructor-led courses and training on Adobe products, employing only Adobe Certified Instructors. A directory of AATCs is available at http://partners.adobe.com.

For information on the Adobe Certified program, visit www.adobe.com/support/certification/main.html.

WHAT'S NEW IN ADOBE ILLUSTRATOR CS4

Adobe Illustrator CS4 is packed with new and innovative features to help you produce artwork more efficiently for print, web, and digital video publication. In this chapter, you'll learn about many of these new features—how they function and how you can use them in your work.

Workspace improvements

You can display multiple documents in a tabbed view or open them side by side, so you can easily compare or drag items from one document to another. Use the intuitive Arrange Documents window to quickly arrange your open documents in a variety of configurations. The Application bar at the top of the application provides menus and options in one easy-to-access place. Use the workspace switcher to quickly jump to different workspace configurations as you work.

Multiple artboards

In Illustrator CS4, you can create multi-page documents using up to 100 artboards of varying sizes in a single document. Artboards can overlap, appear side by side or in a vertical stack. You can save and print multiple artboards together or independently.

You can export multiple artboards, together or independently, to a variety of formats, including PDF, PSD, SWF, JPEG, PNG, and TIFF. You can import an Illustrator file with multiple artboards into Adobe InDesign or Adobe Flash.

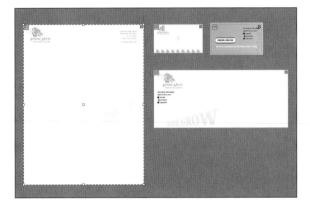

Smart guides

Smart guides are now even more useful, providing unobtrusive guidance to ensure precision in your artwork when you want it. Instant pop-ups display alignment and measurement information, such as the delta between objects and angles of rotation when you move or transform objects. As in previous versions, objects snap to any alignment that you choose, which lets you easily arrange and transform objects exactly how you want.

Gradient enhancements

With the enhanced Gradient tool, you can create elliptical gradients, and edit linear and elliptical gradients on the artboard by adding and changing color stops, applying transparency to color stops, and modifying the direction or angle of a gradient. In the Gradient panel, you can now access a menu of your saved gradients, apply transparency to individual color stops, and more.

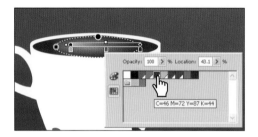

Transparency in gradients

When creating gradients with two or more colors, you can define the opacity of each color individually. By specifying different opacity values for color stops, you can create gradients that fade to transparent, and reveal or hide underlying objects.

The Blob Brush tool

The Blob Brush is a new drawing tool that creates paths that merge with existing artwork that has the same fill and no stroke. Using the Blob Brush, you can merge with existing paths that have complicated appearances, and then edit them with the Blob Brush and the Eraser tools to create uniquely intuitive vector painting.

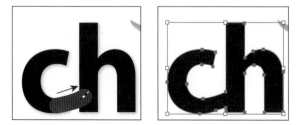

In-panel appearance editing

In the Appearance panel, you can use the enhanced full-featured controls, including direct access to hyperlinks that open dialog boxes for effects, strokes, and fills. To make it even easier to work, you can select and deselect visibility for any attribute to show and hide them on the artboard.

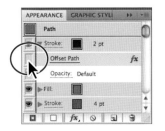

Enriched Graphic Styles panel

In the updated Graphic Styles panel, you can quickly view and apply styles to objects in your document. Using the Text For Preview option, you can view a style as it appears on text, or right-click a thumbnail to preview how that style will look on a selected object. Because effect-only styles display the outlines of the object on which the style was created, you can also see your effect-only styles at a glance. Using the Alt or Option key when applying a style, you can now merge a style with an object's existing style, or merge different styles on an object.

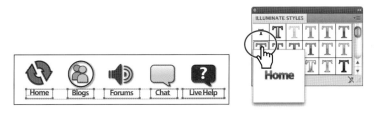

Although this list just touches on just a few of the new features of Illustrator CS4, it exemplifies Adobe's commitment to providing the best tools possible for your publishing needs. We hope you enjoy working with Illustrator CS4 as much as we do.

—The Adobe Illustrator CS4 Classroom in a Book Team

A QUICK TOUR OF ADOBE ILLUSTRATOR CS4

In this interactive demonstration of Adobe Illustrator CS4, you get an overview of the application while using some of the exciting new features.

 This lesson takes approximately an hour to complete. Copy the Lesson00 folder onto your hard disk.

In this interactive demonstration of Adobe Illustrator CS4, you use new and exciting features in the application, like multiple artboards, and transparency in gradients, as well as learn key fundamentals to work effectively in the application.

Getting started

You work with one file during this tour. All art files are on the Adobe Classroom in a Book CD that is included on the inside back cover of this book. Make sure that you copy the Lessons folder from the CD to your hard disk before starting this exercise. Before you begin, you need to restore the default preferences for Adobe Illustrator CS4. This lesson includes a finished art file so that you can view what you will create on your own.

1 To ensure that the tools and panels function as described in this lesson, delete or deactivate (by renaming) the Adobe Illustrator CS4 preferences file. See "Restoring default preferences" on page 3.

2 Start Adobe Illustrator CS4.

● **Note:** If you have not already copied the resource files for this lesson onto your hard disk from the Lesson00 folder on the Adobe Illustrator CS4 Classroom in a Book CD, do so now. See "Copying the Classroom in a Book files" on page 2.

3 Choose File > Open and open the L00end.ai file in the Lesson00 folder in the Lessons folder on your hard disk. This is the final artwork. You can leave it open for reference, or choose File > Close to close it. For this lesson, you start with a blank document.

Working with multiple artboards

1 Choose File > New.

● **Note:** New document profiles in Illustrator are tailored to different kinds of projects—mobile, print, web, and video, for example.

2 In the New Document dialog box, name the file snowboarder and leave the New Document Profile setting as Print. Next, select the Landscape button (⊞) for Orientation, change Number Of Artboards to 2, Units to Inches, Width to 9 in, and Height to 6 in. Click the up arrow to the left of Top Bleed to change the value of all the bleeds to 0.125 in. Click OK. A new blank document window appears.

3   Choose File > Save As. In the Save As dialog box, leave the name as snowboarder.ai and navigate to the Lesson00 folder. Leave the Save As Type option set to Adobe Illustrator (*.AI) (Windows) or the Format option set to Adobe Illustrator (ai) (Mac OS), and click Save. In the Illustrator Options dialog box, leave the Illustrator options at their default settings, and click OK.

4   Choose View > Show Rulers, or use the keyboard shortcut Ctrl+R (Windows) or Command+R (Mac OS) to show vertical and horizontal rulers on the artboard.

5   Select the Artboard tool (⊔) in the Tools panel. Click and drag the rightmost artboard below the leftmost artboard until they do not overlap and a vertical green alignment guide appears in the center of the artboard indicating that it is aligned vertically with the artboard above it.

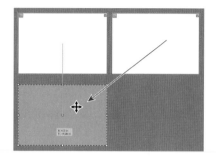

Notice that the options for editing the artboard dimensions, orientation, and more appear in the Control panel, below the menus.

6   Select the Selection tool (▶) to stop editing the artboards. Click the top artboard to make it the active artboard. Choose View > Fit Artboard In Window.

7   Select the Rectangle tool (▭) and click once in the upper left corner of the artboard; do not click and drag. The Rectangle dialog box appears. Enter 9.25 in for the width, and 6.25 in for the height, and then click OK. A rectangle appears on the page. You will reposition it in the next step.

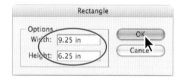

▶ **Tip:** If you don't see in (inches) in the Rectangle dialog box, you can still enter "in" after the value to create the rectangle in inches.

8   Select the Selection tool (▶). With the rectangle still selected, click the Align To Selection button (▦) in the Control panel and choose Align To Artboard from the menu. This aligns the rectangle to the artboard instead of other objects. Click Horizontal Align Center (▦) and then Vertical Align Center (▦) to align the rectangle in the center of the artboard.

9   With the rectangle still selected, notice that there are controls for the fill and stroke at the bottom of the Tools panel. The stroke is essentially a border, and the fill is the interior of a shape. When the Fill box is forward, the selected color is assigned to the interior of the selected object. Activate the fill by clicking the solid Fill box.

Fill selected   Stroke selected

● **Note:** Read more about strokes and fills in Lesson 6, "Color and Painting."

For this example, you assign colors using the Selection tool and the Swatches panel. When you move the pointer over swatches in the Swatches panel, a tooltip appears with the name of the swatch.

10 Click the Swatches panel icon (▦) on the right side of the workspace. With the rectangle still selected click, to select the C=85 M=50 Y=0 K=0 blue swatch in the Swatches panel. The rectangle now has a blue fill.

11 Choose Edit > Copy.

12 Choose Select > Deselect to deselect all the objects on the artboard. Choose File > Save. Leave the file open.

Working with alignment and smart guides

Next you will work with smart guides and navigate between artboards. Smart guides help you align, edit, and transform objects or artboards. The back of the postcard is where a print area for the address will be. Read more about smart guides and navigating artboards in Lesson 4, "Transforming Objects."

1 Choose 2 from the Artboard Navigation menu in the lower left portion of Document window.

2 Click the Layers panel icon (⬤) on the right side of the workspace. In the Layers panel, click the Create New Layer button (▣) to create another layer.

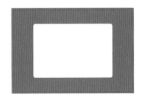

3 Choose Edit > Paste.

4 Choose Object > Lock > Selection.

5 Select the Rounded Rectangle tool (▢) from the Rectangle tool group in the Tools panel. Click on the artboard. In the Rounded Rectangle dialog box, type 6 in into the Width field and 4 in into the Height field. Leave the Corner Radius at its default and click OK.

6 Click the Fill color (■▾) in the Control panel and change the fill to white. Click the Stroke color (▢▾) in the Control panel and make sure it is black.

7 With the Align To Artboard option (▣) still selected in the Control panel, click Horizontal Align Center (⬓) and Vertical Align Center (⬓►) to align the rounded rectangle into the center of the artboard.

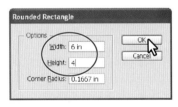

8 Open the snowflake.ai file in the Lesson00 folder located in the Lessons folder on your hard disk.

9 In the snowflake.ai file, click the snowflake with the Selection tool (▶), and then choose Edit > Copy. Choose File > Close to close the snowflake.ai file. In the snowboarder.ai file, choose Edit > Paste.

10 With the Selection tool (▶), drag the snowflake into the upper left corner of the white rounded rectangle. When the center of the snowflake meets the rounded rectangle corner and the word "intersect" appears, as well as green construction guides, release the mouse.

11 With the snowflake still selected, Alt+Shift-drag (Windows) or Option+Shift-drag (Mac OS) the lower right corner down and to the right to make the snowflake bigger. Notice the measurement tooltip (gray box) that appears indicating the size of the object as you scale. Try to get it close to 2.3 in in width and 2 in in height. Release the mouse button, then the keys, when in position.

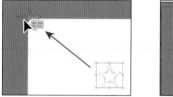 

Drag the snowflake into position and resize it.

12 With the Selection tool, Alt-drag (Windows) or Option-drag (Mac OS) the snowflake to the right to create a copy of it. Drag until the snowflake center is snapped to the upper right corner of the white rounded rectangle (similar to what you did in step 11). Leave the new snowflake selected.

13 With the Selection tool, Shift-click the leftmost snowflake to select both snowflakes. Alt-drag (Windows) or Option-drag (Mac OS) the selected snowflakes down to create a copy of them. Drag until the snowflakes are snapped to the lower corners of the white rounded rectangle. Green construction guides (lines) will alert you when the objects are snapping to the corners.

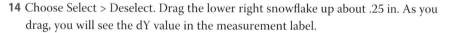

● **Note:** The measurement label (gray box) shows the dX and dY as you drag and copy the snowflakes. This tells you the distance that you have moved the objects on the x and y axes.

14 Choose Select > Deselect. Drag the lower right snowflake up about .25 in. As you drag, you will see the dY value in the measurement label.

15 Shift-click the bottom, left snowflake to select both snowflakes along the bottom.

16 Click the right snowflake on the bottom once more to set it as the key object, as indicated by a thick stroke (border). Choose Vertical Align Center (⊞▶) in the Control panel to align them.

● **Note:** If you don't see the align buttons in the Control panel, click the word Align in the Control panel or choose Window > Align.

17 Repeat steps 16 and 17 for the top two snowflakes. Drag the upper right snowflake down and set it as the key object.

18 Choose Select > Deselect.

19 Choose 1 from the Artboard Navigation menu in the lower left portion of the Document window. Choose File > Save.

Working with the Blob Brush tool

Next you'll create an ellipse on the left side of the page. You can use the Blob Brush tool to paint filled shapes that intersect and merge with other shapes of the same color. Read more about working with the Blob Brush tool and the Eraser tool in Lesson 10, "Working with Brushes."

1 In the first artboard, make sure the Fill color ( ) in the Control panel is white, so that the fill color is white when you paint with the Blob Brush tool. Click the Stroke color in the Control panel and choose None ( ). Click the Stroke color in the Control panel to close the Swatches panel.

2 Click the Layers panel icon ( ) on the right side of the workspace and click Layer 1 to select it. This way all of the content you create is on Layer 1.

3 Select the Ellipse tool ( ) by clicking and holding down the Rounded Rectangle tool ( ) in the Tools panel. Click once on the artboard. In the Ellipse dialog box, change the width to 6 in and the height to 4 in. Click OK.

4 Select the Selection tool ( ) and drag the ellipse off the left edge of the artboard so that the left edge of the ellipse extends off the left edge of the artboard, and the top of the ellipse is about an inch from the top of the artboard. Look at the rulers for guidance. Choose Select > Deselect.

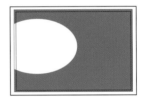

Next you will use the Blob Brush tool to edit the ellipse to make it look like a cloud.

5 Double-click the Blob Brush tool ( ) in the Tools panel. In the Blob Brush Tool Options dialog box, change the size to 70 pt. Click OK.

6 With the pointer, click and drag along the edge of the ellipse to create a bumpy edge. As you drag around the edge, release the mouse button to see how the ellipse shape changes.

7 Select the Selection tool ( ) and click to select the cloud shape. Change the opacity in the Control panel to 20%, and choose Select > Deselect.

Placing Adobe Photoshop images in Illustrator CS4

In Illustrator, you can place Adobe Photoshop files and assign Layer Comps before you place images on the artboard. Layer Comps is a Photoshop feature that lets you save combinations of layers in the Layer Comp panel in Photoshop CS4. Layer Comps can be based on visibility, position, and layer appearance. Read more about Layer Comps and placing Photoshop images in Lesson 14, "Combining Illustrator CS4 Graphics with Other Adobe Applications."

1   Choose File > Place. In the Place dialog box, navigate to the Lesson00 in the Lessons folder, and select the snowboard.psd file. Make sure that the Link options in the lower left corner is selected, and click Place.

Illustrator recognizes when a file has been saved with Layer Comps, and opens a Photoshop Import Options dialog box. The file in this example has been saved with two different Layer Comps.

2   In the Photoshop Import Options dialog box, select Show Preview. Choose Blue Boarder from the Layer Comp menu, and click OK. The image of the snowboarder is placed on the artboard.

● **Note:** By selecting Link in the Place dialog box, you are connecting the Photoshop image to the Illustrator file. If the image is later edited in Photoshop, it is updated in the Illustrator file.

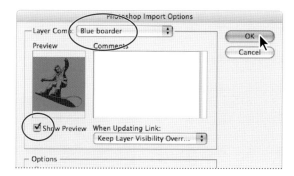

3   Choose File > Save.

Using Live Trace

You can use Live Trace to convert photographs (raster images) into vector artwork. Next you will trace the Photoshop file to create a piece of black and white line art. Read more about Live Trace in Lesson 3, "Creating and Editing Shapes."

1   With the image still selected, click the Live Trace button in the Control panel. The image is converted to vector paths, but it is not yet editable.

2   Click the Expand button in the Control panel. This converts the traced image to paths and breaks the link to the original Photoshop image.

▶ **Tip:** At this point, if the image were linked, and if you were to edit the snowboard.psd image in Photoshop, the Live Trace image would update in Illustrator.

3 Choose Select > Deselect. With the Direct Selection tool ( placeholder), click the white background around the snowboarder. This activates only the white background. Press the Delete or Backspace key to remove the white object. Repeat these steps for the white space between the snowboarder's boots.

4 Choose File > Save. Keep the file open.

Using Live Paint

The Live Paint tool lets you color objects as you would on paper. Read more about Live Paint in Lesson 6, "Color and Painting."

1 With the Selection tool (▶), select the snowboarder. Choose Object > Live Paint > Make to create a Live Paint group.

2 Choose Select > Deselect.

3 Click the Fill color in the Control panel and select the C=5 M=0 Y=90 K=0 yellow swatch.

4 Select the Live Paint Bucket tool (⬦) in the Tools panel and hover the pointer over the snowboarder. Move the pointer over the bottom of the snowboard until the bottom is highlighted in red and colored squares appear above the pointer (⬦). Click to apply the yellow fill color.

The color squares above the paint bucket represent the colors that are before and after the selected color in the Swatches panel.

5 Press the Right Arrow key once to choose the green color (☐) from the three swatches above the Paint Bucket tool. Using the Live Paint Bucket tool, apply the fill to the tip of the snowboard.

6 Click the Left Arrow key twice and paint the pants of both legs with the light orange color.

7 With the Selection tool, select the snowboarder. Double-click the Scale tool (⬓) in the Tools panel. Change Uniform Scale to 70%, and click OK.

8 Select the Selection tool, and drag the snowboarder into the right half of the artboard. Exact positioning isn't important.

9 Choose Select > Deselect.

10 Choose File > Save.

Working with color groups and Edit Color/Recolor Artwork

A color group is an organization tool that lets you group related color swatches together in the Swatches panel. In addition, a color group can be a container for color harmonies, which you create using the Edit Color/Recolor Artwork dialog box or the Color Guide panel. Next you will recolor the snowboarder. Read more about color groups and Edit Color/Recolor Artwork in Lesson 6, "Color And Painting."

1 Select the C=20, M=0, Y=100, K=0 yellow green swatch from the Fill color in the Control panel.

2 Click the Color Guide icon ( ) on the right side of the workspace. Click the Set Base Color To The Current Color icon ( ). Choose Shades from the Harmony Rules menu.

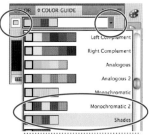

3 Click the Save Color Group To Swatch Panel button ( ). This saves the colors in the Shades harmony rule in the Swatches panel.

4 With the Selection tool ( ), select the snowboarder. Click the Edit Or Apply Colors button ( ) at the bottom of the Color Guide panel.

5 In the Recolor Artwork dialog box, click Color Group 1 in the Color Groups area. Click OK. Choose Select > Deselect.

● **Note:** The Recolor Artwork dialog box maps the colors in the artwork to the colors in the color group you select.

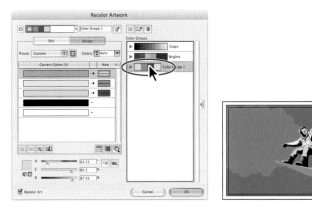

Working with type

Next you will work with the type features in Illustrator. Read more about working with type in Lesson 7, "Working with Type."

1   Choose Essentials from the workspace switcher in the Control panel to reset the panels.

2   Select the Type tool (**T**), and click once on the artboard in an area where there are no objects. You will reposition the text later in the lesson.

3   Type BoardersStore. With the Type tool selected, choose Select > All, or press Ctrl+A (Windows) or Command+A (Mac OS) to select all the text that you typed.

▶ **Tip:** To see the entire Character panel, click the word Character in the Control panel. You can also use the Control panel to access the Stroke, Paragraph, and Transparency panels.

4   In the Control panel, set the font size to 56 pt and press Enter or Return.

Drag to select the font name in the Font field in the Control panel. Begin typing "min" with the font name selected to filter the font list to Minion Pro. You may need to click the arrow to reveal the menu. Select the font name again and begin typing "my" and choose Myriad Pro as the font.

5   Choose Condensed from the Font Style menu.

6   Click the Color panel icon (⬤) on the right side of the workspace. Change the values to C=40, M=0, Y=100, K=0, pressing Tab to navigate to the next field.

● **Note:** If you don't see the CMYK sliders, choose CMYK from the Color panel menu (▾≡).

7   With the Selection tool (▶), drag the text area down toward the lower left corner of the artboard.

Using the Appearance panel

The Appearance panel allows you to control an object's attributes, such as stroke, fill, and effects. Read more about working with the Appearance panel in Lesson 12, "Applying Appearance Attributes and Graphic Styles."

1   Click the Appearance panel icon (◉) on the right side of the workspace.

Note that in the Appearance panel, the current selection is listed as Type.

2   Click the Add New Stroke button (■) at the bottom of the Appearance panel and a new Stroke appears in the Appearance panel. Click the Stroke color, and select the C=5, M=0, Y=90, K=0 yellow swatch. Click the Stroke color to close the Swatches panel.

3   Click the Add New Effect button (*fx*) at the bottom of the Appearance panel, and choose Path > Offset Path. In the Offset Path dialog box, change the Offset to 1 pt and click OK.

4 In the Appearance panel, click the word Type to apply the next effect to the type object. Click the Add New Effect button (fx.), and choose Distort & Transform > Pucker & Bloat. In the Pucker & Bloat dialog box, change Pucker to −10%, and click OK.

5 Click the arrow to the left of the word Stroke in the Appearance panel. Click the eye icon (👁) to hide and disable the Offset Path effect.

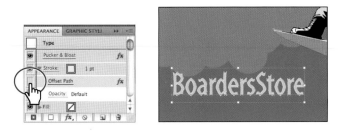

Saving the appearance as a graphic style

Saving a graphic style lets you store attributes, such as stroke and fill, for later use. Read more about working with the graphic styles in Lesson 12, "Applying Appearance Attributes and Graphic Styles."

1 Click the Graphic Styles panel icon (⊡) on the right side of the workspace.

2 Click the New Graphic Style button (⊟) at the bottom of the Graphic Styles panel. Double-click the new graphic style that appears in the panel. In the Graphic Styles Options dialog box, change the name to text, and click OK.

3 With the type area still selected on the artboard, right-click (Windows) or Control-click (Mac OS) on the Arched Green graphic style in the Graphic Styles panel to see a preview of the styling applied to the text. Release the mouse button and then the key.

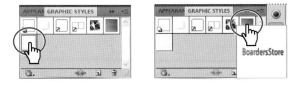

4 Click the Graphic Styles Libraries Menu button (▣。) at the bottom of the Graphic Styles panel. Choose Additive to open the Additive graphic styles library panel.

5 Alt-click (Windows) or Option-click (Mac OS) the Drop Shadow graphic style. This adds the style properties to the text and saves the graphic style in the Graphic Styles panel for later use.

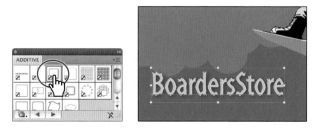

6 Close the Additive graphic styles library panel, and then choose File > Save.

Applying warp to the text

In this next section, you will learn how to apply a warp to objects using the Control panel. Read more about working with envelopes in Lesson 7, "Working with Type."

1 With the type area still selected on the artboard, click the Make Envelope button (▢) in the Control panel. This lets you warp the text using preset templates, such as envelope or flag.

2 In the Warp Options dialog box, leave the default setting at Horizontal and move the slider for Bend to 30%. Select Preview, then change Horizontal Distortion to 51%, and click OK.

3 Choose File > Save.

Creating and editing a gradient

Gradients are color blends that use two or more colors. In Illustrator CS4, gradients can also have transparency applied to one or more colors. Next you will apply a gradient to the cloud shape in the background. Read more about working with gradients in Lesson 9, "Blending Shapes and Colors."

1　With the Selection tool (➤), click to select the cloud shape in the background. Change the Opacity to 100% in the Control panel.

2　Click the Gradient panel icon (▣) on the right side of the workspace.

3　Click the Gradient menu button (▮) and choose Linear Gradient from the menu. This applies a black-to-white gradient to the cloud shape.

4　Double-click the black color stop (♟) on the right side of the gradient bar in the Gradient panel. Click the white color in the lower right corner of the panel that appears to change the color to white. Press Enter or Return to return to the Gradient panel.

5　In the Gradient panel, change the opacity to 10%, and then choose Radial from the Type menu. Notice that the fill of the cloud changes.

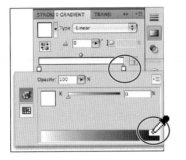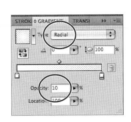

6　Select the Gradient tool (▣) in the Tools panel. Notice the gradient bar that appears on the cloud. Click and drag diagonally from the upper left part of the cloud to just past the lower right edge of the cloud. Dragging with the Gradient tool changes the direction of the gradient.

7　Position the pointer over the gradient slider and it turns into the gradient bar. Notice the color stops beneath the gradient bar, similar to those in the Gradient panel. Position the cursor just below the gradient bar about half way between color stops. When the pointer changes to an arrow with a plus sign (▸₊), click to add another color stop to the gradient slider.

Drag with the Gradient tool to create the gradient. Click to add a color stop and change the opacity of that color stop.

8　Double-click the new color stop and change the opacity to 100% in the panel that appears. Press Enter or Return to close the panel.

9 Choose Select > Deselect.

10 Choose File > Save.

Working with symbols

A symbol is an art object stored in the Symbols panel that you can reuse. You will now create a symbol from artwork. Read more about working with symbols in Lesson 13, "Working With Symbols."

1 Choose View > Fit Artboard In Window.

2 Choose 2 from the Artboard Navigation menu in the lower left portion of the Document window.

3 With the Selection tool (▶), click to select a snowflake and then choose Edit > Copy. Choose 1 from the Artboard Navigation menu in the lower left portion of Document window. In the Layers panel (◈), click to select Layer 1, then choose Edit > Paste and leave the snowflake selected.

4 With the Selection tool, Shift-drag a corner of the selected snowflake to resize proportionally to roughly half the size.

5 Click the Symbols panel icon (♣) on the right side of the workspace.

6 Click the New Symbol button (⬚) at the bottom of the Symbols panel. In the Symbol Options dialog box, name the symbol snowflake and select Graphic as the Type. Click OK.

> **Tip:** Symbols maintain their structure and editability when you copy and paste or import them into Adobe Flash.

A snowflake now appears in the Symbols panel. This symbol is saved in the Symbols panel for use in this document only.

7 In the Symbols panel, drag the snowflake symbol onto the artboard. This creates an instance of the symbol. Drag out several more to create a loose snowflake pattern.

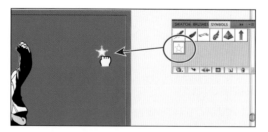

8 With the Selection tool (▶), press the Shift key to resize a snowflake while maintaining its proportions. Change the opacity in the Control panel for some of them as well. Create a large snowflake, change the opacity to 20%, and place it over the snowboarder.

9 With the Selection tool, click to select the snowboarder. You may need to move the snowflake out of the way. Choose Object > Arrange > Bring To Front to bring the snowboarder on top of the snowflake.

10 Choose File > Save, and keep the file open.

Creating a clipping mask

You will now create a clipping mask. A clipping mask blocks or covers the object area not included in the object defined as the mask. Read more about working with clipping masks in Lesson 8, "Working With Layers."

1 In the Tools panel, click and hold down the Ellipse tool (◯) and select the Rounded Rectangle tool (▢).

2 In the Layers panel (◉) on the right side of the workspace, make sure that Layer 1 is still selected.

3 Click once on the artboard to open the Rounded Rectangle dialog box.

4 Change the width to 9 in, the height to 6 in, and the corner radius to .3 in. Click OK. The rounded rectangle appears on the artboard.

5 In the Control panel, choose None (⊘) from the Fill color and None (⊘) from the Stroke color.

6 With the rectangle still selected, click Horizontal Align Center (⊥), and then Vertical Align Center (⊩) in the Control panel to align the shape to the center of the artboard.

7 Choose Select > Deselect.

8 Click the Layers panel icon (◉) on the right side of the workspace. Making sure that Layer 1 is selected in the Layers panel, click the Make/Release Clipping Mask button (◉) at the bottom of the panel.

9 Choose File > Save, and then File > Close.

1 GETTING TO KNOW THE WORK AREA

Lesson overview

In this lesson, you learn how to do the following:

- Use the Welcome Screen.

- Open an Adobe Illustrator CS4 file.

- Select tools in the Tools panel.

- Work with panels, including the Control panel.

- Use viewing options to enlarge and reduce the Document window.

- Navigate multiple artboards and documents.

- Use Illustrator Help.

 This lesson will take approximately 45 minutes to complete. If needed, remove the Lesson00 folder from your hard disk and copy the Lesson01 folder onto it.

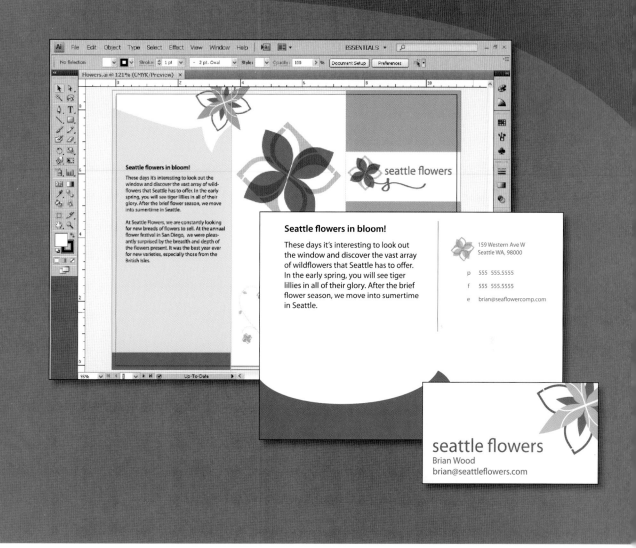

To make the best use of the extensive drawing, painting, and editing capabilities of Adobe Illustrator CS4, it's important to learn how to navigate the workspace. The workspace consists of the menu bar, Tools panel, Control panel, Document window, and the default set of panels.

Getting started

You'll be working in one art file during this lesson, but before you begin, restore the default preferences for Adobe Illustrator CS4. Then, open the finished art file for this lesson to see an illustration.

1   To ensure that the tools and panels function exactly as described in this lesson, delete or deactivate (by renaming) the Adobe Illustrator CS4 preferences file. See "Restoring default preferences" on page 3.

    Note: Due to the differences in Color Settings from one system to another, a Missing Profile dialog box may appear as you open various exercise files. Click OK when you see this. Color Settings are discussed in Lesson 15, "Output."

    Note: If you have not already copied the resource files for this lesson onto your hard disk from the Lesson01 folder on the Adobe Illustrator CS4 Classroom in a Book CD, do so now. See "Copying the Classroom in a Book files" on page 2.

2   Double-click the Adobe Illustrator CS4 icon to start Adobe Illustrator. When started, Adobe Illustrator CS4 displays a Welcome Screen with hyperlinked options.

Tip: If you prefer not to have the Welcome Screen appear at startup, select the Don't show again checkbox. You can open the Welcome Screen at any time by selecting Welcome Screen from the Help menu.

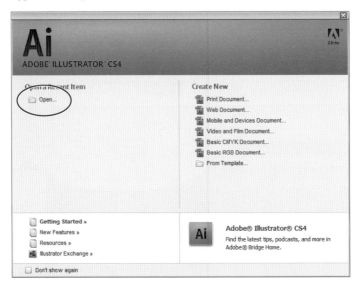

Use the Welcome Screen to find out what's new in Adobe Illustrator CS4 and gain access to resources. The resources include videos, templates, and much more. The Welcome Screen also offers the option to create a new document from scratch, from a template, or to open an existing document. The Open A Recent Item includes the Open link and a list of recently viewed files. This area will be blank when first starting Adobe Illustrator CS4. For this lesson you'll open an existing document.

3 Click Open on the left side of the Welcome Screen, or choose File > Open, and open the L1start.ai file in the Lesson01 folder, located in the Lessons folder on your hard disk.

4 Choose View > Fit Artboard In Window.

5 Choose Window > Workspace > Essentials to ensure that the workspace is set to default.

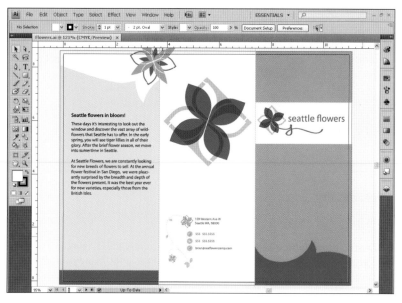

The artwork file contains 2 sides to the brochure, a business card, and a postcard.

When the file is open, and Adobe Illustrator CS4 is fully launched, the menu bar, Tools panel, Control panel and panel groups appear on the screen. Notice that the panels are docked on the right side of the screen. This is where some of the panels are stored by default. Adobe Illustrator CS4 also consolidates many of your most frequently accessed panel items in the Control panel just below the menu bar. This lets you operate with fewer visible panels, giving you a large workspace.

You will use the L1start.ai file to practice navigating, zooming, and investigating an Adobe Illustrator CS4 document and work area.

6 Choose File > Save As. In the Save As dialog box, name the file Flowers.ai, and choose the Lesson01 folder. Leave the Save As Type option set to Adobe Illustrator (*.AI) (Windows) or the Format option set to Adobe Illustrator (ai) (Mac OS), and click Save. If a warning dialog box appears referencing spot colors and transparency, click Continue. In the Illustrator Options dialog box, leave the Illustrator options at their default settings, and click OK.

Artboard overview

Artboards represent the regions that can contain printable artwork. You can use artboards to crop areas for printing or placement purposes. Multiple artboards are useful for creating a variety of things such as multiple page PDFs, printed pages with different sizes or different elements, independent elements for websites, video storyboards, or individual items for animation in Adobe Flash or After Effects.

A. Printable area
B. Nonprintable area
C. Edge of the page
D. Artboard
E. Bleed area
F. Canvas

A B C D E F

Note: You can have 1 to 100 artboards per document depending on the size of the artboards. You can specify the number of artboards for a document when you create it, and you can add and remove artboards at any time while working in a document. You can create artboards of different sizes, resize them with the Artboard tool, and position them on the screen—even overlapping each other.

Note: If you are saving an Illustrator document to be placed in a layout program such as InDesign, the printable and nonprintable areas are irrelevant; the artwork outside the bounds still appears.

A. **Printable area** is bounded by the innermost dotted lines and represents the portion of the page on which the selected printer can print. Many printers cannot print to the edge of the paper. Don't get confused by what is considered nonprintable.

B. **Nonprintable area** is between the two sets of dotted lines representing any nonprintable margin of the page. This example shows the nonprintable area of an 8.5″ x 11″ page for a standard laser printer. The printable and nonprintable area is determined by the printer selected in the Print Options dialog box. (See Lesson 15, "Output" for more information about assigning a printer.)

C. **Edge of the page** is indicated by the outermost set of dotted lines.

D. **Artboard** is bounded by solid lines and represents the entire region that can contain printable artwork. By default, the artboard is the same size as the page, but it can be enlarged or reduced. The U.S. default artboard is 8.5″ x 11″, but it can be set as large as 227″ x 227″.

E. **Bleed Area** is Bleed is the amount of artwork that falls outside of the printing bounding box, or outside the crop area and trim marks. You can include bleed in your artwork as a margin of error—to ensure that the ink is still printed to the edge of the page after the page is trimmed or that an image can be stripped into a keyline in a document.

F. **Canvas** is the area outside the artboard that extends to the edge of the 227″ square window. Objects placed on the canvas are visible on-screen, but they do not print.

—From Illustrator Help

Understanding the workspace

You create and manipulate your documents and files using various elements such as panels, bars, and windows. Any arrangement of these elements is called a workspace. When you first start Illustrator, you see the default workspace, which you can customize for the tasks you perform. For instance, you can create one workspace for editing and another for viewing, save them, and switch between them as you work.

Note: The figures in this chapter are taken in the Windows operating system. Below is a workspace difference worth taking note of if you are on the Mac OS.

Below the areas of the workspace are described:

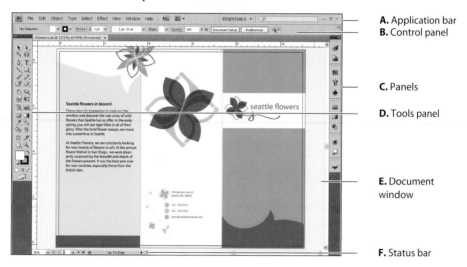

A. Application bar
B. Control panel

C. Panels

D. Tools panel

E. Document window

F. Status bar

A. The Application bar across the top contains a workspace switcher, menus (Windows only), and other application controls.

Note: For the Mac OS, the menu items appear above the Application bar.

B. The Control panel displays options for the currently selected tool.

C. Panels help you monitor and modify your work. Certain panels are displayed by default, but you can add any panel by choosing it from the Window menu. Many panels have menus with panel-specific options. Panels can be grouped, stacked, or docked.

D. The Tools panel contains tools for creating and editing images, artwork, page elements, and so on. Related tools are grouped together.

E. The Document window displays the file you're working on.

F. The Status bar appears at the lower-left edge of the Document window. It contains information such as navigation controls, and more.

Working with the Tools panel

The Tools panel contains selection tools, drawing and painting tools, editing tools, viewing tools, and the Fill and Stroke boxes. As you work through the lessons, you'll learn about the specific function of each tool.

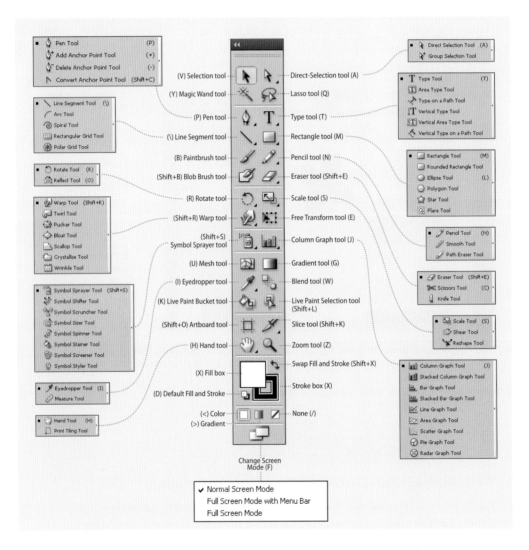

1 Position the pointer over the Selection tool (▸) in the Tools panel. Notice that the name and shortcut are displayed.

▸ **Tip:** You can select a tool by either clicking it in the Tools panel or by using the keyboard shortcut for a particular tool (which appears in parentheses in the tooltip). Because the default keyboard shortcuts work only when you do not have a text insertion point, you can also add other keyboard shortcuts to select tools, even when you are editing text. To do this, use the Edit > Keyboard Shortcuts command. For more information, select Keyboard Shortcuts in Illustrator Help.

▸ **Tip:** You can turn the tool tips on or off by choosing Edit > Preferences > General (Windows) or Illustrator > Preferences > General (Mac OS), and selecting Show Tool Tips.

2 Position the pointer over the Direct Selection tool (▸), click and hold down the mouse button—additional selection tools appear. Drag down and to the right, and release the mouse button over the additional tool to select it. Any tool in the Tools

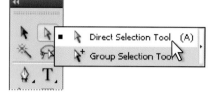

panel that displays a small black triangle at the bottom right corner contains additional tools that can be selected by clicking and holding down the tool.

● **Note:** On Mac OS, the top of the free-floating Tools panel has a dot in the upper left corner (to close the panel) and double arrows in the upper right corner.

Next you will focus on resizing and floating the Tools panel.

3 Select hidden tools using the following methods:

- Click and hold down the mouse button on a tool that has additional hidden tools. Then drag to the desired tool, and release the mouse button.

- Hold down Alt (Windows) or Option (Mac OS), and click the tool in the Tools panel. Each click selects the next hidden tool in the hidden tool sequence.

- Click and hold down the mouse button on the Rectangle tool (▢). Drag to the right of the hidden tools and release on the tearoff arrow. This tears off the tools from the Tools panel so that you can access them at all times.

4 Click the double arrow in the upper left corner of the Tools panel to contract the two columns to one column. This can conserve screen space. Click the same double arrow to expand to two columns again.

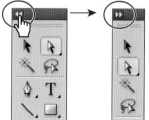

5   Click and drag from the dark gray area at the top of the Tools panel, called the title bar, or from the double line beneath the title bar, into the workspace. The Tools panel is now floating in the workspace.

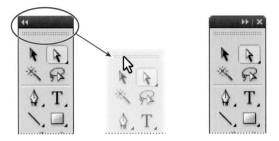

Click and drag to move the Tools panel.

6   With the Tools panel floating in the workspace, click the double arrow in the top left corner of the Tools panel. This gives you a single-column Tools panel. Click again to turn the Tools panel back into two columns.

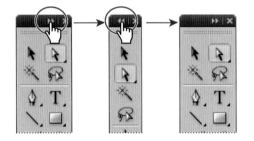

7   To dock the Tools panel again, click and drag from the title bar or the double line below it at the top of the Tools panel to the left side of the application window (Windows) or screen (Mac OS). When the pointer reaches the edge, a translucent blue border to the left appears. This is called the drop zone. Release the mouse button to fit the Tools panel neatly into the side of the workspace.

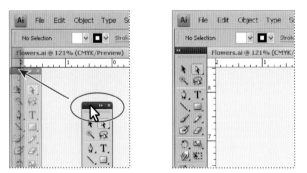

Click and drag to dock the Tools panel.

The Control panel

The Control panel is context-sensitive, meaning that it offers quick access to options, commands, and other panels based on the currently selected object(s). By default, the Control panel is docked at the top of the application window (Windows) or screen (Mac OS); however, you can dock it to the bottom of the application window (Windows) or screen (Mac OS), float it, or hide it altogether. When text in the Control panel is blue and underlined, you can click the text to display a related panel. For example, click the word Stroke to display the Stroke panel.

1 Take a look at the Control panel located below the menus. Select the Selection tool (▶) in the Tools panel and click the middle of orange/blue flower at the top, left of the page. Notice the information that appears in the Control panel. "Group" appears on the left side of the Control panel as well as Stroke, Style, Opacity, etc. for that group of objects. Choose Select > Deselect so the group is no longer selected.

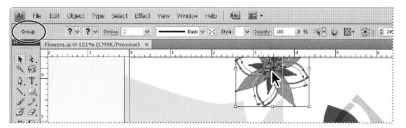

2 With any tool, click the light gray double line on the left side of the Control panel, hold down and drag into the workspace. Once the Control panel is free-floating in the workspace, a dark gray vertical bar is visible on the left side of the Control panel for you to move it to the top or bottom of the workspace.

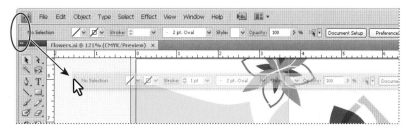

3 Click and drag the left side of the Control panel (the dark gray bar) to the bottom of the workspace (Windows) or screen (Mac OS). Once the pointer reaches the bottom, a blue line appears, indicating the drop zone, telling you that it will be docked when you release the mouse button.

▶ **Tip:** Another way to dock the Control panel is to choose Dock to Top or Dock to Bottom from the Control panel menu (▾☰).

4 If the Control panel is docked at the bottom, click the left side of the Control panel (the light gray double bar) and drag it to the top of the workspace. When the pointer reaches the top (below the AI logo), the blue line appears indicating the drop zone. When you release the mouse button, the panel is docked.

▶ **Tip:** To put the Control panel back at the top of the page you can also choose Window > Workspace > Essentials. This resets the workspace.

Working with panels

Panels, which are located in the Window menu, give you quick access to many tools that make modifying artwork easier. By default, some panels are docked and appear as icons on the right side of the workspace.

Next you'll experiment with hiding, closing, and opening panels.

1 Choose Essentials from the workspace switcher in the Control panel to reset the panels to their original location.

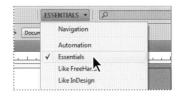

2 Click the Swatches panel icon (⊞) on the right side of the workspace to expand the panel, or choose Window > Swatches. Notice that the Swatches panel appears with two other panels—the Brushes panel and Symbols panel. They are all part of a panel group. Click the Symbols panel tab to view the Symbols panel. Try clicking other panel icons like the Color panel (⬤). After clicking the Color panel icon, notice that a new panel group appears, and the panel group that contained the Swatches panel closes.

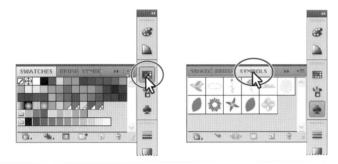

3 Click the Color panel tab (or whichever panel is showing) to collapse the panel back to its icon.

▶ **Tip:** To find a hidden panel, choose the panel name from the Window menu. A check mark to the left of the panel name indicates that the panel is already open and in front of other panels in its panel group. If you choose a checked panel name in the Window menu, the panel and its group collapses.

▶ **Tip:** To collapse a panel back to an icon, you can click its tab, its icon, or the double arrow in the panel title bar.

4 Click the double arrow or dark gray bar at the top of the dock to expand the panels. Once expanded, click the double arrow or dark gray bar to collapse the panels again.

Click to expand.　　Click to collapse.

5 To change the width of all the panels in a dock, drag the left side of the docked panels to the left until text appears. To undo what you just did, click and drag the left side of the docked panels to the right until you can drag no further.

6 Choose Window > Workspace > Essentials. Click the double arrow or dark gray bar at the top of the dock to expand the panels. You are now going to resize a panel group. This can make it easier to see more important panels. Click the Symbols panel tab and drag the dividing line between the Symbols panel group and the Stroke panel group down to resize the group.

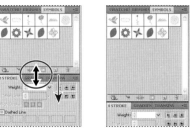

Drag the dividing line between panel groups.

⬤ **Note:** You may not be able drag the divider very far—it depends on your screen size and resolution.

Next you'll reorganize a panel group.

▶ **Tip:** Press Tab to hide all open panels and the Tools panel. Press Tab again to display them all again. You can hide or display just the panels (not the Tools panel) by pressing Shift+Tab.

7 Drag the Symbols panel tab outside the group to remove the panel from the dock and make it a free-floating panel.

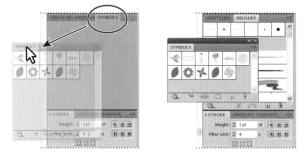

You can also move panels from one panel group to another to create custom panel groups that contain the panels you use most often.

▶ **Tip:** To close a panel, you can drag the panel away from the dock and click the x in the upper right corner (Windows) or dot in the upper left corner (Mac OS). You can also right-click or Ctrl-click a docked panel tab to choose Close from the menu.

8 Drag the Symbols panel by the panel tab, the title bar (behind the panel tab), or the dark grey bar at the top onto the Color and Color Guide panel tabs (or title bar behind). Release the mouse button when you see a blue outline surrounding the Color panel group.

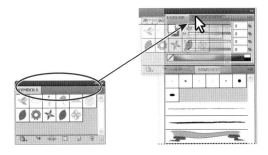

Next you'll organize the panels to create more space in your work area.

9 Click to select the Color panel tab. Double-click the panel tab to reduce the size of the panel. Double-click the tab again to minimize the panel. This can also be done when a panel is free-floating.

Double-click the panel tab.   Double-click again.

Note: Many panels only require you to double-click the panel tab twice to return to the full-size view of the panel.

10 Choose Essentials from the workspace switcher in the Control panel.

Next you'll arrange panel groups. Panel groups can be docked and undocked, or arranged whether they are collapsed or expanded.

11 Choose Window > Align to open the Align panel group. Drag the Align panel by the title bar over to the docked panels on the right side of the workspace. Position the pointer just below the Symbols panel icon (♣) until a single blue line appears. Release the mouse button to add the group to the dock.

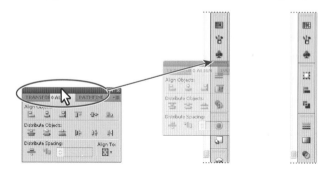

Next you will drag a panel from one group to another in the docked panels.

12 Click and drag the Align panel icon (▤) up so that the pointer is just below the Color panel icon (🎨). A blue line appears and the Color panel group is outlined in blue. Release the mouse button. Arranging the panels in groups that make sense to you can help you work faster.

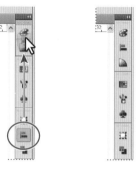

Using panel menus

Most panels have a panel menu in the upper right corner of the panel. Clicking the panel menu button (▾≡) gives you access to additional commands and options for the selected panel. You can also use the panel menu to change the panel display.

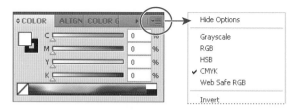

Next you will change the display of the Symbols panel using its panel menu.

1 Click the Symbols panel icon (♣) on the right side of the workspace. You can also choose Window > Symbols to display this panel.

2 Click the panel menu (▾≡) in the upper right corner of the Symbols panel.

3 Choose Small List View from the panel menu. This shows the symbols as a list of names, each with a thumbnail. Because the commands in the panel menu apply only to the active panel, only the Symbols panel is affected.

4 Click the Symbols panel menu, and choose Thumbnail View to return the symbols to their original view. Click the Symbols panel tab to hide it again.

In addition to the panel menus, context-sensitive menus display commands relevant to the active tool, selection, or panel.

To display context-sensitive menus, position the pointer over the artwork, panel list, scrollbar, or Document magnification level. Then click with the right mouse button (Windows), or press Ctrl and hold down the mouse button (Mac OS). The context-sensitive menu at right appears when you right-click (Windows) or Ctrl-click (Mac OS) the artboard with nothing selected.

A context-sensitive menu

Resetting and saving your workspace

You can reset your panels and Tools panel to their default position. You can also save the position of panels and easily access them at any time by creating a workspace. Next you will create a workspace to access a group of commonly used panels.

1 Choose Essentials from the workspace switcher in the Control panel.

2 Choose Window > Pathfinder. Click and drag the Pathfinder panel tab to the right side of the workspace. When the pointer approaches the left side of the docked panels, a blue line appears. Release the mouse button to dock the panel. Click the x in the upper right corner (Windows) or dot in the upper left corner (Mac OS) of the remaining panel group that contains the Align and Transform panels to close it.

▶ **Tip:** Docking panels next to each other on the right side of the workspace is a great way to conserve space. The Pathfinder panel that is now docked can also be collapsed and resized to conserve even more space.

3 Choose Window > Workspace > Save Workspace. The Save Workspace dialog box opens. Enter the name Navigation, and then click OK.

Note: To delete saved workspaces, choose Window > Workspace > Manage Workspaces. Select the workspace name and click the Delete Workspace button.

4 Return to the default panel layout by choosing Window > Workspace > Essentials. Notice that the panels return to their default positions. Toggle between the two workspaces using the Window > Workspace command and selecting the workspace you want to use. Return to the Essentials workspace before starting the next exercise.

▶ **Tip:** To change a saved workspace, you can reset the panels to how you'd like them to appear and then choose Window > Workspace > Save Workspace. In the Save Workspace dialog box, name the workspace the same name, and click OK. A dialog box appears asking if you'd like to overwrite the existing workspace. Click Yes.

Changing the view of artwork

Whether you working with a file that has a single artboard or multiple artboards, you will likely need to change the magnification level and navigate between artboards. The magnification level, which can range from 3.13% to 6400%, is displayed in the title bar next to the filename, and in the lower left corner of the Document window. Using any of the viewing tools and commands affects only the display of the artwork, not the actual size of the artwork.

Viewing artwork

When you open a file, it is automatically displayed in preview mode, which shows how the artwork will print. When you're working with large or complex illustrations, you may want to view only the outlines, or wireframes, of objects in your artwork, so that the screen doesn't have to redraw the artwork each time you make a change. Outline mode can also be helpful when selecting objects, as you will see in Lesson 2, "Selecting and Aligning."

1 Choose View > Fit Artboard In Window to see the entire artboard.

2 Choose View > Outline. Only the outlines of the objects are displayed. Use this view to find objects that might not be visible in preview mode.

3 Choose View > Preview to see all the attributes of the artwork. If you prefer keyboard shortcuts, Ctrl+Y (Windows) or Command+Y (Mac OS) toggles between these two modes.

4 Choose View > Logo Zoom (at the bottom of the View menu) to zoom in to a preset area of the image. This custom view was saved with the document.

Note: When choosing Preview options, it may not be readily apparent that things are visually changing. Zooming in and out (View > Zoom In and View > Zoom Out) may help.

▶ **Tip:** To save time when working with large or complex documents, you can create your own custom views within a document to quickly jump to specific areas and zoom levels. You set up the view that you want to save, and then choose View > New View. Name the view; it is saved with the document.

5 Choose View > Overprint Preview to view any lines or shapes that are set to overprint. This view is helpful for those in the print industry who need to see

how inks interact when set to overprint. See Lesson 15, "Output" for more information on overprinting.

6   Choose View > Pixel Preview to view how the artwork will look when it is rasterized and viewed on-screen in a Web browser. Choose View > Pixel Preview to deselect pixel preview.

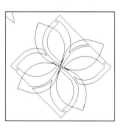
Outline view

Preview view

Overprint preview

Pixel preview

7   Choose View > Fit Artboard In Window to view the entire artboard.

Using the view commands

To enlarge or reduce the view of artwork using the View menu, do one of the following:

• Choose View > Zoom In to enlarge the display of the Flowers.ai artwork.

▶ **Tip:** Ctrl++ (Windows) or Cmd++ (Mac OS) zooms in.

• Choose View > Zoom Out to reduce the view of the Flowers.ai artwork.

▶ **Tip:** Ctrl+– (Windows) or Cmd+–(Mac OS) zooms out.

Each time you choose a Zoom command, the view of the artwork is resized to the closest preset zoom level. The preset zoom levels appear at the lower left corner of the window in a menu, indicated by a down arrow next to the percentage.

You can also use the View menu to fit the artwork to your screen, or to view it at actual size.

1   Choose View > Fit Artboard In Window. A reduced view of the entire document is displayed in the window.

▶ **Tip:** Double-clicking the Hand tool in the Tools panel is another shortcut for fitting the artboard in the window.

◉ **Note:** Because the canvas, which is the area outside the artboard, extends to 227", you can easily lose sight of your illustration. By choosing View > Fit Artboard In Window, or using the keyboard shortcuts, or Ctrl+0 or Command+0, artwork is centered in the viewing area.

2   To display artwork at actual size, choose View > Actual Size. The artwork is displayed at 100%. The actual size of your artwork determines how much of it can be viewed on-screen at 100%.

▶ **Tip:** Double-clicking the Zoom tool in the Tools panel is another shortcut for displaying artwork at 100%.

3   Choose View > Fit Artboard In Window before continuing to the next section.

Using the Zoom tool

In addition to the View commands, you can use the Zoom tool to magnify and reduce the view of artwork. Use the View menu to select predefined magnification levels or to fit your artwork in the Document window.

1 Click the Zoom tool (🔍) in the Tools panel to select the tool, and move the pointer into the Document window. Notice that a plus sign (+) appears at the center of the Zoom tool.

2 Position the Zoom tool over the text "seattle flowers" on the right side of the artboard and click once. The artwork is displayed at a higher magnification.

3 Click two more times on the "seattle flowers" text. The view is increased again, and you'll notice that the area you clicked is magnified. Next you'll reduce the view of the artwork.

4 With the Zoom tool still selected, position the pointer over the text "seattle flowers" and hold down Alt (Windows) or Option (Mac OS). A minus sign (–) appears at the center of the Zoom tool pointer. Keep the key held down for the next step.

Note: The percentage at which the area is magnified is determined by the size of the marquee you draw with the Zoom tool—the smaller the marquee, the higher the level of magnification.

5 While pressing Alt or Option, click the artwork twice. The view of the artwork is reduced.

For a more controlled zoom, you can drag a marquee around a specific area of your artwork. This magnifies just the selected area.

6 Choose View > Fit Artboard In Window before proceeding.

7 With the Zoom tool selected, drag a marquee around the large blue flower in the center of the Document window. Watch as a marquee appears around the area you are dragging, and then release the mouse button. The marqueed area is now enlarged to fit the size of the Document window.

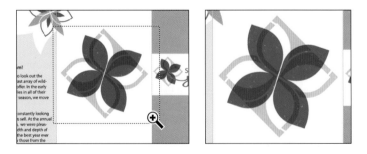

Note: Although you can draw a marquee with the Zoom tool to enlarge the view of artwork, it is not very useful to draw a marquee when reducing the view of artwork.

8 Double-click the Zoom tool (🔍) in the Tools panel to return to a 100% view.

Because the Zoom tool is used frequently during the editing process to enlarge and reduce the view of artwork, you can select it from the keyboard at any time without deselecting any other tool you may be using.

9 Before selecting the Zoom tool from the keyboard, select any other tool in the Tools panel and move the pointer into the Document window.

10 Now hold down Ctrl+spacebar (Windows) or Command+spacebar (Mac OS) to use the Zoom tool without actually choosing that tool. Click or drag to zoom in on any area of the artwork, and then release the keys.

11 To zoom out using the keyboard, hold down Ctrl+Alt+spacebar (Windows) or Command+Option+spacebar (Mac OS). Click the desired area to reduce the view of the artwork, and then release the keys.

12 Double-click the Zoom tool in the Tools panel to return to a 100% view of your artwork.

Note: In certain versions of Mac OS, the keyboard shortcuts for the Zoom tool open Spotlight or Finder. If you decide to use these shortcuts in Illustrator, you may want to turn off or change these keyboard shortcuts in the Mac OS System Preferences.

Scrolling through a document

You use the Hand tool to pan to different areas of a document. Using the Hand tool allows you to push the document around much like you would a piece of paper on your desk.

1 Select the Hand tool (✋) in the Tools panel.

2 Click and drag down in the Document window. As you drag, the artwork moves with the hand.

   As with the Zoom tool (🔍), you can select the Hand tool with a keyboard shortcut without deselecting the active tool.

3 Click any other tool except the Type tool (T) in the Tools panel and move the pointer into the Document window.

4 Hold down the spacebar to select the Hand tool from the keyboard, and then click and drag to bring the artwork back into the center of your view.

   You can also use the Hand tool as a shortcut to fit all the artwork in the window.

5 Double-click the Hand tool to fit the active artboard in the window.

Note: The spacebar shortcut for the Hand tool does not work when the Type tool is active and your cursor is in text.

Navigating multiple artboards

Illustrator CS4 allows for multiple artboards within a single file. This is a great way to create a multi-page document so that you can have collateral pieces like a brochure, a postcard, and business card in the same document. You can easily share content between pieces, create multi-page PDFs and print multiple pages by creating multiple artboards.

Multiple artboards can be added when you initially create an Illustrator document by choosing File > New, or you can add or remove artboards after the document is created using the Artboard tool in the Tools panel. Next you will learn how to efficiently navigate a document with multiple artboards.

1   Select the Selection tool (▴) in the Tools panel.

2   Press Ctrl+– (Windows) or Cmd+– (Mac OS) twice to zoom out. Notice that there are several (four) artboards to the right and below the current artboard.

The artboards in a document can be arranged in any order, orientation, or artboard size. Suppose that you want to create a four page brochure. Every page of the brochure can be a different artboard, and all the artboards can be the same size and orientation. They can be arranged horizontally or vertically or whatever way makes the most sense to you.

The Flowers.ai document has four artboards. The two larger artboards are the front and back of a flyer. The smallest artboard is a business card, and the medium-sized artboard is the front side of a postcard. After zooming out, notice the green logo in the upper left corner of the canvas, which is outside of the artboard. This logo was placed there because it may be used later.

▶ **Tip:** Choose Fit All In Window to see all of the artboards and content in the canvas area.

3   Choose View > **Fit Artboard In Window**. This command fits the current artboard in the window. You can tell which artboard is the current artboard by viewing the Artboard Navigation menu.

● **Note:** Learn how to set the artboard numbering (which numbers in the Artboard Navigation menu related to which artboard), add artboards, and edit artboards in Chapter 3, "Creating and Editing Shapes," and Chapter 4, "Transforming Objects."

4   Choose 2 from the Artboard Navigation menu in the lower left corner of the Document window. This business card appears in the Document window.

5   Choose View > Zoom Out. Notice that zooming occurs on the currently selected artboard.

6   Click the Next button to the right of the Artboard Navigation menu to view the next artboard in the Document window.

7   Click the First button to navigate to the first artboard in the document.

Arranging documents

When you open more than one Illustrator file, the Document windows are tabbed. You can arrange the open documents in a variety of ways including as a default tabbed view or open them side by side to easily compare or drag items from one document to another. You can also use the Arrange Documents window to quickly display your open documents in a variety of configurations. Next you will open several other documents that are versions of the original Flowers.ai you opened in the beginning of the lesson.

1   Choose File > Open and in the Lesson01 folder, Shift-click to select the L1start2.ai and L1start3.ai files located in the Lessons folder on your hard disk. Click Open to open both files at once.

You should now have three Illustrator files open, Flowers.ai, L1start2.ai, and L1start3.ai. Each file has its own tab at the top of the Document window. These documents are considered to be a group of Document windows. You can create multiple document groups to loosely associate files while they are open.

2   Click the Flowers.ai document tab to show the Flowers.ai Document window.

3   Click and drag the Flowers.ai document tab to the right, so that it is between the other two document tabs to the right.

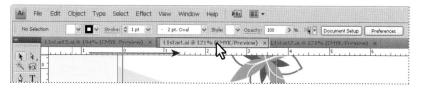

Note: Your tabs may be in a slightly different order. That's OK. Also be careful to drag directly to the right, otherwise you could undock the Document window and create a new group.

Dragging the document tabs allows you to change the order of the documents. This can be very useful if you use the navigate to next or previous document shortcuts:

- Ctrl+F6 (next document), Ctrl+Shift+F6 (previous document) (Windows)
- Cmd+` (next document), Cmd+Shift+` (previous document) (Mac OS)

4   Drag the document tabs in order from left to right, starting with Flowers.ai, and continuing with L1start2.ai, L1start3.ai.

The three documents that are currently open are versions of marketing pieces. To see all of them at one time, you can arrange the Document windows by cascading the windows or tiling them. Cascading allows you to cascade (stack) different document groups and is discussed further in the next section. Tiling shows multiple Document windows at one time in various arrangements.

Next you will tile the open documents so that you can see them all at one time.

5 On the Mac OS (Windows users can skip to the next step), choose Window > Application Frame.

Mac OS users can use the application frame to group all the workspace elements in a single, integrated window similar to working on Windows. If you move or resize the application frame, the elements respond to each other so that they don't overlap.

6 Choose Window > Arrange > Tile.

This shows all three Document windows arranged in a pattern.

7 Click in each of the Document windows. This activates that particular document. Choose View > Fit Artboard In Window for each of the documents.

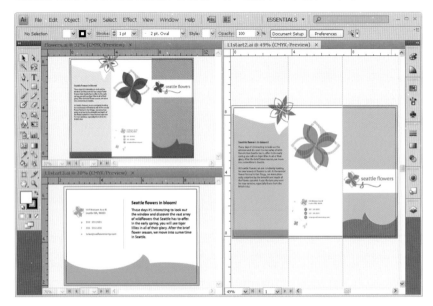

The documents tiled

Note: Your documents may be tiled in a different order and that's OK.

With documents tiled, you may need to drag the dividing lines between each of the Document windows to reveal more or less of a particular document. You can also drag objects between each document to copy them from one document to another.

8 Click in the L1start2.ai Document window. With the Selection tool, click and drag the brown and blue star graphic in the upper left area of the artboard, to the L1start3.ai Document window, and release the mouse button. This copies the graphic from L1start2.ai to L1start3.ai.

Note: After dragging the content in step 8, notice how the document tab for L1start3.ai now has an asterisk to the right of the file name. This indicates that the file needs to be saved.

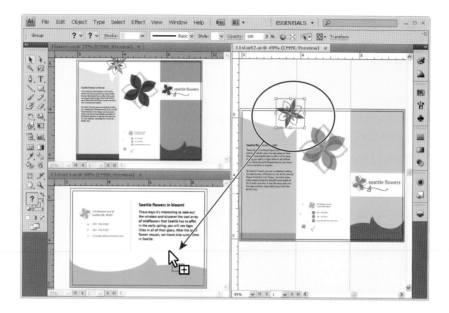

To change the arrangement of the tiled windows, you can drag document tabs around, but that can be difficult to manage. The Arrange Documents window lets you quickly arrange open documents in a variety of configurations.

9 Click the Arrange Documents button (![icon] ▾) in the Control panel to reveal the Arrange Documents window. Select the Tile All Vertically button (![icon]) to see the documents tiled vertically.

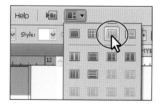

10 Click the 2-Up vertical button (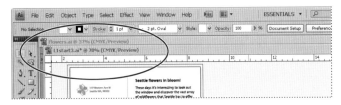) in the Arrange Documents window in the Control panel.

Notice that two of the documents appear as tabs in one of the tiled areas.

11 Click to select the L1start2.ai tab, then click the x on the right side of the L1start2.ai document tab to close the document.

12 Click the Arrange Documents button (▦ ▾) in the Control panel and click the Consolidate All button (▦) in the Arrange Documents window. This returns the two documents to tabs in the same group. Keep the Flowers.ai and L1start3.ai documents open.

Consolidate All arranges the two documents into tabs in the same Document window.

Document groups

Open documents in Illustrator, by default, are arranged as tabs in a single group of windows. You can create multiple groups of files for easier navigation and temporarily associate files together. This can be helpful if you are working on a large project that requires you to create and edit multiple pieces. Grouping documents lets you float the groups so that they are separate from the application window (Windows) or screen (Mac OS). Next you will create and work with two groups of files.

1 Click to select the L1start3.ai file tab.

2 Choose Window > Arrange > Float All In Windows. This creates a separate group for the L1start3.ai file. By default the groups are cascaded with one on top of the other, and the title bars showing.

Document windows floating in separate groups

3 Click the title bar for Flowers.ai and notice that L1start3.ai is not visible. L1star3.ai is now behind Flowers.ai.

4 Choose File > Open and in the Lesson01 folder, select the L1start2.ai file located in the Lessons folder on your hard disk. Click Open. Notice that the newly opened document is added as a document tab to the group that contains Flowers.ai.

● **Note:** When you open a document or create a new document, that document is added to the currently selected group.

5 Choose Window > Arrange > Cascade to reveal both groups.

6 Click the minimize button in the upper right corner (Windows) or the upper left corner (Mac OS) of the L1start3.ai group. Notice that in Windows, the group minimizes to the lower left corner of the application window by default. In the Mac OS, the window minimizes to the operating system Dock.

7 Click the minimize button again or the document tab to show the minimized group (Windows) or click the document thumbnail in the Dock to show the minimized group (Mac OS).

8 Click the Close button in the upper right (Windows) or upper left (Mac OS) to close the L1start3.ai group.

9 If the Save dialog box appears, click Don't Save.

10 Click and drag the document tab for L1start2.ai down until the document appears to float freely. This is another way to create a floating group of documents.

11 Close the L1start2.ai file, and leave Flowers.ai open.

12 On Windows (Mac OS users can skip to the next step), choose Window > Arrange > Consolidate All Windows.

13 On the MacOS, choose Window > Application Frame to deselect the Application frame, then click the green button in the upper left corner of the Document window so that the Document window fits as well as it can.

Using the Navigator panel

The Navigator panel lets you scroll through a document with a single artboard or multiple artboards. This is useful when you need to see all artboards in the document in one window and edit content in any of those artboards in a zoomed in view.

1 Choose View > Fit Artboard In Window.

2 Choose Window > Navigator to open the Navigator panel. It is free-floating in the workspace.

Note: Dragging the slider in the Navigator panel tends to jump in percentage values (be less precise). You may also type in a value in the lower left corner of the Navigator panel.

3 In the Navigator panel, drag the slider to the left to approximately 75% to change the view of the document. As you drag the slider to decrease the level of magnification, the red box in the Navigator panel, called the proxy preview area, becomes larger, showing the area of the document that is being shown.

4 Position the pointer inside the proxy preview area (the red box) of the Navigator panel. The pointer becomes a hand ($\sqrt[3]{}$).

5 Drag the hand in the proxy preview area of the Navigator panel to pan to different parts of the artwork. Drag the proxy preview area over the small artboard in the upper right of the Navigator window. This is a business card.

6 Click the larger mountain icon (⬛) in the lower right corner of the Navigator panel several times to zoom into the business card.

7 In the Navigator panel, move the pointer outside of the proxy preview area and click. This moves the box and displays a different area of the artwork in the Document window.

8 With the pointer (hand) still positioned in the Navigator panel, hold down the Ctrl (Windows) or Command (Mac OS) key. When the hand changes to a magnifier, drag a marquee over an area of the artwork. The smaller the marquee you draw, the higher the magnification level in the Document window.

▶ **Tip:** Choosing Panel Options from the Navigator panel menu allows you to customize the Navigator panel in several ways, including changing the color of the view box.

9 Deselect View Artboard Contents Only from the Navigator panel menu (▾≡). This shows you any artwork that is in the canvas as well. Notice the green version of the logo in the canvas.

● **Note:** You may need to adjust the slider in the Navigator panel to see the logo in the proxy area.

● **Note:** The percentage and proxy preview area in your Navigator panel may appear different, but that's alright.

10 Close the Navigator panel group by clicking the x in upper right corner (Windows) or the dot in the upper left corner (Mac OS) of the title bar. Choose File > Close to close any open files. If a dialog box appears asking you to save changes, you don't need to.

Finding Resources for using Illustrator

For complete and up-to-date information about using Illustrator panels, tools, and other application features, visit the Adobe website. Choose Help > Illustrator Help. You'll be connected to the Adobe Community Help website, where you can search Illustrator Help and support documents, as well as other websites relevant to Illustrator users. You can narrow your search results to view only Adobe help and support documents, as well.

If you plan to work in Illustrator when you're not connected to the Internet, download the most current PDF version of Illustrator Help from www.adobe.com/go/documentation.

For additional resources, such as tips and techniques and the latest product information, check out the Adobe Community Help page at community.adobe.com/help/main.

● **Note:** If Illustrator detects that you are not connected to the Internet when you start the application, choosing Help > Illustrator Help opens the Help HTML pages installed with Illustrator. For more up-to-date information, view the Help files online or download the current PDF for reference.

Searching for a topic in Help

1 In the search box in the Application bar, type artboard and press Enter or Return.

   If you are connected to the internet, the Adobe Community Help website is opened in an available browser. From there, you can explore the different help topics available.

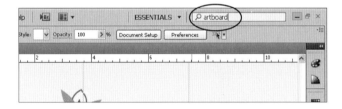

2 Close the browser and return to Illustrator.

Checking for updates

Adobe periodically provides updates to software. You can easily obtain these updates through Adobe Updater, as long as you have an active Internet connection.

1   In Illustrator, choose Help > Updates. The Adobe Updater automatically checks for updates available for your Adobe software.

2   In the Adobe Updater dialog box, select the updates you want to install, and then click Download And Install Updates to install them.

● **Note:** To set your preferences for future updates, click Preferences. Select how often you want Adobe Updater to check for updates, for which applications, and whether to download them automatically. Click OK to accept the new settings.

3   When you are finished investigating Illustrator Help, close the browser window and return to Illustrator.

Exploring on your own

Open a sample file from Adobe Illustrator CS4 to investigate and use some of the navigational and organization features learned in this lesson.

1 Open the file named Yellowstone Map.ai in the Lesson01 folder.

● **Note:** A missing profile dialog box may appear. Click OK to continue.

2 Perform the following on this artwork:

- Practice zooming in and out. Notice that at the smaller zoom levels the text is "greeked," appearing as though it is a solid gray bar. As you zoom in closer, the text can be viewed more accurately.

- Save zoomed in views using View > New View for different areas such as; Mammoth Springs, Tower-Roosevelt and Canyon Village.

- Create a zoomed in view of Madison in the Outline View. Create a Preview view of the entire map.

- Enlarge the Navigator panel and use it to scroll around the artboards and to zoom in and out.

- Navigate between artboards using the Artboard Navigation menu and buttons in the lower left corner of the Document window.

- Create a Saved workspace (View > New View) that shows only the Tools panel, Control panel and Layers panel. Save it as map tools.

Review questions

1 Describe two ways to change the view of a document.

2 Describe a way to navigate between artboards.

3 How do you select tools in Illustrator?

4 Describe three ways to change a panel display.

5 How do you save panel locations and visibility preferences?

6 Describe how arranging Document windows can be helpful.

7 Describe how to get more information about Illustrator.

Review answers

1 You can choose commands from the View menu to zoom in or out of a document, or fit it to your screen; you can also use the Zoom tool in the Tools panel, and click or drag over a document to enlarge or reduce the view. In addition, you can use keyboard shortcuts to magnify or reduce the display of artwork. You can also use the Navigator panel to scroll artwork or change its magnification without using the Document window.

2 Select an artboard by number from the Artboard Navigation menu. Click the Next, Previous, First, or Last buttons to navigate between artboards.

3 To select a tool, you can either click the tool in the Tools panel, or press the keyboard shortcut for that tool. For example, you can press V to select the Selection tool from the keyboard. Selected tools remain active until you click a different tool.

4 You can click a panel's tab or choose Window > [panel name] to make the panel appear. You can drag a panel's tab to separate the panel from its group or to remove it from a dock and create a new group, or drag the panel into another group. You can drag a panel group's title bar to move the entire group. Double-click a panel's tab to cycle through a panel's various sizes. You can also press Shift+Tab to hide or display all panels.

5 Choose Window > Workspace > Save Workspace to create custom work areas and make it easier to find the controls that you need.

6   Arranging Document windows allows you to tile windows or cascade document groups. This can be useful if you are working on multiple Illustrator files and you need to compare or share content between them.

7   Adobe Illustrator contains Help, plus keyboard shortcuts and some additional information and full-color illustrations. Illustrator also has context-sensitive help about tools and commands, and online services for additional information on services, products, and Illustrator tips.

2 SELECTING AND ALIGNING

Lesson overview

In this lesson, you'll learn how to do the following:

- Differentiate between the various selection tools.

- Group and ungroup items.

- Work in isolation mode.

- Work with smart guides.

- Clone items with the Selection tool.

- Lock and hide items for organizational purposes.

- Save selections for future use.

- Use tools and commands to align basic shapes to each other.

 This lesson takes approximately an hour to complete. If needed, remove the previous lesson folder from your hard disk and copy the Lesson02 folder onto it.

In this lesson, you learn how to locate and select objects using the selection tools, as well as how to protect other objects by hiding and locking them. You also learn how to align objects to each other and the artboard.

Getting started

When changing colors or size, and adding effects or attributes, you must first select the object to which you are applying the changes. In this lesson you will learn the fundamentals of using the selection tools. More advanced selection techniques using layers are discussed in Lesson 8, "Working with Layers."

1   To ensure that the tools and panels function as described in this lesson, delete or deactivate (by renaming) the Adobe Illustrator CS4 preferences file. See "Restoring default preferences" on page 3.

2   Start Adobe Illustrator CS4.

● **Note:** If you have not already copied the resource files for this lesson onto your hard disk from the Lesson02 folder on the Adobe Illustrator CS4 Classroom in a Book CD, do so now. See "Copying the Classroom in a Book files" on page 2.

3   Choose File > Open, and open the L2start_01.ai file in the Lesson02 folder, located in the Lessons folder on your hard disk. Choose View > Fit Artboard In Window.

Using the Selection tool

The Selection tool in the Tools panel lets you select entire objects.

1   Select the Selection tool (▸) in the Tools panel. Position the pointer over the different shapes without clicking. The icon that appears as you pass over objects (▸.) indicates that there is an object that can be selected under the pointer. When you hover over an object, it is outlined in blue.

2   Hover the pointer over the edge of one of the black airplanes. A word such as path or anchor may appear because smart guides are selected by default. Smart guides are snap-to guides that help you align, edit, and transform objects or artboards. Smart guides are discussed in more detail in Chapter 3, "Creating and Editing Shapes."

3   Click the black airplane in the upper left corner. A bounding box with eight handles appears.

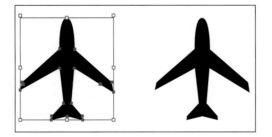

The bounding box is used for transformations such as resizing and rotating. It also indicates that this item is selected and ready to be modified. The color of the bounding box indicates which layer the object is on. Layers are discussed more in Lesson 8, "Working with layers."

4   Using the Selection tool, click the airplane on the right and notice that the left airplane is now deselected and only the second airplane is selected.

5   Add the left airplane to the selection by holding down the Shift key and clicking the airplane on the left. Both airplanes are now selected.

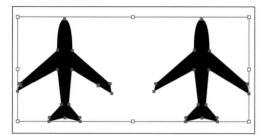

Add other items to a selection by holding down the Shift key.

Note: When you select an item without a fill, you must click on the stroke (border).

▶ Tip: To select all objects, choose Select > All. To select all objects in a single artboard, choose Select > All In Active Artboard. To learn more about artboards, see Chapter 3, "Creating and Editing Shapes."

6   Reposition the airplanes anywhere in the document by clicking in the center of either selected airplane and dragging. Because both airplanes are selected, they travel together.

As you drag, notice the green lines that appear. These are called alignment guides and are visible because smart guides are selected (View > Smart Guides). As you drag, the objects are aligned to other objects on the artboard. Also notice the gray box, or measurement label, that shows the object's distance from its original position. Measurement labels appear because smart guides are selected.

▶ Tip: If you don't want to use smart guides at times, you can deselect them by choosing View > Smart Guides.

7   Deselect the airplanes by clicking the artboard where there are no objects, or by choosing Select > Deselect.

8   Revert to the last saved version of the document by pressing the F12 key or choosing File > Revert. In the Revert dialog box, click Revert.

Using the Direct Selection tool

The Direct Selection tool selects points or path segments within an object. Next you will select anchor points and path segments using the Direct Selection tool.

1   With the same file open, switch to the Direct Selection tool (◄) in the Tools panel. Without clicking, move the pointer over the different points on the airplanes. When the Direct Selection tool is over an anchor point of a deselected or selected path or object, by default an anchor or path label, such as the word anchor or path, appears.

2 Click the top point of the first airplane. Note that only the point you selected is solid, indicating that it is selected, while the other points in the airplane are hollow and not selected.

Notice the direction lines extending from the anchor point. At the end of the direction lines are direction points. The angle and length of the direction lines determine the shape and size of the curved segments. Moving the direction points reshapes the curves.

● **Note:** The gray measurement label that appears as you drag the anchor point has the values dx and dy. Dx indicates the distance the pointer has moved along the x axis (horizontally), and dy indicates the distance the pointer has moved along the y axis (vertical).

3 With the Direct Selection tool still selected, click and drag the individual point down to edit the shape of the object. Try clicking on other points. When you click another point, the previous point is deselected.

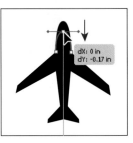

4 Revert to the last saved version by choosing File > Revert. In the Revert dialog box, click Revert.

▶ **Tip:** Using the Shift key, you can select multiple points to move them together.

Selection and anchor point preferences

You can change selection preferences and how anchor points appear in the Preferences dialog box.

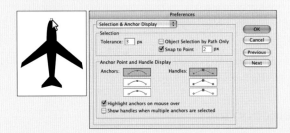

Choose Edit > Preferences > Selection & Anchor Display (Windows) or Illustrator > Preferences > Selection & Anchor Display (Mac OS). You can change the size of anchor points (called anchors in the dialog box) or the display of the direction lines (called handles).

You can also turn off the highlighting of anchor points as the pointer hovers over them. As you move the pointer over anchor points, they are highlighted. Highlighting anchor points makes it easier to determine which point you are about to select. You learn more about anchor points and anchor point handles in Lesson 5, "Drawing with the Pen and Pencil tools."

Creating selections with a marquee

Some selections may be easier to make by creating a marquee around the objects that you want to select.

1   In the same file, switch to the Selection tool (▶). Instead of Shift-clicking to select the first two airplanes, position the pointer above the upper left airplane and then click and drag downward and to the right to create a marquee that overlaps just the tops of the airplanes.

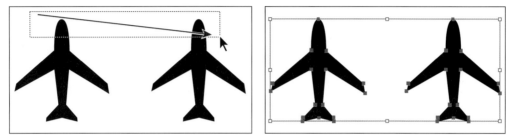

When dragging with the Selection tool, you only need to encompass a small part of an object to include it in the selection.

2   Choose Select > Deselect or click where there are no objects.

3   Now use the Direct Selection tool (▷) to perform the same action. Click outside the first airplane and drag across to select the nose of each airplane in the top row.

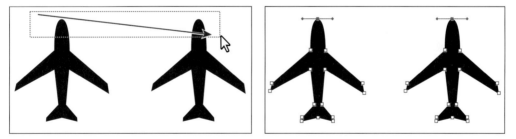

Drag across the top points with the Direct Selection tool selects only those points.

Only the top points become selected. Click one of the anchor points and drag to see how the airplanes reposition together. Use this method when selecting a single point. That way, you don't have to click exactly on the anchor point that you want to edit.

4   Choose Select > Deselect.

Creating selections with the Magic Wand tool

You can use the Magic Wand tool to select all objects in a document that have the same or similar color or pattern fill attributes.

▶ **Tip:** You can customize the Magic Wand tool to select objects based on stroke weight, stroke color, opacity, or blending mode by double-clicking the Magic Wand tool in the Tools panel. You can also change the tolerances used to identify similar objects.

1   Select the Magic Wand tool (✱) in the Tools panel. Click the apple and notice that the fish is selected as well. No bounding box (a box surrounding the two shapes) appears because the Magic Wand tool is still selected.

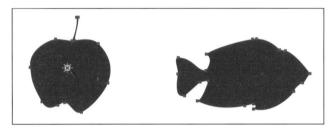

When selecting with the Magic Wand tool, objects with the same color fill are selected as well.

2   Click one of the baseball hats with the Magic Wand tool. Notice that both hats are selected and that the apple and fish are deselected.

3   Holding down the Shift key, use the Magic Wand tool to click the apple. This adds the apple and fish to the selection since they have the same fill color (red). With the Magic Wand tool still selected, hold down Alt (Windows) or Option (Mac OS) and click the apple again to deselect the red objects. Release the keys.

4   Choose Select > Deselect or click where there are no objects.

Grouping items

You can combine objects in a group so that the objects are treated as a single unit. This way, you can move or transform a number of objects without affecting their attributes or relative positions.

1   Select the Selection tool (▶). Click outside the top right airplane and drag a marquee that touches both airplanes, the fish, and apple to select all four objects.

2   Choose Object > Group, and then choose Select > Deselect.

3   With the Selection tool, click the apple. Because it is grouped with the other three objects, all four are now selected. Notice that the word Group appears on the left side of the Control panel.

4   Choose Select > Deselect.

Adding to a group

Groups can also be nested—they can be grouped within other objects or groups to form larger groups.

1 With the Selection tool (➤), click an airplane to select the grouped objects. Shift-click the left hat in the third row to add it to the selection. Choose Object > Group. The bounding box is expanded to include the hat.

2 Shift-click the right hat in the third row and then choose Object > Group.

You have created a nested group—a group within a group. Nesting is a common technique used when designing artwork.

3 Choose Select > Deselect.

4 With the Selection tool, click one of the grouped objects. All objects in the group become selected.

5 Click a blank area on the artboard to deselect the objects.

6 Hold down the Direct Selection tool (➤) in the Tools panel, and drag to the right to access the Group Selection tool (➤⁺).

7 Click once on the left airplane to select the object. Click again to select the object's parent group. The Group Selection tool adds each group to the selection in the order in which it was grouped.

● **Note:** After step 1, notice that the bounding box also goes around the hat on the right in the third row. Look for anchor points to indicate if the object is actually selected.

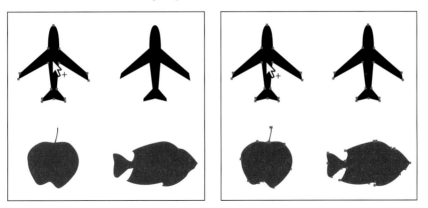

The Group Selection tool adds the object's parent group(s) to the current selection.

8 Choose Select > Deselect.

9 With the Selection tool, click any object to select the group of objects. Choose Object > Ungroup to ungroup the objects. You must repeat this action for each group. For this lesson, to completely ungroup all objects, you need to choose Object > Ungroup three times.

Working in isolation mode

Isolation mode isolates groups or sublayers so that you can easily select and edit specific objects or parts of objects. When you use isolation mode, you don't need to worry about what layer an object is on, nor do you need to manually lock or hide the objects you don't want affected by your edits. All objects outside of the isolated group are locked so that they aren't affected by the edits you make. An isolated object appears in full color, while the rest of the artwork appears dimmed, letting you know which content you can edit.

► **Tip:** To enter isolation mode, you can also select a group with the Selection tool and click the Isolate Selected Object button (⊡) in the Control panel.

1 With the Selection tool (▶), click a blank area of the artboard to deselect, and then drag a marquee across the fish and apple to select them. Choose Object > Group. The word Group appears in the Control panel indicating that a group is now selected.

2 With the Selection tool, double-click the apple to enter isolation mode.

At the top of the Document window, a gray arrow appears with the words Layer 1 and <Group>. This indicates that you have isolated a group of objects that is on layer 1. You learn more about layers in Lesson 8, "Working with Layers." Notice that the rest of the content on the page appears dimmed (you can't select it).

3 Click the fish to select it. Drag it to the left.

When you enter isolation mode, groups are temporarily ungrouped. This enables you to edit objects in the group without having to ungroup.

► **Tip:** To exit isolation mode, you can also click the gray arrow in the upper left corner of the Document window until isolation mode disappears. Or, click the Exit isolation mode button (⊡) in the Control panel.

4 Double-click outside of the objects to exit isolation mode.

5 Click to select the fish. Notice that it is once again grouped with the apple and you can now select other objects on the page.

6 Choose Select > Deselect.

Selecting similar objects

You can also select objects based on fill color, stroke color, stroke weight, and more. The stroke of an object is its outline, and the fill is a color applied to the interior area. Next you will select several objects with the same fill color.

1 With the Selection tool (▶), click to select the baseball hat on the left.

2 Click the arrow to the right of the Select Similar Objects button (▨▾) in the Control panel to reveal a menu. Choose Fill Color to select all objects on the artboard with the same fill color (orange). Notice that both hats are selected.

3 Choose Select > Deselect.

4 Choose File > Close, and don't save the file.

Applying selection techniques

In this lesson, you will use some of the techniques discussed previously in this chapter, as well as other selection options.

1 Choose File > Open, and open the L2start_02.ai file in the Lesson02 folder, located in the Lessons folder on your hard disk. This document has two artboards that you will navigate.

2 Press Shift+Tab to hide the panels. You can also hide the panels individually or by groups using the Window menu.

3 Choose 2 from the Artboard Navigation menu in the lower left corner of the Document window. Make sure that the current artboard is visible by choosing View > Fit Artboard In Window. For information on navigating multiple artboards, see Chapter 1, "Getting to Know the Work Area." Artboard 2 shows the final assembled artwork.

4 Choose 1 from the Artboard Navigation menu to return to the first artboard.

5 Choose View > Zoom Out to see both artboards.

6 Holding down the spacebar to temporarily access the Hand tool (✋), click and drag the artboards to the left until you see both artboards completely.

7 Choose View > Smart Guides to deselect smart guides temporarily.

8 With the Selection tool (▶), select the white daisy flower shape in artboard 1. Notice that it is part of a group of objects, and that the word Group appears in the Control panel. To avoid grabbing a bounding box handle and accidently resizing the shapes, click and drag the yellow center of the flower group to slide it to its new location as the head of the green flower stem on the left.

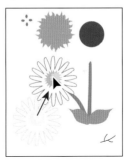

▶ **Tip:** To navigate artboards, you can also click the Previous or Next buttons, or click the First or Last buttons to the left and right of the Artboard Navigation menu.

9 Double-click the yellow center to enter isolation mode. Click to select the light yellow shape and drag it so that it's more centered on the other two shapes.

10 Click outside of the shapes to deselect the yellow center.

11 Press Escape to exit isolation mode.

12 Using the Selection tool, drag the orange sunflower base and the brown sunflower center into position, as shown in the figure at right.

13 With the Selection tool, click and drag across the leaf vein shapes below and to the right of the flowers to select all three shapes. Choose Object > Group.

14 Click and drag the grouped leaf veins onto the right leaf. Click a blank area of the artboard to deselect the group.

15 Select the orange and brown sunflower shapes with the Selection tool by Shift-clicking them. Choose Object > Lock > Selection to keep them in position. You cannot select the shapes until you choose Object > Unlock All. Leave them locked for now.

16 Select the Zoom tool (🔍) in the Tools panel and click three times on the leaves at the bottom of the flowers on the current artboard (artboard 1).

17 Hold down the Group Selection tool (𝅺) in the Tools panel, and drag to the right to access the Direct Selection tool (𝅺). Click the anchor point on the tip of the left leaf. When the individual point is selected, it appears as a solid point (active); the other anchor points are hollow (inactive). Click and drag the individual anchor point to change its position.

If you are having difficulty accessing only one anchor point, choose Select > Deselect. Then, using the Direct Selection tool, click and drag a marquee around the point, encompassing it with the selection marquee.

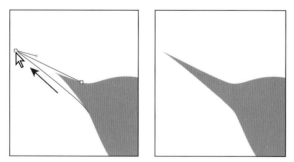

18 Individually select other anchor points in the leaf shape and move them in different directions to reshape the leaf.

19 Double-click the Hand tool () in the Tools panel to fit the artboard in the window.

20 Select the Selection tool. The sunflower center consists of four small, light brown ellipses. Click to select one of the ellipses. In the Control panel, click the Select Similar Objects button () to select all four of the ellipses. Choose Object > Group. Drag the group into position in the center of the orange and brown sunflower.

Note: The Select Similar Objects button remembers the last menu item you chose (fill color for this lesson). When you click the button, it selects objects with the same fill color.

21 Using the Selection tool, hold down Alt (Windows) or Option (Mac OS) to copy, or clone, the group of ellipses. With the key held down, drag the flower center group to the center of the white flower. Position the cloned group as the white flower's center. Make sure to release the mouse button before releasing Alt or Option.

Note: If you also hold down the Shift key when cloning, the cloned object is constrained and snaps to a straight 45°, 90°, or 180° angle.

22 Choose File > Save and then File > Close.

Press Alt or Option and drag to clone, or copy, the center ellipse shapes.

Advanced selection techniques

When working on complex artwork, selections may become more difficult to control. In this section, you'll combine some of the techniques you've already learned with additional features that make selecting objects easier.

1 Open the file named L2start_03.ai in the Lesson02 folder of Lessons folder.

2 The large words in this artwork make it difficult to select items underneath. Using the Selection tool (), select the word "Fries," and choose Object > Hide > Selection or press Ctrl+3 (Windows) or Command+3 (Mac OS). The word is hidden so that you can more easily select other objects.

3 Select any small red star and choose Select > Same > Fill & Stroke. All the other red stars are now selected. Click Fill color in the Control panel and select white in the Swatches panel that appears. The stars all change to white.

4 Close the Swatches panel by pressing Escape.

5 Select one of the shapes within the french fries and then choose Select > Same > Stroke Weight. The french fry shape has a 1.5 pt stroke, so all strokes that are 1.5 pt are now selected.

6 There is another artboard to the right of the current artboard. Choose View > Zoom Out to see both artboards. If necessary, hold down the spacebar to temporarily select the Hand tool (✋) and drag the artboards to the left until you see both of them.

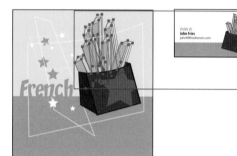

When you use the select similar commands, similar objects on all artboards are selected by default.

7 Choose 3 pt from the Stroke Weight menu to increase the stroke weight.

▶ **Tip:** It is helpful to name selections according to use or function. In step 8, if you name the selection 3 pt stroke, for instance, the name may be misleading if you later change the stroke weight of the object.

8 With the previous selection still active, choose Select > Save Selection. Name the selection french fries, and click OK. You can choose this selection at a later time.

9 Choose Select > Deselect to deselect the objects. Choose Select > french fries from the bottom of the Select menu to make the selection active. Change the stroke weight to 2 pt in the Control panel.

10 Choose Object > Show All. The text Fries now appears and is selected. Keep the file open for the next exercise and the Fries text still selected.

Locking selected objects

As you create more complex artwork, existing objects may get in the way and make it difficult to select objects. Besides hiding objects, a common technique is to lock selected artwork.

* **To lock an object:** Select an object (or objects), then choose Object > Lock > Selection, or Ctrl+2 (Windows) or Command+2 (Mac OS). A locked object cannot be moved or selected although it can still be seen. Unlock all objects at the same time by choosing Object > Unlock All, or use Ctrl+Alt+2 (Windows) or Command+Option+2 (Mac OS).

—From Illustrator Help

Aligning objects

Multiple objects may need to be aligned or distributed relative to each other, the artboard, or the crop area. In this section, you will explore the options for aligning objects and aligning points.

1   In the L2start_03.ai file, Shift-click the text French with the Selection tool (▶) to select the text French and the text Fries. Click the Horizontal Align Left button (⬓) in the Control panel, or if you don't see the Align options, click the word Align in the Control panel to open the Align panel. Notice that Fries moves to align with the word French.

Note: The Align options may not appear in the Control panel, but are indicated by the word Align. Illustrator fits as many options as it can in the Control panel, depending on your screen resolution.

2   Choose Edit > Undo Align to undo the alignment.

Aligning to a key object

A key object is an object that you want other objects to align to. You specify a key object by selecting all the objects you want to align, including the key object, and then clicking the key object again. When selected, the key object has a thick blue outline, and the Align To Key Object icon appears in the Control panel and the Align panel.

3   With the French and Fries text objects still selected, click Fries with the Selection tool. The thick blue outline indicates that it is the key object that other objects align to.

Fries is the key object.

Tip: In the Align panel, you can also choose Align To Key Object from the Align To option. The object that is in front becomes the key object.

4 In the Align options in the Control panel or the Align panel, click the Horizontal Align Left button (![]). Notice that French moves to align with Fries.

5 Choose Select > Deselect.

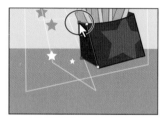

Aligning points

Next you'll align two points to each other using the Align panel.

1 With the Selection tool, Shift-click the words French and Fries and choose Object > Hide > Selection.

2 With the Direct Selection tool (![]), click the bottom left point of the red french fries box, and then Shift-click to select the top left point. You are selecting the points in a certain order because the last selected anchor point is the key anchor. Other points align to the last selected anchor point.

Shift-click to select two anchor points.

3 Click the Horizontal Align Left button (![]) in the Control panel.

● **Note:** If you don't see the Align options, click the word Align in the Control panel to reveal the Align panel.

4 Choose Object > Show All to reveal the text again.

Distributing objects

● **Note:** The Distribute Spacing options in the Align panel distribute the space between the objects, not the left, center, or right edges of the objects.

▶ **Tip:** You can also assign a specific spacing between objects using the Distribute Spacing options.

Distributing objects enables you to select multiple objects and distribute the spacing between those objects equally. The distribute options are also found in the Align panel. For example, if you have three stars and then click Horizontal Distribute Center, the leftmost and rightmost objects stars do not move and the middle star is repositioned so that its center point is halfway between the other two stars.

1 Click the Next button (![]) in the lower left corner of the Document window to go to artboard 2.

2 Choose View > Fit Artboard In Window if the artboard isn't showing in the Document window.

3 With the Selection tool (➤), drag across the four stars above the John Fries text to select them all.

4 Click the Horizontal Distribute Center button (‖↓‖) in the Control panel. This moves the center two stars so that the spacing between the center of each star is equal. Choose Select > Deselect.

5 With the Selection tool, click the rightmost star. Keep the mouse button held down, and Shift-drag to the right to keep the star vertically aligned with the other stars. Drag to the right until the right edge of the star is even with the letter s in John Fries.

Shift-drag the rightmost star to the right.

6 Select all four stars again, and click the Horizontal Distribute Center button again. Notice that with the rightmost star repositioned, the center two stars move to distribute the spacing between all the star center points. Choose Select > Deselect.

Aligning to the artboard

You can also align content to the artboard rather than other objects. With this method, each individual object is aligned separately to the artboard. Next you'll align the words French and Fries to the center of the artboard.

1 Click the Previous button (◀) in the lower left corner of the Document window to return to the first artboard.

2 With the Selection tool (➤), Shift-click to select the words French and Fries.

3 Choose Object > Group to group the objects together.

4 Click the Align To Selection button (▦) and choose Align To Artboard from the menu that appears (if it isn't already selected). Setting this option ensures that all future alignments are aligned to the artboard. Click the Horizontal Align Center (⤼) button to align the objects to the horizontal center of the artboard.

After aligning to the artboard

5 Choose File > Close without saving, unless you want to complete the Exploring on your own section.

● **Note:** When you want to align all content for a poster, for example, to the center of the artboard, grouping the objects is an important step. Grouping moves the objects together as one object, relative to the artboard. If this isn't done, centering everything horizontally moves all the objects to the center independent of each other.

About align options

The Align panel has a lot of features that are very useful in Illustrator. Not only can you align objects, but you can also distribute objects as well. Select the objects to align or distribute, then, in the Align panel, do any of the following:

- To align or distribute relative to the bounding box of all selected objects, click the button for the type of alignment or distribution you want.

- To align or distribute relative to one of the selected objects (a key object), click that object again (you don't need to hold down Shift as you click this time). Then click the button for the type of alignment or distribution you want.

   Note: *To stop aligning and distributing relative to an object, choose Cancel Key Object from the Align panel menu.*

- To align relative to the active artboard, click the Align To Artboard button (⊞) or click the Align menu (arrow to the right of the Align To Artboard button) and choose Align To Artboard. Then click the button for the type of alignment you want.

—From Illustrator Help

Exploring on your own

1   Experiment by cloning a star from L2start_03.ai. Clone it several times using the Alt or Option key.

2   Apply different colors and strokes to the shapes and reselect them using the Select Same menu item.

3   Select three stars from L2start_03.ai and try some of the distribute objects options in the Align panel.

4   Select three stars and click one of them to set it as the key object. Align the other selected stars to the key object using the align options in the Align panel. Keep the stars selected.

5   Choose Object > Group.

6   With the Selection tool, double-click one of the stars in the group to enter isolation mode.

7   Resize several of the stars by clicking and dragging each star's bounding box.

8   Press Escape to exit isolation mode.

9   Close the file without saving.

Review questions

1   How can you select an object that has no fill?

2   Name two ways you can select one item in a group without choosing Object > Ungroup.

3   How do you edit the shape of an object?

4   What should be done after spending a lot of time creating a selection that is going to be used repeatedly?

5   If something is blocking your view of a selection, what can you do?

6   To align objects to the artboard, what must be selected in the Align panel or Control panel before you choose an alignment option?

Review answers

1   You can select items that have no fill by clicking on the stroke or dragging a marquee across the object.

2   Using the Group Selection tool, you can click once for an individual item within a group. Continue to click to add the next grouped items to the selection. Read Lesson 8, "Working with Layers," to see how you can use layers to make complex selections. You can also double-click the group to enter isolation mode, edit the shapes as needed, and then exit isolation mode by pressing Escape or double-clicking outside of the group.

3   Using the Direct Selection tool, you can select one or more individual anchor points and make changes to the shape of an object.

4   For any selection that you need to use again, choose Select > Save Selection. Name the selection and reselect it at any time from the Select menu.

5   If something is blocking your access to a selection, you can choose Object > Hide > Selection. The object is not deleted, just hidden in the same position until you choose Object > Show All.

6   To align objects to artboard, the Align To Artboard option must be selected first.

3 CREATING AND EDITING SHAPES

Lesson overview

In this lesson, you'll learn how to do the following:

- Create a document with multiple artboards.
- Use tools and commands to create basic shapes.
- Use rulers and smart guides as drawing aids.
- Scale and duplicate objects.
- Join and outline objects.
- Work with Pathfinder commands to create shapes.
- Use Live Trace to create shapes.

This lesson will take approximately an hour and a half to complete. If needed, remove the previous lesson folder from your hard disk and copy the Lesson03 folder onto it.

You can create documents with multiple artboards and many kinds of objects by starting with a basic shape and then editing it to create new shapes. In this lesson, you'll add and edit artboards, then create and edit some basic shapes for a technical manual.

Getting started

In this lesson, you'll create several illustrations for a technical manual.

1   To ensure that the tools and panels function as described in this lesson, delete or deactivate (by renaming) the Adobe Illustrator CS4 preferences file. See "Restoring default preferences" on page 3.

2   Start Adobe Illustrator CS4.

● **Note:** If you have not already copied the resource files for this lesson onto your hard disk from the Lesson03 folder on the Adobe Illustrator CS4 Classroom in a Book CD, do so now. See "Copying the Classroom in a Book files" on page 2.

3   Choose File > Open. Locate the file named L3end.ai in the Lesson03 folder in the Lessons folder that you copied onto your hard disk. There are two artboards containing illustrations for a technical manual, including a screwdriver and a wrench with gears. You will create the tools

in this lesson. Choose View > Fit All In Window and leave the file open for reference, or choose File > Close.

Creating a document with multiple artboards

You will now make two illustrations for a technical manual. The document that you create will have several artboards.

● **Note:** When typing values in fields, if the correct unit is showing, you don't need to type the value again.

1   Choose File > New to open a new, untitled document. In the New Document dialog box, change the Name to tools, choose Print from the New Document Profile menu (if it isn't already selected) and change the Units to inches. When you change the units, the New Document Profile becomes [Custom]. Keep the dialog box open for the next step.

Document startup profiles

Using document profiles, you can set up a document for different kinds of output, such as print, web, video, and more. For example, if you are designing a web page mock-up, which you will do in this lesson, you can use a web document profile, which automatically displays the page size and units in pixels, changes the color mode to RGB, and the raster effects to Screen (72 ppi).

2 Change the Number Of Artboards option to 2 to create two artboards. Click the Arrange By Row button (⊡) and make sure that the Left To Right Layout arrow (→) is showing. In the Spacing text field, type 1. Click the word Width and type 7 in the Width field. Type 8 in the Height field. Click OK.

Note: The spacing value is the distance between each artboard.

Note: At left, the New Document dialog box shows the Print Document profile after customizing the options. The Advanced options (click the arrow left of Advanced to toggle open) are context-sensitive, which means that the options change based on which document profile is chosen.

3 Choose File > Save As. In the Save As dialog box, ensure that the name of the file is tools.ai, and choose the Lesson03 folder. Leave the Save As Type option set to Adobe Illustrator (*.AI) (Windows) or the Format option set to Adobe Illustrator (ai) (Mac OS), and click Save. In the Illustrator Options dialog box, leave the Illustrator options at their default settings, and click OK.

Note: If the Document Setup button does not appear in the Control panel, you can also choose File > Document Setup.

4 Choose Select > Deselect (if it's not dimmed) to make sure nothing is selected on either artboard. Click the Document Setup button in the Control panel.

After deselecting, the Document Setup button appears. When you click it, you can change the artboard size, units, bleeds, and more, after a document is created.

5 In the Bleed section of the Document Setup dialog box, change the value in the Top field to .13 in by clicking the up arrow to the left of the field once or typing the value. Click in the Bottom field or press the Tab key to make all the Bleed settings the same. Click OK.

Notice the red line that appears around both artboards. The red line indicates the bleed area. Typical bleeds for printing are about 1/8 of an inch.

Working with basic shapes

You'll begin this exercise by displaying a grid to use as a guideline for drawing and setting up the workspace.

1   Choose Window > Workspace > Essentials.

2   Choose View > Show Grid to display a grid that is useful for measuring, drawing, and aligning shapes. The grid doesn't print with the artwork. Choose View > Snap To Grid. The edges of drawn objects will now snap to, or pull toward, the grid lines.

3   Choose View > Show Rulers, or press Ctrl+R (Windows) or Command+R (Mac OS), to display rulers along the top and left side of the window if they are not already showing. The ruler units are inches because of the change you made in the New Document dialog box.

    You can change the ruler units used for all documents or for only the current document. The ruler unit applies to measuring objects, moving and transforming objects, setting grid and guide spacing, and creating ellipses and rectangles. It does not affect the units in the Character, Paragraph, and Stroke panels. The units used in these panels are controlled by the options in the Units & Display Performance dialog box in the program preferences (Edit > Preferences (Windows) or Illustrator > Preferences (Mac OS)).

> **Tip:** You can change grid properties, such as color and gridline distance by choosing Edit > Preferences > Guides & Grid (Windows) or Illustrator > Preferences > Guides & Grid (Mac OS).

> **Tip:** You can change the units for the current document by right-clicking or Ctrl-clicking the horizontal or vertical ruler and choosing a new unit from the context menu.

Accessing the basic shape tools

In the first part of this lesson, you'll create a screwdriver using the basic shape tools. The shape tools are organized under the Rectangle tool. You can tear this group off the Tools panel to display it as a separate free-floating panel.

1   Hold down the mouse button on the Rectangle tool (□) until a group of tools appears, and then drag to the small triangle at the right end and release the mouse button.

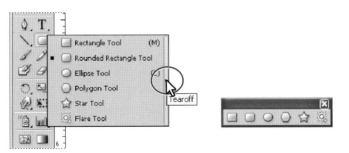

2   Move the Rectangle tool group away from the Tools panel.

Creating with shapes

In Adobe Illustrator CS4, you control the thickness and color of lines that you draw by setting stroke attributes. A stroke is the paint characteristic of a line, or the outline of an object. A fill is the paint characteristic of the inside of an object. The default settings use a white fill and black stroke for objects.

First, you'll draw a series of shapes that make up the illustrations. You'll also use smart guides to align your drawing.

1 Choose View > Fit Artboard In Window.

2 Make sure that 1 is showing in the Artboard Navigation area, which indicates that the first artboard is selected.

3 Choose Window > Transform to display the Transform panel. Then choose Window > Info.

4 Select the Rectangle tool (⬛), and start dragging with pointer crosshairs on a vertical guide in the grid, roughly in the center of the artboard. Drag to draw a rectangle that's approximately 0.75 inches wide and 2.5 inches tall. Use the Info panel to determine the size. This will be part of the body of the first illustration (a screwdriver). Notice that as you drag, the rectangle edge snaps to the grid lines. You can also use the rulers and the grid as guides.

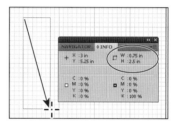

When you release the mouse button, the rectangle is automatically selected, and its center point appears. All objects created with the shape tools have a center point that you can drag to align the object with other elements in your artwork. You can make the center point visible or invisible using the Attributes panel, but you cannot delete it.

● **Note:** The objects that you draw snap, or pull, to the gridlines because View > Snap To Grid is selected (indicated by the check mark). You can deselect the snapping option and use the grid just as a visual guide by choosing View > Snap To Grid again.

▶ **Tip:** If the unit in appears in the Width and Height fields in the Transform panel, you can simply type a value (.75), and Illustrator assumes that it is inches.

5 In the Transform panel, note the rectangle's width and height. If necessary, enter .75 in in the width text field and 2.5 in in the height text field.

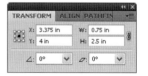

6 Close the Transform panel group by clicking the x in the upper right corner of the group title bar (Windows) or the dot in the upper left corner (Mac OS).

Next you'll draw another rectangle centered inside the first one to continue creating the body of the screwdriver.

7   Choose View > Snap To Grid to deselect snapping.

8   Choose View > Hide Grid to hide the grid.

Next, you will use the smart guides, which are selected by default, to align and size objects.

⬤ **Note:** Choose View > Smart Guides if the smart guides are not selected.

9   With the Rectangle tool still selected, position the pointer over the center point of the rectangle that you just drew. Notice that the word center appears next to the pointer. Hold down Alt (Windows) or Option (Mac OS), and drag out diagonally (down and to the right) from the center point to draw a rectangle that's centered inside the other. Don't release the mouse button yet.

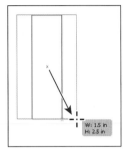

⬤ **Note:** As you draw with the shape tools, smart guides give you feedback in the form of green lines. Most of the time, the green lines indicate that objects are snapping to other objects, or that the edges of the objects are aligned horizontally or vertically.

10 As you drag, notice the tooltip that appears (as a gray box) indicating the width and height of the shape as you draw. Drag down and to the right until the width is approximately 1.5 in and the height is 2.5 in. The pointer should snap to the height (at 2.5 in), and a green line appears indicating that you are snapping to the bottom of the existing rectangle. Release the mouse button and then the Alt or Option key.

Holding down Alt or Option as you drag the Rectangle tool draws the rectangle from its center point rather than from its upper left corner. As you drag the pointer, the smart guides snap the pointer to the edges of the existing rectangle by displaying the word path. The new shape that you drew is on top of the previous shape.

⬤ **Note:** If Snap To Grid is selected, you can't use smart guides.

You will now arrange the new shape behind the old shape.

11 Select the Selection tool (⬧) in the Tools panel. With the second rectangle still selected, choose Object > Arrange > Send To Back. The larger rectangle should now be behind the smaller one.

About smart guides

Smart Guides are temporary snap-to guides and pop-ups that appear when you create or manipulate objects or artboards. They help you align, edit, and transform objects or artboards relative to other objects, artboards, or both by snap-aligning and displaying location or delta values. You can choose what type of guides and values appear with smart guides by setting the Smart Guides preferences.

To activate Smart Guides, choose View > Smart Guides. You can use Smart Guides in the following ways:

- When you create an object with the pen or shape tools, use the Smart Guides to position a new object's anchor points relative to an existing object. Or, when you create a new artboard, use Smart Guides to position it relative to another artboard or an object.

- When you create an object with the pen or shape tools, or when you transform an object, use the smart guides' construction guides to position anchor points to specific preset angles, such as 45 or 90 degrees. You set these angles in the Smart Guides preferences.

- When you move an object or artboard, use the Smart Guides to align the selected object or artboard to other objects or artboards. The alignment is based on the center point or edge of the objects or artboards. Guides appear as the object approaches the edge or center point of another object.

- When you rotate or move an item, use Smart Guides to snap to the last used angle or the nearest alignment option.

- When you transform an object, Smart Guides automatically appear to assist the transformation. You can change when and how Smart Guides appear by setting Smart Guide preferences.

  Note: When Snap To Grid is turned on, you cannot use Smart Guides (even if the menu command is selected).

—From Illustrator Help

Besides dragging on the artboard with a tool to draw a shape, you can select a tool and then double-click the artboard to open a dialog box with options for that tool. Now you'll create a rounded rectangle for another portion of the illustration by setting options in a dialog box.

▶ **Tip:** To automatically enter identical width and height values in the Ellipse or Rectangle dialog boxes, type a width or height value, and then click the name of the other value.

12 Select the Rounded Rectangle tool (⬜), and click once in the artwork to open the Rounded Rectangle dialog box. Type 1.5 in the Width field, press the Tab key, and type 0.5 in the Height field. Press the Tab key again, and type 0.2 in the Corner Radius field. The radius determines the amount of the curve of the corners. Click OK.

You'll use smart guides to help you align the new shape to the existing shapes.

13 Select the Selection tool (▶) in the Tools panel. Select anywhere inside the rounded rectangle and begin dragging toward the right edge of the rectangles. Don't release the mouse button yet.

● **Note:** Notice the gray box that appears when you drag the shape? This Smart Guide tooltip indicates the x and y distance that the pointer has moved.

14 Drag the shape to align with the right side of the larger rectangle. A vertical green smart guide appears in the center to indicate that the rounded rectangle is centered on the other rectangles. When the rounded rectangle is centered horizontally and vertically

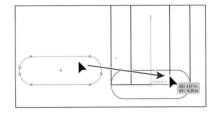

▶ **Tip:** The color of the smart guides can be changed from green to another color by choosing Edit > Preferences > Smart Guides (Windows) or Illustrator > Preferences > Smart Guides (Mac OS).

with the bottom of the larger rectangle, the word intersect appears. Release the mouse button, then the key, to drop the rounded rectangle on top of the larger rectangle.

15 Choose Object > Arrange > Send To Back.

You've been working in preview mode. This default view of a document lets you see how objects are painted (in this case, with a white fill and black stroke). If paint attributes seem distracting, you can work in outline mode.

16 Choose View > Outline to switch from preview to outline mode.

Next you'll create another shape by duplicating the rounded rectangle using the Alt key (Windows) or Option key (Mac OS).

17 Select the Selection tool (▶) in the Tools panel, and with the rounded rectangle still selected, hold down Alt (Windows) or Option (Mac OS) and drag from the bottom edge down until the word intersect appears, indicating that the center of the shape is aligned with the bottom of the rounded rectangle. Release the mouse button, and then the key.

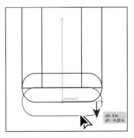

● **Note:** Outline mode removes all paint attributes, such as colored fills and strokes, to speed up selecting and redrawing artwork. You can't select or drag shapes by clicking in the middle since the fill is temporarily gone.

● **Note:** Don't drag a bounding point or the shape will become distorted.

18 With the Selection tool, hold down Alt (Windows) or Option (Mac OS), click and drag the right bounding point of the rounded rectangle toward the center of the shape (to the left) until the right edge is aligned with the right edge of the smaller rectangle. The word intersect appears with a green line, indicating that it's snapping to the rectangle shape.

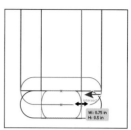

19 With the new rounded rectangle still selected, choose Object > Arrange > Send To Back.

You can control the shape of polygons, stars, and ellipses by pressing certain keys as you draw. You'll draw an ellipse next to represent the top of the screwdriver.

20 Select the Ellipse tool (⬤) from the Rectangle tool group, and position the pointer over the upper left corner of the larger rectangle. Notice the word anchor appear. Click and begin dragging down and to the right. Don't release the mouse button yet.

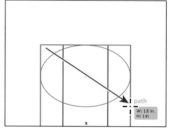

21 Drag the pointer down and to the right until it touches the right edge of the largest rectangle and the word path appears. Without releasing the mouse button, drag up or down slightly until the height is 1 in. in the smart guide measurement label that appears. Don't release the mouse button yet.

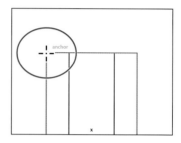

▶ **Tip:** When drawing shapes, holding down the Shift key constrains the proportions of the shape. In the case of the ellipse, it creates a perfect circle.

22 Hold down the spacebar and drag the ellipse up a little bit, making sure that as you drag up, you still see the word path. This ensures that the ellipse is still aligned with the right edge of the larger rectangle. Release the mouse button when the ellipse is positioned and sized as in the figure at right, and then release the keys.

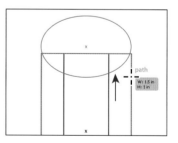

Hold down the spacebar while drawing to reposition the ellipse.

● **Note:** Ensure that the width is 1.5 in, which is the same as the larger rectangle, and that the height is 1 in. To check the width, open the Transform panel (Window > Transform). Click the ellipse, then click the larger rectangle to see if the widths are the same. If not, correct the ellipse by typing the same width value as the larger rectangle.

23 Choose Object > Arrange > Send To Back.

24 Choose Select > All In Active Artboard to select the shapes in this artboard only. Choose Object > Group to group them.

Now you'll create two triangles for the screwdriver tip using the Polygon tool.

25 Choose Select > Deselect.

26 Select the Zoom tool and click three times on the bottom of the screwdriver shapes to zoom in.

27 Select the Polygon tool (⬤) from the Rectangle tool group and position the pointer over the center point of the bottommost rounded rectangle (the word center appears). Don't worry if it's not perfectly centered; that will be fixed later.

28 Drag to begin drawing a polygon, but don't release the mouse button. Press the Down Arrow key three times to reduce the number of sides on the polygon to a triangle. Hold down the Shift key to straighten the triangle. Without releasing the Shift key, drag down and to the right until the smart guide measurement label tells you that the width is 0.5 in. Don't release the mouse button or the Shift key yet.

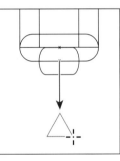

▶ **Tip:** When drawing with the Polygon tool, pressing the Up Arrow and Down Arrow keys changes the number of sides. If you want to change the number of sides quickly while drawing a polygon, hold down one of the arrow keys as you drag out the shape.

29 Hold down the spacebar as well and drag the triangle down to position it below the group of objects. Release the mouse button when the triangle is positioned below the other shapes. Release the keys.

30 Select the Selection tool (▶) in the Tools panel and, holding down the Shift key, click the grouped objects to select both.

● **Note:** Because you are still in outline mode, you may need to either drag across to select objects or click on their strokes.

31 In the Control panel, click the Horizontal Align Center button (⬓) to align the objects to each other.

Hold down the spacebar while drawing to reposition the triangle.

● **Note:** If you don't see the align options in the Control panel, click the word Align. Otherwise, choose Window > Align to open the Align panel.

32 Choose Select > Deselect.

33 With the Selection tool, click to select the triangle shape. Double-click the Rotate tool (↻) in the Tools panel to open the Rotate dialog box. Change the angle value to 180, and click OK.

34 Select the Zoom tool (🔍) in the Tools panel and click the triangle shape twice to zoom in.

35 With the Selection tool, click the triangle, and choose Edit > Copy, and then Edit > Paste In Front to paste a copy directly on top.

36 Select the Selection tool. Holding the Alt key (Windows) or Option key (Mac OS), resize the new triangle from the middle point on the right side of the bounding box until the smart guide measurement label displays a 0.15 in width.

37 With the Selection tool, drag across both triangles and choose Object > Group.

Resize the triangle while pressing Alt or Option.

38 Double-click the Hand tool (✋) in the Tools panel to fit the artboard in the window.

39 Choose File > Save.

Tips for drawing polygons, spirals, and stars

You can control the shapes of polygons, spirals, and stars by pressing certain keys as you draw the shapes. As you drag the Polygon, Spiral, or Star tool, choose any of the following options to control the shape:

- To add or subtract sides on a polygon, points on a star, or number of segments on a spiral, hold down the Up Arrow or Down Arrow key while creating the shape. This only works if the mouse button is held down. When the mouse button is released, the tool remains set to the last specified value.

- To rotate the shape, move the mouse in an arc.

- To keep a side or point at the top, hold down the Shift key.

- To keep the inner radius constant, start creating a shape and then hold down Ctrl (Windows) or Command (Mac OS).

- To move a shape as you draw it, hold down the spacebar. This also works for rectangles and ellipses.

- To create multiple copies of a shape, hold down the ~ (tilde) key as you draw.

Outlining strokes

Paths, such as a line, can only have a stroke color and not a fill color by default. If you create a line in Illustrator and you want to apply both a stroke and a fill, you can outline the stroke, which converts the line into a closed shape (or compound path). Next you will create the shaft of the screwdriver by drawing a line segment. You will then outline that stroke so that you can apply a stroke and a fill to the object.

▶ **Tip:** Outlining strokes lets you add a gradient to a stroke or separate the stroke and fill into two separate objects.

1 Choose Select > Deselect.

2 With the Selection tool (▸), click and drag the grouped objects that make the handle straight up toward the top of the artboard. A smart guide construction guide appears, constraining the movement horizontally as you drag up. At right, you can see the artwork so far.

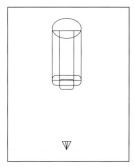

● **Note:** If the construction guide does not appear, make sure the smart guides are selected (View > Smart Guides), and that you are dragging straight up.

3 Select the Line Segment tool (\) in the Tools panel.

4 Place the pointer at the bottom of the handle, in the center, until the word intersect and a green vertical line appear. Hold the Shift key to ensure that the line is straight, and click and drag down. Don't release the mouse button yet.

● **Note:** As you drag to create the line, the smart guide measurement label may show an angle of 270 degrees, but your distance (D:) may be shorter or longer. That's alright.

5 Stop dragging when you reach the grouped triangles and the word intersect appears. Release the mouse button, and then the Shift key.

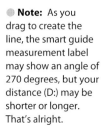

Shift-drag with the Line Segment tool.

Drag to the screwdriver tip to create the line.

6 With the line still selected, type .5 in into the Stroke Weight field in the Control panel. Press Enter or Return to accept the value. Notice that the value changes to points. Make sure the Fill color is None (▨) and the Stroke color is black in the Control panel.

● **Note:** If the line initially has a color fill, a more complex group is created when you choose Outline Stroke.

7 Choose View > Preview to see the thick black stroke on the line.

8 Choose Object > Path > Outline Stroke. This creates a filled rectangle that is 0.5 inches wide. With the new shape selected, click the Fill color (◼▾) in the Control panel and change the color to white, and click the Stroke color (▱▾) to change the color to black.

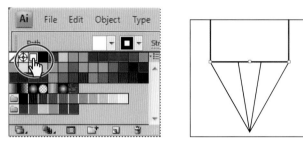

Set the stroke and fill colors.

Align the stroke for the rectangle to the inside.

9 With the object selected, open the Stroke panel by clicking the Stroke icon (≣) on the right side of the workspace.

10 In the Stroke panel, select the Align Stroke To Inside button (▣). This aligns the stroke to the inside edge of the shape.

● **Note:** You may need to zoom in to see the change.

11 With the Selection tool, select the group of triangles and repeat the same step to align the stroke to the inside of both shapes in the group. The rectangle and the group of triangles should now be the same width visibly. Leave the triangle group selected for the next steps.

Align stroke

If an object is a closed path (such as a circle or square), select an option in the Stroke panel to align the stroke along the path:

Align Stroke To Center

Align Stroke To Inside

Align Stroke To Outside

● **Note:** If you try to align paths that use different stroke alignments, the paths may not exactly align. Make sure the path alignment settings are the same if you need the edges to match up exactly.

12 Choose View > Smart Guides to deselect smart guides temporarily.

13 With the Selection tool, Shift-click the rectangle to add it to the selection, so that the triangles and the rectangle are both selected.

14 Click and drag the center point on the right side of the bounding box to the left to make the triangles and rectangle narrower. As you drag, hold down Alt (Windows) or Option (Mac OS) to resize both sides at once. Release the mouse button, and then the key.

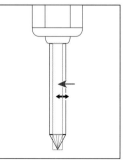

15 Choose Select > All In Active Artboard, and then Object > Group.

16 Choose File > Save.

Working with line segments

Next you'll work with straight lines and line segments to create a screw for the screwdriver. Shapes can be created in many ways in Illustrator, and the simpler way is usually better.

1 With tools.ai open, select the Hand tool (🖑) in the Tools panel, and click and drag up to move to the bottom of the artboard to give yourself room to work.

2 Select the Zoom tool (🔍) in the Tools panel, and click three times below the screwdriver tip to zoom in.

3 Choose View > Smart Guides and make sure that smart guides are selected.

4 Choose Essentials from the workspace switcher in the Control panel.

5 Select the Ellipse tool (◯) from the same group as the Polygon tool (◯) in the Tools panel. Draw an ellipse that has a width of 0.6 in and a height of 0.3 in. To see the size of the shape as you draw, reference the measurement label that appears.

> ▶ **Tip:** Zooming in to the artwork gives you finer control over the size of the shape as you draw.

6 Click the Fill color in the Control panel and select None (⬜). Make sure that the stroke weight is 1 pt.

Note: When you drag to select, make sure that you do not drag across the points on the left and right ends of the ellipse.

7   With the Direct Selection tool (⟨⟩), drag across the lower part of the ellipse to select the bottom half. Choose Edit > Copy, and then Edit > Paste In Front to create a new path. Switch to the Selection tool and press the Down Arrow key about seven times to move the new line down.

8   Select the Line Segment tool (╲) in the Tools panel. Hold down Shift while drawing a line from the left anchor point of the ellipse to the left anchor point of the new path. The anchor points highlight when the line snaps to them. Repeat this on the right side of the ellipse.

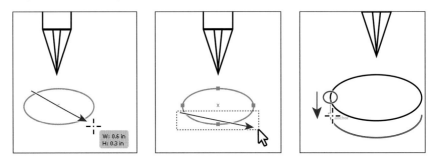

9   Choose File > Save.

Next you will take the three line segments that make up part of the screw head and join them together as one path.

Joining paths

When the end points of an open path are selected, you can join them together to create a closed path (like a circle). You can also join the end points of two separate paths. Next you will join the three open paths to create a single open path.

1   Choose Select > Deselect.

2   Select the Direct Selection tool (⟨⟩) in the Tools panel.

▶ **Tip:** After end points are selected, you can also join paths by choosing Object > Path > Join or pressing Ctrl+J or Cmd+J.

3   Click and drag on the left side of the shapes, where the lower two paths meet (see figure at the top of the next page). This selects the two end points. Click the Connect Selected End Points button (⟨⟩) in the Control panel. This opens the Join dialog box.

4   In the Join dialog box, make sure that the Corner option is selected and click OK.

5   Choose Select > Deselect.

6   Repeat the above two steps where the line segment on the right side and the bottom path meet.

7   With the Direct Selection tool still selected, hold down the Shift key and click the top two points of the selected path (on the right and left). Release the Shift key. Click the Connect Selected End Points button (⟨⟩) in the Control panel. A line appears connecting the two end points.

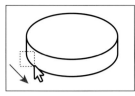
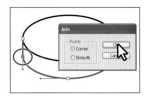
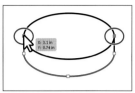

● **Note:** Joining the points in this step is not necessary if you only want to fill the shape with a color, because an open path can have a color fill. It is necessary if you want a stroke to appear around the entire fill area.

8 Select the Selection tool (▶), click a blank area of the artboard, and then reselect the path you just joined.

9 Change the Fill color in the Control panel to a light gray (K=20).

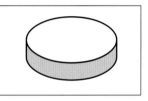

10 Choose Object > Arrange > Send To Back.

11 Click the path of the ellipse shape to select it. In the Control panel, click the Fill color (⬜▾) and choose white. This covers the shape that you just put in the back.

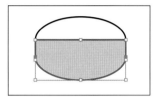

● **Note:** Selecting paths without fills requires that you select them by clicking or dragging across the path.

Join paths

As shown below, if the end points of two separate paths are on top of each other (called coincident points), a dialog box appears when you join them that allows you to specify the type of join you want: corner or smooth, merging the two points together.

If the end points are noncoincident (apart from each other), and you join them, a connecting line is drawn between them, joining the end points.

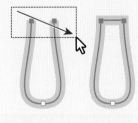

Noncoincident points

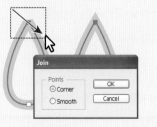

Coincident points

Next you will finish this part of the lesson by drawing with the Star tool.

12 Select the Selection tool, hold down the Shift key, and click both shapes to select them. Choose Object > Group.

13 With the group still selected, choose Object > Lock > Selection. This temporarily locks the group so that it cannot be accidentally selected.

▶ **Tip:** Step 14 uses several keyboard commands for working with stars. Take it slow and understand each as you draw the star.

14 Select the Star tool (☆) from the same group as the Ellipse tool (◯) in the Tools panel. Place the pointer in the center of the ellipse shape. Notice that the word center appears.

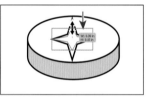

Draw a star using several keyboard commands.

Click and drag to the right to create a star shape. Without releasing the mouse button, press the Down Arrow key once so that the star has four points. Hold down Control (Windows) or Command (Mac OS) and continue dragging to the right. This keeps the inner radius constant. Without releasing the mouse button, release the Control or Command key, and then hold down the Shift key. Resize by dragging until the star fits within the ellipse (about 0.25 in width and 0.25 in height). Release the mouse button, and then the Shift key.

15 Select the Selection tool. Holding down Alt (Windows) or Option (Mac OS), click and drag the top, center anchor point down. This resizes both sides of the star, giving it a more realistic appearance. Release the mouse button, and then the key.

16 Holding down Alt (Windows) or Option (Mac OS), click and drag the center anchor point on the right side of the star to the right.

17 Change the Stroke Weight in the Control panel to 0.5 pt.

18 Choose Object > Unlock All.

19 Choose File > Save.

Using the Eraser tool

The Eraser tool lets you erase any area of your artwork, regardless of the structure. You can use the Eraser tool on paths, compound paths, paths inside Live Paint groups, and clipping paths.

1 Choose Select > Deselect.

2 Select the Zoom tool (🔍) in the Tools panel, and click the star you just created twice to zoom in.

3 With the Selection tool (▸), click to select the star.

4 Select the Eraser tool (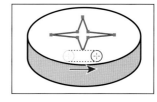) in the Tools panel. With the pointer on the artboard, press the Left Bracket key ([) several times until the eraser diameter becomes smaller. Position the pointer just to the left of the bottom point of the star, hold down the Shift key, and click and drag across the bottom star point to cut part of it off in a straight line. Repeat for the top star point. The path remains closed (the erased ends are joined).

Note: To erase a specific object, select it with the Eraser tool. Otherwise, leave all objects deselected to erase any object that the tool touches.

Note: If you erase and nothing seems to happen, erase more of the star on the bottom and top. Zooming in can also be helpful.

5 Choose Select > Deselect.

6 Choose View > Fit Artboard In Window.

7 Hold down Ctrl+spacebar (Windows) or Command+spacebar (Mac OS) to temporarily access the Zoom tool. Click the tip of the screwdriver (the bottom triangle group) several times to zoom in.

8 Release the keys to return to the Eraser tool. Press the Right Bracket key (]) three times to make the Eraser diameter larger. Drag across the bottom of the screwdriver tip in a "u" shape to create a slightly rounded tip (it's not meant to be perfectly round).

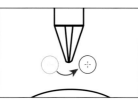

Tip: To change the Eraser tool preferences, such as roundness and diameter, double-click the Eraser tool in the Tools panel to open the Eraser Tool Options dialog box.

Tip: Like many other tools in Illustrator, if it doesn't turn out the way you wanted, you can always drag across again, or choose Edit > Undo Eraser and try again.

9 Choose View > Fit Artboard In Window.

10 Choose Select > All In Active Artboard, and then choose Object > Group.

11 Choose Select > Deselect, and then choose File > Save.

Combining objects

Pathfinder commands let you combine objects to create shapes. There are two types of Pathfinder commands: Pathfinder effects and shape modes.

Pathfinder effects in the Pathfinder panel let you combine shapes in many different ways to create paths or groups of paths by default. When a Pathfinder effect is applied (such as Merge), the original objects selected are permanently transformed. If the effect results in more than one shape, they are grouped automatically.

Shape modes create paths like Pathfinder effects, but they can also be used to create compound shapes. When several shapes are selected, clicking a shape mode while pressing the Alt (Windows) or Option (Mac OS) key creates a compound shape rather than a path. The original underlying objects of compound shapes are preserved. As a result, you can select each object within a compound shape, as shown below.

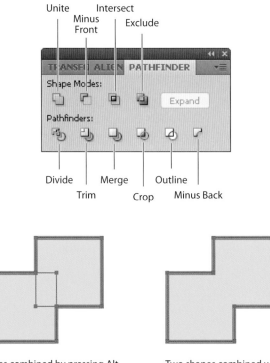

Two shapes combined by pressing Alt (Windows) or Option (Mac OS) and the Unite shape mode.

Two shapes combined with the Unite shape mode

Working with Pathfinder effects

Next, you will create several shapes for a wrench that use Pathfinder effects. But first, you will copy some shapes from an existing document.

1 Click the Next button (▶) in the status bar in the lower left corner of the Document window to navigate to the second artboard.

2 Choose File > Open and open the wrench.ai file in the Lesson03 folder in the Lessons folder.

3 Select the Selection tool (▶) in the Tools panel, and choose Select > All.

4 Choose Edit > Copy. Close the wrench.ai file by clicking the x on the wrench.ai Document window tab.

5 In the tools.ai file, choose Edit > Paste, and then choose Select > Deselect.

6 Select the Rectangle tool (▭) from the same group as the Star tool (☆) in the Tools panel. Position the pointer in the artboard and click. When the Rectangle dialog box opens, change the width to 0.8 in, and then click the word Height to make it the same value. Click OK.

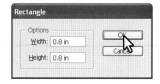

7 With the Selection tool, Shift-click the top circle of the wrench and the rectangle. Release the Shift key and click the circle one more time indicating that it is the key object. Notice the blue outline around it. In the Control panel, click the Horizontal Align Center button (⬒) and the Vertical Align Top button (⬒) to align the objects to each other.

Set the key object.

8 Choose Window > Pathfinder.

9 Click the Minus Front button (⬚) in the Pathfinder panel to subtract the rectangle from the circle. Notice that the fill and stroke are preserved.

10 Choose Select > Deselect.

11 Select the Polygon tool (⬡) in the Tools panel. Click the artboard to open the Polygon dialog box. Change the radius to 0.4 in and the sides to 6. Click OK.

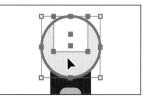

12 With the Selection tool, hold the Shift key and click the bottom circle of the wrench. Click the circle once more to set it as the key object. In the Control panel, click the Horizontal Align Center button (⬒) and the Vertical Align Center button (⬒) to align the two objects to each other.

Note: A compound path contains two or more paths that are painted so that holes appear where the paths overlap.

13 In the Pathfinder panel, click the Minus Front button (▣). With the new shape selected, notice the words Compound Path on the left side of the Control panel.

14 With the Selection tool (▶), double-click the newly created compound path to enter isolation mode. The rest of the content on the artboard is now dimmed and can't be selected and a bar appears at the top of the Document window indicating that the Compound Path is on Layer 1. The compound path is also temporarily ungrouped so that you can select its parts individually. Click the stroke (the edge) of the polygon (in the center of the circle) to select it.

▶ **Tip:** Another way to enter isolation mode is to select the object and click the Isolate Selected Object button (⬚) in the Control panel.

15 In the Control panel, click the Constrain Width And Height Proportions button (⬚). Change the width to 1.125 in by clicking the arrow to the left of the field three times. This also changes the height value proportionally.

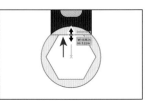

16 With the Selection tool, double-click outside the shapes on the artboard to exit isolation mode.

17 Click to select the rectangle that is the wrench body. Click and drag the bottom, center bounding point up until it snaps the top edge of the polygon. The word intersect appears. Release the mouse button.

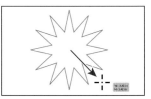

Click and drag the bottom center bounding point up.

18 Choose Select > All In Active Artboard. Choose Object > Group. Drag the wrench to the left side of the artboard.

19 Choose Object > Hide > Selection to give you room to create more content.

Working with shape modes

Next you will use Pathfinder effects and shape modes to create two gears.

1 Select the Star tool (☆) in the Tools panel. Click and drag on the left side of the artboard to create a star. Without releasing the mouse button, press the Up Arrow key until the star has 12 points. Hold down the Shift key and drag toward the center or away until the width and height are approximately 3.42 in in the measurement tooltip. Release the mouse button.

▶ **Tip:** As you are drawing a star, you can hold down Ctrl or Command and drag away from or toward the center of a star to increase or decrease the radius.

2 Click the Fill color in the Control panel and select white in the Swatches panel that appears.

3 Select the Ellipse tool (⬭) in the Tools panel. While holding down Alt (Windows) or Option (Mac OS), click in the center of the star you just created (the word center appears). In the Ellipse dialog box, change the width and height to 2 in and click OK.

4 With the Selection tool, hold down the Shift key, and select both the ellipse and the star. To ensure that the shapes are centered on each other, in the Control panel, click the Horizontal Align Center button (⬓) and the Vertical Align Center button (⬓) to align the two objects to each other.

5 With the objects selected, click the Merge button (⬓) in the Pathfinder panel (Window > Pathfinder). Notice that the shapes are combined but the stroke disappears. With the shape selected, click the Stroke color in the Control panel and select black.

The shapes are combined.

6 Select the Ellipse tool in the Tools panel and click in the center of the star you just created. In the Ellipse dialog box, change the width and height to 2.5 in and click OK.

7 With the Selection tool, hold down the Shift key, and select both the ellipse and the star. In the Control panel, click the Horizontal Align Center button (⬓) and the Vertical Align Center button (⬓) to align the two objects to each other. This is gear A.

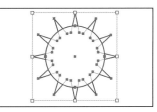

At this point, you have the two shapes selected that will combine to make a gear.

Next, you will create a copy of the selected gear shapes so that you will have two gears when finished. You will combine the shapes to create two gears, but they will be combined in two different ways.

8 With the shapes still selected, choose Edit > Copy, and then Edit > Paste. Drag the copied shapes (called gear B) to the right of gear A. Keep the two copied shapes for gear B selected.

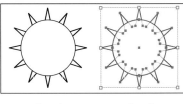

Gear A   Gear B

● **Note:** With the two gears on the artboard, it is a tight fit for the moment. Later you will move the gears to fix this.

9 Click the Intersect button (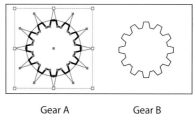) in the Shape Modes section of the Pathfinder panel to trace the outline of the overlapping area.

10 Choose Select > Deselect.

The result is a single gear shape. Notice that you cannot edit the original objects. You will now combine the shapes for gear A so that you can edit the shapes, even after they are combined to form the gear.

11 With the Selection tool, click and drag across both shapes that make up gear A to select them both.

12 Hold down the Alt (Windows) or Option (Mac OS) key, and click the Intersect button () in the Pathfinder panel.

This creates a compound shape that traces the outline of the overlapping area of both objects. It also means that you can still edit the ellipse and the star shape separately.

● **Note:** The stroke weight for gear A in the figure has been exaggerated so that it is easier to see.

▶ **Tip:** To edit the original shapes in a compound shape like gear A, you can also select them individually with the Direct Selection tool ( ).

13 With the Selection tool, double-click gear A to enter isolation mode.

14 Choose View > Outline so that you can see the two pieces (the ellipse and the star). Click to select the circle if it isn't already selected.

● **Note:** In outline mode, notice that gear B is still a single shape.

15 While pressing Shift+Alt (Windows) or Shift+Option (Mac OS), click and drag a corner of the ellipse bounding box toward its center to make it smaller. This resizes the ellipse from the center. Drag until the width and height are roughly 2.3 inches in the measurement tooltip. It does not have to be exact. Release the mouse button, and then the keys.

● **Note:** Resizing a shape precisely can be easier when you zoom in. You can also change the width and height of the selected shape in the Transform panel.

16 Choose View > Preview.

17 With the Selection tool, double-click outside of gear A to exit isolation mode.

You will now expand gear A. Expanding a compound shape maintains the shape of the compound object, but you can no longer select or edit the original objects.

18 Click to select gear A. Click the Expand button in the Pathfinder panel. Close the Pathfinder panel group.

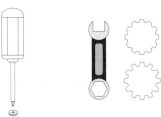

19 Choose Select > Deselect.

20 With the Selection tool, click and drag the gears so that one is on top of the other on the right side of the artboard.

21 Choose Object > Show All. The wrench now appears.

22 Choose View > Fit Artboard In Window.

You may want to position the wrench and gears so that they look something like the figure at right.

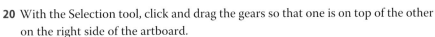

23 Choose File > Save, and then File > Close.

In the next lesson, you'll learn how to work with Live Trace.

Using Live Trace to create shapes

In this part of the lesson, you will learn how to work with the Live Trace command. Live Trace traces existing artwork, like a raster picture from Photoshop. You can then convert the drawing to vector paths or a Live Paint object.

1 Choose File > Open, and open the L3start_02.ai file in the Lesson03 folder.

2 Choose File > Save As, name the file snowboarding.ai, and select the Lesson03 folder in the Save As dialog box. Leave the Save As Type option set to Adobe Illustrator (*.AI) (Windows) or the Format option set to Adobe Illustrator (ai) (Mac OS), and click Save. In the Illustrator Options dialog box, leave the Illustrator options at their default settings, and click OK.

● **Note:** A Missing Profile dialog box may appear. Click OK to continue.

3 Choose View > Fit Artboard In Window.

4 With the Selection tool (▶), select the snowboarder sketch.

Note that the Control panel options change when the scanned image is activated. It says Image on the left side of the Control panel, and you can see the resolution (PPI: 150).

5 Click the Live Trace button in the Control panel. This converts the image from raster to vector.

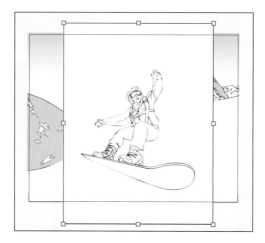

Raster versus vector

Raster images use a rectangular grid of picture elements (pixels) to represent images. Each pixel is assigned a specific location and color value. When working with bitmap images, you edit pixels rather than objects or shapes.

Raster image

Vector graphics (sometimes called vector shapes or vector objects) are made up of lines and curves defined by mathematical objects called vectors, which describe an image according to its geometric characteristics.

—From Illustrator Help

Vector graphic

▶ **Tip:** In the Tracing Options dialog box, the Ignore White option does not trace areas that contain a white fill. The white areas become transparent, which is especially helpful when tracing an image with a white background.

With Live Trace, you can view your changes as you make them. You can change the settings, or even the original placed image, and then see the updates immediately.

6 Click the Tracing Options Dialog button (🖫) in the Control panel, and choose Comic Art from the Preset pop-up menu. Check Preview to experiment with different presets and options. Leave the Tracing Options dialog box open.

▶ **Tip:** For information on Live Trace and the options in the Tracing Options dialog box, see "Tracing artwork" in Illustrator Help.

As you see, the Live Trace feature can interpret black and white sketches as well as full-color images.

7 In the Tracing Options dialog box, change Threshold to 220. After experimenting with other settings in the Tracing Options dialog box, make sure that Comic Art preset is selected, and click Trace.

The snowboarder is now a tracing object (vector), however the anchor points and paths are not yet editable. To edit the content, you must expand the tracing object.

● **Note:** Threshold specifies a value for generating a black and white tracing result from the original image. All pixels lighter than the Threshold value are converted to white, and all pixels darker than the Threshold value are converted to black.

8 With the snowboarder still selected, click the Expand button in the Control panel.

9 Choose Object > Ungroup, and then Select > Deselect.

10 Select the Selection tool (↖) in the Tools panel, and then click the white
background surrounding the snowboarder. Press Delete to remove the
white shape.

11 With the Selection tool, try clicking to select other parts of the snowboarder.
Notice that it is composed of many shapes and paths.

12 Choose File > Save, and close the file.

Exploring on your own

Experiment with shapes by creating a shape such as a circle, star, or rectangle. Clone
it several times using the Alt or Option key.

Open the tools.ai file. Select the gear shapes and create an ellipse that is centered
on the gear. Click the Minus Front button (◻) in the Pathfinder panel to create a
compound path.

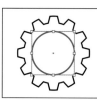

The original gear   Create the ellipse.   Create the compound path.

In the tools.ai file, choose File > Place and place a raster image. Try selecting the
raster image, and then clicking the Live Trace button in the Control panel. Choose a
preset from the Tracing Preset menu in the Control panel.

Review questions

1   What are the basic shape tools? Describe how to tear or separate a group of shape tools away from the Tools panel.

2   How do you select a shape with no fill?

3   How do you draw a square?

4   How do you change the number of sides on a polygon as you draw?

5   How do you combine several shapes into one?

6   How can you convert a raster image to editable vector shapes?

Review answers

1   There are six basic shape tools: Ellipse, Polygon, Star, Flare, Rectangle, and Rounded Rectangle. To tear off a group of tools from the Tools panel, position the pointer over the tool that appears in the Tools panel and hold down the mouse button until the group of tools appears. Without releasing the mouse button, drag to the triangle at the bottom of the group, and then release the mouse button to tear off the group.

2   Items that have no fill must be selected by clicking the stroke.

3   To draw a square, select the Rectangle tool in the Tools panel. Hold down Shift and drag to draw the square, or click the artboard to enter equal dimensions for the width and height in the Rectangle dialog box.

4   To change the number of sides on a polygon as you draw, select the Polygon tool in the Tools panel. Start dragging to draw the shape, and hold the Down Arrow key to reduce the number of sides and the Up Arrow key to increase the number of sides.

5   Using the Pathfinder commands, you can create new shapes out of overlapping objects. You can apply Pathfinder effects by using the Effects menu or the Pathfinder panel.

6   If you want to base a new drawing on an existing piece of artwork, you can trace it. To convert the tracing to paths, click Expand in the Control panel or choose Object > Live Trace > Expand. Use this method if you want to work with the components of the traced artwork as individual objects. The resulting paths are grouped.

4 TRANSFORMING OBJECTS

Lesson overview

In this lesson, you'll learn how to do the following:

- Add and edit artboards in an existing document.
- Select individual objects, objects in a group, and parts of an object.
- Move, scale, and rotate objects using a variety of methods.
- Work with smart guides.
- Reflect, shear, and distort objects.
- Adjust the perspective of an object.
- Apply a distortion filter.
- Position objects precisely.
- Repeat transformations quickly and easily.

 This lesson will take approximately an hour to complete. If needed, remove the previous lesson folder from your hard disk and copy the Lesson04 folder onto it.

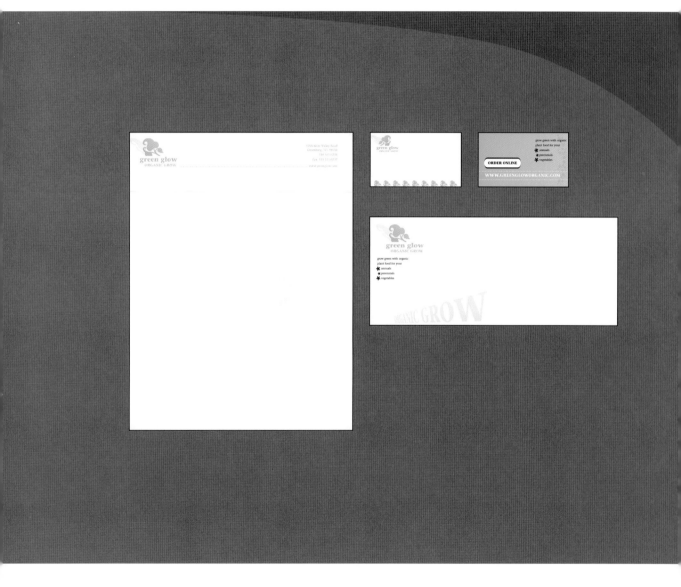

You can modify objects in many ways as you create artwork, including quickly and precisely controlling their size, shape, and orientation. In this lesson, you'll explore creating and editing artboards, the various Transform commands, and specialized tools as you create several pieces of artwork.

Getting started

In this lesson, you'll create a logo and use it in three pieces of artwork to create a letterhead design, an envelope, and a business card. Before you begin, you'll restore the default preferences for Adobe Illustrator, and then open a file containing a composite of the finished artwork to see what you'll create.

1 To ensure that the tools and panels function as described in this lesson, delete or deactivate (by renaming) the Adobe Illustrator CS4 preferences file. See "Restoring default preferences" on page 3.

2 Start Adobe Illustrator CS4.

● **Note:** If you have not already copied the resource files for this lesson onto your hard disk from the Lesson04 folder on the Adobe Illustrator CS4 Classroom in a Book CD, do so now. See "Copying the Classroom in a Book files" on page 2.

3 Choose File > Open, and open the L4end.ai file in the Lesson04 folder, located in the Lessons folder on your hard disk.

This file contains the three pieces of finished artwork: a letterhead, a business card (front and back), and an envelope. The Green Glow logo in the upper left corner of the letterhead has been resized differently for the letterhead, envelope, and business card.

4 Choose View > Zoom Out to reduce the view of the finished artwork. Then adjust the Document window size, and leave the artwork on-screen as you work. Select the Hand tool (✋) to move the artwork where you want it in the window. If you don't want to leave the file open, choose File > Close.

To begin working, you'll open an existing art file set up for the letterhead artwork.

5 Choose File > Open to open the L4start.ai file in the Lesson04 folder, located in the Lessons folder on your hard disk. This file has been saved with the rulers showing, custom swatches added to the Swatches panel, and blue guidelines for scaling objects used to create the logo.

6 Choose File > Save As. In the Save As dialog box, name the file green_glow.ai and navigate to the Lesson04 folder. Leave the Save As Type option set to Adobe Illustrator (*.AI) (Windows) or the Format option set to Adobe Illustrator (ai) (Mac OS), and click Save. In the Illustrator Options dialog box, leave the Illustrator options at their default settings, and click OK.

7 Choose Window > Workspace > Essentials.

Working with artboards

Artboards represent the regions that can contain printable artwork, similar to pages in Adobe InDesign. You can use artboards to crop areas for printing or for placement purposes—they work the same way as crop areas work in Illustrator CS3. Multiple artboards are useful for creating a variety of things, such as multiple page PDF files, printed pages with different sizes or different elements, independent elements for websites, video storyboards, or individual items for animation.

Adding artboards to the document

You can add and remove artboards at any time while working in a document. You can create artboards in different sizes, resize them with the Artboard tool, and position them anywhere in the Document window. All artboards are numbered. The number appears in the upper left corner of the artboard when the Artboard tool is selected.

To begin, this document has one artboard for the letterhead. You will add more artboards to create the business card and envelope.

1 Choose View > Fit Artboard In Window. This is artboard number 1.

2 Press Ctrl++ (Windows) or Cmd++ (Mac OS) twice to zoom in.

3 Pressing the spacebar, click and drag the artboard to the left and down until you see the canvas off the upper right corner of the artboard.

4 Select the Artboard tool (⊡), and to the right of the existing artboard, bring the pointer in line with the top edge of the existing artboard until a green alignment guide appears. Drag down and to the right to create an artboard that is 3.5 inches (width) by 2 inches (height). A measurement label indicates when the artboard is the correct size. This is artboard number 2.

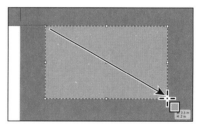

> **Tip:** If you zoom in on an artboard, the measurement labels have smaller increments.

> **Note:** If you haven't scrolled over far enough, you may not be able to see the artboard and measurement label that appears.

5 Click the New Artboard button (⬚) in the Control panel. This creates a duplicate of the last selected artboard. This is artboard number 3.

6 Drag the pointer below the new artboard and line it up with the left edge of the artboard until a vertical green alignment guide appears. Click to create a copy of the artboard.

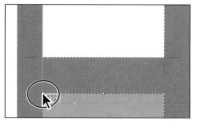

Editing artboards

You can create multiple artboards for your document, but only one can be active at a time. When multiple artboards are defined, you can view them all by selecting the Artboard tool. Each artboard is numbered for easy reference. You can edit or delete an artboard at any time, and you can specify different artboards each time you print or export.

1   Using the Artboard tool (⌗), select the bottom artboard on the right, and change the width to 9.5 in and the height to 4 in in the Control panel.

When resizing artboards using the Artboard Options dialog box, the artboard is resized from its center.

2   Choose View > Fit All In Window.

3   With the Artboard tool, click and drag from the center of the resized artboard so that the left edge of the third artboard lines up with the left edge of the second artboard above it (a green alignment guide appears on the left). Leave about an inch of room between the third artboard and the artboard above it.

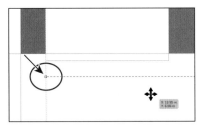

Move the resized artboard.

▶ **Tip:** To duplicate an existing artboard, using the Artboard tool, Alt-drag or Option-drag the artboard that you want to duplicate.

4   With the Artboard tool, click the center of the bottom right artboard to select it. Drag the bottom bounding point of the artboard until the height is 4.25 in in the measurement label.

▶ **Tip:** To delete an artboard, click the artboard and press Delete, click Delete in the Control panel, or click the Delete icon in an artboard's upper right corner. You can delete all but the last remaining artboard.

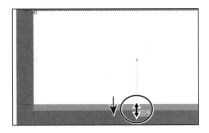

Resize the third artboard.

5   With the top artboard on the right selected (artboard 02), click the Artboard Options button (⊞) in the Control panel to open the Artboard Options dialog box. In the Display Options, select Show Center Mark. Click OK.

6 Select the Selection tool (⬆) in the Tools panel to see the center mark. Also, notice the black outline around the artboard, which indicates the currently active artboard.

Next you will make a copy of the smaller artboard for the front and back side of a business card.

● **Note:** When you drag an artboard with content on it, the art moves with the artboard by default. If you want to move an artboard, but not the art on it, select the Artboard tool, and then click to deselect Move/Copy Artwork With Artboard (⬒).

7 With the Artboard tool, Alt-drag (Windows) or Option-drag (Mac OS) artboard 02 to the right. Drag until the copied artboard clears the original. When creating new artboards, you can place them anywhere, including overlapping them. You just need to leave room between them to account for a bleed, if necessary.

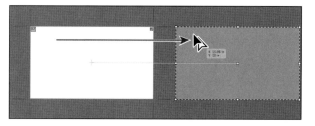

8 Choose View > Fit All In Window to see all the artboards.

9 With the Artboard tool, click to select artboard 01.

▶ **Tip:** Clicking the delete icon (⊠) in the upper right corner of every artboard deletes that artboard.

10 Choose Legal from the Presets menu in the Control panel.

Change the artboard preset to Legal

The Presets menu lets you change a selected artboard to a set size. Notice that the sizes in the Presets menu include web sizes (800x600, for instance) and video sizes (NTSC DV, for instance). You can also fit the artboard to the artwork bounds or the selected art, which is a great way to fit an artboard to a logo, for instance.

11 Choose Letter from the Presets menu in the Control panel to return the artboard to standard letter size.

12 Select the Selection tool in the Tools panel. Click the Document Setup button in the Control panel.

▶ **Tip:** You can also access the Document Setup dialog box by choosing File > Document Setup.

13 In the Document Setup dialog box, change the Top Bleed option to .125 in by clicking the up arrow to the left of the field. Notice that all the values change together, because Make All Settings The Same (⬛) is selected. Click Edit Artboards to commit to the changes and return to the Artboard tool.

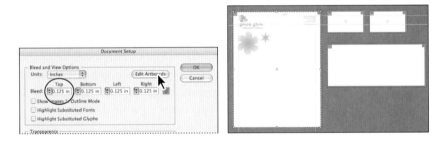

● **Note:** All changes made in the Document Setup dialog box are set for the entire document (all artboards).

14 Select the Selection tool to stop editing the artboards.

15 Choose Window > Workspace > Essentials.

Now that the artboards are set up, you will concentrate on transforming artwork to create the content for the artboards.

Transforming content

Transforming content allows you to move, rotate, reflect, scale, and shear objects. Objects can be transformed using the Transform panel, selection tools, specialized tools, Transform commands, guides, and smart guides. In this part of the lesson, you will transform content using a variety of methods.

Working with rulers and guides

Rulers help you accurately place and measure objects. The point where 0 appears on each ruler is called the ruler origin, which some refer to it as the zero, zero point. The ruler origin can be reset depending on which artboard is active. There are also two types of rulers available: document rulers and artboard rulers. Guides are nonprinting lines that help you align objects. You can create horizontal and vertical ruler guides by dragging them from the rulers.

Note: By default, the ruler origin appears in the lower left corner of the Document window, but you can change the location.

Next you will make the rulers visible, reset the origin point, and create a guide.

1   With the Selection tool (**✎**), click the top right artboard, which is the back of the business card, to make it the active artboard. Choose View > Fit Artboard In Window.

▶ **Tip:** Instead of clicking an artboard to make it active, you can use the First, Next, Previous, or Last buttons in the status bar to make an artboard active.

2   Double-click the upper left corner of the Document window where the rulers intersect. This resets the ruler origin so that the ruler origin appears in the lower left corner of the active artboard.

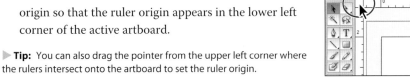

▶ **Tip:** You can also drag the pointer from the upper left corner where the rulers intersect onto the artboard to set the ruler origin.

3   Click the Layers panel icon (🔵) on the right side of the workspace. Click to select the Visibility column to the left of the Business card layer name. Click the Business card layer name to select it. Any new content, including guides, is placed on the selected layer.

4   Shift-drag from the vertical ruler to the right to create a vertical guide at 1/4 inch on the horizontal ruler. The Shift key snaps the guide to the ruler units as you drag.

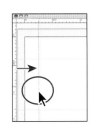

5   Choose View > Guides > Lock Guides to prevent them from being accidentally moved.

6   Choose File > Save.

▶ **Tip:** Choose File > Document Setup or with nothing selected, click the Document Setup button in the Control panel to change the units for a document. You can also right-click or Option-click either ruler to change the units.

Scaling objects

Objects are scaled by enlarging or reducing them horizontally (along the x axis) and vertically (along the y axis) relative to a fixed reference point that you designate. If you don't designate an origin, objects are scaled from their center points. You'll use three methods to scale the objects that make up parts of the business card.

First you'll set the preference to scale strokes and effects. Then you'll scale the logo background by dragging its bounding box and aligning it to the guides provided.

1 Choose Edit > Preferences > General (Windows) or Illustrator > Preferences > General (Mac OS), and select Scale Strokes & Effects. This scales the stroke width of any object scaled in this lesson. Click OK.

2 Select the Rectangle tool (▢) in the Tools panel. Position the pointer in the upper left corner of the red bleed guides and click when the word intersect and the green alignment guides appear.

3 In the Rectangle dialog box, change the width to 3.75 in and the height to 2.25 in. Click OK.

4 Click the Fill color in the Control panel and select the business card swatch.

5 With the rectangle still selected, choose Object > Hide > Selection. This makes it easier to edit content.

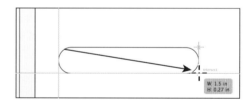

6 Select the Rounded Rectangle tool (▢) from the Rectangle group, and then position the pointer at the vertical guide and in line with the center mark (green cross hairs) until a horizontal alignment guide appears. Click and drag down and to the right to the bottom horizontal guide until the right edge of the shape is aligned with the center mark. The width in the measurement label is 1.5 in.

7 Select black for the fill color in the Control panel.

8 With the Selection tool (▶), Shift-drag the lower right corner of the object's bounding box up and to the left until the width is about 1.4 in in the measurement label.

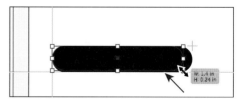

● **Note:** If you do not see the bounding box, choose View > Show Bounding Box.

Next you'll resize the rectangle from the side.

9 With the object still selected, Alt-drag (Windows) or Option-drag (Mac OS) the bottom, middle bounding point down. Drag to just below the lower horizontal guide. This doesn't have to be exact.

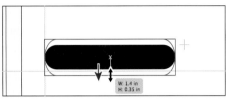

10 Choose 1 from the Artboard Navigation menu in the status bar.

11 Choose View > Outline.

12 With the Selection tool, drag a marquee across the text below the large flower to select it all. Choose Edit > Cut.

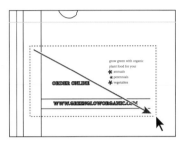

13 Choose 4 from the Artboard Navigation menu in the status bar to return to the business card artboard.

14 Choose Edit > Paste. Choose Select > Deselect.

15 Shift-drag a vertical guide from the vertical ruler to 1½ in on the horizontal ruler.

16 With the Selection tool, select the text "Order Online" and drag it so that the right edge aligns with the new guide as best as you can. Vertically align the text to the center of the rounded rectangle.

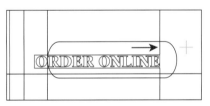

● **Note:** If it is difficult to see the text, use outline mode, and then return to preview mode.

17 Choose View > Preview.

18 In the Control panel, click the word Transform. In the Transform panel that appears, click the middle right reference point of the Reference Point Locator (⊞) to set the reference point from which the objects scale. Click to select the Constrain Width And Height Proportions icon (🔒) between the W and H fields in the Transform panel. Change the width to 1.1 in, and then press Enter or Return to decrease the size of the text.

● **Note:** Depending on your screen resolution, the Transform options may appear in the Control panel. If they do appear you can set the options directly in the Control panel. The figure at left shows clicking the word Transform to reveal the Transform panel.

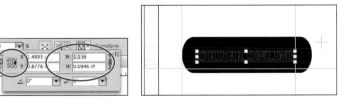

Next you'll position a copy of the rounded rectangle and then use the Scale tool to resize and copy it.

19 With the Selection tool, select the rounded rectangle.

20 Double-click the Scale tool (⬚) in the Tools panel.

21 In the Scale dialog box, select the Preview option. Change Vertical to 80% and click Copy to make a smaller copy on top of the other rounded rectangle.

22 Change the Fill color in the Control panel to white.

Reflecting objects

When you reflect an object, Illustrator creates a reflection of the object across an invisible vertical or horizontal axis. Copying objects while reflecting allows you to create a mirror image of the object based on a point. Similar to scaling and rotating, when reflecting an object, you either designate the reference point or use the object's center point by default. You can also alter the orientation of a reflection by changing its angle.

Next you'll place a symbol on the artboard, and use the Reflect tool to flip and copy it 90° across the vertical axis and then scale and rotate the copy into position.

▶ **Tip:** To learn more about symbols, see Lesson 13, "Working with Symbols."

1 Click the Symbols panel icon (♣) on the right side of the workspace. Drag the Floral symbol onto the business card artboard.

2 With the symbol selected, double-click the Scale tool (⬚) in the Tools panel.

3 In the Scale dialog box, change Uniform Scale to 30%, and click OK.

4 Select the Selection tool (▸) and drag the symbol down below "Order Online," lining the left edge of the symbol with the guide at 1/4". It doesn't have to be exact.

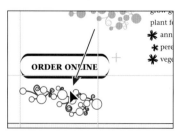

5 Select the Reflect tool (◔) nested within the Rotate tool (◯) in the Tools panel, and then Alt-click (Windows) or Option-click (Mac OS) the right edge of the symbol (the word edge may appear).

● **Note:** Pressing Alt or Option is not necessary, but it sets the reflection point to the right edge of the symbol.

6 In the Reflect dialog box select Preview. Select Vertical, and then click Copy.

Alt-click or Option-click with the Reflect tool. Select Vertical in the Reflect dialog box, and then click Copy.

● **Note:** You can also drag the selected object with the Reflect tool to reflect it.

Rotating objects

Objects are rotated by turning them around a designated reference point. You can rotate objects by displaying their bounding boxes and moving the pointer to an outside corner. When the rotate pointer appears, click to rotate the object around its center point. You can also rotate objects using the Transform panel to set a reference point and a rotation angle.

You'll rotate both symbols using the Rotate tool.

1 With the Selection tool (➤), select the leftmost symbol. Select the Rotate tool (⟳) nested within the Reflect tool (▨) in the Tools panel. Double-click the Rotate tool (⟳) in the Tools panel. Notice that the symbols reference point (◇) is its center.

2 In the Rotate dialog box, make sure that Preview is selected. Change the angle to 20, and then click OK to rotate the symbol around the reference point.

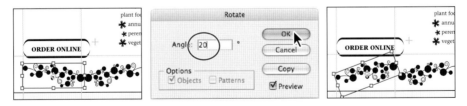

● **Note:** If you select an object, and then select the Rotate tool, you can Alt-click or Option-click anywhere on the object (or artboard) to set a reference point and open the Rotate dialog box.

3 Select the Selection tool, and click the symbol on the right.

4 Double-click the Rotate tool (⟳) in the Tools panel.

5 In the Rotate dialog box, change the angle to –20, and then click OK.

6 With the Selection tool, Shift-click to add the symbol on the left to the current selection.

7 Choose Object > Group.

8 Choose View > Zoom Out twice.

9 Select the Rotate tool. Click the bottom, right edge of the group to set the reference point (⬦). Click and drag from the left side of the group up and to the right. Notice that the movement is constrained to a circle rotating around the reference point. While dragging, press the Shift key to constrain the rotation to 45°. When the group is vertical and the measurement label shows –90°, release the mouse button, and then the key.

10 With the Selection tool, drag the group to the right edge of artboard and visually center it vertically on the artboard. The placement does not have to be exact.

11 Shift-drag the left middle bounding point of the group, and drag to the right to resize it until the group fits within the top and bottom bleed guides.

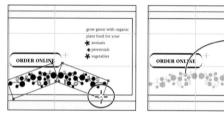 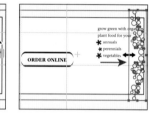

12 With the group still selected, click the word Opacity in the Control panel and change the opacity blending mode to Overlay.

13 Choose Object > Show All to see the business card background.

14 Choose View > Guides > Hide Guides.

15 Choose File > Save.

Distorting objects

You can distort the original shapes of objects in different ways using various tools. Now you'll create a flower, first using the Twist effect to twirl the shape of a star, and then applying the Pucker & Bloat distort filter to transform its center.

1 Click the First button (⏮) in the status bar to navigate to artboard 1.

2 With the Selection tool (▶), click to select the large flower shape below the Green Glow logo.

3 Choose Effect > Warp > Twist. Select Preview in the Warp Options dialog box. Change Bend to 60 and click OK.

Twist distortion is applied as an effect, which maintains the original shape and lets you remove or edit the effect at any time in the Appearance panel. Learn more about using effects in Lesson 11, "Applying Effects."

Now you'll draw the middle part of the flower that's centered on top of the flower.

4 With the flower selected, choose Window > Attributes to open the Attributes panel. Click the Show Center button (▣) to display the center point of the flower.

5 Close the Attributes panel group.

6 Select the Zoom tool (🔍), and click the flower shape three times.

7 Select the Star tool (☆) nested within the Rounded Rectangle tool, and drag from the center point to draw a star over the center of the flower. Press the Up Arrow key once to add a point to the star, making a total of six points on the star. Press the Shift key and drag until the height is approximately .8 inches in the measurement label. Release the mouse button and Shift key, and keep the star selected.

8 Click Fill color in the Control panel and choose the light green swatch (12c 0m 47y 0k). Press Escape to close the Swatches panel that appears.

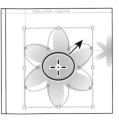

Now you'll distort the frontmost star using the Pucker & Bloat effect. This effect distorts objects inward and outward from their anchor points.

9 Select the Zoom tool (🔍) in the Tools panel and click the flower shapes twice to zoom in.

10 With the center star selected, choose Effect > Distort & Transform > Pucker & Bloat.

11 In the Pucker & Bloat dialog box, select Preview, and drag the slider to the left to change the value to roughly −80% to distort the star. Click OK.

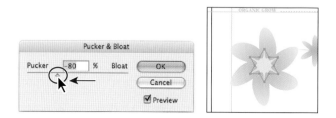

12 Choose View > Smart Guides to deselect smart guides.

13 With the Selection tool, position the pointer off the lower right corner of the star bounding box until the rotate arrows (↻) appear. Click and drag down and to the left until the star points are lined up with the flower shapes.

When you rotate or distort objects in other ways, the bounding box is also rotated or distorted. When necessary, you can reset the bounding box so that it is squared to the object again.

14 With the shape still selected, choose Object > Transform > Reset Bounding Box.

15 With the Selection tool, Shift-click the flower shape behind it and the smaller flower shape to the right to select all three shapes. Choose Object > Group.

16 In the Control panel, change Opacity to 20.

17 With the Selection tool, drag the flower group to the right side of the artboard, and about half way down the page.

18 Choose Select > Deselect, and then File > Save.

Shearing objects

Shearing an object slants, or skews, the sides of the object along the axis you specify, keeping opposite sides parallel and making the object asymmetrical.

Next you'll copy and shear the logo shape.

1   Choose View > Fit Artboard In Window.

2   Choose View > Smart Guides to select the smart guides.

3   Select the Zoom tool (🔍) in the Tools panel and drag a marquee around the green glow logo in the upper left corner of the artboard.

4   Select the Selection tool (▸). Click to select the flower shape above the "green glow" text.

5   Choose Edit > Copy, and then choose Edit > Paste In Front to paste a copy directly on top of the original.

6   Select the Shear tool (◿) nested within the Scale tool (🔲) in the Tools panel. Position the pointer at the bottom edge of the flower shape and click to set the reference point. Shift-drag the flower shape to the left and stop before it reaches the edge of the artboard. Release the mouse button, and then the Shift key.

7   Change the opacity in the Control panel to 20%.

8   Choose Object > Arrange > Send Backward to put the copy behind the original flower shape.

▶ **Tip:** In the Transform panel, you can also change the scale, shear, and rotate, as well as the position on the x and y axes.

9   With the Selection tool, drag a marquee around the two flower shapes, the "green glow" text, and the "organic grow" text to select the logo pieces. Make sure not to select the dotted line to the right of the logo. Choose Object > Group.

10   Choose Select > Deselect.

11   Choose File > Save.

You've completed the letterhead artwork. Keep the file open so that you can use this artwork later in the lesson.

Positioning objects precisely

You can use the smart guides and Transform panel to move objects to exact coordinates on the x and y axes of the page and to control the position of objects in relation to the edge of the artboard.

You'll add content to the envelope by pasting a copy of the logo into the envelope artwork, and then specifying its exact coordinates on the envelope.

1   Choose View > Fit All In Window to see all the artboards.

2   Using the Selection tool (➤), Alt-drag (Windows) or Option-drag (Mac OS) the logo group onto the envelope artboard (artboard 03).

3   With the Selection tool, click the envelope artboard to make that the active artboard. Choose View > Fit Artboard In Window.

4   Double-click in the upper left corner where the rulers intersect. This resets the ruler origin to the lower left corner of the active artboard.

5   With the Selection tool, select the copied logo group again, click Align To Selection (⊡) in the Control panel and choose Align To Artboard from the menu. Click Horizontal Align Left (🖿), and then Vertical Align Top (🔳).

6   Select the Zoom tool (🔍) and drag a marquee around the upper left corner of the artboard. Using the Selection tool, drag the logo group from the corner down and to the right. While dragging, press Shift and when dX: 0.25 in and dY: −0.25 in appears in the measurement label, release the mouse button, and then the Shift key.

7   Choose Select > Deselect.

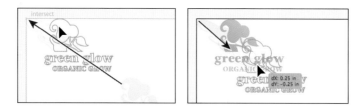

● **Note:** The dY: −0.25 appeared in the measurement label for the previous step because the ruler origin (0,0) starts in the lower left corner of the artboard. Dragging content down on an artboard gives you a negative value by default.

8   Choose 4 from the Artboard Navigation menu in the status bar to view the back of the business card.

9   With the Selection tool, Shift-click the text and small flowers in the upper right corner of the business card.

10 Choose Object > Group, and then choose Edit > Copy.

11 Choose 3 from the Artboard Navigation menu in the status bar to return to the envelope artboard. Choose Edit > Paste.

12 In the Control panel, click the word Transform, then click the middle left reference point (⊞) in the Transform panel. Change the X value 0.25 in and Y to 2.1 in. Press Enter or Return to apply these settings.

● **Note:** Depending on your screen resolution the word Transform may not appear in the Control panel. Instead, the Transform options may appear in the Control panel.

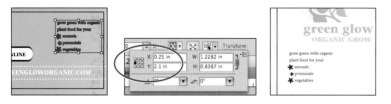

13 Click away from the artwork to deselect it, and then choose File > Save.

Changing the perspective

Now you'll use the Free Transform tool to change the perspective of the text. The Free Transform tool is a multipurpose tool that, besides letting you change the perspective of an object, combines the functions of scaling, shearing, reflecting, and rotating.

1 With the Selection tool (➤), double-click the green glow logo in the upper left corner. This puts the logo in isolation mode.

2 Select the text "organic grow" and choose Edit > Copy.

3 Double-click a blank area of the artboard to exit isolation mode.

4 Choose Edit > Paste. Drag the text to the bottom of the artboard about 1 inch from the left edge of the artboard.

5 Double-click the Hand tool (✋) in the Tools panel to fit the artboard in the window.

6   Select the Scale tool (⊡) nested within the Shear tool (⊿) in the Tools panel, and then Alt-click (Windows) or Option-click (Mac OS) the left side of the "organic grow" text to set the origin point. In the Scale dialog box select Preview, and then change Uniform Scale to 300%. Click OK.

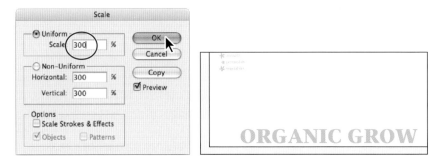

7   With the text selected, select the Free Transform tool (⊠) in the Tools panel.

8   Position the double-headed pointer (↔) over the upper right corner of the bounding box of the object. Extra attention is required in the rest of this step, so follow directions closely. Click and slowly drag the upper right corner handle upward. While dragging, press Shift+Alt+Ctrl (Windows) or Shift+Option+Command (Mac OS) to change the perspective of the object. Release the mouse button, and then the keys.

⬤ **Note:** If you use the modifier keys while clicking to select, the perspective feature does not work.

Pressing Shift as you drag scales an object proportionally. Pressing Alt (Windows) or Option (Mac OS) scales an object from its center point. Pressing Ctrl (Windows) or Command (Mac OS) as you drag distorts an object from the anchor point or bounding box handle that you're dragging.

⬤ **Note:** After rotating, the bottom of the text should be above the bottom of the artboard. If that isn't the case, try a different value in the Rotate dialog.

9   Double-click the Rotate tool (↻), select Preview in the Rotate dialog box, and then change the angle to 8°. Click OK.

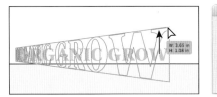 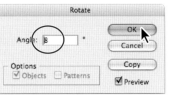

10 If necessary, with the Selection tool, drag the text up until the bottom is above the bottom of the artboard.

11 Change Opacity to 30% in the Control panel.

12 Choose Select > Deselect.

13 Choose File > Save and keep the file open.

Using the Free Distort effect

Now you'll explore a slightly different way of distorting objects. Free Distort is an effect that lets you distort a selection by moving any of its four corner points.

1 Choose File > Open, and open the L4start2.ai file in the Lesson04 folder, located in the Lessons folder on your hard disk. This file has content that you will copy into another file that you create.

2 Choose File > New.

3 In the New Document dialog box, change the name to business cards, ensure that Print is chosen for New Document Profile, change Units to Inches, change the Number Of Artboards to 8, click to select the Grid By Column button (⊞), change Spacing to 0 in, Columns to 2, Width to 3.25 in, Height to 2 in, and Orientation to landscape (⊡). Click the up arrow to the left of the Top Bleed field to make all the bleed values 0.125 in. Click OK.

4 With the Selection tool (▶), click the top left artboard to make it the active artboard.

5 Choose File > Save As. In the Save As dialog box, leave the name as business cards.ai and navigate to the Lesson04 folder. Leave the Save As Type option set to Adobe Illustrator (*.AI) (Windows) or the Format option set to Adobe Illustrator (ai) (Mac OS), and click Save. In the Illustrator Options dialog box, leave the Illustrator options at their default settings, and click OK.

6 Click the Arrange Documents button (▦ ▾) in the Control panel and choose 2-Up from the menu to arrange the documents side by side.

7 Click in the business cards.ai window, and choose View > Fit Artboard In Window. Click in the L4start2.ai window, and choose View > Fit Artboard In Window. Choose Select > All to select the content on the L4start2.ai artboard. Choose Object > Group. Drag the selected content onto the upper left business card artboard (artboard 1).

8 Close the L4start2.ai document without saving.

9 In the business cards.ai file, Align To Artboard (⊞) should still be selected in the Control panel. Click Horizontal Align Center (⬓), and then click Vertical Align Center (⊞➔) to align the artwork in the center of the artboard.

10 With the Selection tool, double-click the group of objects to enter isolation mode. Click to select the sandals.

11 Choose Effect > Distort & Transform > Free Distort.

12 In the Free Distort dialog box, drag one or more of the handles to distort the selection. We dragged the upper anchor points to the outside and the bottom points in toward the center. Click OK.

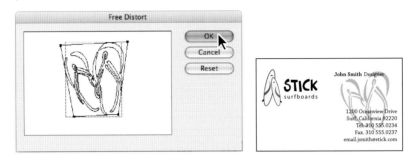

13 Double-click outside the artwork to exit isolation mode and to deselect it.

Making multiple transformations

Now you'll create multiple copies of the business card content.

1 Choose View > Fit All In Window.

2 Choose Select > All to select all the objects on every artboard.

3 Choose Object > Transform > Transform Each.

The Move options in the Transform Each dialog box let you move objects in a specified or random direction.

Now you'll move a copy of the selected objects.

4 In the Transform Each dialog box, select Preview, and type 3.5 in in the Move Horizontal text field. Leave the other settings as they are, and click Copy (don't click OK).

5   Press Ctrl+A (Windows) or Command+A (Mac OS) to select everything on the two business cards, and right-click (Windows) or Control-click (Mac OS) in the Document window to display a shortcut menu. Choose Transform > Transform Each from the shortcut menu.

6   In the Transform Each dialog box, type 0 in in the Move Horizontal text field, and –2.25 in in the Move Vertical text field. Leave the other settings as they are, and click Copy (don't click OK).

▶ **Tip:** You can also apply multiple transformations as an effect, including scaling, moving, rotating, and reflecting an object. After selecting the objects, choose Effect > Distort & Transform > Transform. The dialog box looks the same as the Transform Each dialog box. Transforming as an effect has the advantage of letting you change or remove the transformation at any time.

7   Choose Object > Transform > Transform Again to create one more.

Now you'll use the keyboard shortcut to repeat the transformations.

8   Press Ctrl+D (Windows) or Command+D (Mac OS) to transform, creating a total of eight cards.

9   Choose Select > Deselect. Then choose View > Guides > Hide Guides to hide the red bleed guides, and press Tab to hide the Tools panel and other open panels.

▶ **Tip:** Pressing Shift+Tab alternately hides or shows all panels, except the Tools panel and Control panel.

10 Choose File > Save, and then File > Close.

▶ **Tip:** To print the business cards on a single page, choose File > Print, and select Ignore Artboards to fit all the artboards on a single page.

Exploring on your own

1   In the letterhead project, copy and paste the green glow logo group onto artboard 2.

2   Transform the logo so that it's .5 in wide.

3   Copy other content, including the order online button on artboard 4 onto artboard 2.

4   Try flipping the flower in the green glow logo by double-clicking the logo to enter isolation mode.

5   Select the flower and click the word Transform in the Control panel to reveal the Transform panel (or click X, Y, W, or H). Select the center reference point and choose Flip Horizontal from the Transform panel menu.

Review questions

1 Name two ways to change the size of an existing active artboard.

2 How can you select and manipulate individual objects in a group (as described in this chapter)?

3 How do you resize an object? Explain how you determine the point from which the object resizes. How do you resize a group of objects proportionally?

4 What transformations can you make using the Transform panel?

5 What does the square diagram (▦) indicate in the Transform panel, and how does it affect transformations?

6 What's an easy way to change perspective? List three other types of transformations you can perform with the Free Transform tool.

Review answers

1 Double-click the Artboard tool and edit the dimensions of the active artboard in the Artboard Options dialog box. Select the Artboard tool and position the pointer over an edge or corner of the artboard and drag to resize.

2 You can double-click the group with a selection tool to enter isolation mode. This ungroups content temporarily that allows you to edit content within a group without ungrouping.

3 You can resize an object several ways: by selecting it and dragging handles on its bounding box, by using the Scale tool or the Transform panel, or by choosing Object > Transform > Scale to specify exact dimensions. You can also scale by choosing Effect > Distort & Transform > Transform.

To determine the reference point from which an object scales, select a reference point from the reference point locator in the Transform panel or in the Transform Effect or Transform Each dialog box, or click in the artwork with the Scale tool. Pressing Alt (Windows) or Option (Mac OS) and dragging the bounding box or double-clicking the Scale tool resizes a selected object from its center point.

Shift-dragging a corner handle on the bounding box scales an object proportionally, as does specifying either a uniform scale value in the Scale dialog box or multiples of the dimensions in the Width and Height text fields in the Transform panel.

4 You use the Transform panel for making the following transformations:

- Moving or precisely placing objects in your artwork (by specifying the x and y coordinates and the reference point)
- Scaling (by specifying the width and height of selected objects)
- Rotating (by specifying the angle of rotation)
- Shearing (by specifying the angle of distortion)
- Reflecting (by flipping selected objects vertically or horizontally)

5 The square diagram in the Transform panel indicates the bounding box of the selected objects. Select a reference point in the square to indicate the reference point from which the objects as a group move, scale, rotate, shear, or reflect.

6 An easy way to change the perspective of selected objects is to select the Free Transform tool, press Shift+Alt+Ctrl (Windows) or Shift+Option+ Command (Mac OS), and drag a corner handle on the bounding box.

Other types of transformations that you can perform with the Free Transform tool are distorting, scaling, shearing, rotating, and reflecting.

5 DRAWING WITH THE PEN AND PENCIL TOOLS

Lesson overview

In this lesson, you'll learn how to do the following:

- Draw straight lines.

- Use template layers.

- End path segments and split lines.

- Draw curved lines.

- Select and adjust curve segments.

- Draw and edit with the Pencil tool.

This lesson will take approximately an hour and a half to complete. If needed, remove the previous lesson folder from your hard disk and copy the Lesson05 folder onto it.

While the Pencil tool is preferable for drawing and editing free-form lines, the Pen tool is excellent for drawing precisely, including straight lines, Bezier curves, and complex shapes. You'll practice using the Pen tool on a blank artboard, and then use it to create an illustration of an apple.

Getting started

In the first part of this lesson, you learn how to manipulate the Pen tool on a blank artboard.

1 To ensure that the tools and panels function as described in this lesson, delete or deactivate (by renaming) the Adobe Illustrator CS4 preferences file. See "Restoring default preferences" on page 3.

2 Start Adobe Illustrator CS4.

⬤ **Note:** If you have not already copied the resource files for this lesson onto your hard disk from the Lesson05 folder on the Adobe Illustrator CS4 Classroom in a Book CD, do so now. See "Copying the Classroom in a Book files" on page 2.

3 Open the L5start_01.ai file in the Lesson05 folder, located in the Lessons folder on your hard disk. The top portion of the artboard shows the path that you will create. Use the bottom half of the artboard for this exercise.

4 Choose File > Save As. In the Save As dialog box, navigate to the Lesson05 folder and open it. Type path1.ai in the File Name text field. Choose Adobe Illustrator (.AI) from the Save As Type menu (Windows) or choose Adobe Illustrator (ai) from the Format menu (Mac OS). In the Illustrator Options dialog box, leave the default settings and click OK.

5 Press Ctrl+0 (zero) (Windows) or Command+0 (Mac OS) to fit the entire artboard in the window. Then hold down Shift and press Tab once to close all the panels, except for the Tools panel. You don't need the panels for this lesson.

6 Choose View > Smart Guides to deselect the smart guides.

⬤ **Note:** If you see a crosshair instead of the pen icon, the Caps Lock key is active. Caps Lock turns tool icons into crosshairs for increased precision.

7 Select the Pen tool (✒) in the Tools panel. Notice the x next to the pen icon (✒ₓ), indicating that a starting point has not been selected. Click in the bottom of the artboard and then move the pointer away from the original anchor point. The "x" disappears.

8 Click to the right of the original point to create the next anchor point in the path.

⬤ **Note:** The first segment you draw is not visible until you click a second anchor point. If direction handles appear, you have accidentally dragged with the Pen tool; choose Edit > Undo, and click again. Direction handles are used to reshape curved paths and do not print.

9 Click beneath the initial anchor point to create a zigzag pattern. Create a zigzag that has six anchor points.

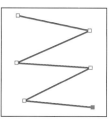

One of the many benefits of using the Pen tool is that you can create custom paths and continue to edit the anchor points that make up the path.

Next, you'll see how the Selection tools work with the Pen tool.

10 Select the Selection tool (➤) in the Tools panel and click the zigzag path. Notice that all the anchor points become solid, signifying that all anchor points are selected. Click and drag the path to a new location anywhere on the artboard. All the anchor points travel together, maintaining the zigzag path.

11 Deselect the zigzag path in one of the following ways:

- With the Selection tool, click an empty area of the artboard.

- Choose Select > Deselect.

- With the Pen tool selected, Ctrl-click (Windows) or Command-click (Mac OS) in a blank area of the artboard to deselect. This temporarily selects the Selection tool. When the Ctrl or Command key is released, you return to the Pen tool.

- Click the Pen tool once. Even though it looks like the path is still active, it will not connect to the next anchor point created.

12 Select the Direct Selection tool (➤) in the Tools panel and click on any point in the zigzag, or drag a marquee selection around an anchor point. The selected anchor point turns solid, and the unselected anchor points are hollow.

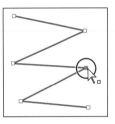

13 With the anchor point selected, click and drag to reposition the anchor point. The anchor point moves but the others remain stationary. Use this technique to edit a path.

14 Choose Select > Deselect. At times you may need to recreate just one line segment in a path. With the Direct Selection tool, click on any line segment that is between two anchor points, and then choose Edit > Cut. This cuts only the selected path from the zigzag.

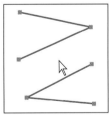

Note: If the entire zigzag path disappears, choose Edit > Undo Clear and try again.

15 With the Pen tool, position the pointer over one of the anchor points that was connected to the line segment. Notice that the Pen tool has a forward slash (/) indicating a continuation of an existing path. When you click the point, it becomes solid. Only active points appear solid.

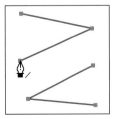

16 Position the pointer over the other point that was connected to the original line segment. The pointer now has a merge symbol next to it () indicating that you are connecting to another path. Click the point to reconnect the paths.

17 Choose File > Save, and then File > Close.

Creating straight lines

In Lesson 4, "Transforming Objects," you learned that using the Shift key in combination with shape tools constrains the shape of objects. The Shift key also constrains the Pen tool, to create paths of 45°.

Next you will learn how to draw straight lines and constrain angles.

1 Open the L5start_02.ai file in the Lesson05 folder, located in the Lessons folder on your hard disk. The top portion of the artboard shows the path that you will create. Use the bottom half of the page for this exercise.

2 Choose File > Save As. In the Save As dialog box, navigate to the Lesson05 folder and open it. Name the file path2.ai. Choose Adobe Illustrator (.AI) from the Save As Type menu (Windows) or choose Adobe Illustrator (ai)from the Format menu (Mac OS). In the Illustrator Options dialog box, leave the default settings and click OK.

3 Choose View > Smart Guides to select smart guides.

4 Select the Pen tool (✒) and click once in the work area of the page.

5 Move the pointer to the right of the original anchor point 1.5 in as indicated by the measurement label. A green construction guide appears when the pointer is vertically aligned with the previous anchor point. Click to set the second anchor point.

The measurement label and construction guide are part of the smart guides.

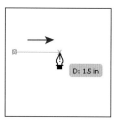

6 Set three more points by clicking the mouse button, creating the same shape as in the top half of the artboard. To create angled lines, press the Shift key, and then move the pointer to the right and down and click to set the anchor point.

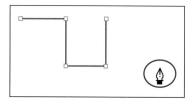

Press the Shift key while clicking to constrain the path.

7 Drag the pointer down and click to set the last anchor point for the shape.

8 Choose File > Save and close the file.

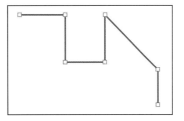

Creating curved paths

In this part of the lesson, you'll learn how to draw smooth, curved lines with the Pen tool. In vector drawing applications such as Adobe Illustrator CS4, you draw a curve, called a Bezier curve, with control points. By setting anchor points and dragging direction handles, you can define the shape of the curve. Although drawing curves this way can take some time to learn, it gives you the greatest control and flexibility in creating paths.

1 Choose File > New to create a new letter-sized document, leaving the settings at the page defaults. Use this file to practice creating a Bezier curve.

2 In the Control panel, click the Fill color and choose the None swatch (⬜) Then click the Stroke color and make sure that the black swatch is selected.

3 Make sure the stroke weight is 1 pt in the Control panel.

4 With the Pen tool (✒), click anywhere on the page to create the initial anchor point. Click in another location, and drag to create a curved path.

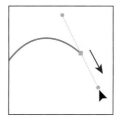

Click and drag to create a curved path.

Continue clicking and dragging at different locations on the page. The goal for this exercise is not to create anything specific, but to get accustomed to the feel of the Bezier curve.

Notice that as you click and drag, direction handles appear. Direction handles consist of direction lines that end in round direction points. The angle and length of the direction handles determine the shape and size of the curved segments. Direction handles do not print and are not visible when the anchor is inactive.

5 Choose Select > Deselect.

6 Select the Direct Selection tool (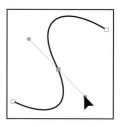) and click a curved segment to display the direction handles. If smart guides are selected, the word path appears when you click. Moving the direction handles reshapes the curve.

● **Note:** Anchor points are square, and are solid when selected; they are hollow squares when not selected. Direction points are round. These lines and points do not print with the artwork.

7 Choose File > Close and do not save the file.

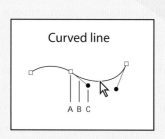

Select anchor points to access the direction handles.

Components of a path

As you draw, you create a line called a path. A path is made up of one or more straight or curved segments. The beginning and end of each segment are marked by anchor points, which work like pins holding a wire in place. A path can be closed (for example, a circle) or open, with distinct end points (for example, a wavy line). You change the shape of a path by dragging its anchor points, the direction points at the end of direction lines that appear at anchor points, or the path segment itself.

Paths can have two kinds of anchor points: corner points and smooth points. At a corner point, a path abruptly changes direction. At a smooth point, path segments are connected as a continuous curve. You can draw a path using any combination of corner and smooth points. If you draw the wrong kind of point, you can always change it.

—From Illustrator Help

Curved line

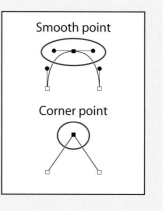

A. Anchor point B. Direction line
C. Direction handle (or point)

Building a curve

In this part of the lesson, you will learn how to control the direction handles to control curves.

1 Open the L5start_03.ai file in the Lesson05 folder. This file contains a template layer that you can trace to practice using the Pen tool (✒). (See Lesson 8, "Working with Layers," for information about creating layers.) The work area below the path is for additional practice on your own.

2 Choose File > Save As. In the Save As dialog box, navigate to the Lesson05 folder. Type path3.ai in the File Name text field. Choose Adobe Illustrator (.AI) from the Save As Type menu (Windows) or choose Adobe Illustrator (ai) from the Format menu (Mac OS). In the Illustrator Options dialog box, leave the default settings and click OK.

3 Press Z to switch to the Zoom tool (🔍) and drag a marquee around the curve labeled A.

4 Choose View > Smart Guides to deselect them.

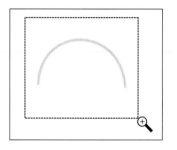

5 Select the Pen tool (✒) in the Tools panel. Click at the base of the left side of the arch and drag up to create a direction line going the same direction as the arch. It helps to remember to always follow the direction of the curve. Release the mouse button when the direction line is slightly above the arch.

▶ **Tip:** As you draw with the Pen tool, if you make a mistake, choose Edit > Undo Pen to undo points.

When a curve goes up, the direction line also go up.

● **Note:** The artboard may scroll as you drag. If you lose visibility of the curve, choose View > Zoom Out until you see the curve and anchor point. Pressing the spacebar temporarily gives you the Hand tool to reposition the artwork.

6 Click the lower right base of the arch path and drag down. Release the mouse button when the top direction point is slightly above the arch.

7 If the path you created is not aligned exactly with the template, use the Direct Selection tool (▷) to select the anchor points one at a time. Then adjust the direction handles until your path follows the template more accurately.

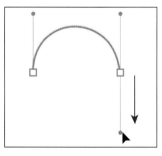

To control the path, pay attention to where the direction handles fall.

● **Note:** Pulling the direction handle longer makes a higher slope, when the direction handle is shorter the slope is flatter.

8 Use the Selection tool (⬉) and click the artboard anywhere there are no other objects, or choose Select > Deselect. If you were to click with the Pen tool while path A was still active, the path connects to the next point you draw. Deselecting the first path allows you to create a new path.

▶ **Tip:** To deselect objects, you can also press Ctrl or Command to temporarily switch to the Selection or Direct Selection tool, whichever was last used, and click the artboard where there are no objects.

9 Choose File > Save.

10 Zoom out to see path B.

11 Using the Pen tool, click and drag at the left base of path B in the direction of the arch. Click and drag down on the next square point, adjusting the arch with the direction handle before you release the mouse button.

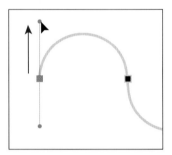

Click and drag up to create the upward arch.

● **Note:** Don't worry if it is not exact. You can correct the line with the Direct Selection tool when the path is complete.

● **Note:** By default, you can undo a series of actions—limited only by your computer's memory—by repeatedly choosing Edit > Undo, or Ctrl+Z (Windows) or Command+Z (Mac OS).

12 Continue along the path, alternating between clicking and dragging up and down. Put anchor points only where there are square boxes. If you make a mistake as you draw, you can undo your work by choosing Edit > Undo Pen.

13 When the path is complete, use the Direct Selection tool and select an anchor point. When the anchor is selected, the direction handles appear, and you can readjust the slope of the path.

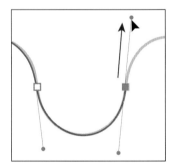

Alternate between dragging up and down with the Pen tool.

14 Practice repeating these paths in the work area.

15 Choose File > Save, and then File > Close.

Converting curved points to corner points

When creating curves, the directional handles help to determine the slope of the path. Returning to a corner point requires a little extra effort. In the next portion of the lesson, you will practice converting curve points to corners.

1 Open the L5start_04.ai file in the Lesson05 folder. On this page you, can see the paths that you will create. Use the top section as a template for the exercise.

Create your paths directly on top of those that you see on the page. The work area below is for additional practice on your own.

2   Choose File > Save As. In the Save As dialog box, navigate to the Lesson05 folder. Type path4.ai in the File Name text field. Choose Adobe Illustrator (.AI) from the Save As Type menu (Windows) or choose Adobe Illustrator (ai) from the Format menu (Mac OS). In the Illustrator Options dialog box, leave the default settings and click OK.

3   Use the Zoom tool (🔍) and drag a marquee around the path A.

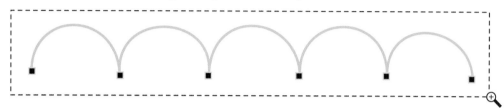

4   Select the Pen tool (✒), and while pressing the Shift key, click the first anchor point and drag up. Click the second anchor point and drag down without releasing the mouse button. As you drag down, press the Shift key. When the curve looks correct, release the mouse button, and then the Shift key.

● **Note:** Pressing the Shift key when dragging constrains the angle of the handle to a straight line.

Next you will split the direction lines to convert a smooth point to a corner point.

5   Press Alt (Windows) or Option (Mac OS) and position the pointer over either the last anchor point created or its direction point. Look for the caret (^) symbol and click and drag a direction line up when the carat is visible. Release the mouse button, and then the Alt or Option key. If you do not see the caret (^), you will create an additional loop.

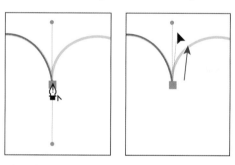

When the caret is visible, click and drag up.

▶ **Tip:** After you draw a path, you can also select single or multiple anchor points and click the Convert Selected Anchor Points To Corner button (⌐) or Convert Selected Anchor Points To Smooth button (⌐) in the Control panel.

● **Note:** If you don't click exactly on the anchor point or the direction point at the end of the direction line, a warning dialog box appears . Click OK and try again.

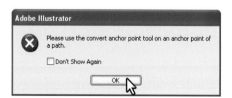

You can practice adjusting the direction handles with the Direct Selection tool when the path is completed.

6 Click the next square point and drag down. Release the mouse button when the path looks correct.

7 Press Alt (Windows) or Option (Mac OS) and, after the caret (^) appears, pull up the last anchor point or direction point for the next curve.

▶ **Tip:** Steps 8 and 9 are a way to convert a point to a corner point while drawing a new point.

8 For the third anchor point, click the next square point on the path and drag down until the path looks correct. Do not release the mouse button.

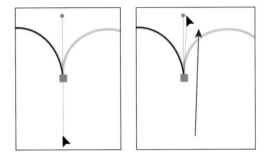

9 Press Alt (Windows) or Option (Mac OS) again and drag up for the next curve. Release the mouse button, and then the key.

10 Continue clicking and dragging, using Alt (Windows) or Option (Mac OS) to create corner points, until the path is completed. Use the Direct Selection tool (⬚) to fine-tune the path, and then deselect the path.

11 Choose File > Save.

12 Choose View > Fit Artboard In Window. You can also use Ctrl+0 (zero) (Windows) or Command+0 (Mac OS). Use the Zoom tool to drag a marquee around path B to enlarge its view.

Next you will go from a curve to a straight line.

13 With the Pen tool, click the first anchor point on the left and drag up. Then click and drag down on the second anchor point. This motion of creating an arch should be familiar to you by now. You will now go from the curve to a straight line. Simply pressing the Shift key and clicking does not produce a straight line, since this last point is a curved anchor point.

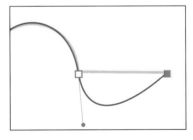

The path when a curved point is not turned into a corner point.

The figure in this step shows what the path would look like if you simply clicked with the Pen tool on the last point.

14 To create the next path as a straight line, click the last point created to delete one direction line from the path. Shift-click to set the next point to the right, creating the straight segment.

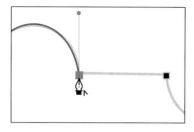

Click the last anchor point to force a straight path from it.

15 For the next arch, hover over the last point created (notice that the carat appears $\mathbf{\mathring{\phi}_\wedge}$) and then click and drag down from the point you just created. This creates a direction line.

16 Click the next point and drag up to complete the downward arch. Click the last anchor point of the arch.

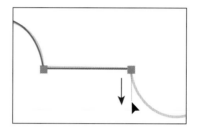

Click the last point and drag away to create a direction line.

17 Shift-click the next point to create the second straight segment.

18 Click and drag up, and then click and drag down on the last point to create the final arch.

19 Practice repeating these paths in the lower portion of the artboard. Use the Direct Selection tool to adjust your path if necessary.

20 Choose File > Save, and then File > Close.

Creating the apple illustration

In this next part of the lesson, you'll create an illustration of an apple pierced by an arrow. You'll use the new skills you learned in the previous exercises, and also learn some additional Pen tool techniques.

1 Choose File > Open, and open the L5end.ai file in the Lesson05 folder, located in the Lessons folder.

2 Choose View > Zoom Out to make the finished artwork smaller to fit on your screen as you work. (Use the Hand tool (🖐) to move the artwork to where you want it.) If you don't want to leave the image open, choose File > Close.

3 Choose File > Open, and open the L5start.ai file in the Lesson05 folder.

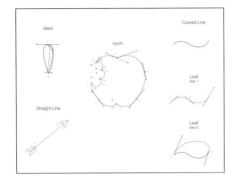

4 Choose File > Save As, name the file apple.ai, and select the Lesson05 folder in the Save As dialog box. Choose Adobe Illustrator (.AI) from the Save As Type menu (Windows) or choose Adobe Illustrator (ai) from the Format menu (Mac OS) and click Save. In the Illustrator Options dialog box, leave the options set at the defaults and click OK.

Creating the arrow

You'll begin by drawing the straight line for the arrow. The template layer lets you draw directly over the artwork.

1 Choose View > Straight Line to zoom into the left corner of the template.

Separate views were saved in this document to show different areas of the template at a higher magnification.

▶ **Tip:** To create a custom view, choose View > New View. For more information, see "To use multiple windows and views" in Illustrator Help.

2 Choose View > Hide Bounding Box to hide the bounding boxes of selected objects. Select the Pen tool (✎) and place it on the dashed line of the arrow in the artwork. Notice that the pointer has an x next to it. If you recall, this indicates that your next click begins a new path.

● **Note:** When drawing with the Pen tool, it can be easier to draw paths with no fill selected. You can also change the fill and other properties of the path after you begin drawing.

3 In the Control panel, make sure that None (▨) is the fill color and black is the stroke color in the Control panel. Also make sure that the stroke weight is 1pt.

4 Click point A at the left end of the line to create the starting anchor point—a small solid square.

5 Click point B to create the ending anchor point.

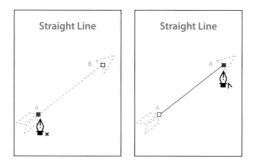

When you click a second time, a caret (^) appears next to the Pen tool. The caret indicates that you can drag out a direction line for a curve by clicking and dragging the Pen tool from this anchor point. The caret disappears when you move the Pen tool away from the anchor point.

6 Choose Select > Deselect to end the path. You must deselect before you can draw other lines that aren't connected to this path.

Now you'll make the straight line thicker by changing its stroke weight.

7 With the Selection tool (➤), click the straight line to select it.

8 In the Control panel, change the Stroke Weight to 3 pt.

Splitting a path

To continue creating the arrow, you'll split the path of the straight line using the Scissors tool and adjust the segments.

1 Choose View > Smart Guides to select smart guides.

2 With the straight line selected, in the Tools panel, click and hold down the Eraser tool (✐) to reveal the Scissors tool (✂). Select the Scissors tool and click the middle of the line to make a cut (the word path appears).

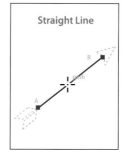

Note: If you click the stroke of a closed shape (a circle, for example) with the Scissors tool, it simply cuts the path so that it becomes open (a path with two end points).

Cuts made with the Scissors tool must be on a line or a curve rather than on an end point.

When you click with the Scissors tool, a new selected anchor point appears. The Scissors tool actually creates two anchor points each time you click, but because they are on top of each other, you can see only one.

3   Select the Direct Selection tool (⬈) and position it over the cut you just made. The hollow square (and the word intersect) on the pointer indicates that it's over the anchor point. Select the new anchor point, and drag it up to widen the gap between the two split segments. As you drag, notice that the word path appears, indicating that the anchor point is snapping to the line. Leave the top path selected.

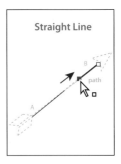

Straight Line

Adding arrowheads

You can add arrowheads and tails to open paths by applying an effect. The benefit to using an effect is that the arrow dynamically changes with the stroke to which it is applied.

When a path with an arrowhead effect is changed, the arrowhead follows the path. Learn more about effects and how to use them in Lesson 12 "Applying Appearance Attributes and Graphic Styles."

Now you'll add an arrowhead to the end point of one line segment and a tail to the starting point of the other line segment.

1   With the top line segment selected, choose Effect > Stylize > Add Arrowheads from the Illustrator Effects.

   ◉ **Note:** The Photoshop effect, which is the second Effect > Stylize command, applies painted or impressionistic effects to RGB images.

2   In the Add Arrowheads dialog box, leave the Start section set to None. For the End section, click an arrow button to select the number 2 style of arrowhead (a thumbnail preview appears in the dialog box), and click OK.

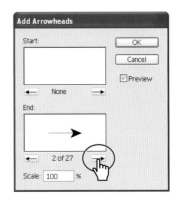

3   Using the Selection tool (▶), select the bottom line segment, and choose Effect > Stylize > Add Arrowheads from the Illustrator Effects to open the Add Arrowheads dialog box. Select the number 17 style of arrowhead in the Start section. In the End section, select None by clicking the left arrow, and click OK to add a tail to the starting point of the line.

4   Choose Select > Deselect, and then File > Save.

Drawing curves

In this part of the lesson, you will review drawing curves by drawing the apple, its stem, and a leaf. You'll examine a single curve and then draw a series of curves together, using the template guidelines to help you.

Selecting a curve

1 Choose View > Smart Guides to deselect the smart guides.

2 Choose View > Curved Line to display a view of a curved line on the template.

3 Using the Direct Selection tool (⬚), click one of the segments of the curved line to view its anchor points and direction handles, which extend from the points. The Direct Selection tool lets you select and edit individual segments in the curved line.

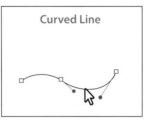

Curved Line

Note: Because you are tracing over existing shapes, the smart guides snap to those shapes. Deselect smart guides to draw more fluidly.

With a curve selected, you can also select the stroke and fill of the curve. When you do this, the next line you draw will have the same attributes. For more on these attributes, see Lesson 6, "Color and Painting."

▶ **Tip:** With the Direct Selection tool, click and drag several of the direction points (at the ends of the direction lines) to change the shape of the curves.

Drawing the leaf

Now you'll draw the first curve of the leaf.

1 Choose View > Leaf, or scroll down to see the guides for Leaf step 1.

Instead of dragging the Pen tool (✒) to draw a curve, you will drag it to set the starting point and the direction of the line's curve.

2 Select the Pen tool and position it over point A on the template. Click and drag from point A to the red dot.

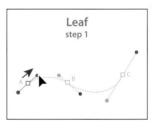

Leaf
step 1

Next you'll set the second anchor point and its direction handles.

3 Click and drag with the Pen tool (✒) from point B to the next red dot. The two anchor points are connected with a curve that follows the direction handles you have created. Notice that if you vary the angle of dragging, you change the degree of the curve.

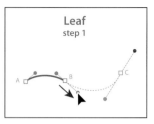

4 To complete the curved line, click and drag with the Pen tool from point C to the last red dot.

5 Control-click (Windows) or Command-click (Mac OS) away from the line to end the path.

▶ **Tip:** You can also end a path by clicking the Pen tool, pressing P for the Pen tool shortcut, or choosing Select > Deselect.

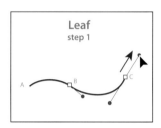

Drawing different kinds of curves

Now you'll finish drawing the leaf by adding to an existing curved segment. Even after ending a path, you can return to the curve and add to it. The Alt or Option key lets you control the type of curve you draw.

1 Click the arrow to the right of the status bar in the lower left corner of the Document window, and choose Show > Current Tool.

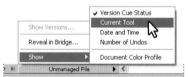

2 Scroll down to the template for Leaf step 2.

You'll now add a corner point to the path. A corner point lets you change the direction of the curve. A smooth point lets you draw a continuous curve.

3 Position the Pen tool (✒) over point A. The slash next to the pen icon indicates that you're aligned with an anchor and are continuing the path of the existing line, rather than starting a new line.

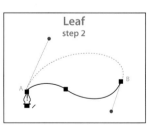

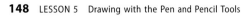

4 Press Alt (Windows) or Option (Mac OS) and notice that the status bar in the lower left corner of the Document window displays Pen: Make Corner. Now Alt-drag (Windows) or Option-drag (Mac OS) the Pen tool from anchor point A to the red dot. Release the mouse button, and then the Alt or Option key.

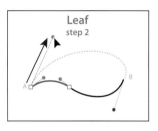

Alt-dragging or Option-dragging creates a corner point.

So far, you have drawn curves that are open paths. Now you'll draw a closed path in which the final anchor point is drawn on the first anchor point of the path. Examples of closed paths include ovals and rectangles.

Next you'll close the path using a smooth point.

5 Position the pointer over anchor point B on the template. An open circle appears next to the Pen tool, indicating that clicking closes the path. Click and drag from this point to beyond the red dot below point B. As you drag, pay attention to the top line segment that you are adjusting.

Notice the direction handles that appear where you close the path. The direction handles on both sides of a smooth point are aligned along the same angle.

⬤ **Note:** The dotted template lines are a guide only. The shapes you create do not need to follow the lines exactly.

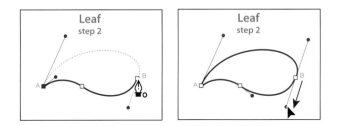

6 Control-click (Windows) or Command-click (Mac OS) away from the line, and choose File > Save.

Convert between smooth points and corner points

Now you'll create the leaf stem by adjusting a curved path. You'll be converting a smooth point on the curve to a corner point, and a corner point to a smooth point.

1 Choose View > Stem to display a magnified view of the stem.

2 Select the Direct Selection tool (⟩), and position the pointer over point A at the top of the curve. When an open square appears next to the pointer, click the anchor point to select it and display its red direction handles for the smooth point.

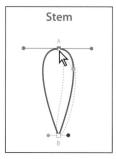

3 Select the Convert Anchor Point tool (⋀) from the same group as the Pen tool (⬦) in the Tools panel, or use the shortcut by pressing the Alt (Windows) or Option (Mac OS) while the Pen tool is selected.

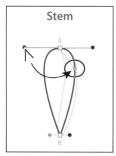

4 Using the Convert Anchor Point tool, select the left direction point on the direction line, and drag it to the gold dot on the template.

● **Note:** If a warning dialog box appears, click OK and try again. Also, if you click without dragging, the direction handle disappears.

Dragging with the Convert Anchor Point tool converts the smooth anchor point to a corner point and adjusts the angle of the left direction line.

5 With the Convert Anchor Point tool, select the bottom anchor point and drag from point B to the red dot to convert the corner point to a smooth point, rounding out the curve. Two direction handles emerge from the anchor point, indicating that it is now a smooth point

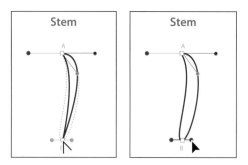

Use the Convert Anchor Point tool to convert corners to curves.

Next you'll continue editing the shape of the stem.

6 With the Direct Selection tool (⤡), click to select point A. In the Control panel, click the Cut Path At Selected Anchor Points button (⬚). Drag the selected anchor point to the left.

7 Shift-click the two points at the top, and then click the Connect Selected End Points button (⟋) in the Control panel to create a straight line across the top of the stem.

8 Select the top-left anchor point with the Direct Selection tool, and click the Convert Selected Anchor Points To Smooth button (⬚) in the Control panel.

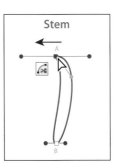

Cut the path and drag the anchor point left.

▶ **Tip:** To join the path, you can also choose Object > Path > Join, or Ctrl+J or Cmd+J.

9 Click and drag the bottom direction line for the upper left point to the right so that the shape follows the guidelines a little more closely.

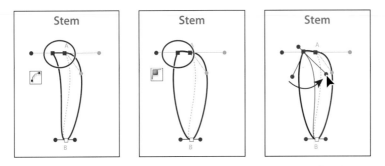

Click the Connect Selected End Points button. Click the Convert Selected Anchor Points To Smooth button, then drag the direction line.

10 Choose File > Save.

Drawing the apple shape

Now you'll draw a single, continuous object that consists of smooth points and corner points. Each time you want to change the direction of a curve at a specific point, you'll press Alt or Option to create a corner point.

1 Choose View > Apple to display a magnified view of the apple.

First you'll draw the side opposite the bite marks on the apple by creating smooth points and corner points.

2 Select the Pen tool (🖋) from the same group as the Convert Anchor Point tool (⊿) in the Tools panel. Starting at the blue square (point A), click and drag from point A to the red dot to set the starting anchor point and direction of the first curve.

⬤ **Note:** You do not have to start at the blue dot (point A) to draw this shape. You can set anchor points for a path with the Pen tool in a clockwise or counter-clockwise direction.

3 With the Pen tool, click and drag from point B to the red dot, creating the direction line that controls the next curve.

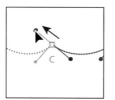

Apple

▶ **Tip:** In step 4, you drag the pointer to the red dot first. This sets the preceding curve. Once the curve matches the template, pressing Alt or Option splits the direction lines and lets you drag the next direction line to control the shape of the next curve.

4 Click and drag from point C to the red dot and keep the mouse button held down. Alt-drag (Windows) or Option-drag (Mac OS) from the red dot to the gold dot. Release the mouse button, and then the key. This splits the direction handles.

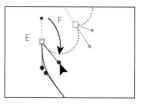

Drag to adjust the curve.

Alt-drag/Option-drag the direction point to set the curve.

5 With the Pen tool, click and drag from point D to the red dot, creating the direction line that controls the next curve.

6 With the Pen tool, click and drag from point E to the red dot. Alt-drag or Option-drag the direction handle from the red dot to the gold dot.

7 Continue drawing to points F, G, H, and I by first dragging from the anchor point to the red dot, and then Alt-dragging or Option-dragging the direction handle from the red dot to the gold dot.

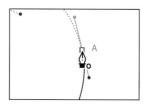

Split the direction lines by pressing Alt (Windows) or Option (Mac OS).

Next, you'll complete the drawing of the apple by closing the path.

8 Position the Pen tool over point A. Notice that an open circle appears next to the pen pointer, indicating that the path closes when you click.

The Pen tool pointer has an open circle when closing a path.

9 Click and drag down and a bit to the right to the red dot below point A. Notice that as you drag down, another direction line appears above the point. As you drag, you are reshaping the path.

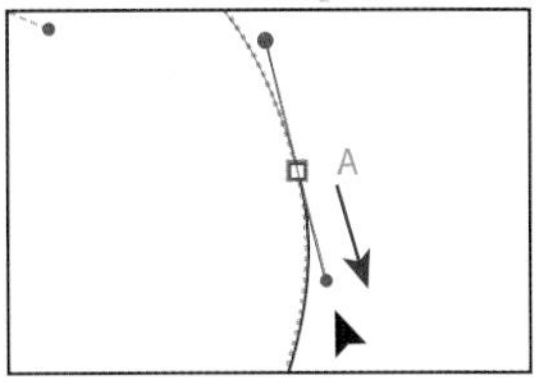

10 Ctrl-click (Windows) or Command-click (Mac OS) away from the path to deselect it, and then choose File > Save.

Editing curves

To adjust the curves you've drawn, you can drag either the curve's anchor points or direction handles. You can also edit a curve by moving the line. You will turn on the smart guides as an aid as you edit the path. You will also hide the template layer so that you can edit the actual path.

1 Choose View > Smart Guides to select them.

2 Choose Essentials from the workspace switcher on the right side of the Control panel. Then click the Layers panel icon (◈) on the right side of the workspace to open the Layers panel. Click the Template Layer icon (◈) in the Layers panel to deselect visibility for the template layer.

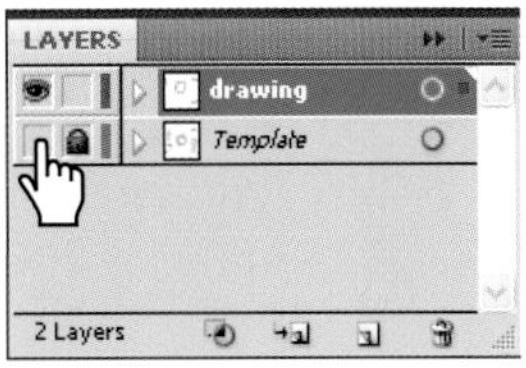

3 Select the Direct Selection tool (◈) and click the outline of the apple when the word path appears next to the pointer.

Clicking with the Direct Selection tool displays the curve's direction handles and lets you adjust the shape of individual curved segments. Clicking with the Selection tool (◈) selects the entire path.

4 Click the anchor point at the bottom of the apple (point C on the template layer) to select it (the word anchor appears when you hover over the bottom anchor point). Press the Down Arrow key to nudge the point down.

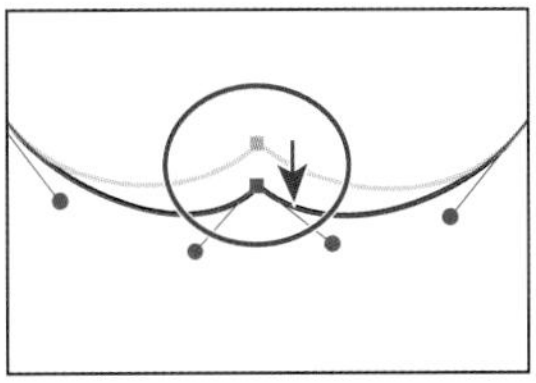

Note: You can also drag the anchor point with the Direct Selection tool.

5 With the Direct Selection tool, click and drag across the bottom of the apple to select the bottom three anchor points. Notice that when all three points are selected, the handles disappear. In the Control panel, click Show Handles For Multiple Selected Anchor Points

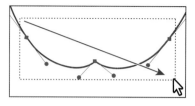

(▣) to see the direction lines for all three points. This lets you edit the anchor points together.

● **Note:** If you don't select all three points the first time, try dragging across them again. If you have at least one of the anchor points selected, you can also Shift-click with the Direct Selection tool on the other remaining anchor points to select them.

6 With the Direct Selection tool, click and drag the bottom direction point for the leftmost point. Align the direction point with the bottom of the apple. When the green alignment guide appears, release the mouse button.

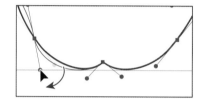

Rotate the left direction line and align it with the bottom of the apple.

7 With the Direct Selection tool, click and drag the bottom direction point for the rightmost point to the right. Align the direction point with the bottom of the apple. When the green alignment guide appears, release the mouse button.

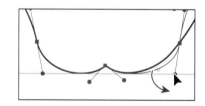

Rotate the right direction line and align it with the bottom of the apple.

● **Note:** The alignment guides are available because smart guides are selected. If you don't see them, choose View > Smart Guides.

8 Choose Select > Deselect.

9 Choose File > Save.

Deleting and adding anchor points

When working with paths, it is best not to add more anchor points than necessary. A path with fewer points is easier to edit, display, and print. You can reduce a path's complexity or change its overall shape by deleting unnecessary points. Next you will delete an anchor point and reshape the bite taken out of the apple.

1 Select the apple with the Selection tool (▶).

2 Select the Pen tool and position the pointer over the path where the bite is taken out of the apple. When a plus sign (+) and the word path appear next to the Pen tool, click to create a new anchor point.

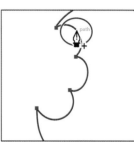

Drag to reshape the path.

▶ **Tip:** Another way to add anchor points is to select the Add Anchor Point tool (◊⁺) in the Tools panel, position the pointer over a path, and click to add a point.

3 With the Direct Selection tool, click and drag the newly created point down and to the left just a bit. Drag the direction lines to the right so that a corner point is created.

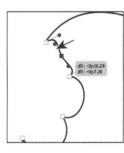  

4 Repeat the above steps to add another anchor point to the bottom of the bite.

Now you will delete an anchor point and reshape the bite.

● **Note:** You can achieve the same effect by adding only one anchor point and reshaping the curves.

5   With the Direct Selection tool, click a point in the bite out of the apple to select it. In the Control panel, click Remove Selected Anchor Points (🖋) to delete the anchor point.

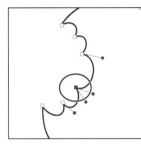   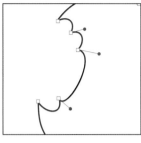

Select the anchor point.   Click Remove Selected Anchor Points to delete the anchor point.

6   With the Direct Selection tool, drag the direction handles for the remaining anchor points so that part of the bite is rounder.

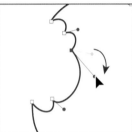

Drag the top direction handle   Drag the bottom direction handle
to reshape the curve.   to reshape the curve.

7   Choose Select > Deselect.

8   Choose File > Save.

Drawing with the Pencil tool

The Pencil tool lets you draw open and closed paths as if you were drawing with a pencil on paper. Anchor points are created as you draw and are placed on the path where Illustrator deems them necessary. However, you can adjust the points when the path is complete. The number of anchor points set down is determined by the length and complexity of the path and by tolerance settings in the Pencil Tool Options dialog box. The Pencil tool is most useful for free-form drawing and creating more organic shapes.

Next you will draw a few leaf veins on the leaf.

1   Choose View > Fit Artboard In Window.

2 Select the Zoom tool (🔍) in the Tools panel and click the leaf shape in the lower right corner of the artboard three times.

3 Double-click the Pencil tool (✎) in the Tools panel. In the Pencil Tool Options dialog box, drag the Smoothness slider to the right until the value is 100%. This makes the paths drawn with the Pencil tool have fewer points and appear smoother. Click OK.

4 With the Pencil tool selected, click the Stroke color in the Control panel, and select black in the Swatches panel that appears, and then click the Fill color in the Control panel and choose None (⬜).

Note: The default settings may already be set to the stroke and fill colors in step 4.

5 Click and drag from the left end of the leaf toward the right end of the leaf in an arc to create a center line for the leaf.

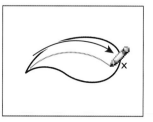

Note: The x that appears to the right of the pointer before you begin drawing indicates that you are about to create a new path.

▶ **Tip:** If you want to create a closed path, like a circle, click and drag with the Pencil tool. As you're dragging, press Alt or Option. The Pencil tool displays a small circle to indicate that you're creating a closed path. When the path is the size and shape you want, release the mouse button, but not the Alt or Option key. After the path closes, release the Alt or Option key. The beginning and ending anchor points are connected with the shortest line possible.

Notice that as you draw, the path may not look perfectly smooth. When you release the mouse button, the path is smoothed based on the Smoothness value that you set.

6 Position the pointer over the newly created path. Notice that the x is no longer next to the Pencil tool pointer. This indicates that if you drag to start drawing, you will edit the leaf vein rather than draw a new path.

Next you will set more options for the Pencil tool.

7 Double-click the Pencil tool in the Tools panel.

8 In the Pencil Tool Options dialog box, deselect Edit Selected Paths. Change the Fidelity value to 20 pixels. Click OK.

▶ **Tip:** The higher the Fidelity value, the greater the distance between anchor points (fewer anchor points are typically created). Fewer anchor points can make the path smoother and less complex.

9 With the Pencil tool, click and drag, starting from the first vein and radiating out to draw several smaller veins in the leaf.

10 Select the Selection tool and draw a marquee around the leaf and veins to select them. Choose Object > Group.

11 Choose Select > Deselect.

Editing with the Pencil tool

You can also edit any path using the Pencil tool and add free-form lines and shapes to any shape. Next you will edit the stem shape using the Pencil tool.

1 Double-click the Hand tool (✋) in the Tools panel to fit the artboard in the window.

2 Select the Zoom tool (🔍) and click the stem in the upper left corner of the artboard three times.

3 With the Selection tool, select the stem.

4 Double-click the Pencil tool. In the Pencil Tool Options dialog box, click Reset. Notice that the Edit Selected Paths option is selected (this is important for the next steps). Change the Smoothness to 15%, and click OK.

Note: Depending on where you begin to redraw the path and in which direction you drag, you may get unexpected results. For example, you may unintentionally change a closed path to an open path, change an open path to a closed path, or lose a portion of a shape.

5 Position the Pencil tool on the top left of the stem path and notice that the x disappears from the pointer. This indicates that you are about to redraw the selected path.

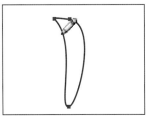

6 Drag up and to the right to round the corner of the stem. When the pointer is back on the path, release the mouse button to see the shape.

▶ **Tip:** If the corner doesn't look good, you can choose Edit > Undo Pencil or try dragging with the Pencil tool again across the same area.

7 Choose Select > Deselect.

● **Note:** Your stem result may not be exactly as you see in the figure to the right. That's OK.

8 Choose File > Save.

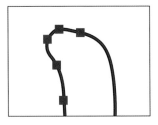

Pencil tool options

The Pencil tool options let you to change how the tool works on paths that you draw or edit. Double-click the Pencil tool to set any of the following options.

- **Fidelity**: Controls how far you have to move the pointer before a new anchor point is added to the path. The higher the value, the smoother and less complex the path. The lower the value, the more the curves match the pointer's movement, resulting in sharper angles. Fidelity can range from 0.5 to 20 pixels.

- **Smoothness**: Controls the amount of smoothing applied when you draw. Smoothness can range from

Pencil Tool Options dialog box

0% to 100%. The higher the value, the smoother the path. The lower the value, the more anchor points are created, and the more the line's irregularities are preserved.

- **Fill New Pencil Strokes**: Applies a fill to pencil strokes that you draw after selecting this option, but not to existing pencil strokes. Remember to select a fill before you draw the pencil strokes.

- **Keep Selected**: Specifies whether to keep the path selected after you draw it. This option is selected by default.

- **Edit Selected Paths**: Specifies whether you can change or merge an existing path when you are within a certain distance of it. You specify the distance with the Within option.

- **Within**: Specifies within how many pixels the pointer must be to an existing path to edit the path. This option is only available when the Edit Selected Paths option is selected.

—From Illustrator Help

Finishing the apple illustration

To complete the illustration, you'll make some minor modifications and assemble and paint the objects. Then you will position parts of the arrow to create the illusion of the apple being pierced.

Assembling the parts

1 Double-click the Hand tool (✋) to fit the artboard in the window.

2 Choose View > Show Bounding Box so that you can see the bounding boxes of selected objects as you transform them.

3 Select the Selection tool (▶) in the Tools panel, and Shift-click to select the two single, curved lines that you no longer need for the leaf. Press Backspace (Windows) or Delete (Mac OS) to delete them.

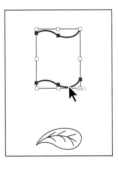

Now you'll make the stem and leaf smaller, and rotate them slightly using the Transform commands.

4 Select the stem and choose Object > Transform > Scale. Select Uniform and enter 50 in the Scale field. Select the Scale Strokes & Effects Option, and click OK.

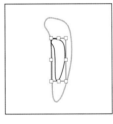

   The Scale Strokes & Effects Option scales stroke weights and effects which keeps the appearance of the shape. You can also set this option as a preference by choosing Edit > Preferences > General (Windows) or Illustrator > Preferences > General (Mac OS).

5 Choose Object > Transform > Rotate. Enter 30 in the Angle field, and click OK.

Now you'll repeat the scaling and rotation on the leaf.

6 Select the leaf group. Choose Object > Transform > Scale. Leave the settings as they are, and click OK to scale the leaf by 50%. Choose Object > Transform > Rotate, and enter 30 (if it's not in the Angle text field), and click OK.

You can also scale and rotate objects with the Scale and Rotate tools, respectively, or by using the Free Transform tool to do either. For more information, see Lesson 4, "Transforming Objects."

7 With the Selection tool, move the stem and the leaf to the top of the apple.

8 With the Selection tool, select the apple shape and choose white from the Fill color in the Control panel.

9 Select the arrow and move the parts of the arrow over the apple to make it look as if the arrow is entering the front of the apple and exiting the back.

Objects are arranged in the order in which they are created, with the most recent (the apple) in front.

● **Note:** If your arrow appears in front of the apple, with the arrow parts selected, choose Object > Arrange > Send To Back.

10 Select the bottom part of the arrow, and then choose Object > Arrange > Bring To Front to arrange it in front of the apple.

11 Select the Pencil tool and draw a small U shape where the tail of the arrow pierces the apple.

12 Change the Stroke Weight to 1pt of the selected U shape in the Control panel if not already set.

13 Choose Select > Deselect.

14 Choose File > Save.

Painting the artwork

In the color illustration, the fills are painted with custom-made gradients called Apple leaf, Apple stem, and Apple body, which are provided in the Swatches panel. We added some detail lines to the stem and painted the veins in the leaf. We also stroked the curve where the arrow pierces the apple.

1 Select an object, and then click the Fill color in the Control panel to view the Swatches panel. Use the swatches named Apple leaf, Apple stem, and Apple body for the appropriate parts.

2 Choose File > Save, and then File > Close.

To learn how to create your own gradients, see Lesson 9, "Blending Shapes and Colors." To learn more about painting options in Illustrator, see Lesson 6, "Color and Painting." For additional practice with the Pen tool, try tracing over images with it. As you practice with the Pen tool, you'll become more adept at drawing the kinds of curves and shapes you want.

Exploring on your own

Find an image, logo, or other simple artwork that you would like to create and save it in an image file format that Illustrator can accept, such as PDF, PSD, TIFF, EPS, JPG, and more.

1　Create a new Illustrator document, choose the size and color mode based on your needs, or simply leave the default settings unchanged.

2　Choose File > Place. Browse to locate the artwork you want to recreate, select it, and select Template. Click OK. The image is placed on a locked template with a blank layer at the top of the stacking order.

3　Select the Pen tool (✍) and start using the techniques you learned throughout this lesson to recreate the graphic.

Review questions

1 Describe how to draw straight vertical, horizontal, or diagonal lines using the Pen tool.

2 How do you draw a curved line using the Pen tool?

3 How do you draw a corner point on a curved line?

4 Name two ways to convert a smooth point on a curve to a corner point.

5 Which tool would you use to edit a segment on a curved line?

6 How can you change the way the Pencil tool works?

Review answers

1 To draw a straight line, click twice with the Pen tool. The first click sets the starting anchor point, and the second click sets the ending anchor point of the line. To constrain the straight line vertically, horizontally, or along a 45˚ diagonal, press the Shift key as you click with the Pen tool.

2 To draw a curved line with the Pen tool, click and drag to create the starting anchor point and set the direction of the curve, and then click to end the curve.

3 To draw a corner point on a curved line, press Alt (Windows) or Option (Mac OS) and drag the direction handle on the end point of the curve to change the direction of the path, and then continue dragging to draw the next curved segment on the path.

4 Use the Direct Selection tool to select the anchor point, and then use the Convert Anchor Point tool to drag a direction handle to change the direction. Another method is to choose a point or points with the Direct Selection tool and then click Convert Selected Anchor Points To Corner (⊤) in the Control panel.

5 To edit a segment on a curved line, select the Direct Selection tool and drag the segment to move it, or drag a direction handle on an anchor point to adjust the length and shape of the segment.

6 Double-click the Pencil tool to open the Pencil Tool Options dialog box, where you can change the smoothness, fidelity, and more.

6 COLOR AND PAINTING

Lesson overview

In this lesson, you'll learn how to do the following:

- Use color modes and color controls.

- Create, edit, and paint with colors using the Control panel and shortcuts.

- Name and save colors, create color groups, and build a color palette.

- Use the Color Guide panel and the Edit Colors/Recolor Artwork features.

- Copy paint and appearance attributes from one object to another.

- Paint with gradients and patterns.

 This lesson takes approximately an hour and a half to complete. If needed, remove the previous lesson folder from your hard disk and copy the Lesson06 folder onto it.

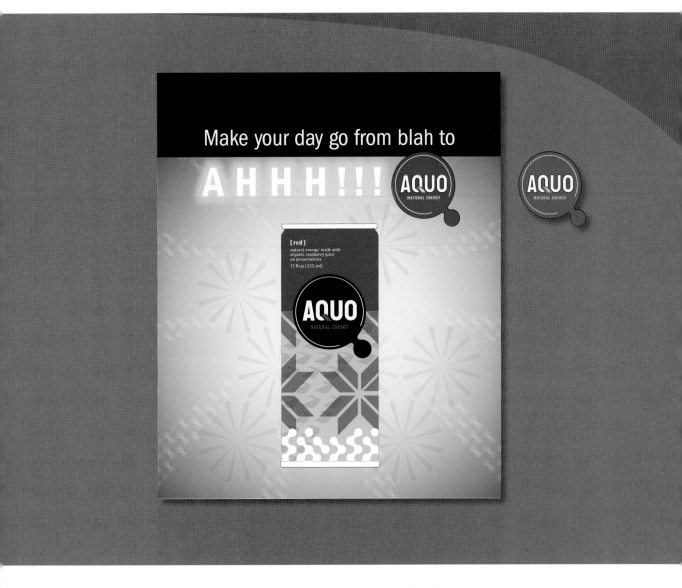

Spice up your illustration with colors by taking advantage of color controls in Illustrator CS4. In this information-packed lesson, you'll discover how to create and paint fills and strokes, use the Color Guide panel for inspiration, work with color groups, recolor artwork, create patterns, and more.

Getting started

In this lesson, you will learn about the fundamentals of color and create and edit colors using the Color panel, Swatches panel, and more.

1   To ensure that the tools and panels function as described in this lesson, delete or deactivate (by renaming) the Adobe Illustrator CS4 preferences file. See "Restoring default preferences" on page 3.

2   Start Adobe Illustrator CS4.

   ● Note: If you have not already copied the resource files for this lesson onto your hard disk from the Lesson06 folder on the Adobe Illustrator CS4 Classroom in a Book CD, do so now. See "Copying the Classroom in a Book files" on page 2.

3   Choose File > Open and open the L6end.ai file in the Lesson06 folder to view a final version of the poster. Leave it open for reference, or choose File > Close.

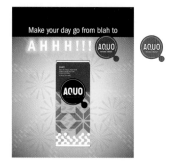

4   Choose File > Open. In the Open dialog box, navigate to the Lesson06 folder in the Lessons folder. Open the L6start.ai file.

   This file has some components already in it. You will create and apply color as necessary to complete the poster.

5   Choose File > Save As. In the Save As dialog box, navigate to the Lesson06 folder and name it aquo_poster.ai. Leave the Save As Type option set to Adobe Illustrator (*.AI) (Windows) or the Format option set to Adobe Illustrator (ai) (Mac OS), and click Save. In the Illustrator Options dialog box, leave the Illustrator options at their default settings, and click OK.

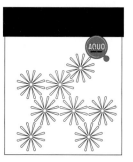

Understanding color

When working with color in Illustrator, you first need to understand color models and color modes. When you apply color to artwork, keep in mind the final medium in which the artwork will be published (print or web, for instance), so that you can use the correct color model and color definitions. First, you will learn about color modes, and then learn the basic color controls.

Color modes

Before starting a new illustration, you must determine which color mode the artwork should use, CMYK or RGB colors.

- **CMYK**—Cyan, magenta, yellow, and black are the colors used in four-color process printing. These four colors are combined and overlapped in a screen pattern to create a multitude of other colors. Select this mode for printing.

- **RGB**—Red, green, blue is the natural method of viewing color using light. Select this mode if you are using images for onscreen presentations or the Internet.

You select a color mode by choosing File > New and picking the appropriate document profile such as Print, which uses CMYK for the color mode. The color mode can be changed by toggling the arrow to the left of Advanced to see the Advanced options.

When a color mode is selected, the applicable panels open, built with colors in either the CMYK or RGB mode. You can change the color mode of a document after a file is created by choosing File > Document Color Mode, and then selecting either CMYK or RGB in the menu.

Understanding the color controls

In this lesson, you will discover the traditional method of coloring objects in Adobe Illustrator CS4. This includes painting objects with colors, gradients, and patterns using a combination of panels and tools—the Control panel, Color panel, Swatches panel, Gradient panel, Stroke panel, Color Guide panel, Color Picker, and the paint buttons in the Tools panel. You'll begin by looking at finished artwork to which color has already been applied.

1   Select the Selection tool (▶), and then click the blue shape in the Aquo logo.

Note: Because of screen resolution, your Tools panel may be double-column rather than the default single-column.

Objects in Illustrator can have a fill, a stroke, or both. In the Tools panel, notice that the Fill box appears in the foreground, indicating that it is selected. This is the default setting. The Fill box is blue for this object. Behind the Fill box, the Stroke box has a black outline.

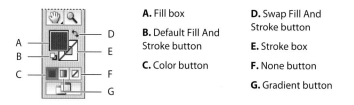

A. Fill box
B. Default Fill And Stroke button
C. Color button
D. Swap Fill And Stroke button
E. Stroke box
F. None button
G. Gradient button

2   Click the Appearance panel icon (◉) on the right side of the workspace.

The Fill and Stroke attributes of the selected object also appear in the Appearance panel. You can edit, delete or save appearance attributes as graphic styles, which you can apply to other objects, layers, and groups. You'll use this panel later in this lesson.

A. Object selected
B. Stroke Color
C. Fill Color

Tip: Shift-click the color spectrum bar at the bottom of the Color panel to rotate through different color modes.

3   Click the Color panel icon (🎨) on the right side of the workspace. The Color panel displays the current color of the fill and stroke. The CMYK sliders show the percentages of cyan, magenta, yellow, and black. At the bottom of the Color panel is the color spectrum bar.

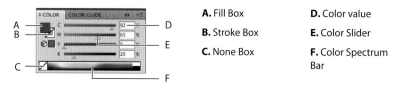

A. Fill Box
B. Stroke Box
C. None Box
D. Color value
E. Color Slider
F. Color Spectrum Bar

The color spectrum bar lets you quickly and visually select a fill or stroke color from a spectrum of colors. You can also choose white or black by clicking the appropriate color box at the right end of the color spectrum bar.

4 Click the Swatches panel icon (▦) on the right side of the workspace. You can name and save document colors, gradients, and patterns in the Swatches panel for instant access. When an object has a fill or stroke that contains a color, gradient, pattern, or tint applied in the Swatches panel, the applied swatch is highlighted in the Swatches panel.

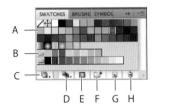

A. Swatch

B. Color group

C. Swatch Libraries menu

D. Show Swatch Kinds menu

E. Swatch Options

F. New Color Group

G. New Swatch

H. Delete Swatch

5 Click the Color Guide panel icon (◢) on the right side of the workspace. Click the blue swatch in the upper left corner of the panel to set the base color as the blue of the selected object (labeled A in the diagram below). Click the Harmony Rules menu, and choose Complementary 2.

The Color Guide can provide color inspiration while you create your artwork. It helps you pick color tints, analogous colors, and much more. In this panel, you can also access the Edit Color feature, which lets you edit and create colors.

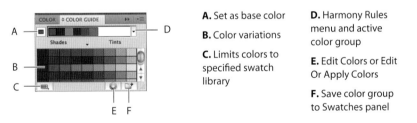

A. Set as base color

B. Color variations

C. Limits colors to specified swatch library

D. Harmony Rules menu and active color group

E. Edit Colors or Edit Or Apply Colors

F. Save color group to Swatches panel

6 Click the Color panel icon (🎨). Using the Selection tool (▶), click various shapes in the aquo_poster.ai file to see how their paint attributes are reflected in the panel.

7 Leave the file open.

Creating color

You are working on artwork in the CMYK color mode, which means that you can create your own color from any combination of cyan, magenta, yellow, and black. You can create color in a variety of ways, depending on the artwork. If you want to create a color that is specific to your company, for instance, you can use a swatch library. If you are trying to match color in artwork, you can use the Eyedropper tool to sample color, or the Color Picker to enter exact values. Next you will create color using different methods and then apply that color to objects.

Building and saving a custom color

Next you will create a color using the Color panel, and then save the color as a swatch in the Swatches panel.

1   Choose Select > Deselect.

   ● **Note:** If objects are selected when you create color, the color is typically applied to the selected object.

2   If the Color panel is not visible, click the Color panel icon (🎨). If the CMYK sliders are not visible, choose CMYK from the Color panel menu (▾≡).

3   Types these values in the CMYK text fields: C=9%, M=100%, Y=100%, K=2%.

▶ **Tip:** To save a color you made in the Color panel, you can also click the New Swatch button in the Swatches panel to open the New Swatch dialog box.

4   Click the Swatches panel icon (▦), and choose New Swatch from the Swatches panel menu (▾≡).

5   In the New Swatch dialog box, name the color logo background, and click OK. Notice that the swatch is highlighted in the Swatches panel.

   New colors added to the Swatches panel are saved with the current file only. Opening a new file displays the default set of swatches that comes with Adobe Illustrator CS4.

   ▶ **Tip:** If you want to load swatches from one saved document into another, click the Swatch Libraries Menu button (📚) and choose Other Library, and then locate the document with the swatches that you want to import.

   ● **Note:** The Swatches panel that appears when you click Fill color in the Control panel is the same as the Swatches panel.

6   With the Selection tool (▶), click the blue aquo logo background shape to select it. Click the Fill color in the Control panel. When the Swatches panel appears, select the logo background swatch.

7   Click Stroke color in the Control panel and choose None (⬚).

8   Select the Zoom tool ( ) and drag a marquee across the logo to zoom into it.

Leave the aquo logo background shape selected.

Editing a swatch

After a color is created and saved in the Swatches panel, you can edit that color. Next you will edit the logo background swatch that you just saved.

1   Select the Fill box in the Tools panel.

2   Click the Swatches panel icon ( ) on the right side of the workspace to open the Swatches panel.

3   With the shape still selected, double-click the logo background swatch in the Swatches panel. In the Swatch Options dialog box, change the K value (black) to 10%. Select Preview to see the changes to the logo shape. Change the K value to 3%, and click OK.

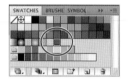

When you create a swatch and then edit it, the objects that have that swatch color applied need to be selected to show the change. Next you will change the logo background swatch to a global color. A global color automatically updates throughout the artwork when you edit it, regardless of whether the objects that use that global color are selected.

4   Double-click the logo background swatch in the Swatches panel to open the Swatch Options dialog box. Select Global, and click OK.

5   Choose Select > Deselect.

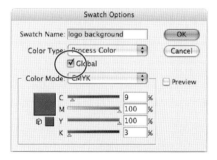

6   Double-click the logo background swatch in the Swatches panel again to open the Swatch Options dialog box. Change the K value (black) to 10%. Select Preview to see the changes. Change the K value to 3%, and click OK.

Note: The white triangle in the lower right corner of the swatch icon ( ) in the Swatches panel indicates a global color.

7   Choose File > Save.

Using Illustrator swatch libraries

Note: Most, but not all, of the libraries that come with Illustrator are CMYK colors.

Swatch libraries, are collections of preset colors such as PANTONE, TOYO, and thematic libraries like Earthtone and Ice Cream. The libraries appear as separate panels and cannot be edited. When you apply color from a library to artwork, the color in the library becomes a swatch that is saved in the Swatches panel for that document. Libraries are a great starting point for creating colors.

Perhaps the Aquo company always uses yellow for the text in their company logo. When this color is defined, it could be a warm, dark, or light yellow. This is why most printers and designers rely on a color matching system, like the PANTONE system, to help maintain color consistency and to give a wider range of colors in some cases. Next you will create a spot color using the PANTONE solid coated library.

Spot versus process colors

You can designate colors as either spot or process color types, which correspond to the two main ink types used in commercial printing.

- A process color is printed using a combination of the four standard process inks: cyan, magenta, yellow, and black (CMYK).

- A spot color is a special premixed ink that is used instead of, or in addition to, CMYK process inks. A spot color requires its own printing plate on a printing press.

Creating a spot color

In this section, you will see how to load a color library, such as the PANTONE color system, and to add a PANTONE (PMS) color to the Swatches panel.

Note: When you exit Illustrator and then relaunch it, the PANTONE library panel does not reopen. To open the panel automatically when Illustrator opens, choose Persistent from the PANTONE Solid Coated panel menu.

1   In the Swatches panel, click the Swatch Libraries Menu button (⛃). Choose Color Books > PANTONE Solid Coated. The PANTONE solid coated library appears in its own panel.

2   Choose Show Find Field from the PANTONE Solid Coated panel menu (▾≡). Type 116 in the Find field. PANTONE 116 C is highlighted. Click the highlighted swatch to add it to the Swatches panel. Close the PANTONE Solid Coated panel.

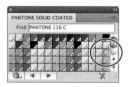

The PANTONE color appears in the Swatches panel.

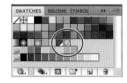

3   With the Selection tool (⬆), Shift-click the tail of the q in the Aquo text and NATURAL ENERGY to select them both. From the Fill color in the Control panel, choose the PANTONE 116 C color to fill the text. Change the Stroke color to None (⬜).

4   Choose Select > Deselect.

5   Choose File > Save. Keep the file open.

Why does my PANTONE swatch look different from the other swatches in the Swatches panel?

In the Swatches panel, you can identify the color type using icons that appear next to the name of the color. You can identify spot-color swatches by the spot-color icon (◉) when the panel is in list view or by the dot in the lower corner (◪) when the panel is in thumbnail view. Process colors do not have a spot-color icon or a dot.

By default, the PANTONE solid coated swatch is defined as a spot color, hence the dot. A spot color is not created from a combination of CMYK inks but is its own solid ink color. A press operator uses a premixed PMS (PANTONE Matching System) color in the press, offering more consistent color.

A triangle indicates that the color is global. If a global color is edited, all color references used in the illustration are updated. Any color can be global, not only PANTONE colors. To learn more about spot colors, choose Help > Illustrator Help and search for "spot colors."

Using the Color Picker

The Color Picker lets you select color in a color field, and spectrum by defining colors numerically or by clicking a swatch. Next you will create a color using the Color Picker, and then save the color as a swatch in the Swatches panel.

1 Double-click the Hand tool (🖐) to fit the artboard in the window.

2 With the Selection tool (▶), click to select one of the star shapes in the background.

3 Double-click the Fill box in the Tools panel to open the Color Picker.

▶ **Tip:** You can double-click the Fill box or Stroke box in the Tools panel or Color panel to access the Color Picker.

▶ **Tip:** If you work in Adobe Photoshop, the Color Picker is probably familiar, because Photoshop also has a Color Picker feature.

4 In the Color Picker dialog box, type these values into the CMYK text fields: C=0%, M=35%, Y=87%, and K=0%.

Notice that the slider in the color spectrum bar and the circle in the color field move as you enter the CMYK values. The color spectrum shows the hue, and the color field shows saturation (horizontally) and brightness (vertically).

5 Select S (saturation) to change the color spectrum displayed in the Color Picker. The color spectrum bar becomes the saturation of the orange color. Drag the color spectrum slider up until the S value is 90%, and click OK.

The star shape is filled with the orange color you made in the Color Picker.

● **Note:** The Color Swatches button in the Color Picker shows you the swatches in the Swatches panel and lets you select one. Then you can return to the color models view you started with by clicking the Color Models button and editing the swatch color values.

6 Change the stroke color in the Control panel to None (⬜).

Next you will save the color in the Swatches panel.

7 Open the Swatches panel by clicking its panel icon (▦).

8 Click the New Swatch button () at the bottom of the Swatches panel and name the color stars in the New Swatch dialog box. Select Global, and click OK to see the color appear as a swatch in the Swatches panel.

9 Choose File > Save.

Creating and saving a tint of a color

A tint is a lighter version of a color. You can create a tint from a global process color or from a spot color. Next you will create a tint of the stars swatch.

1 With the star still selected on the artboard, click the Color panel icon ().

2 Make sure that the Fill box is selected in the panel, and then drag the tint slider to the left to change the tint value to 70%.

Change the tint value.

3 Click the Swatches panel icon () on the right side of the workspace. Click the New Swatch button () at the bottom of the panel to save the tint. Notice the tint swatch in the Swatches panel. Hover the pointer over the swatch icon. The name stars 70% appears.

4 Choose File > Save.

Copying attributes

1 Using the Selection tool (), select one of the stars that has not yet been colored, and then Shift-click to add all other unpainted stars to the selection.

2 Using the Eyedropper tool (), click the painted star. All the stars that are unpainted pick up the attributes from the painted star.

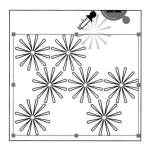 

3 With the Selection tool, Shift-click to select the original star. With all the stars selected, change the opacity to 30% in the Control panel.

4 Choose Object > Group.

5 Choose Select > Deselect, and then File > Save.

Creating color groups

In Adobe Illustrator CS4, you can save colors in color groups, which consist of related color swatches in the Swatches panel. Organizing colors by their use, such as grouping all the colors for the logo, is helpful. Only spot, process, and global colors can be in a group. Next you will create a color group using the logo colors you created.

Note: If objects are selected when you click the New Color Group button, an expanded New Color Group dialog box appears. In this dialog box, you can create a color group from the colors in the artwork and convert the colors to global colors.

1 In the Swatches panel, click a blank area of the panel to deselect the color swatches. Shift-click the logo background swatch and the PANTONE 116 C swatch created earlier to select both.

2 Click the New Color Group button (⬚⁺) at the bottom of the Swatches panel to open the New Color Group dialog box. Change the Name to logo and click OK to save the group.

Next you'll edit a color in the group and then add a color to it.

3 With the Selection tool (➤), click any color in the top of the Swatches panel to ensure that the color group is no longer selected in the Swatches panel.

4 In the Swatches panel, double-click the logo background color in the logo color group to open the Swatch Options dialog box. Change C to 20% and K to 0%. Click OK.

5 Click the K=90 swatch and drag it between the logo background (red) and PANTONE 116 C (yellow) swatches in the color group.

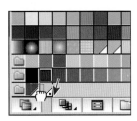

Notice that after you drag and drop, you can reorder the swatches in the group by dragging them. Try dragging the K=90 swatch to the right of the PANTONE 116 C (yellow) swatch.

6 Choose File > Save.

The colors in the logo have now been saved with this document as a color group. You will learn how to edit the color group later in the lesson.

Working with the Color Guide panel

The Color Guide panel can provide color inspiration as you create your artwork. It helps to pick harmony rules such as color tints, analogous colors, and much more. In this panel, you can also access the Edit Color/Recolor Artwork feature, which allows you to edit and create colors. Next you will use the Color Guide panel to select different colors for the logo, and then save those colors as a color group in the Swatches panel.

1 With the Selection tool (▶), drag a marquee across the aquo logo. Alt-drag (Windows) or Option-drag (Mac OS) a copy off the artboard on the right side.

2 Select the Zoom tool (🔍) in the Tools panel and click the copied logo twice to zoom in. Choose Select > Deselect.

3 With the Selection tool, click the red background shape of the copied logo. Make sure that the Fill box is selected in the Tools panel.

4 Click the Color Guide panel icon (◗) on the right side of the workspace to open the panel. Click the Set Base Color To The Current Color button (▣).

This allows the Color Guide panel to suggest colors based on the color showing in the Set Base Color To The Current Color button.

Next you'll experiment with the colors in the logo.

5 Choose Right Complement from the Harmony Rules menu to the right of the Set Base Color To The Current Color button in the Color Guide panel.

6 Click the Save Color Group To Swatch Panel button (▣⁺) to save the colors in the Right Complement harmony rule in the Swatches panel.

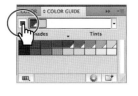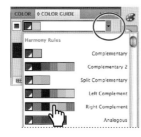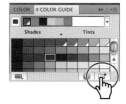

7 Click the Swatches panel icon (▦). Scroll down to see the new group added. You can apply these colors to the artwork or edit them.

8 Click the Color Guide icon (▨) to open the Color Guide panel. Next you'll experiment with the colors.

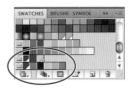

● **Note:** If you choose a different color variation than the one suggested, your color for the rest of this section will differ.

9 In the color variations in the Color Guide panel, select the color in the third row, fourth color from the left (see first figure below). Notice that the copied logo changes color. Click the Set Base Color To The Current Color button (▣) to try a new group of colors using the Right Complement harmony rule. Click the Save Group To Swatch Panel button (▣) to save the colors in the Swatches panel.

10 Choose File > Save.

Next you will edit the colors in the color group before applying them to the logo.

Editing a color group

Adobe Illustrator CS4 has many tools for working with color. When you create color groups, either in the Swatches panel or in the Color Guide panel, you can edit them individually or as a group in the Edit Colors dialog box. You can also rename the color group, reorder the colors in the group, add or remove colors, and more. In this section, you will learn how to edit colors of a saved color group using the Edit Color dialog box.

1 Choose Select > Deselect.

2 Click the Swatches panel icon (▦). Clicking the Swatch Options button (▣) at the bottom of the panel lets you edit a single, selected color.

▶ **Tip:** To edit a color group, you can also double-click the folder icon to the left of the color group in the Swatches panel.

3 Click the folder icon to the left of the last color group to select the group (you may need to scroll down in the Swatches panel). Notice that the Swatch Options button (▣) changes to the Edit Color Group button (⚙) when the group is selected.

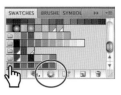

4 Click the Edit Color Group button (⚙) to open the Edit Color dialog box.

5 In the Edit Colors dialog box, the group you are about to edit is shown at the top. Rename the group to logo 2. In the color wheel, you see markers (circles) that represent each color in the group. Click and drag the bright red color (circled in the figure below, right) in a counter-clockwise direction into the green area. Notice that all the other colors change as well.

● **Note:** The larger marker in the color wheel with the double circle is the base color in the color group.

6 Change the Brightness (☼) by dragging the Adjust Brightness slider to the right to brighten all the colors at once.

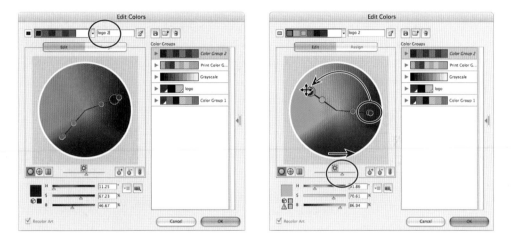

The Recolor Art selection at the bottom of the Edit Colors dialog box is dimmed because no artwork is selected. If artwork is selected when you open this dialog box, the dialog box is called the Recolor Artwork dialog box, and any edits you make change the artwork as well.

Next you will edit one of the colors in the group, and then save the colors as a new named group.

7 Click the Unlink Harmony Colors button (🔓) in the Edit Colors dialog box to edit the colors independently (you should then see the Link Harmony Colors button (🔗). The lines between the color markers (circles) and the center of the color wheel become dotted, indicating that the colors can be edited independently.

8 Click and drag the light red marker up and to the left on the color wheel to adjust the color a bit. When selected, you can edit the color using the HSB (hue, saturation, and brightness) sliders below the color wheel.

9 Click the Color Mode button (▾≡), and choose CMYK from the menu if the CMYK sliders are not already visible. Click to select one of the green markers in the color wheel, as shown in the figure on the right below. Change the K (black) value to 39 to change the color. Notice the green color marker move in the color wheel. Drag the C (cyan) slider to the right to add more cyan. Try adjusting the other color sliders and other colors in the group.

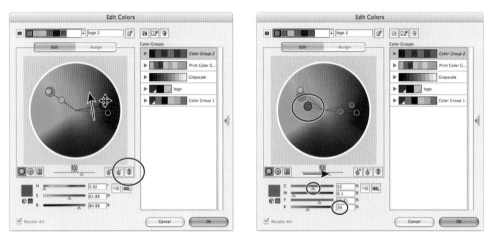

● **Note:** The color markers in your Edit Colors dialog box may be different from the figure above, and that's alright.

10 Click the Color Mode button (▾≡), and choose HSB from the menu so that next time you edit colors, it will be using the HSB sliders.

▶ **Tip:** To edit a color group and save the changes without creating a new color group, click the Save Changes To Color Group button (💾).

11 Click the New Color Group button (🗀) to save the colors you've edited as a new color group named logo 2. The color groups that are available in the document appear on the right side of the Edit Colors dialog box.

12 Click OK to close the Edit Colors dialog box and save the logo 2 color group in the Swatches panel. If a dialog box appears, click Yes to save the changes to the color group in the Swatches panel.

13 Choose File > Save.

Editing color options

You can use the options in the lower portion of the Edit Colors dialog box to edit color. The figure below briefly describes these options.

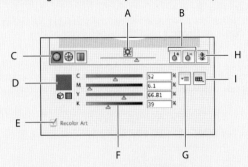

A Show saturation and hue on color wheel.

B Add and subtract color marker tools.

C Color display options (smooth color wheel, segmented color wheel, color bars)

D Color of the selected color marker or color bar

E Selected artwork is recolored when checked (dimmed when artwork is not selected).

F Color sliders

G Color mode button

H Unlink harmony colors.

I Limit the color group to colors in a swatch library.

Editing colors in artwork

You can edit all the colors in selected artwork at one time in the Recolor Artwork dialog box. Next you will edit the colors in the copied logo, save the edited colors as a color group, and apply the color group to other artwork in the document.

1   With the Selection tool (➤), drag a marquee across the copied logo on the canvas to select all of it.

2   Choose Edit > Edit Colors > Recolor Artwork to open the Recolor Artwork dialog box.

   You use the Recolor Artwork dialog box to reassign or reduce the colors in your artwork, and to create and edit color groups. All the color groups that you create for a document appear in the Color Groups storage area of the Recolor Artwork dialog box and in the Swatches panel. You can select and use these color groups at any time.

3 In the Recolor Artwork dialog box, click the Hide Color Group Storage icon (◀) on the right side of the dialog box.

4 Click the Edit tab to edit the colors in the artwork using a color wheel.

5 Click the Link Harmony Colors icon (🕸) to edit all the colors at the same time. The icon should now look like this 🖇.

▶ **Tip:** If you want to return to the original logo colors, click the Get Colors From Selected Art button (🗃).

6 Shift-drag the yellow color circle to the left into the green area of the color wheel.

▶ **Tip:** You can save the edited colors as a color group by clicking the Show Color Group Storage icon (▶) on the right side of the dialog box, and then clicking the New Color Group button (🗀).

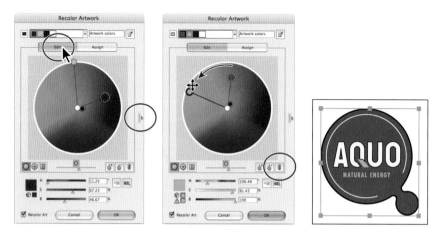

The edit options in the Recolor Artwork dialog box are the same as the options in the Edit Color dialog box. Instead of editing color and creating color groups to apply later, you are dynamically editing colors in the selected artwork. Notice the Recolor Art selection in the lower left corner of the dialog box. When selected, you are editing the selected artwork.

7 Click OK.

8 Choose File > Save.

Next you will get a color group from a community of users using the Kuler panel.

Working with the Kuler panel

The Kuler panel is a portal to themed color groups, such as ice cream, created by an online community of designers. You can browse lots of the groups and download themes to edit or use. You can also create themed color groups to share with others. Next you will download a themed color group for a soda can and apply color to it.

1 Choose Select > Deselect.

2 Choose View > Fit Artboard In Window.

3 Choose Window > Extensions > Kuler.

🔵 **Note:** You need an Internet connection to access the Kuler themes.

4 In the Kuler panel, click the Highest Rated menu and choose Most Popular. The Kuler panel lets you see the newest themes, highest rated themes, and more.

🔵 **Note:** Because the themes are constantly updated and are brought into the Kuler panel via the Internet, your Kuler panel may show different themes from the figures shown.

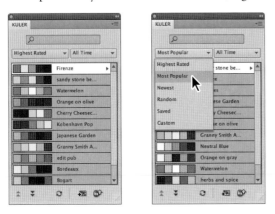

5 To search for themes, type soda in the Search field and press Enter or Return. This brings in the themes related to soda.

6 Click the City Soda theme in the Browse panel (below the search field). If the City Soda theme does not appear, select another. Click the Add Selected Theme To Swatches button (⊞) to add it to the Swatches panel for the open document.

7 Select the Cola theme and click the Add Selected Theme To Swatches button (⊞). Once again, if you don't see that theme in the Kuler panel, select another.

8 Close the Kuler panel.

9 Click the Swatches panel icon (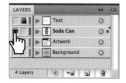) to open the Swatches panel if it isn't already open. Notice that the two new color groups appear in the panel list of swatches (scroll down, if necessary).

10 Choose File > Save.

Kuler panel options

The Kuler panel allows you to not only search, view, and save color themes as groups in the Swatches panel, but you can also view themes online, save searches and more. Here are a few more options in the Kuler panel:

View a theme online on Kuler:

1 In the Browse panel, select a theme in the search results.

2 Click the triangle on the right side of the theme and select View Online in Kuler.

Saving frequent searches:

1 Select the Custom option in the first pop-up menu in the Browse panel.

2 In the dialog box that opens, enter your search terms and save them.

When you want to run the search, select it from the first pop-up menu.

To delete a saved search, select the Custom option in the pop-up menu and clear the searches you'd like to delete.

—From Illustrator Help

Assigning colors to your artwork

The Assign tab of the Recolor Artwork dialog box lets you assign colors from a color group to your artwork. You can assign colors in several ways, including using a new color group chosen from the Harmony Rules menu. Next, you will assign new colors to a soda can that is currently hidden.

1 Click the Layers panel icon () on the right side of the workspace.

2 In the Layers panel, select the Visibility column to the left of the Soda Can layer to show a soda can on the artboard.

3 With the Selection tool (▶), click to select the gray area behind the aquo logo on the can. This selects a group of objects, including the pattern of shapes at the bottom of the can.

4 Choose Edit > Edit Colors > Recolor Artwork.

5 Click the Show Color Group Storage icon (▶) to show the color groups on the right side of the dialog box (if they aren't showing).

6 Select the City Soda color group (or the color group you selected) you saved from the Kuler panel.

7 If necessary, drag the dialog box by the title bar away from the artwork to see the changes to the soda can.

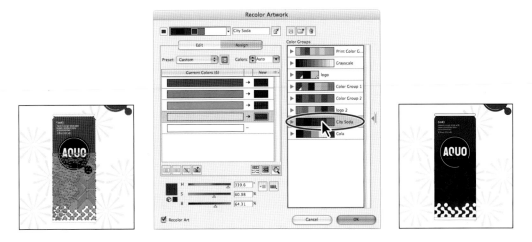

● **Note:** If the colors of the soda can do not change, make sure that Recolor Art is selected at the bottom of the Recolor Artwork dialog box.

8 Select the logo 2 color group to apply those colors to the soda can.

In the Recolor Artwork dialog box, notice that the gray colors of the can group have new colors assigned to them. The colors of the color group are assigned to the colors in the soda can objects by applying the colors in the logo 2 group from left to right. The colors in the can are listed in the Assign area from darkest on top to lightest on bottom. The color group colors are applied in order.

9 Click the Hide Color Group Storage icon (◀) to hide the color groups.

10 In the Recolor Artwork dialog box, click and drag the pink color on top of the light green color above it in the New column. This swaps the green and pink colors in the artwork.

11 Drag the colors back to their original order.

The colors in the New column show what you see in the artwork. If you click one of the colors, notice the HSB sliders at the bottom of the dialog box that let you edit that one color.

12 Double-click the green color at the top of the New column.

13 In the Color Picker dialog box, click the Color Swatches button to see the document swatches. Select logo background in the Color Swatches list. Click OK to return to the Recolor Artwork dialog box.

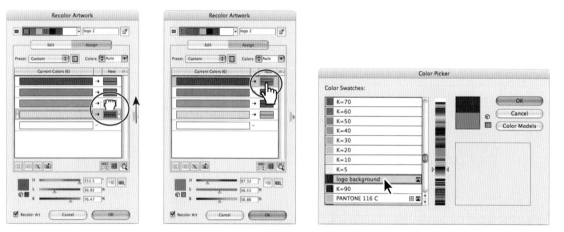

14 Drag the Recolor Artwork dialog box out of the way to see the artwork, if necessary.

Next you will make a few more changes to the colors in the soda can, and then save the color edits to the logo 2 color group.

15 Click the arrow between the light gray in the Current Color column and the pink color in the New column. In the artwork, the pattern on the soda can changes slightly.

By clicking the arrow between a current color and a new color, you exclude the row in the current color (the light gray) from being reassigned to the new color (pink).

16 Drag that same light gray bar on top of the darkest gray bar at the top of the current color list. Notice that the artwork changes again.

When you drag a color in the current color column onto another row in the same column, you are telling Illustrator to apply the same new color (logo background in this case) to both colors. The red color in the New column is split into three different sections (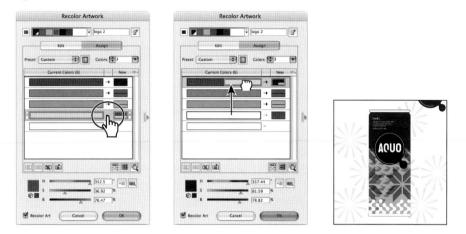). The darkest color in the row (the dark gray) is replaced with the red. The lighter gray color is replaced with a proportionally lighter tint of the red.

17 Click the Show Color Group Storage icon (▶) to show the color groups on the right side of the dialog box.

18 Click the Save Changes To Color Group button (▣) to save the changes to the logo 2 color group without closing the dialog box.

There are many color edits that can be made to selected artwork in the Recolor Artwork dialog box. To learn more about the many things you can do in the Edit Colors/Recolor Artwork dialog box, search for "working with color groups" in Illustrator Help.

19 Click OK. The color changes that you made to the color group are not saved in the Swatches panel.

20 Choose Select > Deselect, and then File > Save.

● **Note:** If you would like to force the selected artwork to have one color applied, you can choose 1 from the Colors menu above the New column in the Recolor Artwork dialog box. Just be careful to finish the steps in this lesson before attempting this.

Reassigning colors in artwork

Do any of the following to reassign colors in selected artwork:

- To assign a current color to a different color, drag the current color up or down in the Current Colors column until it's adjacent to the new color you want.

- If a row contains multiple colors and you want to move them all, click the selector bar at the left of the row and drag up or down.

- To assign a new color to a different row of current colors, drag the new color up or down in the New column. (To add a new color to or remove a color from the New column, right-click in the list and choose Add New Color or Remove Color.)

- To change a color in the New column, right-click it and choose Color Picker to set a new color.

- To exclude a row of current colors from being reassigned, click the arrow between the columns. To include it again, click the dash.

- To exclude a single current color from being reassigned, right-click the color and choose Exclude Colors, or click the icon.

- To randomly reassign colors, click the Randomly Change Color Order button . The New colors move randomly to different rows of current colors.

- To add a row to the Current Colors column, right-click and choose Add A Row, or click the icon.

—From Illustrator Help

Adjusting colors

Next, you will change the original aquo logo to a CMYK logo. Right now, the yellow is a PANTONE color that needs to be CMYK.

1 Select the Selection tool (▶) and drag a marquee across the original logo to select it, being careful not to select the stars group.

2 Choose Edit > Edit Colors > Convert To CMYK. The colors in the selected logo, including the yellow PANTONE 116 C, are now CMYK.

There are many options in the Edit > Edit Colors menu for converting color, including Recolor With Preset. This command lets you change the color of selected artwork using a chosen number of colors, a color library, and a specific color harmony (such as complementary colors). To learn more about adjusting colors this way, search for "reduce colors in your artwork" in Illustrator Help.

3 Choose Select > Deselect, and then File > Save.

Painting with gradients and patterns

In addition to process and spot colors, the Swatches panel can also contain pattern and gradient swatches. Adobe Illustrator CS4 provides sample swatches of each type in the default panel and lets you create your own patterns and gradients. Next you will fill a shape with a gradient and then make edits to the gradient.

To learn about working with gradients, see Lesson 9, "Blending Shapes and Colors." Next you will turn on the visibility for a layer that contains a gradient.

1   Choose Window > Workspace > Essentials.

2   Double-click the Hand tool (✋) to fit the artboard in the window.

3   Click the Layers panel icon (✿).

4   In the Layers panel, click to select the Visibility column to the left of the Background layer. Click the eye icon (👁) to the left of the Soda Can and Artwork layers to deselect visibility.

Using patterns

You can use preset patterns that load with Adobe Illustrator CS4, or create your own. In this section, you will do both.

1   Click the Swatches panel icon (▦). In the Swatches panel, click the Swatch Libraries menu button (▦▴) at the bottom of the panel and choose Patterns > Basic Graphics > Basic Graphics_Dots to open the pattern library.

2   Using the Selection tool (▶), select the group of shapes radiating from the center of the artboard.

3   In the Control panel, change the Stroke color to None (◻).

4   Make sure that the Fill box is selected in the Tools panel.

5   Select the 10 dpi 60% pattern swatch in the Basic Graphics_Dots panel to fill the group of objects with the pattern.

▶ **Tip:** Because some supplied patterns have a clear background, you can create a second fill for the object using the Appearance panel. For more information, see lesson 12, "Applying Appearance Attributes And Graphic Styles."

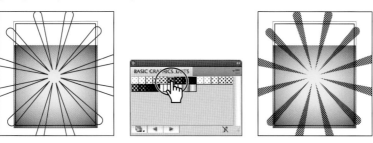

6   Close the Basic Graphics_Dots panel.

7 With the group of shapes still selected, double-click the Scale tool (⬚) in the Tools panel to make the pattern larger without affecting the shape. In the Scale dialog box, deselect Scale Strokes & Effects (if necessary) and Objects, which selects Patterns. Change the uniform scale to 160, and click OK. Only the pattern is enlarged. Leave the group selected.

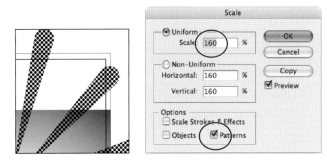

8 Click the Transparency panel icon (⬤) on the right side of the workspace. Choose Soft Light from the Blending Mode menu. Change the opacity to 70%.

9 To get rid of the shapes hanging off of the page, you can create a mask. With the Selection tool (▶), select the rectangle in the background with the gradient applied, and choose Edit > Copy and then Edit > Paste In Front to paste a copy directly on top of the copied shape.

⬤ **Note:** To learn more about working with masks, see Lesson 14, "Combining Illustrator CS4 Graphics with Other Adobe Applications."

10 With the shape still selected, choose Object > Arrange > Bring To Front.

11 Click the Layers panel icon (⬤) to open the Layers panel.

12 Click the Background layer to select it, and then click the Make/Release Clipping Mask button (◉) at the bottom of the Layers panel to mask the objects with the shape that you just arranged. Leave the Layers panel open.

13 Choose Select > Deselect.

14 Choose File > Save.

Creating your own pattern

In this section of the lesson, you will create your own custom pattern and add it to the Swatches panel. You will then learn how to edit an existing pattern and update it in the Swatches panel.

1   In the Layers panel, click to select the Visibility column to the left of the Artwork layer.

2   With the Selection tool (➤), click the small shape off the right side of the artboard to select it.

3   Change the fill in the Control panel to a dark gray color.

4   Click the Swatches panel icon (▦) to reveal the Swatches panel. With the Selection tool, click and drag the selected shape into the Swatches panel. You have created a new pattern.

● **Note:** A pattern swatch can be composed of more than one shape. For instance, to create a flannel pattern for a shirt, you can create three overlapping rectangles or lines, each with varying colors. Then select all three shapes and drag them as one into the Swatches panel.

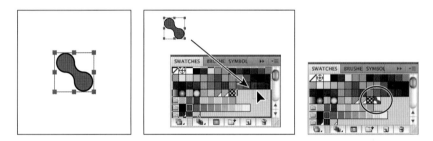

5   Double-click the pattern swatch you added and assign the name background. Click OK.

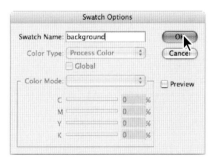

6   With the Selection tool, click to select the small shape off the artboard that you used to make the pattern swatch and delete it.

7   In the Layers panel, click to deselect the eye icon (👁) to the left of the Artwork layer to hide its contents.

Applying a pattern

You can assign a pattern using a number of different methods. In this lesson, you will use the Swatches panel to apply the pattern. You can also apply the pattern using the Fill color in the Control panel.

1 Select the Selection tool (↖) and click the group of shapes radiating from the center of the artboard to select the group.

2 Select the background pattern swatch from the Fill color in the Control panel.

3 Choose Select > Deselect, and then File > Save.

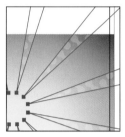

> **Tip:** As you add more custom swatches, it may be beneficial to view the Swatches panel by the swatch names. To change the view, choose List View from the Swatches panel menu.

Editing a pattern

You can edit a saved pattern and then update all instances in your artwork.

1 In the Layers panel, click to select the Visibility column to the left of the Artwork layer to view its contents on the artboard. Then select the Artwork layer so that you can add content to that layer.

2 Click the Swatches panel icon (▦).

3 Using the Selection tool (↖), click and drag the background swatch from the Swatches panel to an empty location on the right side of the artboard.

This places the shape you used to make the pattern onto the artboard or canvas.

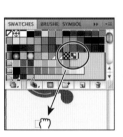

4 With the Selection tool, select the shape on the artboard, and choose Object > Ungroup.

5 Choose Select > Deselect.

6 Select the shape with the Selection tool.

7 Choose None (⊘) from the Stroke color in the Control panel.

Next you will edit the shape, and then use it to update the pattern swatch.

8 Double-click the Scale tool () in the Tools panel. Change Uniform Scale to 60%, and click OK.

9 Make sure that the Fill box is selected in the Tools panel.

10 Click the Gradient panel icon () on the right side of the workspace. Choose Radial Gradient 1 from the Gradient menu ().

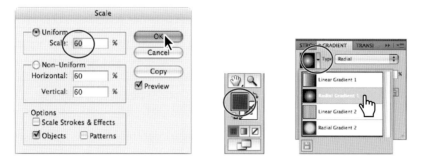

11 In the Gradient panel, click to select the black color stop (see figure below). Change the opacity to 30%.

12 Click the Swatches panel icon (). Using the Selection tool, select the shape and Alt-drag (Windows) or Option-drag (Mac OS) it back on top of the existing pattern swatch called Background in the Swatches panel. The swatch is updated.

13 Select the shape off the artboard that you edited to create the updated pattern and delete it.

14 Open the Layers panel and make all layers visible by selecting the Visibility column to the left of the Text and Soda Can layers.

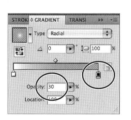 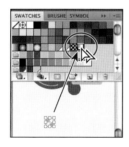 

15 Choose File > Save, and then File > Close.

Working with Live Paint

Live Paint lets you paint vector graphics intuitively by automatically detecting and correcting gaps that previously would have affected how fills and strokes were applied. Instead of planning every detail of an illustration, you can work more as you might if you were coloring by hand on paper.

1 Choose File > Open and open the L6start2.ai file in the Lesson06 folder.

2 Choose File > Save As. In the Save As dialog box, name the file snowboarder.ai and navigate to the Lesson06 folder. Leave the Save As Type option set to Adobe Illustrator (*.AI) (Windows) or the Format option set to Adobe Illustrator (ai) (Mac OS), and click Save. In the Illustrator Options dialog box, leave the Illustrator options at their default settings, and click OK.

3 Use the Selection tool (▶) to select the snowboarder traced image, and choose Object > Live Paint > Make. This creates a Live Paint group that you can now paint.

There are some gap issues to work with before painting. Gaps are the little openings in shapes that allow paint to leak from one shape to another.

▶ **Tip:** The Close Gaps With Paths button closes detected gaps by inserting paths into the artwork. This is a very useful option for traced artwork.

4 Before starting to paint, choose Object > Live Paint > Gap Options.

5 In the Gap Options dialog box, select Gap Detection, if it is not selected. The Gap Preview Color is set to highlight in red.

6 Choose Medium Gaps from the Paint Stops At menu. This stops paint from leaking through some of the larger gaps as you paint. Change the Gap Preview Color to Green. Look at the artwork, moving the Gap Options dialog box out of the way if necessary. Any gaps found are shown in green. Click OK.

7 Select the Live Paint Bucket tool (⬗) in the Tools panel. Before painting, click the Fill color in the Control panel and select the Snowboarder swatch (red) in the Swatches panel.

8 Click the Color Guide panel icon (◗) on the right side of the workspace. Choose Left Complement from the Harmony Rules menu. Click the Save Color Group To Swatch Panel button (▣⁺).

9 Open the Swatches panel (▦) to see the color group. You may have to scroll down to see it. Click the red color (the color farthest to the left) in the color group to select it and ensure that you will paint with the colors in that group.

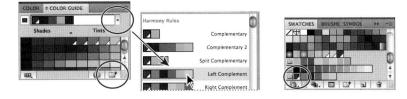

10 Move the mouse over the snowboarder's left leg. As you move over Live Paint objects, they highlight and three color swatches appear above the pointer. The swatches represent the three swatches next to each other in the Swatches panel group that you just made. Click when part of the leg becomes highlighted. Click the other leg to paint it as well.

11 Move the pointer over the snowboard. Click the Left Arrow key to cycle to the light green color in the Swatches panel group. Click to apply the color to the snowboard.

● **Note:** You can also look in the Swatches panel to see which color in the group is selected and switch to another color by clicking it in the Swatches panel.

12 In the Swatches panel, select the Black swatch. Click to fill in the top edge of the snowboard.

13 With the Selection tool, click and drag a marquee around the snow trail to the left of the snowboarder, making sure to include all the pieces. Choose Object > Live Paint > Make.

14 Select a light blue from the Fill color in the Control panel.

If the Live Paint Bucket is selected when you click to fill the snow trail with color, you soon realize that each piece is a separate object. To make it easier to select a series of objects in a Live Paint group, you can use the Live Paint Selection tool. You can either Shift-click to select multiple objects to colorize or drag across the objects.

15 Select the Live Paint Selection tool (▥) in the Tools panel and click and drag across the left half of the snow trail. Select another blue in the Swatches panel to paint the selection.

16 Choose Select > Deselect.

17 Open the L6end2.ai file and use it as a guide to finish painting this artwork. You can use the colors in the example or create your own interpretation. Also, move the snow trail to the left side of the snowboard where it belongs.

It is helpful to zoom in to see details. Don't worry if you fill a region with the wrong color—just choose the right color and fill again.

18 When completed, choose File > Save, and close all open files.

Editing Live Paint regions

When you make a Live Paint group, each path remains editable. When you move or adjust a path, the colors that were previously applied don't just stay where they were, like they do in natural media paintings or image editing software. Instead, the colors are automatically reapplied to the new regions that are formed by the edited paths.

Next you will create a new file and create a simple illustration.

1 Choose File > New, and create a letter-sized document. Click OK.

2 Select the Ellipse tool (⬭) from the same group as the Rectangle tool (▭) in the Tools panel. Pressing the Shift key, create a circle on the artboard. The size of the circle is not important.

3 With the Selection tool (▸), press Alt (Windows) or Option (Mac OS) to clone the circle shape and drag it to the right so that the duplicated circle is overlapping the original circle.

4 Choose Select > All. In the Control panel, choose None () for both the fill and stroke colors.

5 Select the Live Paint Bucket tool (), and cross over the overlapping area. When the circles become highlighted, click once to activate the center shape as a Live Paint group.

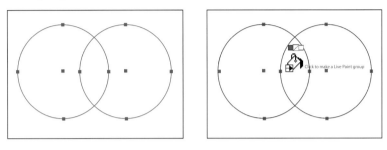

6 Select a color in the Swatches panel and click the center Live Paint group to color it. Select another color in the Swatches panel and then click inside the left Live Paint group. Repeat using a different color for the right Live Paint group.

7 Choose Select > Deselect. Select the Direct Selection tool () in the Tools panel. Click in the left circle, and then click to select the rightmost anchor point of the circle. Drag it to the right. Notice that the intersecting area is dynamic. It changes the fill based on the relationship of the two circles.

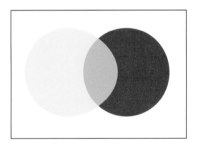 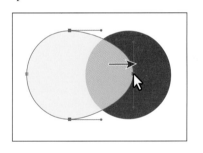

You can use different selection tools, depending on what you want to paint. For instance, use the Live Paint Selection tool () to apply different gradients across different faces in a Live Paint group, and use the Selection tool () to apply the same gradient across the entire Live Paint group.

8 Choose Select > Deselect. Select the Selection tool and double-click the right circle to enter isolation mode. Click and drag one of the circles. Notice that you can edit each circle independently and the intersecting area is still dynamic.

9 Double-click outside of the circles to exit isolation mode.

10 Choose File > Close, and do not save the file.

Exploring on your own

1   Choose File > Open. In the Open dialog box, navigate to the Lesson06 folder in the Lessons folder. Open the file named color.ai.

2   Using the Selection tool, select the letters in the center of the poster.

3   Fill the letters with a color from the Fill color in the Control panel, and then save the color as a swatch in the Swatches panel by Ctrl-clicking (Windows) or Command-clicking (Mac OS) the New Swatch button. Name the color text.

4   With the swatch applied to the text fill, create a tint of the text color, and then save it in the Swatches panel.

5   Apply a 3 pt stroke to the text and paint the stroke with the saved tint, making sure that the fill of the text is just the text color, not the tint.

6   Select the Ellipse tool in the Tools panel and create a circle on the artboard. Select a swatch from the Fill color in the Control panel. Create a pattern out of the circle you drew.

7   Apply the pattern to the star shape behind the text.

8   Edit the pattern and resize the pattern fill in the star shapes by double-clicking the Scale tool.

9   Choose File > Close without saving.

Review questions

1 Describe at least three ways to fill an object with color.

2 How can you save a color?

3 How do you name a color?

4 How do you assign a transparent color to an object?

5 How can you choose color harmonies for colors?

6 Name two things that the Edit Colors/Recolor Artwork dialog box allows you to do.

7 How do you add pattern swatches to the Swatches panel?

Review answers

1 To fill an object with color, select the object and the Fill box in the Tools panel. Then do one of the following:

- Double-click the Fill or Stroke box in the Control panel to access the Color Picker.

- Drag the color sliders, or type values in the text boxes in the Color panel.

- Click a color swatch in the Swatches panel.

- Select the Eyedropper tool, and click a color in the artwork.

- Choose Window > Swatch Libraries to open another color library, and click a color swatch in the Color Library panel.

2 You can save a color for painting other objects in your artwork by adding it to the Swatches panel. Select the color, and do one of the following:

- Drag it from the Fill box and drop it over the Swatches panel.

- Click the New Swatch button at the bottom of the Swatches panel.

- Choose New Swatch from the Swatches panel menu.

You can also add colors from other color libraries by selecting them in the Color Library panel and choosing Add To Swatches from the panel menu.

3 To name a color, double-click the color swatch in the Swatches panel, or select it and choose Swatch Options from the panel menu. Type the name for the color in the Swatch Options dialog box.

4 To paint a shape with a semi-transparent color, select the shape and fill it with any color. Then adjust the opacity percentage in the Transparency panel or Control panel to less than 100%.

5 The Color Guide panel is a tool for inspiration while you create your artwork. The panel suggests color harmonies based on the current color in the Tools panel.

6 You use the Edit Colors/Recolor Artwork dialog box to create and edit color groups and to reassign or reduce the colors in your artwork, and more.

7 Create a pattern (patterns cannot contain patterns themselves), and drag it into the Swatches panel.

7 WORKING WITH TYPE

Lesson overview

In this lesson, you'll learn how to do the following:

- Import text.
- Create columns of type.
- Change text attributes.
- Use and save styles.
- Sample type.
- Wrap type around a graphic.
- Reshape text with a warp.
- Create text on paths and shapes.
- Create type outlines.

 This lesson will take approximately an hour to complete. If needed, remove the previous lesson folder from your hard disk, and copy the Lesson07 folder onto it.

Text as a design element plays a major role in your illustrations. Like other objects, type can be painted, scaled, rotated, and so on. In this lesson, discover how to create basic text and interesting text effects in Illustrator CS4.

Getting started

You'll be working in one art file during this lesson, but before you begin, restore the default preferences for Adobe Illustrator CS4. Then open the finished art file for this lesson to see the illustration.

1   To ensure that the tools and panels function as described in this lesson, delete or deactivate (by renaming) the Adobe Illustrator CS4 preferences file. See "Restoring default preferences" on page 3.

2   Start Adobe Illustrator CS4.

● **Note:** If you have not already copied the resource files for this lesson onto your hard disk from the Lesson07 folder on the Adobe Illustrator CS4 Classroom in a Book CD, do so now. See "Copying the Classroom in a Book files" on page 2.

3   Choose File > Open. Locate the file named L7end.ai in the Lesson07 folder in the Lessons folder that you copied onto your hard disk. In this lesson, you will create the text for this poster. Leave it open for reference, or choose File > Close.

4   Choose File > Open. In the Open dialog box, navigate to the Lesson07 folder in the Lessons folder. Open the L7start.ai file.

This file already has non-text components in it. You will build all the text elements to complete the poster.

5   Choose File > Save As. In the Save As dialog box, navigate to the Lesson07 folder and name the file yoga.ai. Leave the Save As Type option set to Adobe Illustrator (*.AI) (Windows) or the Format option set to Adobe Illustrator (ai) (Mac OS), and click Save. In the Illustrator Options dialog box, leave the Illustrator options at their default settings, and click OK.

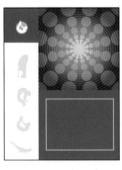

6   Choose View > Smart Guides to deselect smart guides.

7   Choose Window > Workspace > Essentials.

Working with type

Some of the most powerful aspects of Adobe Illustrator are its type features. You can add a single line of type to your artwork, create columns and rows of text like in Adobe InDesign, flow text into a shape or along a path, and work with letterforms as graphic objects.

You can create text in three different ways: as point type, area type, and text along a path. Following is a short description of each type of text:

- **Point type** is a horizontal or vertical line of text that begins where you click and expands as you enter characters. Each line of text is independent—the line expands or shrinks as you edit it, but doesn't wrap to the next line. Entering text this way is useful for adding a headline or a few words to your artwork.

- **Area type** uses the boundaries of an object to control the flow of characters, either horizontally or vertically. When the text reaches a boundary, it automatically wraps to fit inside the defined area. Entering text this way is useful when you want to create one or more paragraphs, such as for a brochure.

- **Type on a path** flows along the edge of an open or closed path. When you enter text horizontally, the characters are parallel to the baseline. When you enter text vertically, the characters are perpendicular to the baseline. In either case, the text flows in the direction in which points were added to the path.

Next you will create point type, and then you will create area type. Later in this lesson you will also create type on a path.

Creating point type

When typing text directly into a document, you select the Type tool and click where you'd like the text. You can then begin typing when the cursor appears. Next you will enter a subhead on artboard 1 (of 2).

1   Select the Zoom tool (🔍) in the Tools panel and click the bottom yoga figure on the left three times.

2   Select the Type tool (T) and click above and to the left of the bottom yoga figure. The cursor appears on the artboard. Type info@transformyoga.com.

By clicking with the Type tool, you create point type. Point type is a line of text that keeps going until you stop typing or press Return or Enter. It's very useful for headlines.

3 Select the Selection tool (🔧) in the Tools panel and notice that the text has a bounding box around it. Click and drag the bounding point on the right to the right. Notice that the text stretches as you drag.

● **Note:** Point type that is scaled as in step 3 is still printable, but the font size may not be a whole number (such as 12pt).

4 Choose Edit > Undo Scale.

Creating area type

To create area type, you click with the Type tool, and drag to create an area type object where you'd like the text. When the cursor appears, you can type. You can also convert an existing shape or object to a type object by clicking with the Type tool on or within the edge of the object. Next you will create area type and enter an address.

1 With the Selection tool (🔧), hold down the spacebar and drag the artboard down to pan to the top yoga figure in the white area on the left side of the artboard.

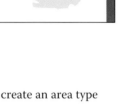

2 Select the Type tool (T), and then click and drag from the upper left to the lower right to create a rectangle above the top yoga figure. The cursor appears in the new type object.

3 Type 1000 Lombard Ave. Central, Washington. The text wraps inside of the type object. You will now adjust how the text wraps.

● **Note:** For now, keep the default settings for type formatting.

● **Note:** If the text is already wrapping correctly, try dragging the edge of the bounding box to see the effect.

4 Select the Selection tool and notice that the bounding box appears around the address. Click and drag the right, center bounding point to the right and left, noticing how the text wraps within the object. Drag until only the text 1000 Lombard Ave. appears on the first line.

5 Choose Select > Deselect.

6 Choose File > Save.

Area type versus point type

How can you tell the difference between point type and area type visually? With the Selection tool, click to select text and its bounding box.

Area type has two extra boxes, called ports. Ports are used to thread (flow) text from one type area to another. Working with ports and threading is covered later in this lesson. Point type, when selected, does not have ports, but it has a point before the first letter in the first line.

Area type   **Point type**

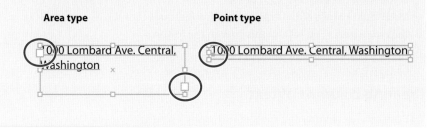

Importing a plain text file

You can import text into artwork from a file that was created in another application. Illustrator supports the following formats for importing text:

- Microsoft Word for Windows 97, 98, 2000, 2002, 2003, and 2007
- Microsoft Word for Mac OS X and 2004
- RTF (Rich Text Format)
- Plain text (ASCII) with ANSI, Unicode, Shift JIS, GB2312, Chinese Big 5, Cyrillic, GB18030, Greek, Turkish, Baltic, and Central European encoding

You can also copy and paste text, but formatting can be lost when text is pasted. One of the advantages of importing text from a file rather than copying and pasting it, is that imported text retains its character and paragraph formatting. For example, text from an RTF file retains its font and style specifications in Illustrator.

Next you will place text from a simple text file.

1   Double-click the Hand tool (✋) to fit the artboard in the window. Choose View > Smart Guides to select the smart guides.

2   Before importing text, create an area type object by selecting the Type tool (T) and clicking and dragging from the upper left corner of the provided guide box to the lower right corner.

3   Choose File > Place. Navigate to the Lesson07 folder in the Lessons folder, select the L7copy.txt file, and click Place.

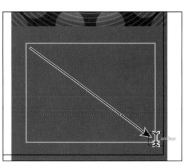

● **Note:** If you place
text without a type area,
the text is placed in a
type area that is created
automatically. The type
area spans most of the
artboard by default.

4 In Text Import Options dialog box,
which has options that you can set
prior to importing text, leave the
default settings, and click OK.

The text is now placed in a type object.
Don't be concerned about formatting
the text. You will learn how to apply
attributes later in this lesson. Also,
if you see a red plus sign (⊞) in the
lower right corner of the type object, this indicates that the text does not fit in
the type object. You will fix this later in the lesson.

5 Choose File > Save, and leave this file open.

Creating columns of text

You can create columns and rows of text easily by using the Area Type options.

1 If the type object is no longer selected, use the Selection tool (▶) to select it.

● **Note:** If the cursor is still in the type object, you don't have to select the text area with the
Selection tool to access the Area Type options.

2 Choose Type > Area Type Options.

3 In the Area Type Options dialog box, select Preview. In the Columns section of
the dialog box, change Number to 2, and click OK.

4 Choose Select > Deselect.

5 Choose File > Save. Leave this document open.

Area type options

You can use the Area Type options to create rows and columns of text. Read about additional options below:

- **Number** specifies the number of rows and columns you want the object to contain.

- **Span** specifies the height of individual rows and the width of individual columns.

- **Fixed** determines what happens to the span of rows and columns if you resize the type area. When this option is selected, resizing the area can change the number of rows and columns, but not their width. Leave this option deselected if you want row and column widths to change when you resize the type area.

- **Gutter** specifies the distance between rows or columns.

- **Inset** controls the margin between the text and the bounding path. This margin is referred to as the inset spacing.

- **First Baseline** controls the alignment of the first line of text with the top of the object.

- **Text Flow** determines how text flows between rows and columns.

—From Illustrator Help

Understanding text flow

For this next section, you will place a Microsoft Word document (.doc) into a rectangle shape to create area type in the second artboard of the currently open file, yoga.ai. This will add text to a postcard that accompanies the poster.

1   Click the Next button in the status bar in the lower left of the Document window to navigate to the second artboard. Choose View > Fit Artboard In Window if the entire postcard is not showing.

2   Select the Rectangle tool (▢) in the Tools panel.

3   Press D to set the default fill (white) and stroke (black).

4   Click and drag in the upper left corner of the square guide in the center of the artboard down and to the right to create a rectangle about 1 inch in height. The word path appears when the pointer snaps to the guide.

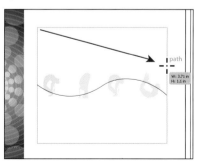

● **Note:** The square that appears after you drag may have a black fill and/or stroke that covers the content. When the shape is converted into a type area, the fill and stroke change to None.

5   Select the Type tool (**T**) and cross it over the edge of the rectangle shape. The word paths appears when you are close enough to the edge of the rectangle. The text insertion cursor is in parentheses ($\mathcal{I}$), indicating that when you click, the cursor will appear inside this shape. Click to insert the cursor.

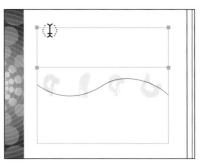

6   With the cursor active in the rectangle, choose File > Place and navigate to the Lesson07 folder in the Lessons folder on your hard disk. Select the file yoga_pc.doc, and then click Place. You are placing a native Microsoft Word document, so you will have additional options to set.

7   In the Microsoft Word Options dialog box, ensure that Remove Text Formatting is deselected to keep the Word formatting. Leave the remaining settings at their default. Click OK. The text appears in the square.

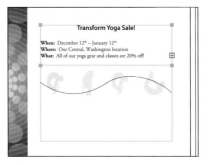

Notice the red plus sign that appears in the lower right corner of the type object. This indicates that the text does not fit in the object. You will fix this in the next section.

Note: When you place a Word document and do not select Remove Text Formatting, paragraph styles that were used in Word are brought into Illustrator. Paragraph styles are discussed later.

Working with overflow text and text reflow

Each area type object contains an in port and an out port. The ports enable you to link to other objects and create a linked copy of the type object. An empty port indicates that all the text is visible and that the object isn't linked. A red plus sign (⊞) in an out port indicates that the object contains additional text, which is called overflow text.

n Yoga Sale!

ary 12th
gton location
d classes are 20% off!

⊞

There are two main methods for remedying overflow text:

- Thread the text to another type object
- Resize the type object

Threading text

To thread, or continue, text from one object to the next, you have to link the objects. Linked type objects can be of any shape; however, the text must be entered in an object or along a path, not at a point. Next you will thread the overset text to another type object.

1   Use the Selection tool (➤) to select the type object.

2   With the Selection tool, click the out port of the selected type object. The pointer changes to the loaded text icon (⬛).

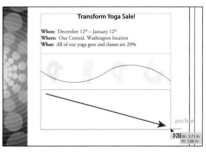

● **Note:** If you double-click, a new type object appears. If this happens, you can either drag the new object into place, or choose Edit > Undo Link Threaded Text and the loaded text icon reappears.

3   Click and drag below the yoga figures starting on the left edge of the guide box and dragging down and to the right corner of the guide box.

● **Note:** With the loaded text icon, you can simply click the artboard instead of dragging to create a new type object.

▶ **Tip:** Another way to thread text between objects is to select an area type object, select the object (or objects) you want to link to, and then choose Type > Threaded Text > Create.

4   Choose File > Save.

With the bottom type object still selected, notice the line between the two objects. This line is the thread that tells you that the two objects are connected. Notice the out port (▣) of the top object and the in port (▣) of the bottom object. The arrow indicates that the object is linked to another object.

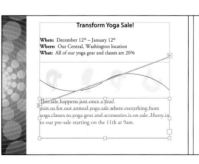

● **Note:** Your text may not look exactly like the figure. That's OK. In the next part of the lesson, you will resize the text areas.

● **Note:** If you delete the second type object (created in step 3), the text is pulled back into the original object as overflow text. Although not visible, the overflow text is not deleted.

Resizing type objects

For this next lesson, you will see how to resize type objects to make room for additional text.

1 Select the Selection tool (▶) and click the text in the top area type object.

2 Double-click the out port (▣) in the lower right corner of the type object.

Double-click the out port to break the thread.

Because the type objects are threaded, double-clicking the out port or the in port breaks the connection between them. Any text threaded between the two type objects flows back into the first object. The bottom object is still there, but it has no stroke or fill.

3 Choose View > Smart Guides to deselect them.

4 Using the Selection tool, click and drag the bottom, middle handle of the bounding box down to the top of the yoga figures. The type object changes in size vertically. Notice that the further you drag down, the more text is revealed.

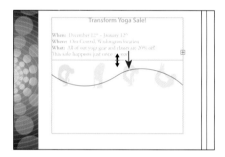

5 With the Selection tool, click the out port (⊞) in the lower right corner of the top type object. The pointer changes to the loaded text icon (▤).

6 Choose View > Outline to reveal the bottom type object.

7 Hover the loaded text icon (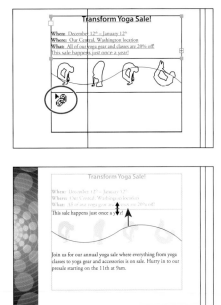) over the edge of the bottom type object. The pointer changes to (). Click to thread the two objects together.

8 Choose View > Preview.

9 Choose Select > Deselect.

10 With the Selection tool, click to select the top type object. Drag the bottom, middle handle up until the text "This sale happens just once a year!" is no longer highlighted in blue. This indicates that it will move to the next type object when the mouse button is released. Release the mouse button to see the text.

When type objects are threaded, you can move them anywhere and the connection between them remains. You can even thread between artboards. When type objects are resized, especially those in the beginning of the thread, text can reflow.

11 Choose File > Save.

▶ **Tip:** You can create unique type object shapes by deselecting the type object and choosing the Direct Selection tool (). Click and drag the edge or corner of the type object to adjust the shape of the path. This method is easier to use when View > Hide Bounding Box is selected. Adjusting the type path with the Direct Selection tool is easiest when you're in Outline view.

● **Note:** If you edit the type object by following the previous tip, choose Edit > Undo before continuing.

With the Direct Selection tool, you can click and drag the bottom, middle handle of the bounding box to resize the type object.

Formatting type

In this section, you'll discover how to change text attributes, such as size, font, and style. You can quickly change most attributes in the Control panel.

1   With the yoga.ai file still open, click the Previous button (◀) in the status bar to return to artboard 1 (the poster).

2   Choose View > Fit Artboard In Window if the poster isn't completely visible in the window.

▶ **Tip:** If you double-click text with the Selection or Direct Selection tool, the Type tool becomes selected.

3   Select the Type tool (**T**) in the Tools panel and insert the cursor anywhere in the two column text area that you created earlier.

4   Choose Select > All, or press Ctrl+A (Windows) or Command+A (Mac OS) to select all the text in the type object.

In this next section, you'll learn two different methods for selecting a font.

First, you'll change the font of selected text using the Font menu in the Control panel.

5   Click the arrow to the right of the Font menu and scroll until you find Adobe Garamond Pro, and select it.

● **Note:** The Adobe Garamond Pro font is in the G section of the menu.

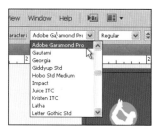

● **Note:** You may need to click the arrow that appears at the bottom of the font list to scroll through the list.

6   With the text still selected, choose Type > Font to see a list of available fonts. Select Myriad Pro > Regular. Scrolling down to find this font may take a little time, particularly if your font list is longer.

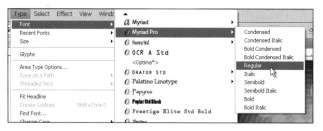

7   Make sure that the text is still selected and then follow the instructions below. This next method is the most dynamic method for selecting a font.

- Click the word Character in the Control panel to reveal the Character panel.

- With the font selected in the Character panel, begin typing the name Minion Pro. Illustrator filters through the list and fills the field with the name.

- Press Enter or Return to accept the font.

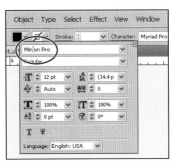

▶ **Tip:** To keep the Character panel open, choose Window > Type > Character.

8 Click the arrow in the Font Style menu to see the available styles for Minion Pro and make sure Regular is selected.

Font styles are specific to each font family. Although you may have the Minion Pro font family on your system, you may not have the bold and italic styles of that family.

Fonts installed and on the Illustrator CS4 DVD

The following fonts and accompanying documentation are installed, and included in the Documentation folder on the Illustrator CS4 product DVD, or in the packaged download file if you download Illustrator CS4 from the Adobe Store. For trial customers, the fonts are not available until after purchase.

Adobe® Caslon® Pro
Adobe® Garamond® Pro
Bell Gothic Std
Birch Std
Cooper Black Std
Giddyup Std
Letter Gothic Std
MESQUITE STD
Myriad Pro
OCRA Std
Prestige Elite Std
ROSEWOOD STD
Tekton Pro
Adobe Kaiti Std
KozGoPro
KozMinPro

Blackoak Std
Brush Script Std
Chaparral Pro
CHARLEMAGNE STD
ECCENTRIC STD
Hobo Std
Adobe Fangsong Std
LITHOS PRO
Minion Pro
Nueva Std
ORATOR STD
Poplar Std
STENCIL STD
TRAJAN PRO
* Kozuka Mincho Pr6N
* Kozuka Gothic Pr6N

* On DVD only

What is OpenType?

If you frequently send files back and forth between platforms, you should be designing your text files using the OpenType format.

OpenType is a cross-platform font file format developed jointly by Adobe and Microsoft. Adobe has converted the entire Adobe Type Library into this format and now offers thousands of OpenType fonts.

The two main benefits of the OpenType format are its cross-platform compatibility (the same font file works on Macintosh and Windows computers), and its ability to support widely expanded character sets and layout features, which provide richer linguistic support and advanced typographic control.

OpenType fonts can include an expanded character set and layout features, providing broader linguistic support and more precise typographic control. Feature-rich Adobe OpenType fonts can be distinguished by the word "Pro," which is part of the font name and appears in application font menus. OpenType fonts can be installed and used alongside PostScript Type 1 and TrueType fonts.

—From Adobe.com/type/opentype

Changing the font size

1 If the two column text is not active, use the Type tool (**T**) to insert the cursor in the area type object and choose Select > All.

2 Type 13 pt in the Font Size field in the Control panel. Notice the text change. Choose 12 pt from the Font Size menu. Leave the text selected.

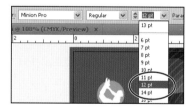

The Font Size menu has preset sizes. If you want a custom size, select the value in the Font Size field, enter a value in points, and then press Enter or Return.

▶ **Tip:** You can change the font size of selected text dynamically using keyboard shortcuts. To increase the font size in increments of 2 pts, press Ctrl+Shift+> (Windows), or Command+Shift+> (Mac OS). To reduce the font size, press Ctrl+Shift+< (Windows), or Command+Shift+< (Mac OS).

Changing the font color

You can change the font color of the fill and stroke of selected text. In this example, you will change only the fill.

1 With the text still selected, click the Fill color in the Control panel. When the Swatches panel appears, select White. The text fill changes to white.

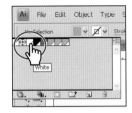

2 With the Type tool, click and drag to select the first line of text, "Transform Yoga" in the area type object, or triple-click the text.

▶ **Tip:** Double-click to select a word; triple-click to select an entire paragraph. The end of a paragraph is defined by where a hard return is entered.

3 Change the Fill color in the Control panel to Aqua.

4 Keep the first line of text selected. Select the text in the Font Size field in the Control panel and change the font size by typing 13. Press Enter or Return.

5 Choose Bold from the Font Style menu in the Control panel to change the font style for the selected text.

6 Choose Select > Deselect.

7 Chose File > Save.

Changing additional text attributes

In the Character panel, which you can access by clicking the blue, underlined word Character in the Control panel, you can change many other text attributes. In this lesson, you will apply some of the attributes, although there are more that are worth investigating to learn the different ways you can format text.

A. Font	**H.** Language
B. Font Style	**I.** Leading
C. Font Size	**J.** Tracking
D. Kerning	**K.** Vertical Scale
E. Horizontal Scale	**L.** Character Rotation
F. Baseline Shift	**M.** Strikethrough
G. Underline	

1   With the Type tool, click the address above the top yoga figure on the left side of the artboard. With the cursor in the text, triple-click to select the entire paragraph.

2   Select the Zoom tool (Q) and click the selected text several times to zoom in.

Tip: To return the leading value to the default, choose Auto from the Leading menu.

3   Click Character in the Control panel to reveal the Character panel. Click the up arrow to the left of the Leading field a few times to increase the leading to 16 pt. Keep the Character panel open.

Notice that the vertical distance between the lines changes. Leading is the vertical space between lines. Adjusting the leading is useful for fitting text into a text area.

Next you will change the spacing between letters.

4   With the text still selected, click the Tracking icon in the Character panel to select the Tracking field. Type 60, and press Enter or Return.

● **Note:** If the text becomes overflow text, as indicated by the red plus sign, you can fit the text by decreasing the Tracking value, or changing the size of the area type object with the Selection tool.

Tracking changes the spacing between characters. A positive value pushes the letters apart horizontally; a negative value pulls the letters closer together.

5   Double-click the Hand tool (✋) in the Tools panel to fit the artboard in the window.

6   Select the Zoom tool in the Tools panel and drag a marquee around the headline, "Transform Yoga," at the top of the first column in the type object.

7   Select the Type tool (T) in the Tools panel and click to place the cursor at the end of the headline, "Transform Yoga."

8   Choose Type > Glyphs to open the Glyphs panel.

The Glyphs panel is used to insert type characters like trademark symbols (™) or bullet points(·). It shows all the characters (glyphs) available for a given font.

Next you will insert a copyright symbol.

9   In the Glyphs panel, scroll down until you see a copyright symbol (©). Double-click the symbol to insert it at the text insertion cursor. Close the Glyphs panel.

> **Tip:** The Glyphs panel lets you select another font in the bottom of the panel. You can also increase the size of the glyph icons by clicking the larger mountain (⟰) in the lower right corner or make them smaller by clicking the smaller mountain (⟰).

10 With the Type tool, select the copyright symbol (©) you just inserted.

11 Choose Window > Type > Character to open the Character panel.

12 Choose Superscript from the Character panel menu (▾≡).

13 Click with the Type tool between "Yoga" and the copyright symbol to insert the cursor.

> **Tip:** To remove kerning changes, insert the cursor in the text, and choose Auto from the Kerning menu.

14 Choose 75 from the Kerning menu in the Character panel. Close the Character panel group, and choose File > Save.

Kerning is similar to tracking, but it adds or subtracts space between a pair of characters. It's useful for situations such as this one, when you're working with a glyph.

Changing paragraph attributes

Just like with character attributes, you can set paragraph attributes, such as alignment or indenting, before you enter new type, or reset them to change the appearance of existing type. If you select several type paths and type containers, you can set attributes for them all at the same time.

Now you'll add more space before all the paragraphs in the column text.

1 Choose View > Fit Artboard In Window.

2 Using the Type tool (T), insert the cursor in either column of the text, and choose Select > All.

3 Click the word Paragraph in the Control panel to open the Paragraph panel.

4 Type 5 in the Space After Paragraph text field (in the bottom right corner), and press Enter or Return. Setting a spacing value after paragraphs, rather than pressing the Return key, is recommended when working with large type objects.

5 Choose Select > Deselect.

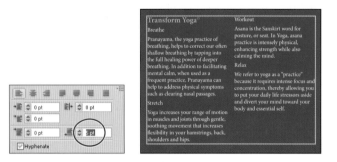

● **Note:** Your text may not look exactly like the figure above. That's OK.

6 With the Type tool, click the address above the top yoga figure on the left side of the artboard to insert the cursor.

7 Click the Align Center button (▤) in the Control panel.

● **Note:** If you don't see alignment options in the Control panel, click the blue, underlined word Paragraph to open the Paragraph panel.

> 1000 Lombard Ave.
> Central, Washington

8 Choose Select > Deselect.

9 Choose File > Save.

Document setup options

By choosing File > Document Setup, you can access the Document Setup dialog box. In this dialog box, there are many text options, including the Highlight Substituted Fonts and Highlight Substituted Glyphs options, which are in the Bleed And View Options section.

In the Type Options at the bottom of the dialog box, you can set the document language, change double and single quotes, edit Superscript, Subscript, Small Caps, and more.

Saving and using styles

Styles allow for consistent text formatting and are helpful when text attributes need to be globally updated. Once a style is created, you only need to edit the saved style. Then, all text formatted with that style is updated.

There are two types of styles in Adobe Illustrator CS4:

- **Paragraph**—Retains text and paragraph attributes and applies them to an entire paragraph.

- **Character**—Retains the text attributes and applies them to selected text.

Creating and using a paragraph style

1 Using the Type tool (**T**), select the subhead "Breathe." Choose Bold from the Font Style menu in the Control panel.

2 With the Type tool, place the cursor in the text "Breathe." You do not need to select text to create a paragraph style, but you do have to place the text insertion point in the line of text that has the attributes you want to save.

3 Choose Window > Type > Paragraph Styles, and choose New Paragraph Style from the panel menu (▾≣).

4 In the New Paragraph Style dialog box, type the name Subhead, and click OK. The text attributes used in the paragraph have been saved in a paragraph style named Subhead.

5 Apply the new paragraph style by selecting the text "Breathe" and then selecting the Subhead style in the Paragraph Styles panel. The text attributes are applied to the selected text.

● **Note:** If you see a plus sign (+) to the right of the style name, the style has an override. An override is any formatting that doesn't match the attributes defined by the style, for example, if you changed the font size for the selected paragraph. Press Alt or Option when you select the style name to overwrite existing attributes if you see the plus sign (+).

Notice the Normal style in the Paragraph Styles panel. When you placed the Word document earlier in this lesson, the Normal style from Word was brought into the Illustrator document.

6 Select the text "Stretch", and Alt-click (Windows) or Option-click (Mac OS) the Subhead style in the Paragraph Styles panel. Repeat this step to apply the style to the text, "Workout" and "Relax" as well.

Creating and using a character style

Whereas paragraph styles apply attributes to an entire paragraph, character styles can be applied to selected text only.

1 Using the Type tool (**T**), select the first occurrence of the text "Pranayama" in the first column of the paragraph text.

2 Choose Bold from the Font Style menu in the Control panel.

Now you will save these attributes as a character style, and apply it to other instances in the text.

3 In the Paragraph Styles panel group, click the Character Styles panel tab.

4 In the Character Styles panel, Alt-click (Windows) or Option-click (Mac OS) the Create New Style button (▣) at the bottom of the Character Styles panel. Alt or Option-clicking the New Style button lets you name the style as it is added to the panel. You can also double-click a style to name and edit it.

5 Name the style Bold and click OK. The style records the attributes applied to your selected text.

Now you will apply that character style to other text.

6 With the "Pranayama" text still selected, Alt-click (Windows) or Option-click (Mac OS) the style named Bold in the Character Styles panel to assign the style to that text. Remember, Alt-clicking or Option-clicking removes any existing attributes from the text that are not part of the character style.

7 Select the next occurrence of "Pranayama" and apply the Bold style again.

● **Note:** You must select the entire word rather than just placing the cursor in the text.

8 Choose Select > Deselect.

Perhaps you decide that you want to change the color of all text that is formatted with the Bold character style. Using styles (either character or paragraph), you can change the type attributes of the original style, and all instances are updated.

Next you will change the color of the Bold character style.

9   Double-click the Bold style name in the Character Styles panel. In the Character Style Options dialog box, click the Character Color category on the left side of the dialog box and make sure that the Fill box is selected. Click the Mustard swatch in the Swatches panel that appears.

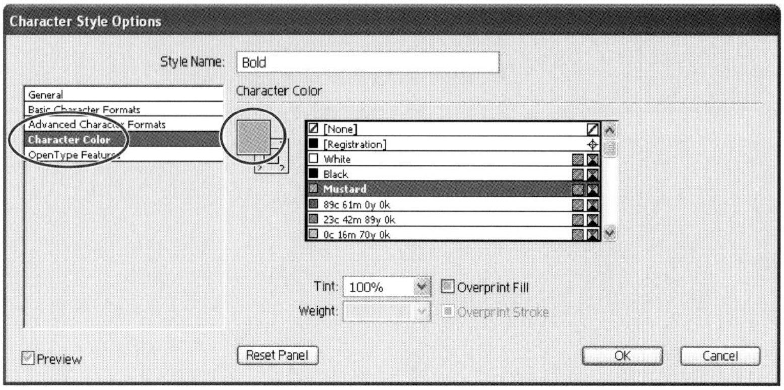

10 Select the Preview checkbox in the lower left corner of the Character Style Options dialog box if it isn't already selected. As you change the style formatting, the text that uses the Bold style changes automatically.

11 Click OK, and close the Character Style panel group.

12 Choose File > Save. Leave the file open.

Sampling text

Using the Eyedropper tool, you can quickly sample type attributes and apply them to text without creating a style.

1   Choose View > Fit Artboard In Window.

2   With the Zoom tool (Q), click and drag a marquee across the text "1000 Lombard Ave. Central, Washington" above the top yoga figure on the left.

3   Using the Type tool (T), triple-click to select the paragraph.

4   In the Control panel, change the Fill color to blue (C=89, M=61, Y=0, K=0), the Font to Myriad Pro (if it isn't already selected), and the Font Style to Condensed.

| 1000 Lombard Ave.
Central, Washington |

● **Note:** If "Central" appears in the first line of text, use the Type tool to place the cursor before "Central" and press Shift+Enter or Shift+Return to add a soft return, pushing the text to the next line.

5   Double-click the Hand tool (✋) to fit the artboard in the window.

6   Choose View > Smart Guides to select them.

7   With the Type tool, select the text "info@transformyoga.com" above the bottom, left yoga figure on the artboard.

8 Select the Eyedropper tool (![eyedropper]) in the Tools panel and click anywhere in the line of text "1000 Lombard Ave. Central, Washington." A letter "T" appears above the eyedropper pointer. The attributes are immediately applied to your selected text. If the e-mail address shifts to the left, move it to its original position with the Selection tool.

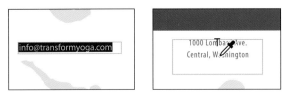

9 Choose Select > Deselect.

10 Choose File > Save. Leave the file open.

Reshaping text with an envelope warp

Warping text is fun because it allows you to give text a more interesting shape. An envelope warp lets you fit the text into a shape that you create or that is created for you. An envelope is an object that distorts or reshapes selected objects. You can use a preset warp shape or a mesh grid as an envelope, or you can create and edit your own using objects on the artboard.

1 Select the Type tool (T) in the Tools panel. Before typing, in the Control panel, change the font family to Myriad Pro (if it is not already chosen), the font style to Bold Condensed, and the font size to 48 pt.

2 With the Type tool, click the poster below the two columns of text once. Exact placement is not important. A cursor appears.

3 Type the word transform.

4 Select the Selection tool (![arrow]). If the text overlaps the text in the two columns above, drag it down until it no longer does. Change the Fill color in the Control panel to white.

▶ **Tip:** With the Type tool selected, you can temporarily switch to the Selection tool by pressing Ctrl or Command.

5 With the text selected with the Selection tool, click the Make Envelope button (![icon]) in the Control panel. In the Warp Options dialog box, select Preview. The text appears as an arc.

6 Choose Arc Upper from the Style menu. Drag the Bend slider to the right to see it bend up further. You can experiment with many different combinations. Drag the Horizontal and Vertical Distortion sliders to see the effect on the text. When you are finished using this dialog box, drag the Distortion sliders to 0%, and click OK.

● **Note:** The Make Envelope button (◻) does not apply an effect. It just turns the text into an envelope object. The same visual result is achieved by choosing Effect > Warp > Arc Upper. For more information about envelopes, see "Reshape using envelopes" in Illustrator Help.

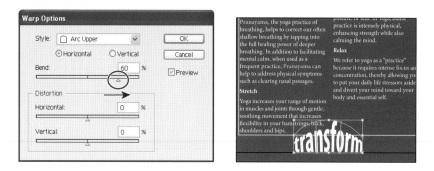

7 Use the Selection tool to move the envelope object (warped text) until the bottom of the warped text is aligned roughly with the bottom of the two columns of text.

If you want to make any changes, you can edit the text and shape separately. Next you will edit the text "transform", and then the warp shape.

8 With the warped text still selected, click the Edit Contents button (▣) in the Control panel. This is how you edit the text in the warped shape.

9 Using the Type tool, hover the cursor over the warped text. Notice the blue line and blue "transform" text. The smart guides are showing you the original text. Click "transform" to insert the cursor, and then double-click to select it.

● **Note:** If you double-click with the Selection tool instead of the Type tool, you enter isolation mode. Press Escape to exit isolation mode.

10 Type workout and notice the text warps automatically in the arc upper shape. Choose Edit > Undo Typing to return to the original text.

● **Note:** It may seem strange that the text you are editing seems to float in the warped shape. It just shows you that the text is being forced into the shape, but it is still editable as text.

11 In the Control panel, change the Stroke Weight to .75 pt, and the Stroke color to Mustard. Press Escape to close the Swatches panel.

Notice that the attributes are applied to the warped text. Next you will edit the warp shape.

12 With the Selection tool, make sure that the warped text is still selected. Click the Edit Envelope button (🔲) in the Control panel.

13 Choose Bulge from the Select Warp Style menu in the Control panel. Notice the other options in the Control panel, such as Horizontal, Vertical, and Bend. Choose Arc Upper to return to the arc upper shape.

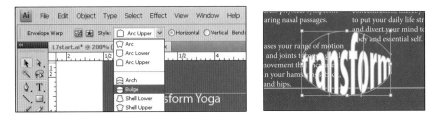

Note: You may have to reposition the warped text to align it with the bottom of the columns of text. Changing the warp style may move the text on the artboard.

14 Select the Direct Selection tool (▷) in the Tools panel. Notice the anchor points around the warped shape. First, click to select the anchor point above the "n" in "transform." Then, drag the selected point up to change the warp shape.

▶ **Tip:** To take the text out of the warped shape, select the text with the Selection tool and choose Object > Envelope Distort > Release. This gives you two objects: the text and the arc upper shape.

15 Choose Edit > Undo Move to return the shape to the arc upper shape.

Next you will add a drop shadow effect to the warped text.

16 Switch to the Selection tool and click "transform."

17 Choose Effect > Stylize > Drop Shadow from the Illustrator effects. In the Drop Shadow Options dialog box, change Opacity to 30%, X Offset to 3 pt, Y Offset to 3 pt, and Blur to 3 pt, and click OK.

18 Choose Select > Deselect, and File > Save. Leave the file open.

Wrapping text around an object

You can create interesting and creative results by wrapping text around an object. Next you will wrap text around the warped text.

1   With the Selection tool, click to select the warped text, "transform."

2   Choose Object > Text Wrap > Make. The text in the two columns wraps around the warped text, "transform."

● **Note:** To wrap text around an object, the wrap object must be in the same layer as the text and located directly above the text in the layer hierarchy.

3   With the Selection tool, click and drag "transform" to see the effect on the text in the two columns.

4   If text is flowing in areas where you don't want it, choose Object > Text Wrap > Text Wrap Options. In the Text Wrap Options dialog box, change Offset to 4 and select Preview to see the change. Click OK.

5   Using the Selection tool, reposition "transform" to create a better text flow. For this example, it is alright if some of your text overflows out of the text area.

6   Choose Select > Deselect.

7   Choose File > Save. Keep the file open.

Creating text on paths and shapes

Using the Type tools, you can type on paths and shapes to flow text along the edge of an open or closed path.

1   Click the Next button (▶) in the status bar in the lower left of the Document window to navigate to the second artboard.

2   Choose View > Fit Artboard In Window if the entire postcard is not showing.

3   With the Selection tool (▶), select the wavy path crossing the yoga figures.

▶ **Tip:** To quickly switch to the Selection tool and back to the Type tool, press Ctrl or Command.

4 With the Type tool (**T**), cross the cursor over the left side of the path to see an insertion point with an intersecting wavy path (ꭕ). Click when this cursor appears. The stroke attributes change to None and a cursor appears. Don't type yet.

5 Change the font size to 20 pt in the Control panel. Change the Fill color to blue (C=89, M=61, Y=0, K=0). Make sure that the font is Myriad Pro and change the font style to Condensed.

6 Type breathe and press the spacebar to add a space. Note that the newly typed text follows the path.

7 Choose Type > Glyphs, and find a bullet point in the Glyphs panel. Double-click to insert the bullet point. Keep the Glyphs panel open. Insert a space after the inserted bullet.

8 Type stretch · relax · transform yourself. Add a space before and after each bullet point.

9 Close the Glyphs panel.

● **Note:** If the text doesn't fit on the path, a small box with a plus sign (+) appears at the bottom of the bounding box. You can make the font size smaller or the line bigger, among other options.

10 Choose Select > Deselect.

11 Click in the text you just typed with the Type tool. In the Control panel, make sure the Align Center button (≡) is selected to center the text on the path.

● **Note:** You can apply any character and paragraph formatting to the text on the path if you like.

12 With the Selection tool, make sure that the text path is still selected. In the Control panel, change Opacity to 60% to make the text semi-transparent.

● **Note:** If you don't see the opacity settings in the Control panel, you can open the Transparency panel by choosing Window > Transparency.

13 Choose Select > Deselect, and then File > Save.

Now you will put text on a closed path.

1 Click the Previous button in the status bar in the lower left of the Document window to navigate to the first artboard.

2 Choose View > Fit Artboard In Window if the entire poster is not showing. Select the Zoom tool (🔍) in the Tools panel and click the blue circle in the upper left corner of the poster three times to zoom in.

3 With the Selection tool (▶), select the aqua circle behind the yoga figure.

Next you will copy the blue circle so that you can put text on it. You are making a copy because putting text on the aqua circle that is there would remove the stroke and fill of that circle. Remember, putting text on a path removes the stroke and fill from the path.

4 Double-click the Scale tool (⬚) in the Tools panel to open the Scale dialog box. In the Scale dialog box, change Uniform Scale to 130, and click Copy to make a copy of the circle. This makes a copy that is 130% larger than the original circle.

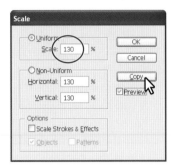

⬤ **Note:** Read more about transforming objects in Lesson 4, "Transforming Objects."

5 Switch to the Type tool. While pressing Alt (Windows) or Option (Mac OS), cross over the left side of the circle. The insertion point with an intersecting wavy path (𝕀) appears. Click, but don't type. The path now has a stroke and fill of none, but the type will have a black fill, and a cursor is on the path.

⬤ **Note:** If you do not want to use Alt or Option, you can select the Type On A Path tool by holding down the Type tool in the Tools panel.

6 In the Control panel, change the font size to 30 pt, the font to Myriad Pro (if not already selected), the font style to Condensed, and the Fill color to white.

7 Click the Align Left button (▤) in the Control panel.

8 Type transform yoga. The text flows on the circular path.

9 To adjust the placement on the path, switch to the Selection tool. The type object is selected. Brackets appear at the beginning of the type, at the end of the path, and at the midpoint between the start and end brackets.

⬤ **Note:** It may look like there are only two brackets. That's because the starting and end brackets are next to each other on the left side of the circle.

10 Position the cursor over the center bracket until a small icon (⊾) appears next to the cursor. Drag the center bracket along the outside of the path. Press Ctrl (Windows) or Command (Mac OS) to prevent the type from flipping to the other side of the path. Position the text so that it is relatively centered across the top of the circle.

Cross over the closed shape with the Type tool while pressing Alt or Option.

11 With the path type object selected with the Selection tool, choose Type > Type On A Path > Type On A Path Options. In the Type On A Path Options dialog box, select Preview, and then choose Skew

from the Effect menu. Select other options from the Effect menu, and then change the effect to Rainbow. Choose Descender from the Align To Path menu. Click OK.

● **Note:** Read more about Type On A Path options in Illustrator Help. Search for, "Creating type on a path."

12 Choose Select > Deselect.

13 Choose File > Save, and leave the file open.

Creating text outlines

When creating artwork for multiple purposes, it is a good idea to create outlines of text so that the recipient doesn't need your fonts to open and use the file correctly. You always want to keep an original of your artwork because you cannot change outline text back to editable text.

1 Click the Next button in the status bar in the lower left of the Document window to navigate to the second artboard.

2 Choose View > Fit Artboard In Window if the entire postcard is not showing.

3 Select the Type tool (**T**) in the Tools panel and click off the left edge of the postcard artboard on the canvas.

4 Change the Fill color in the Control panel to blue (C=89, M=61, Y=0, K=0).

5 Type transform yourself.

6 Double-click the Rotate tool (⟳) in the Tools panel. In the Rotate dialog box, type 90 in the Angle field. Click OK. The text is rotated 90 degrees counterclockwise.

7 With the Selection tool (▶), position the text in the lower right corner of the blue background image on the left.

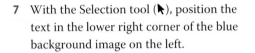

8 Using the Selection tool, Shift-click and drag the upper right handle of the bounding box of the text to proportionally enlarge the text to the height of the postcard.

● **Note:** If the descender of the letters appear in the white area to the right, then drag the text to the left.

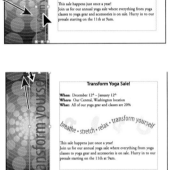

Shift-click and drag to proportionally resize the text.

9 Click the word Opacity in the Control panel to open the Transparency panel. Choose Screen from the Blending Mode menu.

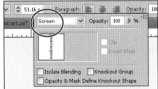

10 With the text area still selected with the Selection tool, choose Type > Create Outlines. The text is no longer linked to a particular font. Instead, it is now artwork, much like any other vector art in your illustration. Choose Select > Deselect.

11 Choose File > Save.

Exploring on your own

Experiment with text features by integrating paths with illustrations. Use the clip art provided in the Lesson07 folder and try some of these type techniques:

- pizza.ai—Using the Pen tool, create paths representing steam rising from the slice. Create text on the wavy paths and apply varying levels of opacity.

- airplane.ai—Complete a banner following the airplane with text of your own.

Take the project further by using this artwork in a one-page sales flyer that has the following text elements on the page:

- Using the placeholder.txt file in the Lesson07 folder, create a three-column text area.

- Use the graphic of the pizza or plane for a text wrap.

- Create a masthead across the top of your page that has text on a curve.

- Create a paragraph style.

- On the yoga poster, choose View > Outline to see all the paths on the page. Notice a spiral shape at the top of the page. Try adding text to that spiral path and choose Type > Type On A Path > Type On A Path Options to change the attributes.

Review questions

1 Name two methods for creating a text area in Adobe Illustrator CS4.

2 What are two benefits of using an OpenType font?

3 What is the difference between a character and paragraph style?

4 What are the advantages and disadvantages of converting text to outlines?

Review answers

1 Following are several methods for creating text areas:

   • With the Type tool, click the artboard, and start typing when the cursor appears. A text area is created to accommodate the text.

   • With the Type tool, click and drag to create a text area. Type when a cursor appears.

   • With the Type tool, click a path or closed shape to convert it to text on a path or a text area. Alt-clicking or Option-clicking when crossing over the stroke of a closed path creates text around the shape.

2 The two main benefits of OpenType fonts are cross-platform compatibility (they work the same on both Windows and Mac OS), and support of widely expanded character sets and layout features, which provide richer linguistic support and advanced typographic control.

3 A character style can be applied to selected text only. A paragraph style is applied to an entire paragraph. Paragraph styles are best for indents, margins, and line spacing.

4 Converting type to outlines eliminates the need to send the fonts along with the file when sharing with others. You can also fill the type with a gradient and create interesting effects on individual letters. However, when you create outlines from text, you should consider the following:

   • Text is no longer editable. The content and font cannot be changed for outlined text. It is best to save a layer with the original text, or use the Outline Object effect.

   • Bitmap fonts and outline-protected fonts cannot be converted to outlines.

   • Outlining text that is less than 10 points in size is not recommended. When type is converted to outlines, the type loses its hints—instructions built into outline fonts to adjust their shape to display or print optimally at many sizes. When scaling type, adjust its point size before converting it to outlines.

   • You must convert all type in a selection to outlines; you cannot convert a single letter within a string of type. To convert a single letter into an outline, create a separate type area containing only that letter.

8 WORKING WITH LAYERS

Lesson overview

In this lesson, you'll learn how to do the following:

- Work with the Layers panel.

- Create, rearrange, and lock layers, nested layers, and groups.

- Move objects between layers.

- Paste layers of objects from one file into another.

- Merge layers into a single layer.

- Apply a drop shadow to a layer.

- Make a layer clipping mask.

- Apply an appearance attribute to objects and layers.

- Isolate content in a layer.

 This lesson will take approximately 45 minutes to complete. If needed, remove the previous lesson folder from your hard disk and copy the Lesson08 folder onto it.

Layers let you organize your work into distinct
levels that can be edited and viewed individually or
together. Every Illustrator document has at least one
layer. Creating multiple layers in your artwork lets you
easily control how artwork is printed, displayed,
and edited.

Getting started

In this lesson, you'll finish the artwork of a wall clock as you explore the various ways to use the Layers panel.

1 To ensure that the tools and panels function as described in this lesson, delete or deactivate (by renaming) the Adobe Illustrator CS4 preferences file. See "Restoring default preferences" on page 3.

2 Start Adobe Illustrator CS4.

● **Note:** If you have not already copied the resource files for this lesson onto your hard disk from the Lesson08 folder on the Adobe Illustrator CS4 Classroom in a Book CD, do so now. See "Copying the Classroom in a Book files" on page 2.

3 Choose File > Open, and open the L8end.ai file in the Lesson08 folder, located in the Lessons folder on your hard disk.

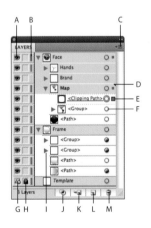

Note: If the Layers panel in your workspace does not look exactly like the figure below, that's okay. At this point, you just need to familiarize yourself with the panel.

Separate layers are used for the objects that make up the clock's frame, face, hands, and numbers, as indicated by the layer names listed in the Layers panel. Below you can see the Layers panel (Window > Layers) and descriptions of the icons.

A. Visibility column

B. Layer color

C. Layers panel menu

D. Current layer indicator

E. Selection column

F. Target column

G. Template layer icon

H. Edit column (lock/unlock)

I. Expand/collapse triangle

J. Make/Release Clipping Mask

K. Create New Sublayer

L. Create New Layer

M. Delete Selection

4 Choose View > Fit Artboard In Window. If you like, you can leave the file open as a visual reference. Otherwise, choose File > Close.

To begin working, you'll open an existing art file that is incomplete.

5 Choose File > Open, and open the L8start.ai file in the Lesson08 folder, located in the Lessons folder on your hard disk.

6 Choose File > Save As, name the file clock.ai, and select the Lesson08 folder. Leave the Save As Type option set to Adobe Illustrator (*.AI) (Windows) or the Format option set to Adobe Illustrator (ai) (Mac OS), and click Save. In the Illustrator Options dialog box, leave the Illustrator options at their default settings, and click OK.

About layers

When creating complex artwork, it's a challenge to keep track of all the items in your document window. Small items get hidden under larger items, and selecting artwork becomes difficult. Layers provide a way to manage all the items that make up your artwork. Think of layers as clear folders that contain artwork. If you reshuffle the folders, you change the stacking order of the items in your artwork. You can move items between folders and create subfolders within folders.

The structure of layers in your document can be as simple or complex as you want it to be. By default, all items are organized in a single parent layer. However, you can create new layers and move items into them, or move elements from one layer to another at any time. The Layers panel provides an easy way to select, hide, lock, and change the appearance attributes of artwork.

—From Illustrator Help

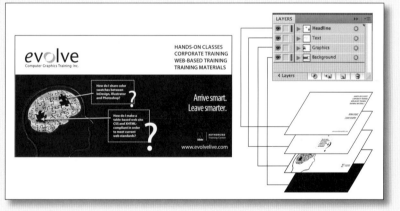

Example of composite art and how layers break out individually.

Creating layers

By default, every document begins with one layer. You can rename and add layers at any time as you create artwork. Placing objects on separate layers lets you easily select and edit them. For example, by placing type on a separate layer, you can change the type all at once without affecting the rest of the artwork.

Next you'll change the default layer name, and then create a layer and a sublayer.

1 If the Layers panel isn't visible, click the Layers panel icon (⬢) on the right side of the workspace, or choose Window > Layers.

Layer 1 (the default name for the first layer) is highlighted, indicating that it is active. The layer also has a triangle (◥) in the upper right corner, indicating that objects on the layer can be edited.

2 In the Layers panel, double-click the layer name to open the Layer Options dialog box. Type Clock in the Name text field, and then click OK.

Now you'll create a layer for the clock face elements and a sublayer for the clock numbers. Sublayers help you organize content within a layer.

3 Click the Create New Layer button (▣) at the bottom of the Layers panel, or choose New Layer from the Layers panel menu (▾≡).

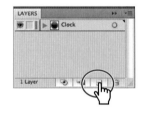

4 Double-click Layer 2. In the Layer Options dialog box, change the name to Face, make sure red is chosen in the Color menu, and click OK.

The new Face layer is added above the Clock layer and becomes active.

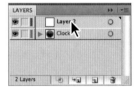

Note: To create a new sublayer without setting options or naming the sublayer, click the Create New Sublayer button without using Alt or Option. Layers and sublayers that aren't named are numbered in sequence, for example, Layer 2.

5 Click the layer named Clock once and then Alt-click (Windows) or Option-click (Mac OS) the Create New Sublayer button (⤵▣) at the bottom of the Layers panel to create a new sublayer. The Layer Options dialog box appears. Creating a new sublayer opens the layer to show existing sublayers.

A sublayer is a layer within another layer. Sublayers are used to organize content within a layer without grouping or ungrouping content.

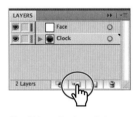

Alt-click or Option-click to create a sublayer.

6 In the Layer Options dialog box, change the name to Numbers, and click OK. The new sublayer appears directly beneath its main layer, Clock, and is selected.

Layers and color

By default, Illustrator assigns a unique color (up to nine colors) to each layer in the Layers panel. The color displays next to the layer name in the panel. The same color displays in the illustration window in the bounding box, path, anchor points, and center point of a selected object.

You can use this color to quickly locate an object's corresponding layer in the Layers panel, and you can change the layer color to suit your needs.

—From Illustrator Help

Each layer and sublayer can have a unique color.

Moving objects and layers

By rearranging the layers in the Layers panel, you can reorder layered objects in your artwork. You can also move selected objects from one layer or sublayer to another. Layers higher in the Layers panel list are in front of objects on the artboard that are in layers lower in the list. First you'll move the clock numbers into their own sublayer.

1 In the Layers panel, click and drag the row for the 11 object and drag it onto the Numbers sublayer. Release the mouse button when you see the large black triangles at either end of the Numbers sublayer. The large triangles indicate that you are adding something to that layer. Notice the arrow that appears to the left of the Numbers sublayer after releasing the mouse button. This indicates that the sublayer has content.

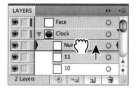

Tip: Keeping layers and sublayers closed can make it easier to navigate content in the Layers panel.

2 Click the triangle to the left of the Numbers sublayer thumbnail to open the sublayer and see its contents.

3 Repeat step 1 for each of the remaining numbers in the Layers panel. This better organizes the Layers panel and makes it easier to find content later.

4 Click the triangle to the left of the Numbers sublayer to hide its contents. Hiding layer and/or sublayer contents makes the Layers panel easier to work with.

Tip: To select multiple layers or sublayers quickly, select a layer and then Shift-click additional layers.

5 Choose File > Save.

Now you'll move the clock face to the Face layer, to which you'll later add the map, hands, and brand name of the clock. You'll also rename the Clock layer to reflect the new organization of the artwork.

6 In the artwork, with the Selection tool (▶), click behind the numbers to select the clock face. In the Layers panel, an object named <Path> becomes active, as indicated by the selected-art indicator (■) to the right of the top <Path> layer.

Selected-art indicator showing that <Path> is selected.

7 Click and drag the selected-art indicator (■) on the <Path> sublayer in the Layers panel up to the right of the target icon (O) on the Face layer.

This action moves the <Path> object to the Face layer. The color of the selection lines in the artwork changes to the color of the Face layer, which is red in this case.

Because the Face layer is on top of the Clock layer and the Numbers sublayer, the clock numbers are covered. Next you'll move the Numbers sublayer into a different layer and rename the Clock layer.

8 Choose Select > Deselect.

9 In the Layers panel, drag the Numbers sublayer into the Face layer. Release the mouse button when you see the indicator bar with large black triangles at either end of the Face layer in the Layers panel.

Now you can see the numbers again because they are on the top (Face) layer.

10 Double-click the Clock layer to display the Layer Options dialog box. Change the layer name to Frame, and then click OK.

11 Choose File > Save.

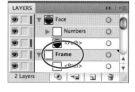

Locking layers

As you edit objects on a layer, use the Layers panel to lock other layers and prevent selecting or changing the rest of the artwork.

Now you'll lock all of the layers except the Numbers sublayer so that you can easily edit the clock numbers without affecting objects on other layers. Locked layers cannot be selected or edited in any way.

1 Click the triangle to the left of the Frame layer to collapse the layer view.

2 Select the edit column to the right of the eye icon on the Frame layer to lock the layer. The lock icon (🔒) indicates that a layer and all its content are locked.

3 Repeat the previous step for the <Path> sublayer below the Numbers sublayer.

You can unlock individual layers by deselecting the lock icon (🔒). Clicking again in the edit column relocks the layer. Pressing Alt (Windows) or Option (Mac OS) as you click in the edit column alternately locks and unlocks all other layers.

Now you'll change the type size and font of the numbers.

4 Click the Selection column to the right of the Numbers sublayer in the Layers panel to select all the content on that layer.

The Numbers sublayer now has a large green square, indicating that everything on that sublayer is selected. On the artboard, you can see that the numbers are selected as well.

Next you will change the font, font style, and font size for the selected numbers.

5 In the Control panel, choose Myriad Pro from the Font menu, Semibold from Font Style menu, and type 28 in the Font Size field.

● **Note:** Myriad Pro is an OpenType font that is included with Illustrator CS4.

6 Use the Color panel () if you want to change the color of the selected numbers.

7 In the Layers panel, deselect the lock icons (🔒) next to the <Path> and Frame layers to unlock them.

8 Choose Select > Deselect.

9 Choose File > Save.

With the Numbers layer selected, you can change the font, font style, and font size of the numbers.

Viewing layers

The Layers panel lets you hide layers, sublayers, or individual objects from view. When a layer is hidden, the content on the layer is also locked and cannot be selected or printed. You can also use the Layers panel to display layers or objects individually in either preview or outline mode.

Now you'll edit the frame on the clock, using a painting technique to create a three-dimensional effect on the frame.

▶ **Tip:** Alt-clicking or Option-clicking the layer eye icon alternately hides and shows a layer. Hiding layers prevents them from being changed.

1 In the Layers panel, click the Frame layer to select it, and then Alt-click (Windows) or Option-click (Mac OS) the eye icon (👁) to the left of the Frame layer name to hide the other layers.

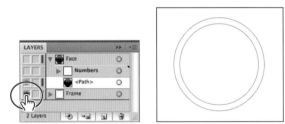

Alt-click or Option-click the eye icon to deselect visibility for all other layers.

2 Using the Selection tool (▶), on the artboard, click the inside circle of the frame to select it. Then Shift-click the next largest circle to add it to the selection.

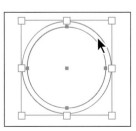

3 With the two circles selected, click Fill color in the Control panel, and then select the clock.frame swatch in the Swatches panel that appears to paint the circles with a custom gradient.

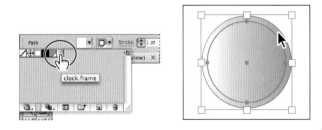

4 Shift-click the largest circle to deselect it. The inside circle remains selected.

5 Select the Gradient tool () in the Tools panel. Drag the tool in a vertical line from below the top of the circle straight down to the bottom to change the direction of the gradient. Release the mouse button.

The Gradient tool works only on selected objects that are filled with gradients. To learn more about the Gradient tool, see Lesson 9, "Blending Shapes and Colors."

● **Note:** When you first select the Gradient tool, a horizontal line appears in the selected circle. This is the default direction of the gradient fill.

6 Choose Select > Deselect, and then File > Save. Try selecting the larger circle and changing the direction of the gradient with the Gradient tool.

7 In the Layers panel, choose Show All Layers from the panel menu (▾≣).

As you edit objects in layered artwork, you can display individual layers in outline mode, keeping the other layers in preview mode.

8 Ctrl-click (Windows) or Command-click (Mac OS) the eye icon (👁) next to the Face layer to switch to outline mode for that layer.

This action lets you see the gradient-filled circle behind the clock face. Displaying a layer in outline mode is also useful for viewing the anchor points or center points on objects without selecting them.

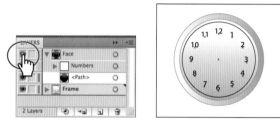

Ctrl-click/Command-click the eye icon to enter outline mode.

9 Control-click (Windows) or Command-click (Mac OS) the eye icon (👁) next to the Face layer to return to preview mode for that layer. Choose Select > Deselect.

Pasting layers

To complete the clock, you'll copy and paste the finishing pieces of artwork from another file. You can paste a layered file into another file and keep the layers intact.

1 Choose File > Open, and open the Details.ai file, located in the Lesson08 folder in the Lessons folder on your hard disk.

2 To see how the objects in each layer are organized, Alt-click (Windows) or Option-click (Mac OS) the eye icons in the Layers panel to alternately display each layer and hide the others. You can also click the triangles (▶) to the left of the layer names to expand and collapse the layers for further inspection. When you're finished, make sure that all the layers are showing and that they are collapsed.

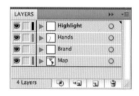

3 Choose Select > All, and then Edit > Copy to select and copy the clock details to the clipboard.

4 Choose File > Close. If a warning dialog box appears, click No (Windows) or Don't Save (Mac OS) to close the Details.ai file without saving any changes.

5 In the clock.ai file, choose Paste Remembers Layers from the Layers panel menu (▾≣). A check mark next to the option indicates that it's selected.

Selecting the Paste Remembers Layers option indicates that when multiple layers from another file are pasted into the artwork, they're added as individual layers in the Layers panel. If the option is not selected, all objects are pasted into the active layer.

6 Choose Edit > Paste In Front to paste the details into the clock. Choose Select > Deselect.

The Paste In Front command pastes the objects from the clipboard to a position relative to the original position in the Details.ai file. The Paste Remembers Layers option causes the Details.ai layers to be pasted as four separate layers at the top of the Layers panel (Highlight, Hands, Brand, Map).

Now you will reposition some of the layers.

7 Close any open layers by toggling the arrow to the left of the layer names. Move the Frame layer above the Highlight layer, and then the Face layer above the Frame layer. If necessary, drag the bottom of the Layers panel down to reveal all the layers.

▶ **Tip:** As you drag layers in the Layers panel, the panel scrolls up or down for you.

Release the mouse button when the indicator bar with black triangles extends the full column width above the Frame and Highlight layers. (You want to create a separate layer, not a sublayer.) If any content is still selected on the artboard, choose Select > Deselect.

Now you'll move the Hands and Brand layers into the Face layer, and the Highlight layer in front of the Frame layer.

8 In the Layers panel, select the Highlight layer, and drag it up between the Face and Frame layers.

9 Click the arrow to the left of the Face layer to show the sublayers.

10 Click the Hands layer, and Shift-click the Brand layer.

11 Drag the selected layers up between the Numbers and <Path> sublayers. When the insertion bar appears between those sublayers, release the mouse button to make the Hands and Brand layers sublayers of the Face layer.

● **Note:** You may want to resize the Layers panel by clicking and dragging the bottom of the Layers panel down so it is easier to see the layers.

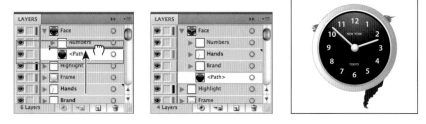

12 Choose File > Save.

Creating clipping masks

The Layers panel lets you create clipping masks to control whether artwork on a layer (or in a group) is hidden or revealed. A clipping mask is an object or group of objects whose shape masks artwork below it so that only artwork within the shape is visible.

Now you'll create a clipping mask with the circle shape in the Face layer. You'll group it with the Map sublayer so that only the map shows through the circle shape.

1   Drag the bottom of the Layers panel down to reveal all the layers.

2   In the Layers panel, drag the Map layer up until the double lines of the insertion bar are highlighted above the <Path> sublayer within the Face layer. Release the mouse button when the indicator bar appears.

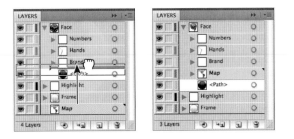

In the Layers panel, a masking object must be above the objects it masks. Because you want to mask only the map, you'll copy the circular <Path> object to the top of the Map sublayer before you create the clipping mask.

3   Click the selection column in the Layers panel to the right of the <Path> sublayer. Notice that the path is selected on the artboard.

4   Hold down Alt (Windows) or Option (Mac OS), and click and drag the selected-art indicator (■) on the <Path> sublayer straight up to the right of the target icon (○) on the Map sublayer.

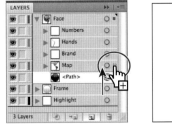

5   Click the triangle (▶) to the left of the Map sublayer in the Layers panel to expand the layer view.

6 Make sure that the <Path> sublayer is at the top of the Map sublayer, moving it if necessary. (Clipping masks must be the first object in a layer or group.)

7 Choose Select > Deselect.

● **Note:** Deselecting is not necessary to complete the next steps, but it can be helpful for viewing the artwork.

8 Select the Map sublayer to highlight it in the Layers panel.

● **Note:** You may not be able to see the entire name <Clipping Path> in the Layers panel.

9 Click the Make/Release Clipping Mask button (⬛) at the bottom of the Layers panel. Notice that all the sublayer dividing lines are now dotted and the first path name has changed to <Clipping Path>. The clipping path name is also underlined to indicate that it is the masking shape. On the artboard, the <Path> sublayer has clipped the parts of the map that extended outside of the clock face.

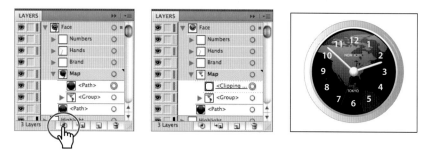

10 Click the triangle next to the Map sublayer name to collapse the layers in the Layers panel.

11 Choose File > Save.

Merging layers

To streamline your artwork, you can merge layers. Merging layers combines the contents of all selected layers into one layer.

● **Note:** Layers can only merge with other layers that are on the same hierarchical level in the Layers panel. Likewise, sublayers can only merge with other sublayers that are in the same layer and at the same hierarchical level. Objects can't be merged with other objects.

1 Click the Numbers sublayer in the Layers panel to highlight it, and then Shift-click to highlight the Hands sublayer.

Notice the current layer indicator (◥) shows the last highlighted layer as the active layer. The last layer you select determines the name and color of the merged layer.

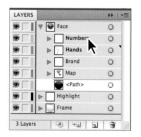

Shift-click to select the Numbers and Hands sublayers.

2 Choose Merge Selected from the Layers panel menu (▾≣) to merge the Numbers sublayer into the Hands sublayer.

The objects on the merged layers retain their original stacking order, and are added above the objects in the destination layer.

3 Now click the Highlight layer to select it, and then Shift-click the Frame layer.

4 Choose Merge Selected from the Layers panel menu (▾≣) to merge the objects from the Highlight layer into the Frame layer.

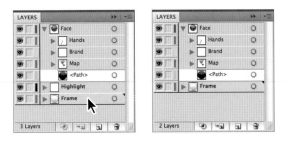

5 Choose File > Save.

To consolidate layers and groups

Merging and flattening layers are similar in that they both let you consolidate objects, groups, and sublayers into a single layer or group. With merging, you can select which items you want to consolidate; with flattening, all visible items in the artwork are consolidated in a single layer. With either option, the stacking order of the artwork remains the same, but other layer-level attributes, such as clipping masks, aren't preserved.

- To flatten layers, click the name of the layer into which you want to consolidate the artwork. Then select Flatten Artwork from the Layers panel menu.

—From Illustrator Help

Applying appearance attributes to layers

You can apply appearance attributes such as styles, effects, and transparency to layers, groups, and objects using the Layers panel. When an appearance attribute is applied to a layer, any object on that layer takes on that attribute. If an appearance attribute is applied only to a specific object on a layer, it affects only that object, not the entire layer. To learn more about working with Appearance attributes, see Lesson 12, "Applying Appearance Attributes and Graphic Styles."

You will apply an effect to an object on one layer. Then you'll copy that effect to another layer to change all objects on that layer.

1 In the Layers panel, collapse the Face layer and expand the Frame layer to reveal all its content.

2 Click to select the bottom <Path> sublayer in the Frame layer.

● **Note:** Clicking the target icon also selects the object(s) on the artboard.

3 Click the target icon (◎) to the right of the bottom <Path> sublayer name. Clicking the target icon indicates that you want to apply an effect, style, or transparency change.

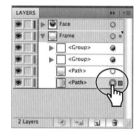

4 Choose Effect > Stylize > Drop Shadow from the Illustrator Effects. In the Drop Shadow dialog box, leave the settings at their default values, and click OK. A drop shadow appears on the outer edge of the clock.

● **Note:** There are two Stylize commands in the Effect menu. Choose the first Stylize menu command, which is in the Illustrator Effects.

Notice that the target icon (◉) is now shaded on the bottom <Path> sublayer, indicating that the object has appearance attributes applied to it.

5 Click the Appearance panel icon (◉) on the right side of the workspace to reveal the Appearance panel. If the Appearance panel isn't visible, choose Window > Appearance. Notice that Drop Shadow has been added to the list of appearance attributes for the selected object.

6 Change Stroke Weight to 0 pt in the Control panel.

7 Choose Select > Deselect.

You will now use the Layers panel to copy an appearance attribute into a layer and then edit it.

8 Click the Layers panel icon on the right side of the workspace to open the Layers panel. Click the arrow to the left of the Face layer to reveal its contents. If necessary, drag the bottom of the Layers panel down to display the entire list. Make sure that the triangles to the left of the Hands, Brand, and Map sublayers are toggled closed.

9 With the Selection tool (▶), click the clock hands in the artwork to select them.

10 Choose Locate Object from the Layers panel menu (▾≡). This selects and scrolls to the group (<Group> appears in the Layers panel) that contains the clock hands in the Layers panel. You may need to scroll in the Layers panel for the next step.

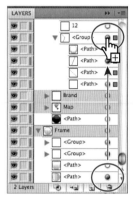

11 Alt-drag (Windows) or Option-drag (Mac OS) the shaded target icon of the bottom <Path> sublayer in the Frame layer to the target icon of the clock hands <Group> sublayer, without releasing the mouse button. The hand pointer with a plus sign indicates that the appearance is being copied.

● **Note:** You can drag and copy the shaded target icon to any layer or sublayer to apply the properties found in the Appearance panel.

12 When the target icon of the <Group> sublayer turns light gray, release the mouse button, and then the Alt or Option key. The drop shadow is now applied to the entire <Group> sublayer, as indicated by the shaded target icon.

Now you'll edit the drop shadow attribute for the type and clock hands to tone down the effect.

13 Click the triangle to the left of the <Group> sublayer under the Hands layer to toggle it closed.

14 In the Layers panel, click the target icon (◉) for the <Group> sublayer that contains the clock hands. This automatically selects the objects on the <Group> sublayer and deselects the object on the Frame layer.

15 In the Appearance panel, scrolling down if necessary, click the words Drop Shadow.

16 In the Drop Shadow dialog box, change X Offset, Y Offset and Blur to 3 pt. Click OK.

17 Choose Select > Deselect.

18 Choose File > Save.

For information on opening layered Photoshop files in Illustrator and working with layered Illustrator files in Photoshop, see Lesson 14, "Combining Illustrator CS4 Graphics with other Adobe applications."

Isolating layers

When a layer is in isolation mode, objects on that layer are isolated so that you can easily edit them without affecting other layers. Next you will enter isolation mode for a layer and make some simple edits.

1 Open the Layers panel by clicking the Layers panel icon.

2 Click the triangles to the left of the sublayers in the Layers panel to close them all. Make sure that the sublayers of the Face layer are showing.

3 Click to select the Map sublayer in the Layers panel.

4 Choose Enter Isolation Mode from the Layers panel menu (▾≡).

In isolation mode the contents of the Map sublayer appear on top of all the objects on the artboard. The rest of the content on the artboard is dimmed and locked.

The Layers panel now shows a layer called isolation mode and a sublayer that contains the map content.

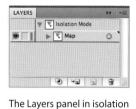

The Layers panel in isolation mode

5   Select the Selection tool (▶), and click the map on the artboard to select it.

6   Choose View >Smart Guides to deselect them temporarily.

7   Drag the map up so that the map is toward the top of the black inner circle.

8   Press Escape to exit isolation mode. Notice that the content is no longer locked and the Layers panel reveals all the layers and sublayers again.

9   Chose Select > Deselect.

10 Choose File > Save.

11 Choose File > Close.

Now that the artwork is complete, you may want to place all the layers into a single layer and delete the empty layers. This is called flattening artwork. Delivering finished artwork in a single layer file can prevent accidents, such as hiding layers and not printing parts of the artwork.

▶ **Tip:** To flatten specific layers without deleting hidden layers, select the layers you want to flatten, and then choose Merge Selected from the Layers panel menu.

For a complete list of shortcuts that you can use with the Layers panel, see "Keyboard Shortcuts" in Illustrator Help.

Exploring on your own

When you print a layered file, only the visible layers print in the same order in which they appear in the Layers panel—with the exception of template layers, which do not print even if they're visible. Template layers are locked, dimmed, and previewed. Objects on template layers neither print nor export.

Now that you know how to work with layers, try creating layered artwork by tracing an image on a template layer. For practice, you can use the bitmap photo image of a goldfish, or your own artwork or photo images.

1   Choose File > New to create a new file for your artwork.

2   Choose File > Place. In the dialog box, select the goldfish.eps file, located in the Lesson08 folder, in the Lessons folder on your hard disk; or locate your file containing the artwork or image you want to use as a template and click Place to add the placed file to Layer 1.

3   Create the template layer by choosing Template from the Layers panel menu or choosing Options for Layer 1 and selecting Template in the Layer Options dialog box.

4   Click the Create New Layer button to create a new layer on which to draw.

5   With Layer 2 active, use any drawing tool to trace over the template, creating new artwork.

6   Create additional layers to separate and edit various components of the new artwork.

7   If you want, delete the template layer after you finish to reduce the size of the file.

▶ **Tip:** You can create custom views of your artwork with some layers hidden and other layers showing, and display each view in a separate window. To create a custom view, choose View > New View. To display each view in a separate window, choose Window > New Window.

For information on custom views, search for "Use multiple windows and views" in Illustrator Help.

Review questions

1   Name two benefits of using layers when creating artwork.

2   How do you hide layers? How do you display individual layers?

3   Describe how to reorder layers in a file.

4   How can you lock layers?

5   What is the purpose of changing the selection color for a layer?

6   What happens if you paste a layered file into another file? Why is the Paste Remembers Layers option useful?

7   How do you move objects from one layer to another?

8   How do you create a layer clipping mask?

9   How do you apply an effect to a layer? How can you edit that effect?

10 What is the purpose of entering isolation mode?

Review answers

1   The benefits of using layers when creating artwork include: protecting artwork that you don't want to change, hiding artwork that you aren't working with so that it's not distracting, and controlling what prints.

2   To hide a layer, click to deselect the eye icon to the left of the layer name. Select the blank, leftmost column (the Visibility column) to show a layer.

3   You reorder layers by selecting a layer name in the Layers panel and dragging the layer to its new location. The order of layers in the Layers panel controls the document's layer order—topmost in the panel is frontmost in the artwork.

4   You can lock layers several different ways:

    •   You can click in the edit column to the left of the layer name. A lock icon appears, indicating that the layer is locked.

    •   You can choose Lock Others from the Layers panel menu to lock all layers but the active layer.

    •   You can hide a layer to protect it.

5 The selection color controls how selected anchor points and direction lines are displayed on a layer, and helps you identify the different layers in your document.

6 The paste commands paste layered files or objects copied from different layers into the active layer by default. The Paste Remembers Layers option keeps the original layers intact when the objects are pasted.

7 Select the objects you want to move, and drag the selected-art indicator (to the right of the target icon) to another layer in the Layers panel.

8 Create a clipping mask on a layer by selecting the layer and clicking the Make/Release Clipping Mask button. The topmost object in the layer becomes the clipping mask.

9 Click the target icon for the layer to which you want to apply an effect. Then choose an effect from the Effect menu. To edit the effect, make sure that the layer is selected, and then click the name of the effect in the Appearance panel. The effect's dialog box opens, and you can change the values.

10 Isolation mode isolates objects so that you can easily select and edit content on a single layer or sublayer.

9 BLENDING SHAPES AND COLORS

Lesson overview

In this lesson, you'll learn how to do the following:

- Create and save gradients.

- Add colors to a gradient.

- Adjust the direction of a gradient blend.

- Adjust the opacity of color in a gradient blend.

- Create smooth-color blends between objects.

- Blend the shapes of objects in intermediate steps.

- Modify a blend, its path, shape, and color.

 This lesson will take approximately an hour to complete. If needed, remove the previous lesson folder from your hard disk and copy the Lesson09 folder onto it.

Gradient fills are graduated blends of two or more colors. Using the Gradient tool and Gradient panel, you can create or modify a gradient fill. With the Blend tool, you can blend the shapes and colors of objects together into a new blended object, or a series of intermediate shapes.

Getting started

You'll explore various ways to create your own color gradients, and blend colors and shapes together using the Gradient panel and the Blend tool.

Before you begin, you'll restore the default preferences for Adobe Illustrator. Then you'll open the finished art file for this lesson to see what you'll create.

1 To ensure that the tools and panels function as described in this lesson, delete or rename the Adobe Illustrator CS4 preferences file. See "Restoring default preferences" on page 3.

2 Start Adobe Illustrator CS4.

● **Note:** If you have not already copied the resource files for this lesson onto your hard disk from the Lesson09 folder on the Adobe Illustrator CS4 Classroom in a Book CD, do so now. See "Copying the Classroom in a Book files" on page 2.

3 Choose File > Open, and open the L9end.ai file in the Lesson09 folder, located in the Lessons folder on your hard disk.

4 The text, background, steam, and coffee liquid are all filled with gradients. The objects that make up the colored beans on the coffee cup, and the coffee beans to the left of the cup have been blended to create new objects.

5 Choose View > Zoom Out to make the finished artwork smaller if you want to leave it on your screen as you work. (Use the Hand tool (✋) to move the artwork where you want it in the window.) If you don't want to leave the image open, choose File > Close.

To begin working, you'll open an existing art file.

6 Choose File > Open, and open the L9start.ai file in the Lesson09 folder, located in the Lessons folder on your hard disk.

7 Choose File > Save As, name the file coffee.ai, and select the Lesson09 folder in the Save In menu. Leave the Save As Type option set to Adobe Illustrator (*.AI) (Windows) or the Format option set to Adobe Illustrator (ai) (Mac OS), and click Save. In the Illustrator Options dialog box, leave the Illustrator options at their default settings, and click OK.

Working with gradients

A gradient fill is a graduated blend between two or more colors. You can create your own gradients, or you can use the gradients provided with Adobe Illustrator, edit them, and save them as swatches for later use.

You can use the Gradient panel (Window > Gradient) or the Gradient tool (▮) to apply, create, and modify gradients. In the Gradient panel, the Gradient Fill box displays the current gradient colors and gradient type. When you click the Gradient Fill box, the selected object is filled with the gradient. The Gradient menu (▮) lists the default and saved gradients.

A. Gradient Fill box	**F.** Location
B. Reverse colors	**G.** Gradient type
C. Gradient slider	**H.** Aspect Ratio
D. Color stop	**I.** Angle
E. Opacity	**J.** Delete Stop

By default, the panel includes a start and end color stop. You can add more color stops by clicking below the gradient slider. Double-clicking a color stop opens a panel where you can choose a color from swatches, color sliders, or the eyedropper.

In the Gradient panel, the left gradient stop under the gradient slider marks the starting color; the right gradient stop marks the ending color. A gradient stop is the point at which a gradient changes from one color to the next.

Creating and applying a linear gradient

To begin the lesson, you'll create a gradient fill for the background.

1   Choose Essentials from the workspace switcher in the Control panel.

2   Choose View > Fit Artboard In Window.

3   Using the Selection tool (▶), click to select the rounded rectangle in the background of the artboard.

The background is painted with a brown color fill and a red stroke, as shown in the Fill and Stroke boxes toward the bottom of the Tools panel. The Gradient box below the Fill and Stroke boxes shows the last used gradient. The default gradient fill is a black-and-white gradient. If you select a gradient-filled object or a gradient swatch in the Swatches panel, the gradient fill in the Tools panel changes to the fill of the selected object or swatch.

4 Click the Gradient box (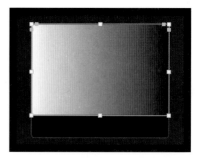) near the bottom of the Tools panel.

The default black-and-white gradient appears in the Fill box, and is applied to the fill of the selected background shape.

5 Choose Window > Gradient if the Gradient panel is not visible on the right side of the workspace.

6 In the Gradient panel, double-click the white, leftmost gradient stop to select the starting color of the gradient. The tip of the gradient stop appears darker to indicate that it's selected.

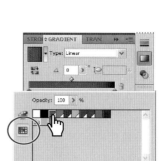

A new panel appears when you double-click a color stop. In this panel, you can change the color of the stop using swatches or the Color panel.

7 In the panel that appears below the Gradient panel, click the Swatches button (⊞). Click to select the swatch named Light Brown. Notice the gradient change on the artboard. Press Escape to close the panel with swatches.

8 Double-click the black color stop in the Gradient panel to edit the color.

▶ **Tip:** To move between text fields, press Tab. Press Enter or Return to apply the last value typed.

9 In the panel that appears below the Gradient panel, click the Color button (🖌) to open the Color panel. Choose CMYK from the Color panel menu (▾≡) if not already showing. Change the values to C=45, M=62, Y=82, and K=44. Press Enter or Return to return to the Gradient panel.

Next you'll save the gradient in the Swatches panel.

10 To save the gradient, click the Gradient menu button (⬐), and then click the Save To Swatches Library button (💾) at the bottom of the panel that appears.

The Gradient menu lists all the default and pre-saved gradients that you can choose. Next you will rename the gradient swatch in the Swatches panel.

▶ **Tip:** You can save a gradient by selecting an object with a gradient fill, clicking the Fill box in the Tools panel, and then clicking the New Swatch button (🔲) at the bottom of the Swatches panel.

11 Click the Swatches panel icon on the right side of the workspace to open the Swatches panel. In the Swatches panel, double-click New Gradient Swatch 1 to open the Swatch Options dialog box. Type Background in the Swatch Name field, and click OK.

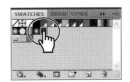

12 To display only gradient swatches in the Swatches panel, click the Show Swatch Kinds Menu button (⬐) at the bottom of the Swatches panel, and choose Show Gradient Swatches from the menu.

13 With the rectangle still selected in the artboard, try some of the different gradients by clicking them in the Swatches panel. Click the Background gradient you just saved to make sure it is applied before continuing to the next step.

Notice that some of the gradients have several colors. You'll learn how to make a gradient with multiple colors later in this lesson.

14 Choose Select > Deselect.

15 Choose File > Save.

Adjusting the direction and angle of a gradient blend

Once you have painted an object with a gradient fill, you can adjust the direction, origin, and the beginning and end points of a gradient using the Gradient tool. Now you'll adjust the gradient fill in the background shape.

1　Use the Selection tool (▶) to select the rectangle in the background.

2　Select the Gradient tool (▭) in the Tools panel.

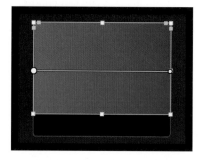

The Gradient tool works only on selected objects that are filled with a gradient. Notice the horizontal gradient bar that appears in the middle of the rectangle. The bar indicates the direction of the gradient, and the larger circle shows the starting point of the gradient, and the smaller circle is the ending point.

A gradient bar appears when you select the Gradient tool.

> **Note:** If you move the pointer to different areas of the gradient slider, the pointer may change. This indicates different functionality.

3　Hover the pointer over the gradient bar. It turns into the gradient slider, much like the one in the Gradient panel. You can use the gradient slider to edit gradient colors and more, without opening the Gradient panel.

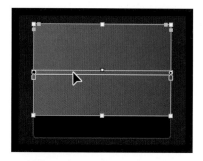

The gradient bar becomes the gradient slider.

4　With the Gradient tool, Shift-click and drag down from the top to the bottom of the rectangle to change the position and direction of the starting and ending colors of the gradient. Holding down the Shift key constrains the gradient to 45 degree angles.

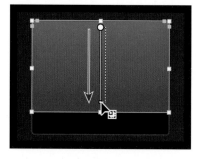

Practice changing the gradient in the rectangle. For example, drag in the rectangle to create a short gradient with distinct color blends; drag a longer distance outside the rectangle to create a longer gradient with more subtle color blends. You can also drag up to transpose the colors and reverse the direction of the blend.

Next you will rotate and reposition the gradient.

5 With the Gradient tool, position the
   pointer just off the bottom color stop in
   the gradient slider. A rotation icon (⟳)
   appears. Click and drag to the right to
   rotate the gradient in the rectangle.

   The gradient bar and the gradient rotate,
   but the gradient bar stays in the center of
   the rectangle when you release the
   mouse button.

Rotate the gradient.

Next you will change the rotation in the
Gradient panel.

6 Click the Gradient icon (▣) on the right side of the
   workspace to show the Gradient panel, if it isn't
   already showing. Change the rotation angle in the
   Angle field to -90 to return the gradient to vertical.
   Press Enter or Return to accept the value.

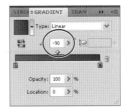

● **Note:** Entering the
gradient rotation in
the Gradient panel,
rather than adjusting it
directly on the artboard,
is useful when you want
to achieve consistency
and precision.

7 With the background rectangle still selected, choose
   Object > Lock > Selection.

8 Choose File > Save.

Creating a radial gradient

You can create linear or radial gradients. Both types of gradient have a starting and
ending color. With a radial gradient, the starting color (leftmost color stop) of the
gradient defines the center point of the fill, which radiates outward to the ending
color (rightmost color stop). Next you will create and edit a radial gradient.

9 Open the Layers panel by clicking the Layers panel
   icon on the right side of the workspace. Click to
   select the Visibility column to the left of the Coffee
   Cup layer (you may need to scroll in the
   Layers panel).

10 Use the Selection tool (▶) to select the brown-
   filled ellipse at the top of the coffee cup. This
   is the coffee in the cup.

11 Select the Zoom tool (◌) in the Tools panel
   and click the coffee cup several times to
   zoom in.

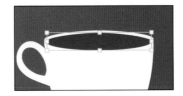

12 With the ellipse selected, click the Gradient box (■) at the bottom of the Tools panel to apply the last selected gradient (the Background gradient). The Gradient panel appears on the right side of the workspace.

The linear gradient that you created and saved earlier fills the ellipse. Next you will change the linear gradient to a radial gradient, and then edit it.

13 In the Gradient panel, choose Radial from the Type menu to convert the gradient to a radial gradient. Keep the ellipse selected.

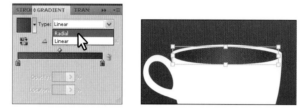

Changing colors and adjusting the gradient

Once you have filled an object with a gradient, you can use the Gradient tool to add or edit gradients, including changing the direction, color, and origin. You can also move the beginning and end points of a gradient.

Next you will use the Gradient tool to adjust the color of each color stop.

1 Select the Zoom tool (🔍) and click once to zoom into the ellipse at the top of the coffee cup.

2 With the Gradient tool (▭), hover over the gradient bar to reveal the gradient slider, which has a dashed circle around it, indicating that it is a radial gradient. Double-click the rightmost color stop to edit the color. In the panel that appears, click the Color button (🎨), if it's not already selected.

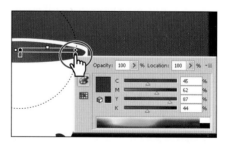

3 Shift-click and drag the Cyan slider a bit to the right to darken the color overall. Press Enter or Return to accept the change and close the panel.

Shift-drag the Cyan slider.

4 In the gradient slider on the artboard, double-click the leftmost color stop. In the panel that appears, click the Color button (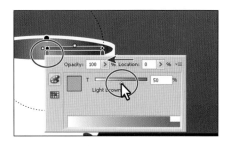) and change the tint to 50% by dragging the tint slider to the left (or by typing 50 into the Tint field). Press Enter or Return to accept the color change and close the panel.

Next you will change the aspect ratio, origin, and radius for the gradient.

5 In the Gradient panel, change Aspect Ratio to 20, and press Enter or Return to commit to the change.

Note: The aspect ratio is a value between 0.5 and 32767%. As the aspect ratio gets smaller, the ellipse flattens and widens.

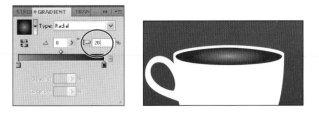

The aspect ratio changes a radial gradient into an elliptical gradient. This makes the coffee appear more realistic.

Next you will edit the aspect ratio using the Gradient tool.

6 With the Gradient tool, click and drag the top black circle on the dotted path up to change the aspect ratio. When you release the mouse button, notice the gradient in the ellipse on the artboard. If the Gradient panel isn't showing, click the Gradient panel icon. The Aspect Ratio is now larger than the 20 set previously.

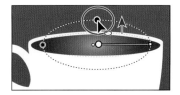

Make the aspect ratio larger.

7 Drag the top black circle on the dotted path back down so that the Aspect Ratio is roughly 14% in the Gradient panel.

Next you will drag the gradient slider to reposition the gradient in the ellipse.

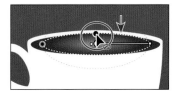

Make the aspect ratio smaller.

8 With the Gradient tool, click and drag the gradient slider down a little bit to move the gradient in the ellipse.

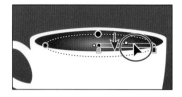

9 Choose Edit > Undo Gradient to move it back.

10 Choose File > Save.

You will now change the radius and origin of the gradient.

▶ **Tip:** To change the radius, you can also drag the second color stop to the right or left.

11 With the Gradient tool, hover the pointer over the ellipse to reveal the gradient slider. Click and drag the black circle on the left of the dotted path to the right to make the radius smaller. This shortens the transition between the leftmost and rightmost color stops.

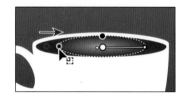

Try dragging the black circle on the left of the dotted path to the left and to the right to see the effect on the gradient. Make sure to drag it to match the figure above once you are done experimenting. Next you'll change the origin of the gradient.

12 With the Gradient tool, click and drag the small white dot to the left of the leftmost color stop to the left. This dot repositions the center of the gradient (the leftmost color stop) without moving the entire gradient bar, and changes the radius of the gradient.

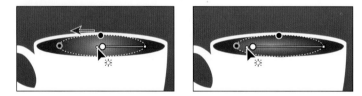

Every gradient has at least two color stops. By editing the color mix of each stop and by adding color stops either in the Gradient panel or using the Gradient tool, you can create custom gradients.

Now you'll add a third color to the coffee ellipse, and then you'll edit it.

13 With the Gradient tool, hover the pointer over the bottom edge of the gradient slider. The pointer changes to a white arrow with a plus sign (▶₊). Click just below the gradient slider in the middle to add another color stop.

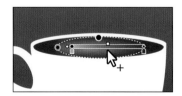

14 Double-click the new color stop to edit the color. In the panel that appears, click the Swatches button (▦), and select the dark brown swatch (C=46, M=72, Y=87, K=44). Press Enter or Return to accept the color change and close the panel.

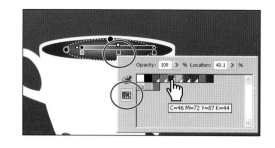

Now that you have three color stops, you will adjust the colors by reordering them.

15 With the Gradient tool, click and drag the leftmost color stop to the right, stopping before the middle color stop.

16 Drag the middle color stop all the way to the left end of the gradient slider to swap the two colors.

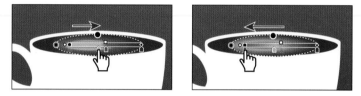

Drag the leftmost color stop to the right, and the middle color stop to the left.

17 Choose Select > Deselect, and then File > Save.

Applying gradients to multiple objects

You can apply a gradient to multiple objects by selecting all the objects, applying a gradient color, and then dragging across the objects with the Gradient tool. Now you'll paint type that has been converted to path outlines with a linear gradient fill, and then edit the colors in it.

1 Choose View > Fit Artboard In Window.

2 Click the Layers panel icon to open the Layers panel. Click to select the Visibility column to the left of the Logo layer (you may need to scroll up in the Layers panel). Click the eye icon (👁) to the left of the Background layer to deselect visibility for that layer.

● **Note:** The text, coffee beans, and ellipse are still showing.

3 Use the Selection tool (➤) and click to select the text Mike's Coffee.

The Mike's Coffee type has already been converted to path outlines so that you can fill it with a gradient.

● **Note:** To convert type to path outlines, select it with the Selection tool, and choose Type > Create Outlines. See Lesson 7, "Working with Type," for more information.

The Mike's Coffee shapes are grouped together. By grouping the letters, you can fill each letter with the same gradient at once. Grouping them also lets you edit the gradient fill globally.

● **Note:** Notice that each letter is filled with the gradient independently. You can adjust this with the Gradient tool.

4 Click the Gradient panel icon (▣) on the right side of the workspace to open the Gradient panel. Click the Gradient menu button (▯), and then select Linear Gradient from the Gradient menu. This applies a white-to-black gradient.

5 In the Gradient panel, double-click the leftmost color stop to select it so that you can adjust the starting color of the gradient. Click the Swatches button (▦), and select the Light Red swatch. Press Enter or Return to accept the color change and close the panel.

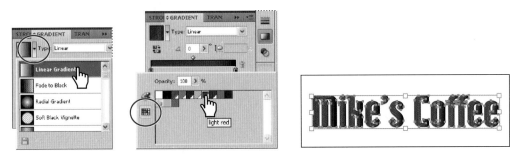

Now you'll adjust the gradient on the letters so that it blends across all the letters and add intermediate colors to the gradient to create a fill with multiple blends between colors.

6 Select the Gradient tool (▣) in the Tools panel. Shift-click and drag across the letters from top to bottom to apply the gradient to all the letters.

Next you will add a color to the gradient by adding a color stop. When you add a color stop, a new diamond appears above the gradient slider to mark the color's new midpoint.

7 In the Gradient panel, click the color bar below the gradient slider to add a stop between the other gradient stops.

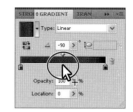

8 Double-click the new color stop to edit the color. In the panel that appears, click the Swatches button and select the Dark Red swatch. Press Enter or Return to close the panel.

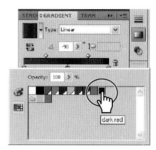

9 To adjust the midpoint between colors, drag the diamond icon between the dark red and black color stops to the right. This gives the gradient more red and less black.

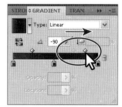

● **Note:** You can delete a color in a gradient by dragging its gradient stop downward and out of the Gradient panel.

Next you will reverse the gradient colors.

10 With the text still selected, click the Reverse Gradient button (⊞) in the Gradient panel. The leftmost and rightmost color stops switch positions. You can also reverse the colors in a gradient by drawing in the opposite direction with the Gradient tool, among other ways.

Another way to apply a color to a gradient is to sample the color from the artwork using the Eyedropper tool or drag a color swatch onto a color stop.

11 Click the center gradient stop in the Gradient panel. Select the Eyedropper tool (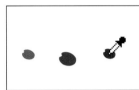) in the Tools panel. In the artwork, Shift-click the coffee bean on the far right of the coffee cup.

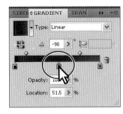

Shift-clicking with the Eyedropper tool applies the color sample to the selected gradient box in the gradient rather than replacing the entire gradient with the color in the selected artwork. Try sampling other areas of the artwork, finishing with the purple color in the coffee bean.

Next you'll save the new gradient.

12 Click the Gradient menu button (▤), and then click the Save To Swatches Library button (▤) at the bottom of the panel that appears.

13 Open the Layers panel by clicking the Layers panel icon on the right side of the workspace. Click to select the Visibility column to the left of the Background layer.

14 Choose Select > Deselect, and then File > Save.

Adding transparency to gradients

You can define the opacity of colors used in gradients. By specifying different opacity values for the different color stops in your gradient, you can create gradients that fade in or out and reveal or hide underlying images. Next you will create a mirror reflection of the coffee cup and apply a gradient that fades to transparent.

1   Using the Selection tool (▶), click to select the coffee cup.

2   Choose Object > Transform > Transform Each. In the Transform Each dialog box, click the bottom, middle point of the reference point locator (▦). Select Reflect X and change Angle to 180. Select Preview to see the changes. Click Copy to reflect, rotate, and copy the coffee cup.

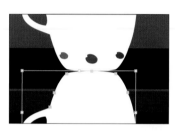

3   With the copy of the coffee cup still selected, open the Gradient panel by clicking the Gradient panel icon. Click the Gradient menu button (▦), and then select Linear Gradient. This fills the coffee cup with a white-to-black gradient.

Select the linear gradient.

▶ **Tip:** There are two gradients with transparency, Fade to Black and Soft Black Vignette. These can be great starting points for fading to transparency.

4   In the Angle field, change the value to -90. Double-click the rightmost color stop (the black color). In the panel that appears, click the Swatches button (▦) and select the white color swatch.

● **Note:** It may seem strange to create a gradient from white to white. Next, you will change the transparency of the rightmost color stop to 0% so that the coffee cup appears to fade away.

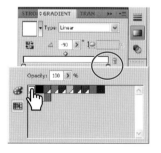

5 Press Enter or Return to accept the color change and return to the Gradient panel.

6 Click the rightmost color stop. Type 0 in the Opacity field or click the arrow to the right of the field and drag the slider all the way to the left. Press Enter or Return.

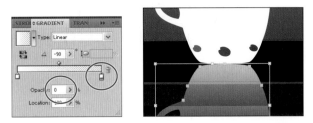

7 Click the leftmost color stop in the Gradient panel and change Opacity to 70.

8 Select the Gradient tool (▇) in the Tools panel. Click and drag from the top of the selected coffee cup reflection to just above the outer edge of the dark red rectangle in the background.

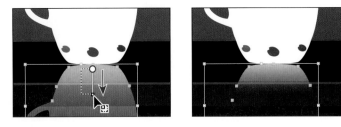

Working with gradients and transparency can lead to a lot of creative fun. Try changing the opacity for the color stops in the coffee cup and changing the direction and distance with the Gradient tool.

9 Choose Select > Deselect.

10 Choose File > Save.

Working with blended objects

You can blend two distinct objects to create and distribute shapes evenly between two objects. The two shapes you blend can be the same or different. You can also blend between two open paths to create a smooth transition of color between objects, or you can combine blends of colors and objects to create color transitions in the shape of a particular object.

When you create a blend, the blended objects are treated as one object, called a blend object. If you move one of the original objects, or edit the anchor points of the original object, the blend changes accordingly. You can also expand the blend to divide it into distinct objects.

Blend between two of the same shape

Blend between same shape, different colors

Blend between two different shapes and colors

Blend along a path

Smooth color blend between two stroked lines

Blend options for the Blend tool

There are three types of spacing options for a blend: Specified Steps, Specified Distance, and Smooth Blend. Each is explained below:

- **Specified Steps**: Controls the number of steps between the start and end of the blend.

- **Specified Distance**: Controls the distance between the steps in the blend. The distance specified is measured from the edge of one object to the corresponding edge on the next object (for example, from the rightmost edge of one object to the rightmost edge of the next).

- **Smooth Color**: Lets Illustrator auto-calculate the number of steps for the blends. If objects are filled or stroked with different colors, the steps are calculated to provide the optimum number of steps for a smooth color transition. If the objects contain identical colors, or if they contain gradients or patterns, the number of steps is based on the longest distance between the bounding box edges of the two objects.

The Orientation options determine the orientation of blended objects.

- **Align to Page**: Orients the blend perpendicular to the x axis of the page.

- **Align to Path**: Orients the blend perpendicular to the path.

—From Illustrator Help

Creating a blend with specified steps

Now you'll use the Blend tool to create a series of blended shapes using three different-colored shapes that make up the design on the coffee cup by specifying the number of steps in the blend.

1 Double-click the Blend tool (⊞) in the Tools panel to open the Blend Options dialog box.

2 Choose Specified Steps from the Spacing menu, and change the number of steps to 2. Click OK.

▶ **Tip:** You can also make a blend by selecting objects and choosing Object > Blend > Make.

3 Using the Blend tool, hover over the coffee bean on the far left until the pointer has an X (⊞ₓ), and then click. Then, hover over the red coffee bean in the middle until the pointer displays a plus sign (⊞₊), indicating that you can add an object to the blend. Click the red coffee bean to add it. There is now a blend between these two objects.

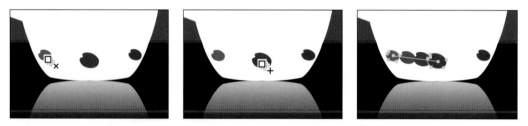

4 Click the rightmost coffee bean with the Blend tool pointer (with the plus sign) to add it to the blend and complete the blended path.

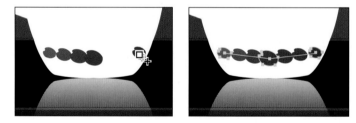

● **Note:** To end the current path and continue blending other objects on a separate path, click the Blend tool in the Tools panel first, and then click the other objects.

Modifying the blend

Now you'll modify the blend object using the Blend Options dialog box. You'll also edit the shape of the path, called the spine, that the coffee beans blend along using the Convert Anchor Point tool.

1   With the blended beans still selected, choose Object > Blend > Blend Options. In the Blend Options dialog box, change the Specified Steps to 1, and click OK.

Tip: To edit the blend options for objects, you can also select the blend, and then double-click the Blend tool.

2   Choose Select > Deselect.

3   Select the Direct Selection tool (⟨) in the Tools panel. Click the center of the red, center coffee bean to select that anchor point. In the Control panel, click the Convert Selected Anchor Points To Smooth button (⬛) to smooth the curve. With the Direct Selection tool, drag the anchor point down.

Note: You are editing the spine. Any way you edit the spine, the blend objects will follow.

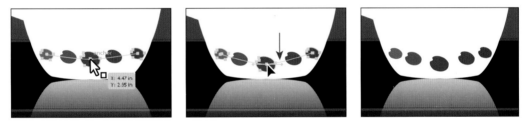

To edit the spine of a blend, select the anchor point, convert it to a smooth point, and drag.

4   Choose Select > Deselect.

Tip: A quick way to reshape the spine of a blend is to wrap it around another path or object. Select the blend, select the other object or path, and then choose Object > Blend > Replace Spine.

You can modify the blend instantly by changing the shape, color, or position of the original objects. Next you will edit the color and position of the middle, red coffee bean and see the effect on the blend.

Tip: When you converted the bottom anchor point to a smooth point, the spacing changed between the coffee beans. To even out the spacing, convert the leftmost and rightmost anchor points on the spine to smooth points and then adjust the direction lines with the Direct Selection tool.

5   Select the Zoom tool (🔍) in the Tools panel and drag a marquee across the beans to zoom into them.

6 With the Selection tool (▶), click the blended objects to select them.

7 Double-click the red coffee bean in the center of the blend to enter isolation mode. This temporarily ungroups the blended objects and lets you edit each original bean (not the beans created by blending), as well as the spine. Click to select the red coffee bean.

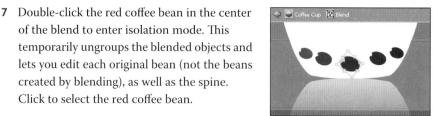

8 Choose View > Outline to see the pieces of the blend. Choose View > Preview to see the filled objects again.

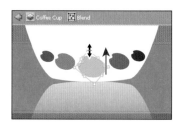

9 Change the fill color of the selected bean to light green (C=48, M=0, Y=62, K=0) in the Control panel. Notice that the rest of the blend changes.

10 With the Selection tool, press Shift+Alt (Windows) or Shift+Option (Mac OS), and click and drag a corner bounding point of the selected coffee bean to make the bean bigger.

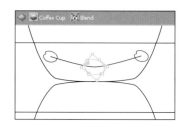

Try changing the shape of the coffee bean by rotating it, changing the shape with the Direct Selection tool (▷), and more.

11 Press Escape to exit isolation mode.

12 With the Selection tool, click to select the blended objects again. Choose Object > Blend > Reverse Spine. This reverses the order of the beans. Keep the blended objects selected.

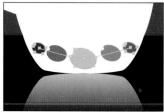

The blended objects are considered a single blend object. If you need to edit all the coffee beans (including the beans that the blend created), you can expand the blend. Expanding the blend converts the blend to individual objects. You can no longer edit the blend as a single object because they become a group of beans. Now you will expand the beans.

13 Choose Object > Blend > Expand. With the beans still selected, notice the word Group on the left side of the Control panel. The blend is now a group of individual shapes that you can edit independently.

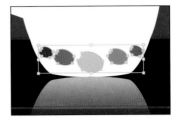

14 Choose Select > Deselect.

15 Choose File > Save.

Creating smooth color blends

You can choose several options for blending the shapes and colors of objects to create a new object. When you choose the Smooth Color blend option, Illustrator combines the shapes and colors of the objects into many intermediate steps, creating a smooth graduated blend between the original objects.

Now you'll combine two shapes for a coffee bean into a smooth color blend.

1 Chose View > Fit Artboard In Window.

2 Open the Layers panel, and click to select the Visibility column to the left of the Blends layer and the Coffee Beans layer. You are going to blend colors to make the coffee bean look more realistic.

3 Click the eye icon (👁) to deselect visibility for the Coffee Beans layer to make it easier to see the two objects you will blend next.

4 Select the Zoom tool (🔍) in the Tools panel and drag a marquee around the lines that appear to the left of the coffee cup.

5 Double-click the Blend tool (🔧) in the Tools panel to open the Blend Options dialog box.

6 Choose Smooth Color from the Spacing menu to set up the blend options, which remain set until you change them. Click OK.

▶ **Tip:** To release, or remove, a blend from the original objects, select the blend and choose Object > Blend > Release.

Next you'll create a smooth color blend from the two lines to the left of the coffee cup. Both objects have a stroke and no fill. Objects that have strokes blend differently than those that have no stroke.

7 With the Blend tool pointer that has an X (⊡ₓ), click the top line with the Blend tool pointer. Click the bottom line with the Blend tool pointer that has a plus sign (⊡₊) to add it to the blend. There is a smooth blend between the lines.

8 Choose Select > Deselect.

Tip: Creating smooth color blends between paths can be tricky in certain situations. For instance, if the lines intersect or the lines are too curved, unexpected results can occur.

When you make a smooth color blend between objects, Illustrator automatically calculates the number of intermediate steps necessary to create a smooth transition between the objects. You can apply a smooth color blend to objects, and then edit it. Next you will edit the paths that make up the blend.

9 Using the Selection tool (▶), double-click the color blend to enter isolation mode. Click to select one of the paths, and change the stroke color in the Control panel to any color you want. Notice how the colors are blended. Choose Edit > Undo Apply Swatch to return to the original stroke color.

10 Double-click away from the blend paths to exit isolation mode.

11 Open the Layers panel and click to select visibility for the Coffee Beans layer and the Steam layer to make those objects visible on the artboard.

12 To complete the bean, select the blended paths with the Selection tool and choose Edit > Copy, and then Edit > Paste to paste a copy of the blend.

13 Move the blend to the bottom part of the same coffee bean, to the left of the coffee cup.

14 Select the Rotate tool (↻) in the Tools panel. Click and drag to rotate the blend so that it fits into the bottom part of the bean. You will need to switch to the Selection tool to move the blend into position.

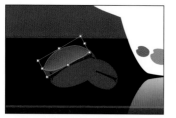

Copy the blend.

Paste and move into position.

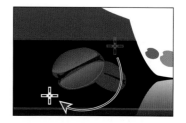

Rotate and position the blend.

15 Choose View > Fit Artboard In Window.

16 Choose Select > Deselect, and then File > Save.

Exploring on your own

There are many ways to be creative with gradients and blends. To explore more, you will create a blend for coffee steam, and then create a new document for a more complex path that you will blend.

1   With the Steam layer visible, select the steam on the artboard with the Selection tool.

2   Open the Gradient panel and select Fade To Black from the Gradient menu (🔽).

3   Select the Gradient tool (▭) in the Tools panel and hover the pointer over the steam. Click and drag from the top of the steam to the bottom of the steam to change the direction of the gradient.

4   Add a color stop so that three appear in the gradient slider.

5   Change the color of each color stop to white by double-clicking each color stop using the Gradient tool. Change Opacity to 10 for the topmost color stop and 5 for the bottommost color stop.

Try changing the color and opacity of each color stop.

Next you'll create a more complex blend.

1   Choose File > New to create a new document and draw a straight line using the Line Segment tool.

2   Select the line, remove the fill, paint the stroke with a color, and increase the stroke weight to 20 pt.

3   If the Stroke panel is not showing, choose Window > Stroke. With the line selected, select the Dashed Line option. Type 25 in the first dash field, and press Enter or Return.

4   Choose Object > Path > Outline Stroke.

Notice that the stroke color and fill color values have switched, so now you can fill the object with a gradient.

5   Fill the object with a gradient of your choice.

6   Copy and paste the object, moving them apart with the Selection tool. Double-click the Blend tool (🖌) in the Tools panel. Choose Smooth Color in the Blend Options dialog box. Click each of the two objects with the Blend tool to create the blend. Practice editing the individual objects in the blend.

Review questions

1 What is a gradient fill?

2 Name two ways to fill a selected object with a gradient.

3 What is the difference between a gradient fill and a blend?

4 How do you adjust the blend between colors in a gradient?

5 Name two ways you can add colors to a gradient.

6 How do you adjust the direction of a gradient?

7 Describe two ways to blend the shapes and colors of objects.

8 What is the difference between selecting a smooth color blend and specifying the number of steps in a blend?

9 How do you adjust the shapes or colors in the blend? How do you adjust the path of the blend?

Review answers

1 A gradient fill is a graduated blend between two or more colors, or tints of the same color.

2 Select an object and do one of the following:
   - Click the Gradient box in the Tools panel to fill an object with the default white-to-black gradient or with the last selected gradient.
   - Click a gradient swatch in the Swatches panel.
   - Make a new gradient by clicking a gradient swatch in the Swatches panel and mixing your own in the Gradient panel.
   - Use the Eyedropper tool to sample a gradient from an object in your artwork, and then apply it to the selected object.

3 The difference between a gradient fill and a blend is the way that colors combine together—colors blend together within a gradient fill and between objects in a blend.

4 You drag the diamond icons or color stops of the gradient in the Gradient panel.

5 In the Gradient panel, click beneath the gradient bar to add a gradient stop to the gradient. Then use the Color panel to mix a new color, or in the Swatches panel

Alt-click (Windows) or Option-click (Mac OS) a color swatch. You can select the Gradient tool in the Tools panel and position the pointer over the gradient-filled object. Click beneath the gradient slider that appears to add a color stop.

6   You click and drag with the Gradient tool to adjust the direction of a gradient. Dragging a long distance changes colors gradually; dragging a short distance makes the color change more abrupt. You can also rotate the gradient using the Gradient tool, change the radius, aspect ratio, and starting point.

7   You can blend the shapes and colors of objects by doing one of the following:

*   Clicking each object with the Blend tool to create a blend of intermediate steps between the objects according to preset blend options.

*   Selecting the objects and choosing Object > Blend > Blend Options to set the number of intermediate steps, and then choosing Object > Blend > Make to create the blend.

Objects that have painted strokes blend differently than those with no strokes.

8   When you choose Smooth Color blend, Illustrator automatically calculates the number of intermediate steps necessary to create a seamlessly smooth blend between the selected objects. Specifying the number of steps lets you determine how many intermediate steps are visible in the blend. You can also specify the distance between intermediate steps in the blend.

9   You can use the Direct Selection tool to select and adjust the shape of an original object, thus changing the shape of the blend. You can change the colors of the original objects to adjust the intermediate colors in the blend. Use the Convert Anchor Point tool to change the shape of the path, or spine, of the blend by dragging anchor points or direction handles on the spine.

10 WORKING WITH BRUSHES

Lesson overview

In this lesson, you'll learn how to do the following:

- Work with the Blob Brush tool and the Eraser tool.
- Use the four brush types: Art, Calligraphic, Pattern, and Scatter.
- Change the brush color and adjust brush settings.
- Create new brushes from Adobe Illustrator artwork.
- Apply brushes to paths created with drawing tools.
- Work with the Scribble effect.

 This lesson takes approximately an hour to complete. If needed, remove the previous lesson folder from your hard disk and copy the Lesson10 folder onto it.

The variety of brush types in Adobe Illustrator CS4 lets you create a myriad of effects simply by painting or drawing on paths. You can choose from the Blob brush, as well as Art, Calligraphic, Pattern, and Scatter brushes, or create new ones based on your artwork. Use the Paintbrush tool or the drawing tools to apply brushes to artwork.

Getting started

In this lesson, you learn how to work with the Blob Brush tool and the Eraser tool. You also learn how to use the four brush types in the Brushes panel, including changing brush options and creating your own brushes. Before you begin, you need to restore the default preferences for Adobe Illustrator CS4. Then you open the finished art file for the first part of this lesson to see the finished artwork.

1 To ensure that the tools and panels function as described in this lesson, delete or deactivate (by renaming) the Adobe Illustrator CS4 preferences file. See "Restoring default preferences" on page 3.

2 Start Adobe Illustrator CS4.

● **Note:** If you have not already copied the resource files for this lesson onto your hard disk from the Lesson10 folder on the Adobe Illustrator CS4 Classroom in a Book CD, do so now. See "Copying the Classroom in a Book files" on page 2.

3 Choose File > Open, and open the L10end.ai file in the Lesson10 folder, located in the Lessons folder on your hard disk.

4 If you like, choose View > Zoom Out to make the finished artwork smaller, and then adjust the window size and leave the artwork on your screen as you work. (Use the Hand tool (🖐) to move the artwork where you want it in the window.) If you don't want to leave the image open, choose File > Close.

To begin working, you'll open an existing art file.

5 Choose File > Open to open the L10start.ai file in the Lesson10 folder in the Lessons folder on your hard disk.

6 Choose File > Save As. In the Save As dialog box, name the file Check_logo.ai, and choose the Lesson10 folder. Leave the Save As Type option set to Adobe Illustrator (*.AI) (Windows) or the Format option set to Adobe Illustrator (ai) (Mac OS), and click Save. In the Illustrator Options dialog box, leave the Illustrator options at their default settings, and click OK.

Working with the Blob Brush tool

You can use the Blob Brush tool to paint filled shapes that intersect and merge with other shapes of the same color. Unlike the Paintbrush tool, which lets you create open paths, with the Blob Brush tool, you can draw with Paintbrush tool artistry, but create a closed shape with a fill only (no stroke) that you can edit with the Eraser or Blob Brush tool. Shapes that have a stroke cannot be edited with the Blob Brush tool.

Path created with the
Paintbrush tool

Shape created with the
Blob Brush tool

Drawing with the Blob Brush tool

First you use the Blob Brush tool to create shapes to add to the check logo.

1 Choose Essentials from the workspace switcher in the Control panel.

2 Select the Zoom tool (Q) in the Tools panel and click three times above the letter "e" to zoom in.

3 Change the fill color to black and the stroke color to None (⟋) in the Control panel.

4 Select the Blob Brush tool (🖌) in the Tools panel.

5 Click the Appearance panel icon (◉) on the right side of the workspace. Click the Add New Effect button (*fx,*) at the bottom of the Appearance panel and choose Stylize > Drop Shadow from the Illustrator Effects.

6 In the Drop Shadow dialog box, change Opacity to 40%, X Offset to 3 pt, Y Offset to 3 pt, and Blur to 2 pt. Click OK.

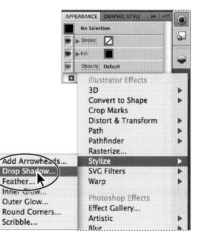

● **Note:** To learn more about working with the Appearance panel, see Lesson 12, "Applying Appearance Attributes and Graphic Styles."

● **Note:** When drawing with the Blob Brush tool, if a fill and stroke are set before drawing, the stroke becomes the fill of the shape made by the Blob Brush tool. If only a fill is set before drawing, it becomes the fill of the shape created.

7 Above the letter "e" in the word "check" click and drag down, then up and to the right to create a check mark. Notice that any appearance properties set before drawing with the Blob Brush tool, such as a drop shadow, are applied.

8 Select the Selection tool (▶) in the Tools panel and click to select the shape you just drew.

● **Note:** When you draw with the Blob Brush tool, you create filled, closed shapes. Those shapes can contain any type of fill, including gradients, solid colors, patterns, and more.

9 With the shape selected, click the Fill color box to the right of the Fill attribute name in the Appearance panel and select the orange color (C=0, M=50, Y=100, K=0). Make sure that the stroke color is still set to None.

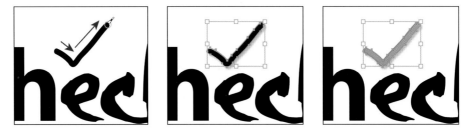

10 Choose Select > Deselect. Next you will edit the check mark shape you created to give it a more stylized look.

Editing with the Blob Brush and Eraser tools

1 Select the Blob Brush tool in the Tools panel. In the Appearance panel menu (▾≣), deselect New Art Has Basic Appearance.

● **Note:** For the Blob Brush tool to function properly in the next steps, make sure that the orange color is still selected as the fill color in the Control panel and that the stroke color is set to None (◿).

2 With the Blob Brush tool, click and drag across the middle of the check mark to thicken the angle.

You can only use the Blob Brush tool to edit shapes that have a stroke color of None. To edit shapes with the Blob Brush tool, the appearances of the Blob Brush tool need to match those of the shape to be edited.

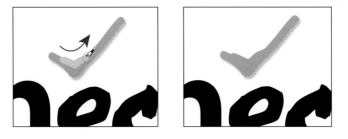

The Blob Brush tool pointer contains a circle that indicates the diameter of the brush. Next you will change the brush size to help edit the check mark.

3 Press the left bracket key ([) several times to decrease the size of the brush.

4 With the Blob Brush tool, draw across the check mark a few more times to give it a rougher look and to fill in the middle. Precision is not necessary, because you are trying to give the check mark a rough, hand-drawn look. See the figure for some guidance.

Next, you will use the Eraser tool to help mold the shape and correct any changes you don't like.

> **Tip:** As you draw with the Blob Brush tool, it is recommended to use shorter strokes and release the mouse button often. You can undo the edits that you make, but if you draw in one long stroke without releasing the mouse button, undo removes the entire stroke.

The check mark now has a rougher look.

> **Tip:** You can also set the brush size by double-clicking the Blob Brush tool, and changing the size in the Blob Brush Tool Options dialog box.

5 With the Selection tool (▶), click to select the check mark shape. Select the Eraser tool (◢) in the Tools panel.

Selecting the shape before the Eraser tool limits the Eraser tool, so that it erases only the selected shape. Otherwise, the Eraser tool erases anything on the artboard that is not hidden or locked. This next step is going to be a little more free-form, so take it slowly and remember that you can always stop and undo.

> **Tip:** The Blob Brush and the Eraser tools work well together. Using these tools is a more free-form approach to creating organic shapes than creating with the Pen tool, for instance.

6 With the Eraser tool, drag along the two ends of the check mark so that they come to more of a point (see figure for guidance).

7 Switch to the Blob Brush tool and add more area to the bottom, right of the check mark. Using the Eraser tool, erase the top end so that it has a bit of curve to the right.

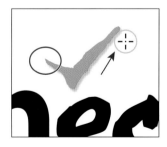 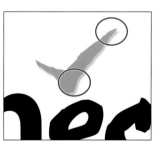

> **Tip:** The Blob Brush tool and the Eraser tool brush diameters can both be changed by pressing the left bracket ([) to make the brush smaller or the right bracket (]) to make the brush bigger.

8 Choose File > Save.

Merge paths with the Blob Brush tool

Besides drawing and editing with the Blob brush tool, you can use it to intersect and merge shapes of the same color. Next you will merge the "c" and "h" letters.

1 With the Selection tool (▶), click to select "ch" on the artboard. Choose Type > Create Outlines to turn the text into paths.

   The Blob Brush tool draws free-form shapes, or intersects and merges shapes. You must convert the text to paths to edit it with the Blob Brush tool.

2 With the letters still selected, choose Object > Ungroup.

3 With the Selection tool, drag a marquee across all the letters to select them, making sure to exclude the check mark.

4 In the Appearance panel, click the Add New Effect button (*fx*,) at the bottom, and choose Stylize > Drop Shadow from the Illustrator Effects. In the Drop Shadow dialog box, change Opacity to 35%, X Offset to 3 pt, Y Offset to 3 pt, and Blur to 2 pt. Click OK.

5 Choose Select > Deselect.

6 With the Selection tool, Shift-click to select the "c" and "h." In the Appearance panel, make sure that the fill color is black, the stroke color is None, and the Drop Shadow effect is applied. If Mixed Appearances is listed in the panel, you cannot merge the letters with the Blob Brush tool. Choose Select > Deselect.

7 Double-click the Blob Brush tool (✎) in the Tools panel. In the Blob Brush Tool Options dialog box, change Smoothness to 30, and Size to 20 pt. Click OK.

8 With the Blob Brush tool selected in the Tools panel, make sure that you see the same attributes as the letter shapes (with the drop shadow) in the Appearance panel. Click and drag from the bottom part of the "c" to the right to connect the "c" shape with the "h" shape.

9 With the Selection tool, drag a marquee across the "c" and "h" to see that the final shape selected is merged.

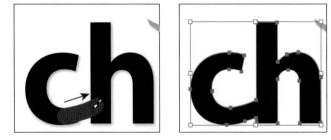

10 Choose Select > Deselect, and then File > Save.

> **Note:** Objects merged with the Blob Brush tool need to have the same appearance attributes and no stroke, be on the same layer or group, and adjacent to each other in the stacking order.

> **Note:** Notice that the drop shadow is applied to the entire shape as you draw and edit.

Experiment with the letters in the logo using the Blob Brush tool and the Eraser tool together to give the letters a more distressed look. Try matching the first "c" with the second "c".

11 When you are finished experimenting, choose File > Save, and then File > Close.

Blob Brush tool options

Double-clicking the Blob Brush tool in the Tools panel will allow you to set the following options:

- **Keep Selected:** When you draw a merged path, all paths are selected and remain selected as you continue to draw. This option is useful for viewing all paths that are included in the merged path. When you select this option, the Selection Limits Merge option is disabled.

- **Selection Limits Merge:** If artwork is selected, the Blob Brush merges only with the selected artwork. If nothing is selected, the Blob Brush merges with any matching artwork.

- **Fidelity:** Controls how far you have to move your mouse or stylus before Illustrator adds a new anchor point to the path. For example, a Fidelity value of 2.5 means that tool movements of less than 2.5 pixels aren't registered. Fidelity can range from 0.5 to 20 pixels; the higher the value, the smoother and less complex the path.

- **Smoothness:** Controls the amount of smoothing that Illustrator applies when you use the tool. Smoothness can range from 0% to 100%; the higher the percentage, the smoother the path.

- **Size:** Determines the size of the brush.

- **Angle:** Determines the angle of rotation for the brush. Drag the arrowhead in the preview, or enter a value in the Angle text box.

- **Roundness:** Determines roundness of the brush. Drag a black dot in the preview away from or toward the center, or enter a value in the Roundness text box. The higher the value, the greater the roundness.

—From Illustrator Help

Working with brushes

Using brushes, you can decorate paths with patterns, figures, textures, or angled strokes. You can modify the brushes provided with Adobe Illustrator CS4 and create your own brushes. Four types of brushes appear in the Brushes panel: Art, Calligraphy, Pattern, and Scatter.

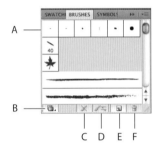

A. Brushes

B. Brush Libraries menu

C. Remove Brush Stroke

D. Options Of Selected Object

E. New Brush

F. Delete Brush

Using Art brushes

Art brushes, which include arrow brushes, decorative brushes, artistic brushes, and others, stretch artwork evenly along a path. Art brushes include strokes resembling various graphic media, such as the Charcoal-Feather brush.

You apply brushes to paths using the Paintbrush tool or drawing tools. To apply brushes with the Paintbrush tool, you choose a brush from the Brushes panel and draw in the artwork. The brush is applied directly to the paths as you draw. To apply brushes using a drawing tool, you draw in the artwork with a drawing tool, select a path in the artwork, and then choose a brush in the Brushes panel. The brush is applied to the selected path.

You can change the color, size, and other features of a brush. You can also edit paths after brushes are applied.

The start file has locked paths that you can use to create and align your artwork. In this section, you'll use the Charcoal-Feather brush to draw the trunk and limbs of a tree.

1 Choose File > Open, and open the L10end2.ai file in the Lesson10 folder, located in the Lessons folder on your hard disk.

2 If you like, choose View > Zoom Out to make the finished artwork smaller. If you don't want to leave the image open, choose File > Close.

To begin working, you'll open an existing art file set up with guides to draw the artwork.

3 Choose File > Open to open the L10start2.ai file in the Lesson10 folder in the Lessons folder on your hard disk.

4 Choose File > Save As. In the Save As dialog box, name the file Brushes.ai, and choose the Lesson10 folder. Leave the Save As Type option set to Adobe Illustrator (*.AI) (Windows) or the Format option set to Adobe Illustrator (ai) (Mac OS), and click Save. In the Illustrator Options dialog box, leave the Illustrator options at their default settings, and click OK.

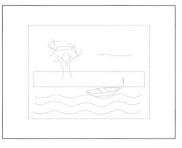

Drawing with the Paintbrush tool

Now you'll use the Paintbrush tool to apply a brush to the artwork.

1 Choose Essentials from the workspace switcher in the Control panel.

2 Choose Window > Brushes to open the Brushes panel.

By default, brushes appear as icons. You can also view brushes by name. When viewed by name, a small icon to the right of the brush name indicates the brush type.

3 In the Brushes panel, choose List View from the panel menu (▾≣).

In the Brushes panel menu, you can also choose which types of brushes are displayed in the Brushes panel to reduce the panel size and make it easier to find the brushes that you want to use.

4 Open the Brushes panel menu and deselect Show Calligraphic Brushes, Show Scatter Brushes, and Show Pattern Brushes, leaving only the Art brushes visible in the Brushes panel.

● **Note:** A check mark next to the brush type in the Brushes panel menu indicates that the brush type is visible in the panel.

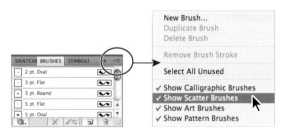

5 Select the Charcoal-Feather art brush in the Brushes panel.

Brushes are applied to paths as a stroke color. If you have a fill color selected when you apply a brush to a path, the path is stroked with the brush and filled with the fill color. You may want to use a fill of None when applying brushes to prevent the brushed paths from being filled. Later in this lesson, you'll use a fill color with a brush. For more information on stroke and fill color, see Lesson 6, "Color and Painting."

6 Select the Zoom tool (🔍) in the Tools panel and drag a marquee around the entire tree to zoom into it.

7 In the Control panel, click Fill color and choose None (▱).

8 Select the Paintbrush tool (🖌) in the Tools panel, and draw a long, upward stroke to create the left side of the tree trunk, tracing over the guides as you draw. Don't worry if your stroke doesn't follow the guide exactly. You'll remove the guides at the end of the lesson, so they won't show in the finished artwork.

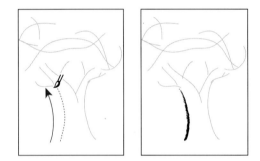

9 Double-click the Paintbrush tool (🖌) to display the Paintbrush Tool Options dialog box. You use this dialog box to change the way the Paintbrush tool functions.

10 Select the Keep Selected option, and click OK. Paths now remain selected after you finish drawing them.

11 Draw a second upward stroke to create the right side of the tree trunk, using the guide to place your drawing.

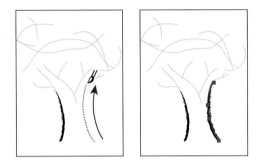

12 Choose File > Save.

Editing paths with the Paintbrush tool

Now you'll use the Paintbrush tool to edit a selected path.

1 With the Paintbrush tool still selected, move the pointer near the top of the selected path (the right side of the tree trunk) and draw upward to extend the trunk up and to the right.

The selected path is edited from the point where you began drawing. Because you selected Keep Selected in the Paintbrush Tool Options dialog box, the new path is added to the selected path instead of becoming a separate path.

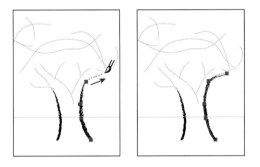

When drawing with the Paintbrush tool, you may want paths to be deselected after you draw them so that you can draw a new path. Next you will deselect the Keep Selected option for the Paintbrush tool.

2 Choose Select > Deselect.

3 In the Tools panel, double-click the Paintbrush tool (✎).

4 Deselect the Keep Selected option, and click OK. Now paths do not remain selected after you finish drawing them, and you can draw overlapping paths without altering previously drawn paths.

Next you'll draw the limbs of the tree.

5 Draw shorter strokes to create the limbs of the tree, as shown in the figure below.

When the Keep Selected option is deselected, you can edit a path by selecting it with the Selection tool (▶) or by selecting a segment or point on the path with the Direct Selection tool (▷), and then redrawing over the path with the Paintbrush tool.

6 Press Ctrl (Windows) or Command (Mac OS) to toggle to the Selection tool, and select a limb that you want to redraw.

Pressing Ctrl (Windows) or Command (Mac OS) temporarily selects the last selected selection tool (Selection tool, Direct Selection tool, or Group Selection tool, whichever was used last) when another tool is selected.

7 Use the Paintbrush tool to draw over the selected path.

You can also edit paths drawn with the Paintbrush tool using the Smooth tool (✐) and the Path Eraser tool (✐), located under the Pencil tool (✐) in the Tools panel. After you apply a brush to an object, it's easy to apply another brush to change the appearance of the object.

8 With the Selection tool (▶), drag a marquee to select the tree trunk and branches.

9 Click the Brush Libraries Menu button (▣.) at the bottom of the Brushes panel and choose Artistic > Artistic_Ink.

10 Choose List View from the Artistic_Ink brush library panel menu (▾≡). Click the Dry Ink 1 brush. The new brush is applied to the selected paths in the artwork. Close the Artistic_Ink brush library panel.

Notice that the Dry Ink 1 brush is added to the Brushes panel. Every brush you apply from a library is added to the Brushes panel.

11 Click outside the artwork to deselect it and view the tree without selection highlights.

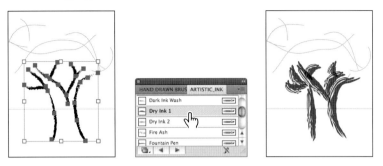

12 Drag a selection marquee to select the tree shapes again.

13 Click several other brushes in the Brushes panel to see the effects of those brushes. When you have finished, click the Charcoal-Feather brush again to reapply that brush.

14 Click outside the artwork to deselect it.

15 Choose File > Save.

As you complete the rest of this lesson, use the methods you learned in this section to edit paths as you draw with the Paintbrush tool. You can use brushes to edit paths with the Keep Selected option if you want strokes to remain selected as you draw, or you can use the Selection tool to select strokes to be edited.

Using Scatter brushes

Scatter brushes randomly spread an object, such as a leaf, ladybug, or strawberry, along a path. In this section, you'll use the Fall Leaf Scatter brush to create leaves on the tree. You'll start by adjusting options for the brush to change its appearance in the artwork.

Changing brush options

You can change the appearance of a brush by adjusting its settings in the Brush Options dialog box, either before or after brushes have been applied to the artwork. The changes that you make appear when you apply the brush to artwork, but do not appear in the brush icon in the Brushes panel.

1 In the Brushes panel, choose Show Scatter Brushes from the panel menu (▾≡), and then deselect Show Art Brushes.

2 Double-click the Fall Leaf brush to open the Scatter Brush Options dialog box for that brush.

Brush options vary according to the type of brush. For Scatter brushes, you can set either fixed values or a range of values for the brush size, spacing, scatter, and rotation. If you are using a pressure-sensitive drawing tablet, you can also set the pressure of the stylus using the Pressure option.

3 Set the following values by either dragging sliders or entering values. Press the Tab key to move to the next text field:

- For Size, set the size of the brush object relative to the default (100%) by choosing Random and entering 40% and 60%.

- For Spacing, set the distance between brush objects on a path relative to 100% (objects touching but not overlapping) by choosing Random and entering 10% and 30%.

- For Scatter, indicate how far objects can deviate from either side of the path, where 0% is aligned on the path, by choosing Random and entering −40% and 40%.

- For Rotation relative to the page or path, enter −180° and 180° and Random. The Rotation Relative To option should be set to Page by default.

4 Click OK.

In addition to the features you adjusted in this section, you can change the color of a brush. You'll change the color of the Fall Leaf brush and another brush later in this lesson.

Applying a Scatter brush to paths

Now you'll use the Fall Leaf brush to draw leaves on the tree. First you'll select and lock the tree to prevent it from being altered while you work on other objects.

1 Use the Selection tool (▶) to drag a marquee around all parts of the tree to select them.

2 Choose Object > Lock > Selection. The bounding box around the tree disappears, and the tree is locked.

3 Select the Fall Leaf brush in the Brushes panel.

4 Use the Paintbrush tool (✐) to draw strokes with the Fall Leaf brush above the tree branches, using the guides to help place your paths. Remember that if you want to edit paths as you draw, you can select the Keep Selected option in the Paintbrush Tool Options for the Paintbrush tool or select paths with the Selection tool.

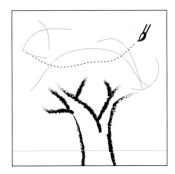  

5 Choose File > Save.

Changing the color attributes of brushes

Before you change the brush color, it's helpful to understand how color is applied to brushes.

To change the color of Art, Pattern, and Scatter brushes, you use one of three color-ization methods. To change the color of Calligraphic brushes, you select the brush and choose a stroke color. You can change the color attributes of a brush before and after you apply the brush to artwork.

When you apply a brush to artwork, the current stroke color for the brush is used only if a colorization method is chosen. If you have not set a colorization method, the default color for that brush is used. For example, the Fall Leaf brush was applied with its default color of red (not the current stroke of black), because its colorization method was set to None.

To colorize Art, Pattern, and Scatter brushes, select one of the following options in the Brush Options dialog box:

- Tints displays the brush stroke in tints of the stroke color. Portions of the art that are black become the stroke color, portions that aren't black become tints of the stroke color, and white remains white. If you use a spot color as the stroke, selecting Tints generates tints of the spot color. Choose Tints for brushes that are in black and white, or when you want to paint a brush stroke with a spot color.

- Tints And Shades displays the brush stroke in tints and shades of the stroke color. Tints And Shades maintains black and white, and everything between becomes a blend from black to white through the stroke color. Because black is added, you may not be able to print to a single plate when using Tints And Shades with a spot color. Choose Tints And Shades for brushes that are in grayscale.

- Hue Shift uses the key color in the brush artwork, as shown in the Key Color box. (By default, the key color is the most prominent color in the art.) Everything in the brush artwork that is the key color becomes the stroke color. Other colors in the brush artwork become colors related to the stroke color. Hue Shift maintains black, white, and gray. Choose Hue Shift for brushes that use multiple colors.

● **Note:** Brushes colorized with a stroke color of white may appear entirely white. Brushes colorized with a stroke color of black may appear entirely black. Results depend on which brush colors were originally chosen.

Changing the brush color using Hue Shift colorization

Now you'll change the color of the Fall Leaf brush using the Hue Shift colorization method.

1 With the Selection tool (↖), drag a marquee to select the paths with the Fall Leaf brush applied in the artwork.

2 Pressing the Shift key, click the Stroke color in the Control panel to open the Color panel. Or, choose Window > Color.

3 Click in the color spectrum bar to select a color for the Fall Leaf brush. (We chose an orangish-red color.)

4 In the Brushes panel, double-click the Fall Leaf brush to view the Scatter Brush Options dialog box. Move the dialog box off to the side to see your artwork as you work.

You must choose a colorization method before you can change the brush color. Brushes set to the Tints, Tints And Shades, or Hue Shift colorization method, by default, automatically apply the current stroke color to the brush when you use it in the artwork.

5 In the Colorization section of the Scatter Brush Options dialog box, select Preview, and then choose Hue Shift from the Method menu.

The Key Color box displays the default key color (in this case, the leaf's red color) or the key color you select. Everything in the artwork that is the key color changes to the new stroke color when the stroke color is changed. For this lesson, you'll use the default key color.

It can be useful to select a new key color if a brush contains several colors and you want to shift different colors in the brush. To select a different key color, you click the Key Color Eyedropper () in the dialog box and position it on the desired color in the preview (such as one of the black veins in the leaf), and then click. The new key color shifts to the stroke color when you use the brush (and other colors in the brush shift correspondingly).

6   Select Preview to see the color applied by the colorization method.

The selected Fall Leaf strokes are colorized with the current stroke color. This color appears when you apply the Hue Shift colorization method.

7   If desired, choose the Tints or Tints And Shades colorization method from the menu to preview the change. Then return to the Hue Shift method.

8   Click OK. In the warning dialog box, click Apply To Strokes to apply the colorization change to the strokes in the artwork. You can also choose to change only subsequent brush strokes and leave existing strokes unchanged.

When you select a colorization method for a brush, the new stroke color applies to selected brush strokes and to new paths painted with the brush.

9   Choose Window > Color. Click the Stroke Box to bring it forward, and then click the color spectrum bar in several different places to try other stroke colors for the selected brush strokes.

10 When you are satisfied with the color of the Fall Leaf brush strokes, click away from the artwork to deselect it.

11 Choose File > Save.

Changing the brush color using Tints colorization

Now you'll apply a new color to the Charcoal - Feather brush in the Brushes panel, and then use the brush to draw bark for the tree in the artwork.

1   Open the Brushes panel ( ) and select Show Art Brushes from the Brushes panel menu ( ). Deselect Show Scatter Brushes.

2   Select the Charcoal - Feather brush in the Brushes panel. Change the Stroke color in the Control panel to black if not already selected.

3 Select the Paintbrush tool (), and draw two paths to fill the center of the tree.

4 With the Selection tool (▶), Shift-click both paths to select them.

5 Click the Options Of Selected Object button ( ) in the Brushes panel to reveal the Stroke Options (Art Brush) dialog box. The color of the brush is black. The Options Of Selected Object button lets you edit just the selected paths.

In the Stroke Options (Art Brush) dialog box, note that the Charcoal-Feather brush is set by default to the Tints colorization method.

The Tints colorization method replaces black with the stroke color. Neither the Tints And Shades nor the Hue Shift colorization method works with black brushes. Because the original brush color is black, neither the Tints And Shades nor the Hue Shift methods changes the brush color.

6 Change the width to 350% to make the size more appropriate for drawing in the artwork. Click OK.

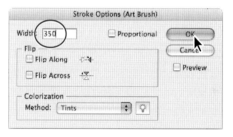

7 With the two paths still selected, Shift-click the Stroke color in the Control panel and choose a light brown color for the tree. Choose Select > Deselect.

Because the Charcoal - Feather brush is one color, the Tints colorization method applies the new stroke color as one color (rather than varied tints of the color). When the original brush contains several colors, the Tints colorization method applies a different tint for each color in the brush.

Note: If strokes disappear as you create new ones, deselect Keep Selected in the Paintbrush options.

Using a fill color with brushes

When you apply a brush to an object's stroke, you can also apply a fill color to paint the interior of the object with a color. When you use a fill color with a brush, the brush objects appear on top of the fill color in places where the fill and the brush objects overlap.

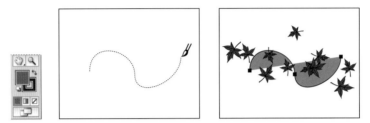

When you apply a brush to an object's stroke, you can apply a fill as well.

Now you'll use the Paintbrush tool to draw a canoe at the edge of the grass with an Art brush. You'll begin by selecting the brush in the Brushes panel.

1   Choose View > Fit Artboard In Window.

2   In the Brushes panel, click the Brush Libraries Menu button (▣.) at the bottom of the panel, and choose Artistic > Artistic_Ink. Click the Tapered Stroke brush to add it to the Brushes panel. Close the Artistic_Ink brush library panel.

The Tapered Stroke brush uses the Tints colorization method by default. To change the color of the Tapered Stroke brush, you'll simply select a stroke color.

3   Click the Stroke color in the Control panel, and select the Canoe Stroke swatch for the edges of the canoe. (It is one of the brown swatches.)

Now you'll use the Paintbrush tool to draw the edges of the canoe. Use the guides to align your drawing.

4   Select the Zoom tool (🔍) in the Tools panel and drag a marquee around the boat.

5   Use the Paintbrush tool (🖌) to draw a crescent shape to make the side and bottom of the canoe:

- Draw a long stroke from left to right to make the side edge of the canoe. Do not release the mouse button.

- While still holding down the mouse button, draw a second long stroke beneath the first, from right to left, connecting the two strokes at the left end point of the object, to make a crescent shape. When you have drawn the second stroke, release the mouse button.

You may have to draw the crescent shape more than once to create a shape with a single path. Remember that you can edit paths as you draw. Use the Direct

Selection tool (⬚) to select a segment of the path that you want to redraw. If you edit a segment, deselect the objects before continuing on.

Don't worry if your drawing doesn't match the guides exactly. What's important is to draw the shape as one path, without releasing the mouse button, so that you can fill the object correctly. If a shape is made of separate paths, the fill color is applied to each path separately, yielding unpredictable results.

6 Draw a third long stroke from left to right for the top side of the canoe. Then draw two shorter strokes for the crossbars. Draw the top side and crossbars as separate paths, releasing the mouse button after each one.

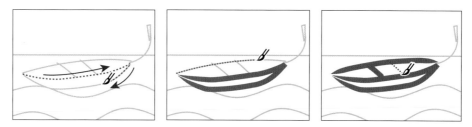

Now you'll fill the side of the canoe with a color.

7 With the Selection tool (▶), select the crescent shape that you drew for the lower side and bottom of the canoe.

8 Click the Fill color in the Control panel, and select the Canoe Fill swatch.

9 Click outside the artwork to deselect it.

10 Choose File > Save.

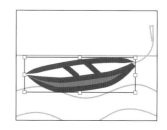

Using Calligraphic brushes

Calligraphic brushes resemble strokes drawn with the angled point of a calligraphic pen. Calligraphic brushes are defined by an elliptical shape whose center follows the path. Use these brushes to create the appearance of hand-drawn strokes made with a flat, angled pen tip.

You'll use a Calligraphic pen to draw water below the canoe. You'll begin by selecting the brush, and then choose a color for the brush.

1 Choose View > Fit Artboard In Window.

2 Choose Show Calligraphic Brushes from the Brushes panel menu (▾≣), and then deselect Show Art Brushes.

3 In the Brushes panel, select the 40 pt. Flat brush.

4   In the Control panel, click the Stroke color and choose the Waves swatch (blue).

Calligraphic brushes use the current stroke color when you apply the brushes to artwork. You do not use colorization methods with Calligraphic brushes.

5   Click the Color panel icon (🖌) to open the Color panel. Click the Fill box and select None (⬚). A fill of None prevents paths from being filled when you apply the brush.

6   Select the Paintbrush tool (✐) in the Tools panel, and draw wavy lines for the water surface. The paths you draw use the stroke color you selected in step 4.

Now you'll change the shape of the 40 pt. Flat brush in the Brush Options dialog box to change the appearance of the strokes made with the brush.

7   In the Brushes panel, double-click the 40 pt. Flat brush to display the Calligraphic Brush Options dialog box.

You can change the angle of the brush (relative to a horizontal line), the roundness (from a flat line to a full circle), the diameter (from 0 to 1296 points) to change the shape that defines the brush's tip, and the appearance of the stroke that the brush makes. Now you'll change the diameter and angle of the brush.

8   In the Name text field, type 35 pt Oval. Enter 35 pt for Diameter. Select Preview and notice that the weight of the Calligraphic brush strokes in the artwork decreases. Enter –20 for the angle. The preview window in the dialog box shows the changes that you make to the brush.

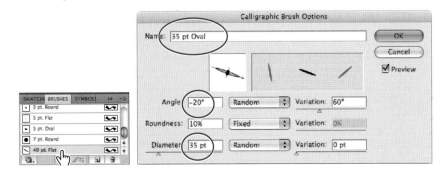

9   Click OK. In the warning dialog box, click Apply To Strokes to apply the change to the strokes in the artwork.

10 With the Selection tool, Shift-click the three blue wavy lines.

11 Click the Transparency panel icon (⬤), or choose Window > Transparency to open the Transparency panel. Type 45 for the opacity of the wavy lines.

12 Choose Select > Deselect.

13 Choose File > Save.

Using Pattern brushes

Pattern brushes paint a pattern made up of separate sections, or tiles. When you apply a Pattern brush to artwork, different tiles of the pattern are applied to different sections of the path, depending on where the section falls on the path—end, middle, or corner. There are hundreds of interesting pattern brushes that you can choose from when creating your own projects—from dog tracks to teacups. Next you'll open an existing Pattern Brush library and choose a Dashed Circle pattern to represent a chain.

1 In the Brushes panel, choose Show Pattern Brushes from the panel menu (▾☰).

2 Click the Brush Libraries Menu button (▤↓) and choose Borders > Borders_Dashed. A brush library panel with various dashed borders appears.

3 Choose List View from the Borders_Dashed brush library panel menu (▾☰).

4 Click the Dashed Circles 1.4 brush to add it to the Brushes panel. Close the Borders_Dashed brush library panel.

5 Double-click the Dashed Circles 1.4 pattern brush in the Brushes panel to open the Pattern Brush Options dialog box for the brush.

The Pattern Brush Options dialog box shows the tiles in the Dashed Circles 1.4 brush. The first tile on the left is the side tile, which is used to paint the middle sections of a path. The second tile is the outer corner tile. The third tile is the inner corner tile.

Pattern brushes can have up to five tiles—the side, start, and end tiles, plus an outer corner tile and an inner corner tile to paint sharp corners on a path. Some brushes have no corner tiles because the brush is designed for curved paths. In the next part of this lesson, you'll create your own Pattern brush that has corner tiles.

Now you'll change the scale of the Pattern brush so that the brush is in scale with the rest of the artwork when you apply it.

6 In the Pattern Brush Options dialog box, change the scale to 20%, and click OK.

7 Select the Zoom tool (🔍) in the Tools panel and drag a marquee loosely across the right end of the boat and the rope to zoom in.

8 Select the Paintbrush tool (✏), and set the opacity value in the Control panel to 100%. Draw a path that loops around the stake from left to right. Draw a second path that wraps around the backside of the stake. Then draw a third path that leads from the loop around the stake to the canoe.

Draw the stroke as three separate paths, rather than one path, to avoid creating a path with a sharp angle. Because the Dashed Circle brush does not include corner tiles, the brush uses side tiles to paint sharp angles. The side tiles may appear severed at sharp corners, and the chain may appear to be cut.

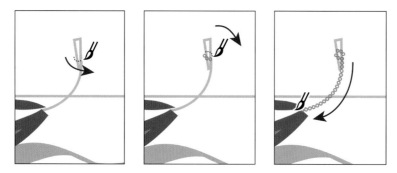

Now you'll draw the stake and wrap the chain around it.

9 Choose Select > Deselect if any content is selected.

10 Select the Pen tool (✎) in the Tools panel, and click four times around the stake guides to create a closed path, clicking back on the first point drawn to close the path.

● **Note:** If the stake shape has the Dashed Circles 1.4 brush applied, click the Remove Brush Stroke button at the bottom of the Brushes panel.

11 With the Selection tool, click back on the stake shape you just drew. From the Fill color in the Control panel, choose a dark brown color. Make sure that the Stroke is set to None (⬜).

Now you will select a portion of the chain you created earlier in the lesson and move it in front of the stake to make the chain appear to go around the stake.

12 Choose Select > Deselect.

13 With the Selection tool (▶), Shift-click to select the first and third portions of chain you drew. (Be careful not to select the stake.)

● **Note:** You may need to zoom in to see the chain parts more clearly.

14 Choose Object > Arrange > Bring To Front.

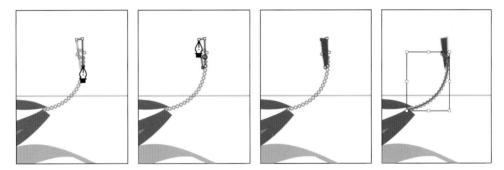

15 Choose Select > Deselect, and then File > Save.

Creating brushes

You can create new brushes using all four brush types that are based on artwork in an Adobe Illustrator CS4 file. In this section, you'll use artwork provided with the lesson to create a new Pattern brush with three tiles: a yellow bar for the side tile, and a blue circle for the outer corner tile and inner corner tile.

Creating swatches for a Pattern brush

You create Pattern brushes by first creating swatches in the Swatches panel with the artwork that you are using for the Pattern brush tiles. In this section, you'll use the yellow line and blue circle drawings included with the artwork file to create swatches.

1 Choose View > Fit Artboard In Window.

2 Use the scroll bars, the Hand tool (🖐), or the Navigator panel to display the canvas area to the right of the artboard where there is a yellow line and a blue circle.

The shapes that make up the pattern brush

3 Choose Object > Unlock All.

Bounding boxes and selection highlights appear around the objects, indicating that the objects are unlocked and selected. The tree, which you locked earlier in the lesson, is unlocked and selected. The tree can be unlocked because you've finished drawing in the area of the tree.

4 Using the Selection tool (▶), click outside the artwork to deselect the objects.

5 Click the Swatches panel icon (▦), or choose Window > Swatches.

Now you'll create a pattern swatch.

6 With the Selection tool, drag the blue circle group into the Swatches panel. The new swatch appears in the Swatches panel.

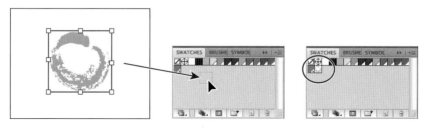

7 Click away from the artwork to deselect.

8 In the Swatches panel, double-click the pattern swatch that you just created. Double-clicking the swatch changes the current fill or stroke box to that swatch and opens the Swatch Options dialog box.

9 Name the swatch Corner, and click OK.

10 Repeat steps 6 through 8 to create a pattern swatch of the yellow line art that is below the blue circle on the canvas area of the right side of the artboard. Name the swatch Side.

▶ **Tip:** For more information on creating pattern swatches, see "About patterns" in Illustrator Help.

11 With the Selection tool, select the original shapes off the right side of the artboard and delete them.

Creating a Pattern brush from swatches

To create a new Pattern brush, you apply swatches from the Swatches panel to tiles in the Brush Options dialog box. Now you'll apply the pattern swatches that you just made to tiles to create a new Pattern brush.

First you'll open a Brush Options dialog box for a new Pattern brush.

1 Click the Brushes panel tab to view the panel, or choose Window > Brushes.

2 Choose Select > Deselect if there is content selected.

3 In the Brushes panel, click the New Brush button (▣).

4 In the New Brush dialog box, select New Pattern Brush and click OK.

Now you'll apply the Side swatch to the side tile for the new Pattern brush.

5 In the Pattern Brush Options dialog box, select the Side tile box on the far left tile box.

6 In the pattern swatches list, below the tile boxes, select the Side swatch. The Side swatch appears in the Side tile box.

Next you'll apply the Corner swatch to the outer corner and inner corner tiles for the new Pattern brush.

7 In the Pattern Brush Options dialog box, select the Outer Corner tile box (the second tile box from the left). In the pattern swatches list, select the Corner swatch. The Corner swatch appears in the Outer Corner tile box.

8 In the Pattern Brush Options dialog box, select the Inner Corner tile box (the middle tile box). In the pattern swatches list, select the Corner swatch. The Corner swatch appears in the Inner Corner tile box.

9 Name the brush Border, and then click OK.

Note: When you create a new brush, the brush appears in the Brushes panel of the current document only.

You won't create a start or end tile for the new brush because you'll apply the new brush to a closed path in the artwork later in the lesson. When you want to create a Pattern brush that includes start and end tiles, you add those tiles the same way as you did the side and corner tiles.

The Border brush appears in the Pattern brush section in the Brushes panel.

▶ **Tip:** To save a brush and reuse it in another file, you can create a brush library with the brushes you want to use. For more information, see "Work with brush libraries" in Illustrator Help.

Painting with the Pattern brush

So far in this lesson, you've used the Paintbrush tool to apply brushes to paths. You can also apply brushes to paths created with any drawing tool—including the Pen, Pencil, Ellipse, and Rectangle tools—and the other basic shape tools. In this section, you'll use the Rectangle tool to apply the Border brush to a rectangular border around the artwork.

When you use drawing tools to apply brushes to artwork, you first draw the path with the drawing tool, and then select the brush in the Brushes panel to apply the brush to the path.

1 In the Tools panel, click the Fill box and select None (⬚). Then click the Stroke box and select None (⬚).

2 Use the Navigator panel or the Zoom tool (🔍) to zoom out.

Now you'll draw a border with the Rectangle tool and apply the brush to the path.

3 Select the Rectangle tool (▭). Drag to draw a rectangle on the artboard, following the outer guide.

4 In the Brushes panel, choose Thumbnail View from the panel menu (▾≣).

5 Click the Border brush in the Brushes panel.

The rectangle path is painted with the Border brush, with the Side tile on the sides and the Corner tile on the corners.

6 Ctrl-click (Windows) or Command-click (Mac OS) outside the art to deselect it.

Now you'll draw a curved path using the Border brush.

7 In the Brushes panel, double-click the Border pattern brush to open the Pattern Brush Options dialog box.

You'll change the scale and spacing of the brush for a different look.

8 For Scale, type 130%, and click OK.

9 In the Brush Change Alert dialog box, click Leave Strokes to keep the border brush strokes as they are.

The Leave Strokes option preserves paths that are already painted with the brush. The changes you made to the brush apply to subsequent uses of the brush. Now you'll use the brush to paint a curved path in the artwork.

10 Select the Paintbrush tool ( ) and draw a smooth curve to the right of the tree. Use the guide for placement.

The path is painted with the Side swatch from the Border brush, which the Side tile is used for. Because the path does not include sharp corners, the outer corner and inner corner tiles are not applied to the path.

Applying the Scribble effect

The Scribble effect lets you apply loose or mechanical-looking scribbling to fills and strokes. This includes fills of gradients and patterns.

You will create the grass using the Scribble effect and its options.

1 With the Rectangle tool ( ), create a rectangle in front of the tree, which will be the area for the grass. Set the stroke to None ( ) first, then fill the rectangle with the Green swatch in the Control panel.

2 With the grass area still selected, choose Object > Arrange > Send To Back.

3 Choose Effect > Stylize > Scribble from the Illustrator Effects.

The Scribble Options dialog box appears, giving you choices that range from changing the width of the scribbled stroke to curviness and spacing.

4 Choose options in the Scribble Options dialog box to make the grass look more like grass, such as Angle 67°, Path Overlap 0 pt, Variation 5 pt, Stroke Width 3 pt. Curviness is set to be more angular with a setting of 5%, but you can use variations to make the strokes look less mechanical. Set Curviness Variation to 1%, and spacing between the strokes to 6 pt with a variation of .5 pt. Select Preview to see the changes, and then click OK.

Scribble Options

Settings: Custom

Angle: 67 °

Path Overlap: 0 pt   Variation: 5 pt

Inside   Centered   Outside   None   Wide

Line Options

Stroke Width: 3 pt

Curviness: 5 %   Variation: 1 %

Angular   Loopy   None   Wide

Spacing: 6 pt   Variation: 0.5 pt

Tight   Loose   None   Wide

OK

Cancel

☐ Preview

5   Select the Type tool (T), and click above the curved shape to the right of the tree. Before typing, set character attributes. Click the word Character in the Control panel or choose Window > Type > Character and choose a font. We chose Myriad Pro Bold, which comes with Adobe Illustrator CS4. Change the font size and leading to 24 pt.

6   Type Lakeside Designs on the artboard.

You've completed the artwork for the lesson. Now you'll hide the guides so that you can view the artwork in its finished form.

7   Click the Layers panel icon ( ) to open the Layers panel. Deselect the eye icon ( ) to the left of the Guides layer to hide the drawn guides.

8   Choose File > Save, and then File > Close.

Exploring on your own

The Blob Brush tool

Open the file Check_logo.ai and practice adding other content as well as shaping and merging letters using the Blob Brush tool. Fill the letters with a pattern, and then try editing and merging shapes.

Applying brushes

Practice applying brushes to paths that you create with drawing tools, just as you applied the Pattern brush to a path drawn with the Rectangle tool in the final section of the lesson.

1   Choose File > New, and create a document to use for practice.

2   Click the Brushes Libraries Menu button (▥) in the Brushes panel, and choose Decorative > Decorative_Scatter.

3   Use the drawing tools (the Pen or Pencil tool, and any of the basic shape tools) to draw objects. Use the default fill and stroke colors when you draw.

4   With one of the objects selected, click a brush in the Decorative Scatter panel to apply the brush to the object's path.

    As you select a Scatter brush, it is automatically added to the Brushes panel.

5   Repeat step 4 for each object you drew.

6   In the Brushes panel, double-click one of the Scatter brushes that you used in Step 4 to display the Scatter Brush Options dialog box. Change the color, size, or other features of the brush. After you close the dialog box, click Apply To Strokes to apply your changes to the brush in the artwork.

Creating brushes

Use one of the basic shape tools to create artwork to use as a new Scatter brush.

1   Select a basic shape tool in the Tools panel, and draw an object, keeping it selected.

2   Click the New Brush button at the bottom of the Brushes panel.

    ● **Note:** You can use more than one object to create the new brush. All selected objects in the artwork are included in the brush. If you use a brush to create artwork for a new brush, remember to expand the brush strokes before creating the new brush.

3   In the New Brush dialog box, select New Scatter Brush, and click OK.

    The Brush Options dialog box appears with the selected objects displayed in the brush example. The new brush is named Scatter Brush 1 by default.

4   Rename the brush, and then click OK to accept the settings for the brush.

5   Select the Paintbrush tool and draw a path. The new brush is applied to the path.

6   Double-click the new brush to display the Brush Options dialog box. Change the brush settings to try out different versions of the brush. When you are finished, click OK.

Review questions

1 What does the Blob Brush tool allow you to create?

2 Describe each of the four brush types: Art, Calligraphic, Pattern, and Scatter.

3 What is the difference between applying a brush to artwork using the Paintbrush tool and applying a brush to artwork using one of the drawing tools?

4 Describe how to edit paths with the Paintbrush tool as you draw. How does the Keep Selected option affect the Paintbrush tool?

5 How do you change the colorization method for an Art, Pattern, or Scatter brush? (Remember, you don't use colorization methods with Calligraphic brushes.)

6 How can you make the Scribble effect more mechanical rather than loose and flowing?

Review answers

1 Use the Blob Brush tool to edit filled shapes that you can intersect and merge with other shapes of the same color or create artwork from scratch.

2 The following are the four brush types:

- Art brushes stretch artwork evenly along a path. Art brushes include strokes that resemble graphic media, such as the Charcoal-Feather brush used to create the tree. Art brushes also include objects, such as the Arrow brush.

- Calligraphic brushes are defined by an elliptical shape whose center follows the path. They create strokes that resemble hand-drawn lines made with a flat, angled calligraphic pen tip.

- Pattern brushes paint a pattern made up of separate sections, or tiles, for the sides, ends, and corners of the path. When you apply a pattern brush to artwork, the brush applies different tiles from the pattern to different sections of the path, depending on where the section falls on the path.

- Scatter brushes scatter an object, such as a leaf, along a path. You can adjust the size, spacing, scatter, and rotation options to change the appearance of the brush.

3 To apply brushes using the Paintbrush tool, you select the tool, choose a brush in the Brushes panel, and draw on the artboard. The brush is applied directly to the paths as you draw. To apply brushes using a drawing tool, you select the tool and draw in the

artwork. Then you select the path in the artwork and choose a brush in the Brushes panel. The brush is applied to the selected path.

4   To edit a path with the Paintbrush tool, drag over a selected path to redraw it. The Keep Selected option keeps the last path selected as you draw with the Paintbrush tool. Leave the Keep Selected option selected (the default setting) when you want to easily edit the previous path as you draw. Deselect the Keep Selected option when you want to draw layered paths with the paintbrush without altering previous paths. When Keep Selected is deselected, you can use the Selection tool to select a path and then edit it.

5   To change the colorization method of a brush, double-click the brush in the Brushes panel to open the Brush Options dialog box. Use the Method menu in the Colorization section to select another method. If you choose Hue Shift, you can use the default color displayed in the dialog box preview, or you can change the key color by clicking the Key Color Eyedropper, and clicking a color in the preview. Click OK to accept the settings, and close the Brush Options dialog box. Click Apply To Strokes in the alert dialog box if you want to apply the changes to existing strokes in the artwork.

Existing brush strokes are colorized with the stroke color that was selected when the strokes were applied to the artwork. New brush strokes are colorized with the current stroke color. To change the color of existing strokes after applying a different colorization method, select the strokes and select a new stroke color.

6   Using the Scribble Option, you can keep the options for Curviness Variation and Spacing Variation to a minimum to make the scribble more mechanical.

11 APPLYING EFFECTS

Lesson overview

In this lesson, you'll learn how to do the following:

- Use Pathfinder and Distort & Transform effects.

- Use Photoshop effects to add texture to objects.

- Use Warp effects to create a banner logotype.

- Create 3D objects from 2D artwork.

- Map artwork to the faces of 3D objects.

This lesson will take approximately an hour to complete. If needed, remove the previous lesson folder from your hard disk and copy the Lesson11 folder onto it.

Effects change the look of an object. Effects are live, which means you can apply an effect to an object and then modify or remove it at any time using the Appearance panel. Using effects, it's easy to apply drop shadows, turn two-dimensional artwork into three-dimensional shapes, and much more.

Getting started

In this lesson, you'll create objects using the Distort & Transform, Pathfinder, Texture, Warp, 3D effects. Before you begin, you'll need to restore the default preferences for Adobe Illustrator. Then you'll open a file containing the finished artwork to see what you'll create.

1   To ensure that the tools and panels function exactly as described in this lesson, delete or rename the Adobe Illustrator CS4 preferences file. See "Restoring default preferences" on page 3.

2   Start Adobe Illustrator CS4.

● **Note:** If you have not already copied the resource files for this lesson onto your hard disk from the Lesson11 folder on the Adobe Illustrator CS4 Classroom in a Book CD, do so now. See "Copying the Classroom in a Book files" on page 2.

3   Choose File > Open, and open the L11end.ai file in the Lesson11 folder, located in the Lessons folder on your hard disk.

This file displays a completed illustration of a gift certificate.

4   Choose View > Zoom Out to make the finished artwork smaller. Adjust the window size, and leave it on your screen as you work. (Use the Hand tool (🖑) to move the artwork where you want it in the window.) If you don't want to leave the image open, choose File > Close.

Using live effects

● **Note:** When you apply a raster effect, the original vector data is rasterized using the document's raster effects settings, which determine the resolution of the resulting image. To learn about document raster effects settings, see Lesson 15, "Output."

The Effect menu commands alter the appearance of an object without changing the underlying object. Applying an effect automatically adds the effect to the object's appearance attribute. You can apply more than one effect to an object. You can edit, move, delete, or duplicate an effect at any time in the Appearance panel. To edit the points that the effect creates, you must first expand the object.

There are two types of effects in Illustrator: vector effects and raster effects.

• **Vector effects:** The top half of the Effects menu contain vector effects. You can apply these effects only to vector objects or to the fill or stroke of a bitmap object in the Appearance panel. Some vector effects can be applied to both vector and bitmap objects: 3D effects, SVG filters, Warp effects, Transform effects, Drop Shadow, Feather, Inner Glow, and Outer Glow.

• **Raster effects:** The effects in the bottom half of the Effects menu are raster effects. You can apply them to either vector or bitmap objects.

Applying an effect

In this part of the lesson, you'll apply three effects to a lime—a Pathfinder effect to make the inner part of the lime, a Distort & Transform effect to finish the inner part of the lime, and a texture using a Photoshop effect called Grain to create the rind.

1   Choose File > Open, and open the L11start.ai file in the Lesson11 folder, located in the Lessons folder on your hard disk.

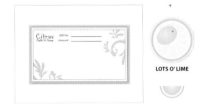

2   Choose Essentials from the workspace switcher in the Control panel to reset the workspace.

3   Choose File > Save As, name the file Gift.ai, and select the Lesson11 folder in the Save In menu. Leave the Save As Type option set to Adobe Illustrator (*.AI) (Windows) or the Format option set to Adobe Illustrator (ai) (Mac OS), and click Save. In the Illustrator Options dialog box, leave the Illustrator options at their default settings, and click OK.

4   Use the Hand tool (✋) to move the artwork to the left so that you can see off the right side of the artboard. There are several pieces to the logo for the gift certificate, including a lime.

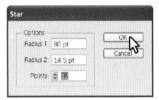

Select the Star tool (☆) which is nested in the Rectangle tool in the Tools panel. Click once off the right edge of the artboard in the canvas. In the Star dialog box, enter 80 pt for Radius 1, 14.5 pt for Radius 2, and 12 for Points. Click OK.

Don't worry about the star's stroke or fill. You are using the star to punch through a shape to create lime wedges.

5   With the Selection tool (▶), drag the star over the lime in the lower right corner off the artboard and position it roughly on top. Keep the star selected.

6   Shift-click the center lime shape to choose the star and the top gradient-filled shape. Click the center lime shape once more to make it the key object for aligning. Click the Horizontal Align Center button (⊟) and the Vertical Align Bottom button (⊞) in the Control panel to align them horizontally and vertically.

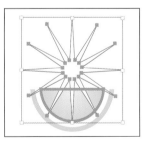

7 Choose Object > Group to group the lime and star together.

8 Choose Effect > Pathfinder > Subtract to subtract the top shape (the star) from the bottom shape (the lime object). It still looks like two separate shapes when selected. Keep the group selected.

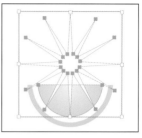

● **Note:** To subtract shapes, you can also use the Pathfinder panel, but the shapes are expanded immediately by default. Using the Effect menu lets you edit shapes independently.

Next you will see the effect in the Appearance panel.

● **Note:** To remove the Subtract effect that you just applied, click the Subtract effect in the Appearance panel, and then click the Delete Selected Item button (🗑) at the bottom of the panel.

9 Click the Appearance panel icon (◉) on the right side of the workspace. Notice that the Subtract effect appears in the Appearance panel. Clicking Subtract would allow you to edit the effect.

● **Note:** You'll learn more about the Appearance panel in Lesson 12, "Applying Appearance Attributes and Graphic Styles."

Next you will edit the star shape, and then expand the effect into editable vector shapes.

10 Choose View > Smart Guides to deselect them.

11 With the Selection tool, double-click the group to enter isolation mode. Choose View > Outline to see the outline of the shapes.

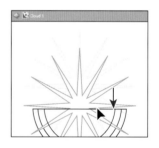

12 In outline mode, Shift-click the star shape and drag it down until the leftmost and rightmost star points are just above the lime shape (see figure at right). Release the mouse button, and then the Shift key.

13 Double-click anywhere outside of the grouped objects to exit isolation mode and return to preview mode. With the Selection tool, click to select the star group and keep it selected. You now have lime wedges.

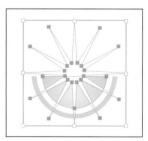

Next you will change the appearance of the wedges you just created using the Roughen effect. This applies a second effect to the grouped objects.

14 Choose Effect > Distort & Transform > Roughen. In the Roughen dialog box, change Size to 3%, Detail to 13/in, and select the Smooth option. Select Preview to see the change. Try different settings to see their effect, and then click OK.

15 Choose Select > Deselect.

⬤ **Note:** To see the change in the lime wedges, you may need to zoom in.

16 With the Selection tool, click to select the green outer edge of the lime.

You will next apply a Photoshop effect to the lime rind to make it look more realistic.

17 With the lime rind shape selected, choose Effect > Texture > Grain to open the Effect Gallery. In the Grain settings on the right, type 50 for Intensity, 55 for Contrast, and choose Clumped from the Grain Type menu.

⬤ **Note:** After you apply the raster effect, the rind shape is composed of pixels.

In the Effect Gallery, you can apply a single raster effect or multiple raster effects to an object. The raster effects are in the middle panel, organized in folders that correlate to the menu item in the Effect menu. You can try more effects and adjust their settings if you like. Click OK to accept the Grain options.

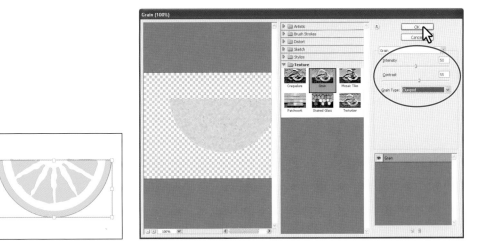

Next you will expand the lime wedges, and then add a Drop Shadow effect to the entire lime wedge. Expanding an object with an effect changes the underlying object and lets you edit the anchor points.

18 With the Selection tool, select the lime wedges (the star group).

19 Choose Object > Expand Appearance to see the anchor points of the lime wedges. With the group selected, notice that the effects no longer appear in the Appearance panel. The Appearance panel tells you that a group of objects is selected with the opacity set at the default.

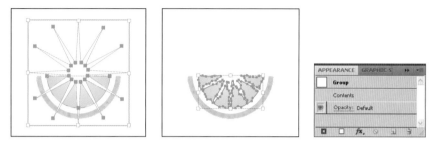

20 With the Selection tool, drag a marquee across the lime wedges and the other shapes beneath them to select the entire lime slice.

21 Choose Object > Group to group them together.

22 In the bottom of the Appearance panel, click Add New Effect (*fx.*) and choose Stylize > Drop Shadow.

23 In the Drop Shadow dialog box, change Opacity to 20%, X Offset to 2 pt, Y Offset to 2 pt, and Blur to 2. Select Preview to see the formatting. Click OK.

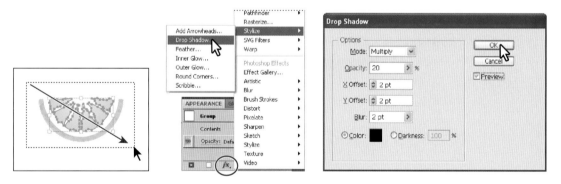

24 Choose Select > Deselect.

When you apply an effect to a group, if the objects later become ungrouped, the effect is removed. If you had simply selected the shapes (as you did in previous steps) and applied the drop shadow without grouping, each object would have a drop shadow, not the group as a whole.

25 Choose File > Save.

Editing an effect

Effects are live, so they can be edited after they are applied to an object. You can edit the effect in the Appearance panel by either clicking the name of the effect or double-clicking the attribute row. This displays the dialog box for that effect. Changes you make to the effect update in the artwork. In this section, you will edit the Roughen effect applied to the lime wedges.

1 With the Selection tool (▶), click the grouped lime shapes and make sure that the Appearance panel is showing. If it isn't, choose Window > Appearance or click its panel icon (●).

Notice the Drop Shadow effect listed in the Appearance panel. To edit an effect, you simply click the name of the effect, and a dialog box opens.

2 Click Drop Shadow in the Appearance panel.

3 In the Drop Shadow dialog box, change Opacity to 40% and select Preview to see the change. Try different settings to see their effects, and then click OK.

4 With the Selection tool, drag the lime slice onto the logo above it.

● **Note:** If you've zoomed in, you may need to zoom out to see the artwork.

5 Select the Rotate tool (⟲) in the Tools panel. From the upper right corner, click and drag around the right corner to rotate the lime slice. Choose Select > Deselect.

6 Choose File > Save.

Next you will remove an effect from an object.

▶ **Tip:** It may be easier to select the shape by choosing View > Outline.

7 With the Selection tool, click the largest light green circle in the back of the logo with the drop shadow applied.

8 In the Appearance panel, click to the right or left of the blue, underlined name Drop Shadow to highlight the attribute row for the Drop Shadow effect. Be careful not to click the blue, underlined name Drop Shadow (that opens the Drop Shadow dialog box). After highlighting the attribute row, click the Delete Selected Item button (🗑) at the bottom of the panel.

● **Note:** Only the background ellipse is selected in the figure at right.

9 Choose Select > Deselect.

10 Choose File > Save.

Next you will create a Warp effect with text, and then edit the effect.

Creating a banner logo with the Warp effect

Warp effects distort objects, including paths, text, meshes, blends, and raster images. After you apply a Warp affect to your artwork, you can continue to modify or remove it at any time using the Appearance panel. You will use a Warp effect to create the banner logo.

Creating the logotype

You can make a warp from objects in your artwork, or you can use a preset warp shape or mesh object as an envelope.

1   Select the Selection tool (▶) in the Tools panel, and then select the "Lots O' Lime" type.

2   Choose Effect > Warp > Rise.

3   In the Warp Options dialog box, to create a ribbon effect, set Bend to 93%. Select Preview to preview the changes. To see the type in the artwork, move the Warp Options dialog box by dragging its title bar. Click OK. Keep the text selected.

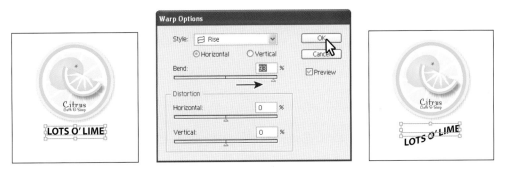

4   With the Selection tool, drag the "Lots O' Lime" type bounding box up into the center of the Citrus logo. As you drag press Shift to keep the type aligned. When the type is in the correct position, release the mouse button, and then the Shift key. Keep the text selected.

● **Note:** With the text selected from step 3, if you press the Shift key first, then attempt to drag the type, it will be deselected. This is why you drag first, then press the Shift key.

5   Choose Object > Arrange > Bring To Front if the type is not on the top of the other objects.

6   Choose Select > Deselect.

7   Choose File > Save.

Stylizing the banner and logotype

To complete the banner and logotype, you'll add some sophistication by offsetting a stroke around the text and adding a colored drop shadow.

1   With the Selection tool (▶), click the "Lots O' Lime" type to select it.

2   If the Appearance panel is not visible, choose Window > Appearance.

Notice that the Appearance panel lists the Warp: Rise effect that has been applied to the text.

3   Click the Add New Stroke button (■) at the bottom of the Appearance panel. Leave the stroke weight at 1 pt.

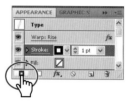

4   Click the Stroke Color in the Appearance panel and select the stem swatch in the Swatches panel. Press Enter or Return to close the Swatches panel and return to the Appearance panel.

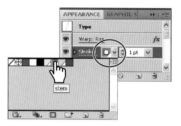

5   Click the word Stroke in the Appearance panel to open the Stroke panel. Select Dashed Line and type .5 into the first Dash field and make sure that the remaining Gap and Dash fields are empty. Press Enter or Return to close the Stroke panel and return to the Appearance panel.

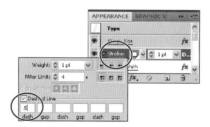

You can add multiple strokes to an object and apply different effects to each one, giving you the opportunity to create unique and interesting artwork.

6   Select the Zoom tool (🔍) and click twice on the logo to zoom in to see the dashed stroke applied.

7 With Stroke selected in the Appearance panel, click Add New Effect (*fx*) at the bottom of the Appearance panel. Choose Path > Offset Path. Change Offset to 2 pt, and click OK. This creates an outline around the text.

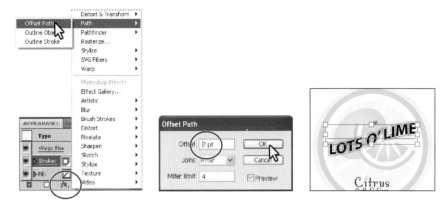

Now you will add a colored drop shadow to the text.

8 In the Appearance panel, click the arrow to the left of the word Stroke to toggle it open. Notice that Offset Path is subset underneath Stroke. This indicates that the Offset Path is applied to the Stroke only.

9 Click the word Type at the top of the Appearance panel. This will apply the drop shadow you create in the next step to the text rather than just the offset stroke.

● **Note:** You may need to scroll up in the Appearance panel or resize the panel for easier viewing.

10 Click Add New Effect (*fx*) and choose Stylize > Drop Shadow from the Illustrator Effects section.

11 In the Drop Shadow dialog box, select Preview, and change Opacity to 40%, X Offset to 4 pt, Y Offset to 4 pt, and Blur to 2 pt. Click the square to the right of Color. This opens the Color Picker dialog box.

12 In the Color Picker, click the Color Swatches button to see the document's color swatches. Select the stem swatch. Click OK.

13 Click OK to close the Drop Shadow dialog box.

14 Choose View > Zoom Out.

15 With the Selection tool, drag a marquee around all the logo parts. Choose Object > Group to group them.

16 Click the Symbols panel icon (♣), or choose Window > Symbols to open the Symbols panel. Drag the grouped logo onto the Symbols panel to create a symbol. In the Symbol Options dialog box, name the symbol Can top, and select Graphic as the symbol type. Click OK.

▶ **Tip:** To learn more about symbols, see Lesson 13, "Working with Symbols."

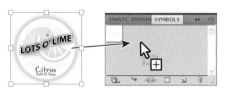

17 Choose Select > Deselect, and then File > Save. Keep the file open.

Creating the 3D cylinder

Using the 3D effect, you can control the appearance of 3D objects with lighting, shading, rotation, and other attributes. In this part of the lesson, you'll use two-dimensional shapes as the foundation for creating three-dimensional objects.

There are three ways to create a 3D object:

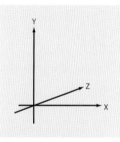

- **Extrude & bevel**—Extends a 2D object along the object's z axis to add depth to the object. For example, if you extrude a 2D ellipse, it becomes a cylinder.

- **Revolve**—Sweeps a path or profile in a circular direction around the global y axis (revolve axis) to create a 3D object.

- **Rotate**—Uses the Z axis to rotate 2D artwork in 3D space and change the artwork's perspective.

The 3D effect takes advantage of the x, y, and z axes.

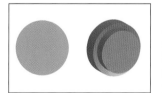

Extrude & bevel

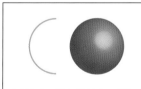

Revolve

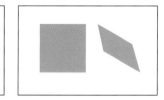

Rotate

Using the 3D Extrude & Bevel effect

In this next lesson, you will create a soap can for the Citrus logo label.

1 Select the Ellipse tool (⬭) from the Star tool group in the Tools panel. Off the artboard on the right, click once below the Lots O' Lime logo. In the Ellipse dialog box, type 285 pt in the Width text field, and click the word Height to enter the same value in this field. Click OK.

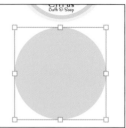

2 Select the Selection tool (▶) in the Tools panel. Click the Stroke color in the Control panel and set the stroke color to None (⬜). Click the Fill color in the Control panel and select Can Green in the Swatches panel.

3 Choose Effect > 3D > Extrude & Bevel. Drag the title bar of the dialog box to a location that allows you to see your artwork. In the 3D Extrude & Bevel Options dialog box, select Preview.

The Extrude & Bevel effect has been applied to the 2D circle using the default settings. You will now change several options, including the depth and edges.

4 Click the aqua-colored track cube face on the left side of the dialog box. Experiment with rotating the object by clicking and dragging the cube. When you are finished experimenting, choose Off-Axis Bottom from the Position menu. Keep the dialog box open.

5 Make the cylinder taller by typing 75 into the Extrude Depth text field. Deselect, and then reselect, Preview to refresh the image. Keep the dialog box open.

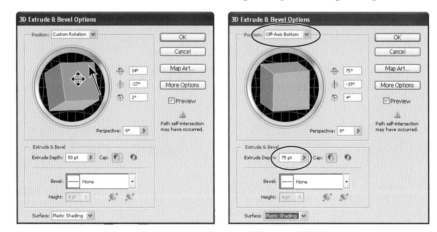

Cap on or cap off?

In the 3D Options dialog box for the Extrude & Bevel effect and the Revolve 3D effect , you can choose to make your object appear solid or hollow.

- Click the Cap On button (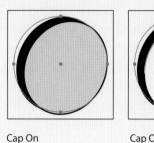) to make the object appear solid.
- Click the Cap Off button () to make the object appear hollow.

Cap On   Cap Off

6 Using the Bevel menu, experiment with the different options to see the variations of edge effects that you can create.

After you choose a bevel from the Bevel menu, you can add beveling properties to carve away from or add to the object's surface.

- The Extent Out ( ) button adds the bevel to the object's shape.
- The Extent In ( ) button carves the bevel out of the object's original shape.

7 When you are finished experimenting, choose None from the Bevel menu.

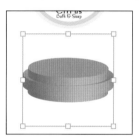
Complex 1 bevel

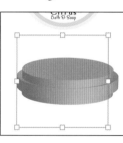
Complex 1 bevel with Extent Out selected

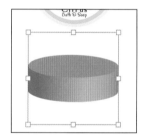
None

Note: 3D objects may display anti-aliasing artifacts on screen, but these artifacts disappear when the object is rasterized. Read more about rasterization in the flattening section of Lesson 15, "Output."

8 Click OK to close the dialog box. Leave the object selected.

9 Choose File > Save. Leave the file open for the next lesson.

Applying a symbol as mapped artwork

You can apply any 2D artwork stored as a symbol in the Symbols panel to selected surfaces on your 3D object.

Every 3D object is composed of several surfaces. For example, the shape that you just created has three external surfaces. It has a top, a bottom, and a side surface that wraps around the shape. In this next lesson, you will take the Lots O' Lime logo that you created and map it to the cylinder.

1 Since you are editing the existing Extrude & Bevel effect, open the Appearance panel (Window > Appearance). In the Appearance panel, click the blue words 3D Extrude & Bevel. Drag the 3D Extrude & Bevel Options dialog box to the side so that you can see your artwork as you make changes.

⬤ **Note:** Any time that you apply an effect, click the effect name in the Appearance panel to edit it. If you choose Effect > 3D > Extrude & Bevel again with the can still selected, it adds another instance of the effect.

2 In the 3D Extrude & Bevel Options dialog box, click Map Art. In the Map Art dialog box, select Preview.

The Map Art dialog box has a window for positioning mapped artwork. You can select the symbol and surface to work with.

3 Click the Surface next arrow button to navigate from one surface to another. Notice that as you go through the surfaces, a red highlight appears on the ellipse object, indicating which surface is active in the preview window.

4 Surface 1 of 3 should be selected. If not, click the next or previous Surface arrow button. You see the top of the cylinder in the preview panel.

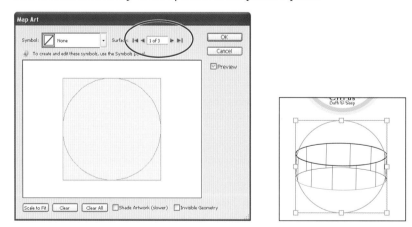

5 Choose Can top from the Symbol menu. The Can top symbol appears in the preview window.

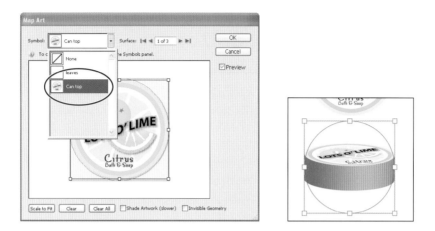

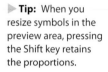

6 Click the next Surface arrow button twice to navigate to 3 of 3.

7 Choose leaves from the Symbol menu.

8 Click the Scale To Fit button to scale the symbol so that it fills the side of the soap can. Press Shift+Alt (Windows) or Shift+Option (Mac OS), and click and drag the top bounding point of the Leaves symbol down to make the symbols smaller. Release the mouse button, and then the keys. In the preview window, the light gray area is the visible area of the can, and the dark gray areas are in back, and therefore not visible. If you like, select Shade Artwork (Slower) to shade the side and top art.

▶ **Tip:** When you resize symbols in the preview area, pressing the Shift key retains the proportions.

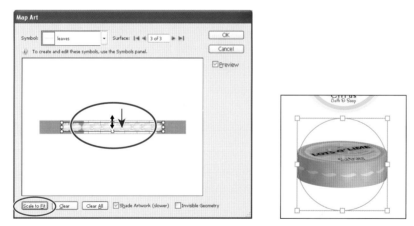

9 Click OK to close the Map Art dialog box, and click OK again to close the 3D Extrude & Bevel Options dialog box. The soap can is now done.

10 Choose Select > Deselect, and then File > Save.

To map artwork to a 3D object

Following is some helpful information about mapping artwork to 3D objects.

- To move the symbol, position the cursor inside the bounding box and drag. To scale, drag a side or corner handle. To rotate, drag outside and near a bounding box handle.

- To remove artwork from a single surface, select the surface using the Surface options, and then either choose None from the Symbol menu or click Clear.

- To remove all maps from all of the 3D object's surfaces, click Clear All.

- To show only the artwork map, not the geometry of a 3D object, select Invisible Geometry. This is useful when you want to use the 3D mapping feature as a three-dimensional warping tool. For example, you could use this option to map text to the side of an extruded wavy line so that the text appears warped as if on a flag.

—From Illustrator Help

Creating a revolved object

In this next lesson, you will create soap in the shape of a sphere. To begin with, you will create an arc that will be revolved to create the sphere.

1 Choose Window > Workspace > Essentials.

2 Select the Rectangle tool (▢) from the Ellipse tool group, and click once on the canvas to the right of the artboard. When the Rectangle dialog box appears, type 85 pt for Width, and 100 pt for Height. Click OK.

3 Select the Selection tool (▸), and move the rectangle away from any other artwork.

4 Press the D key to return the rectangle back to the default colors of black stroke and white fill.

5 Press Ctrl+5 (Windows) or Command+5 (Mac OS), or choose View > Guides > Make Guides, to turn the rectangle into a custom guide.

6 By default, guides are locked. To verify that guides are locked, choose View > Guides. If there is a check mark to the left of Lock Guides, they are locked. If there is no check mark, choose Lock Guides to lock them.

7 With the Zoom tool (🔍), click the guides several times to zoom in. Choose View > Smart Guides to select them.

8 Select the Pen tool (✒), click the lower right corner of the rectangle guide when the word anchor appears, and drag to the left until the end point of the direction line reaches the lower left corner, and release. This creates a direction line.

9 Click the upper right corner when the word anchor appears. Shift-drag to the right until the end point of the directional line reaches the upper left corner, and release. You have created an arc.

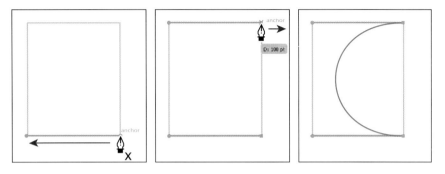

10 Choose View > Guides > Clear Guides.

11 Using the Selection tool, select the arc.

12 Click the Stroke color in the Control panel and choose None (⬜).

13 Click the Fill color in the Control panel and select Can Green.

14 Choose Effect > 3D > Revolve. In the 3D Revolve Options dialog box, select Preview to see your changes.

● **Note:** The stroke color would override the fill color of the object when revolved.

Although options in the 3D Revolve Options dialog box appear similar to the Extrude & Bevel options, they have a very different effect.

15 Choose Off-Axis Front from the Position menu if not already chosen.

16 For the Offset option choose Right Edge. This is the edge that your arc revolves around. The result varies dramatically depending on the side that you choose and whether you have a stroke or fill applied to the original object. Click OK.

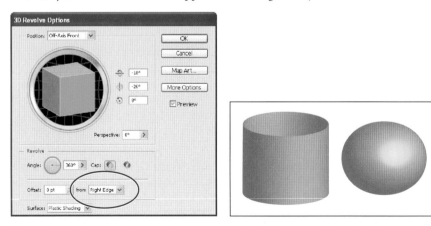

Choose which edge to revolve around.

Revolve with Left Edge selected.

Revolve with Right Edge selected.

17 Choose File > Save, and keep the file open.

Changing the lighting

In this lesson, you will change the strength and direction of the light source.

1 With the lime soap shape selected, click 3D Revolve in the Appearance panel. If the Appearance panel is not visible, choose Window > Appearance. You may also need to scroll in the Appearance panel, or resize it for easier viewing.

2 Select Preview in the 3D Revolve Options dialog box, and click More Options.

You can create custom lighting effects on your 3D object. Use the preview window in the lower left to reposition the lighting and change the shade color.

3 Choose Diffuse Shading from the Surface menu.

4 In the Surface options preview pane, click and drag the white square that represents the light source. This changes the direction of the lighting. Drag the light source to the top of the object. Click the New Light button (⬚) to add another light source to the lime shape. Drag the second light source to the right.

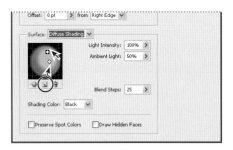

5 Choose Custom from the Shading Color menu. Click the colored red square to the right of Custom and use the Color Picker to select a dark green color, or enter values in the color text fields to the right of the picker window (we used C=62%, M=50%, Y=100%, B=45%), and then click OK.

The green shape now has a dark green shading.

6 In the 3D Revolve Options dialog box, change Ambient Light to 40%, and then click OK. Ambient light controls the brightness on the surface uniformly.

7 Using the Selection tool (▶), position the soap shape closer to the soap can.

8 Choose Select > Deselect.

9 Choose File > Save.

What are Blend Steps?

Clicking More Options in the 3D options dialog box reveals the Surface option called Blend Steps. Blend Steps control how smoothly the shading appears across the object's surfaces. Enter a value between 1 and 256. Higher numbers produce smoother shades and more paths than lower numbers.

As a default, this amount is low to quickly generate the blend and provide the optimum number of steps for artwork that is viewed on your computer monitor or on the Internet. This low number may cause banding (large, visible shifts of value from one tone to the next) when printing.

—From Illustrator Help

Mapping a Photoshop image

You can map artwork from Illustrator and also import artwork from other applications, such as Photoshop. In this part of the lesson, you will place a Photoshop texture into the document and apply it to the soap.

1 Choose File > Place, and locate the image named limeskin.psd in the Lesson11 folder. Make sure that Link is not selected in the Place dialog box. Files to be used as symbols must be embedded. Click Place. In the Photoshop Import Options dialog box, click OK.

Note: The limeskin.psd image will cover existing artwork.

2 Open the Symbols panel by clicking the Symbols panel icon (♣). With the Selection tool (▶), drag the image onto the Symbols panel. In the Symbol Options dialog box, enter the name newTexture, and select Graphic as the Type option. Click OK.

3 Delete the placed image.

4 Select the soap shape with the Selection tool, and open the Appearance panel. Click 3D Revolve in the Appearance panel.

5 Click Map Art in the 3D Revolve Options dialog box. Choose newTexture from the Symbol menu. Select Preview if not already selected.

● **Note:** If the arc edges are not perfectly aligned you will see more than one surface (2 of 2). Use the Next Surface arrow to navigate through the surfaces and choose the one that highlights the outer surface.

● **Note:** If you select the wrong surface, choose Clear and map to another surface.

6 Click the Scale To Fit button, and select Shade Artwork (Slower). Click OK to close the Map Art dialog box. In the 3D Revolve Options dialog box, click OK.

The texture now wraps around the soap shape. Next you will clone the 3D objects to add more to the artboard.

7 Make sure the soap shape you just created is selected with the Selection tool. Alt-drag (Windows) or Option-drag (Mac OS) the shape to the left and down. Release the mouse button, and then the key. This clones the soap shape and gives you a total of two. Drag a marquee around both soap shapes to select them, and move them closer to the can.

Adjusting the lighting

Because 3D objects do not share lighting, you will edit the existing Extrude & Bevel effect applied to the ellipse that you used to create the soap can.

1 With the Selection tool (➤), click to select the soap can.

2 In the Appearance panel, click 3D Extrude & Bevel (Mapped).

3 In the 3D Extrude & Bevel Options dialog box, in the Surface options preview pane, drag the light to the top center of the sphere. This makes the lighting more

▶ **Tip:** Whenever artwork is mapped to a 3D object, the word (Mapped) appears in the Appearance panel.

consistent with the soap shapes. We added a second light source to the can in a similar position to where it was on the sphere. Change the surface by choosing Diffuse Shading from the Surface menu and change the ambient light to 40%. Click OK.

● **Note:** If you don't see the Surface options, click More Options in the 3D Extrude & Bevel dialog box.

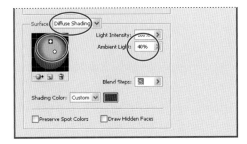

4 With the Selection tool, Shift-click the soap can and both spheres to select them. Move them onto the artboard in the middle of the gift certificate.

5 There is a green stem off the artboard on the right. You can place the stem on one of the limes if you like. Choose Object > Arrange > Bring To Front if the stem disappears when you drag it into place.

6 When you have rearranged objects to your satisfaction, choose File > Save, and keep the file open for the Exploring on Your Own section, or choose File > Close.

▶ **Tip:** When you apply a 3D effect to an object, you can change the scale of the object or change the color, and the 3D effect remains.

● **Note:** Do not rotate objects that have 3D effects applied to them, because you will get unexpected results. To rotate a 3D object, click the name of the effect in the Appearance panel, and rotate the item in space using the position preview window.

Exploring on your own

Next you will work with another effect to add a nice touch to the Gift.ai file you still have open.

1 With the Selection tool, click to select the green rectangle around the outside of the gift certificate.

2 Choose Effect > Convert to Shape > Rounded Rectangle.

3 In the Shape Options dialog box, select the Relative option, and then change Extra Width and Extra Height to 0. Select Preview, and then adjust the corner radius to the desired corner radius.

4 Click OK.

5 Choose File > Save, and then File > Close.

Try to create an additional item for the artwork in this lesson.

1　Choose File > Open, and locate the L11start2.ai file in the Lesson11 folder.

2　Choose the Selection tool, and then Select > All.

3　Drag the artwork into the Symbols panel.

4　In the Symbols Options dialog box, change the name to Soap, and select Graphic as the type.

5　With the artwork still selected, choose Edit > Clear, or press the Delete key.

6　Select the Rectangle tool (■), and click the artboard once. Type 325 pt for the width and 220 pt for the height. Click OK.

7　Choose Effect > 3D > Extrude & Bevel, and experiment with different positions and settings.

8　Click Map Art, and map the Soap symbol that you created to the top of the box.

9　Close both dialog boxes when you are finished.

Take the illustration further by creating your own symbols and applying them to the other faces of the box.

10 Choose File > Close and don't save the file.

Review questions

1 Name two ways to apply an effect to an object.

2 Where can the effects applied to an object be edited once they are applied?

3 What are the three types of 3D effects that are available? Give an example of why you would use each one.

4 How can you control lighting on a 3D object? Does the lighting of one 3D object affect other 3D objects?

5 What are the steps to map artwork to an object?

Review answers

1 You can apply an effect to an object by selecting the object, and then choose the effect from the Effect menu. You can also apply an effect by selecting the object, then clicking Add New Effect (*fx.*) in the Appearance panel, and choosing the effect from the menu that appears.

2 You can edit effects in the Appearance panel.

3 The types of 3D effects are extrude & bevel, revolve, and rotate.

   • Extrude & bevel—Uses the Z axis to give a 2D object depth by extruding the object. For example, a circle becomes a cylinder.

   • Revolve—Uses the Y axis to revolve an object around an axis. For example, an arc becomes a circle.

   • Rotate—Uses the Z axis to rotate 2D artwork in 3D space and change the artwork's perspective.

4 By clicking the More Options button in the various 3D dialog boxes, you can change the light, the direction of the light, and the shade color. Options for one 3D object's lighting do not affect other 3D objects.

5 Map artwork to an object by following these steps:

   1 Select the artwork and Alt-click (Windows) or Option-click (Mac OS) the New Symbol button in the Symbols panel.

   2 Select the object and choose Effect > 3D > Extrude & Bevel or Effect > 3D > Revolve.

   3 Click Map Art.

   4 Navigate to the surface using the arrow keys. Select the symbol from the Symbol menu. Close both dialog boxes.

12 APPLYING APPEARANCE ATTRIBUTES AND GRAPHIC STYLES

Lesson overview

In this lesson, you'll learn how to do the following:

- Create and edit an appearance attribute.

- Add a second stroke to an object.

- Reorder appearance attributes and apply them to layers.

- Copy, turn on and off, and remove appearance attributes.

- Save an appearance as a graphic style.

- Apply a graphic style to an object and a layer.

- Apply multiple graphic styles to an object or layer.

 This lesson will take approximately an hour to complete. If needed, remove the previous lesson folder from your hard disk and copy the Lesson12 folder onto it.

Without changing the structure of an object, you can change its look using appearance attributes, including fills, strokes, effects, transparency and blending modes. You can save appearance attributes as graphic styles and apply them to another object. You can also edit an object that has a graphic style applied to it, and then edit the graphic style—an enormous time-saver!

Getting started

In this lesson, you'll enhance the design for a web page by applying appearance attributes and graphic styles to the type, background, and buttons. Before you begin, you'll restore the default preferences for Adobe Illustrator CS4. Then you will open the finished art file for this lesson to see what you'll create.

1   To ensure that the tools and panels function as described in this lesson, delete or deactivate (by renaming) the Adobe Illustrator CS4 preferences file. See "Restoring default preferences" on page 3.

2   Start Adobe Illustrator CS4.

⬤ **Note:** If you have not already copied the resource files for this lesson onto your hard disk from the Lesson12 folder on the Adobe Illustrator CS4 Classroom in a Book CD, do so now. See "Copying the Classroom in a Book files" on page 2.

3   Choose File > Open. Locate the L12end.ai file in the Lesson12 folder in the Lessons folder that you copied onto your hard disk to view the finished artwork. In this lesson, you will apply styling to the web buttons and other objects. Leave the file open for reference, or choose File > Close.

The design for the completed web page includes several graphic styles and effects, including gradients, semi-transparent type, drop shadows, and texturized and shaded graphics.

4   Open the L12start.ai file in the Lesson12 folder, located in the Lessons folder on your hard disk.

5   Choose File > Save As. In the Save As dialog box, navigate to the Lesson12 folder and open it. Name the file tech_design.ai. Leave the Save As Type option set to Adobe Illustrator (*.AI) (Windows) or the Format option set to Adobe Illustrator (ai) (Mac OS), and click Save. In the Illustrator Options dialog box, leave the Illustrator options at their default settings, and click OK.

Using appearance attributes

You can apply appearance attributes to any object, group, or layer by using effects and the Appearance panel and Graphic Styles panel. An appearance attribute is an aesthetic property—such as a fill, stroke, transparency, or effect—that affects the look of an object, but does not affect its basic structure. An advantage of using appearance attributes is that they can be changed or removed at any time without changing the underlying object or any other attributes applied to the object.

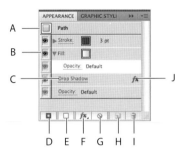

A. Path with stroke, fill, and drop shadow effect

B. Visibility column

C. Link to options

D. Add New Stroke

E. Add New Fill

F. Add Effect

G. Clear Appearance

H. Duplicate Selected Item

I. Delete Selected Item

J. Path with effect

For example, if you apply the Drop Shadow effect to an object, you can change the drop shadow distance, blur, or color. You can also copy that effect and apply it to other shapes, groups, or layers. You can even save it as a graphic style and use it for other objects or files.

The Appearance panel contains the following types of editable attributes:

- Stroke (weight, color, and effects)
- Fill (type, color, transparency, and effects)
- Transparency, including opacity and blending mode
- Effect menu

Editing and adding appearance attributes

You'll start by selecting an arrow shape and adding to its basic appearance using the Appearance panel.

1   Choose Window > Workspace > Essentials.

2   In the tech_design.ai file, using the Selection tool (￼), select the top green arrow shape in the Home button.

3   Open the Appearance panel (￼) from the right side of the workspace, and click the Stroke attribute row to select it. Do not click the blue underlined word Stroke. Click to the right or left of the word.

Selecting the Stroke attribute row lets you change just the stroke in the artwork.

4 Click the word Opacity in the Control panel to reveal the Transparency panel. In the Transparency panel, choose Multiply from the menu of blending modes. Change Opacity to 50%. Press Enter or Return to close the Transparency panel.

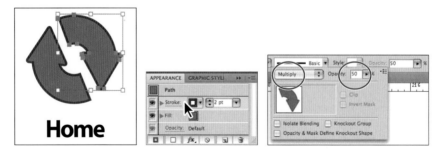

5 With the Selection tool, press Ctrl+spacebar (Windows) or Command+spacebar (Mac OS) and click the arrow shape several times to zoom in about 200%. Inspect the stroke around the arrow to see how it has changed. The effect of the Multiply blending mode is similar to drawing on a page with transparent marker pens.

Strokes are centered on a path outline—half of the stroke color overlaps the filled arrow shape, and half of the stroke color overlaps the white background. Next you will edit the stroke of the arrow using the Appearance panel.

6 In the Appearance panel, expand the stroke attributes by clicking the triangle (▶) to the left of the word Stroke in the panel list.

7 Click the word Opacity to open the Transparency panel.

8 In the Transparency panel, change Opacity to 70%. Click the Opacity attribute row in the Appearance panel to hide the Transparency panel.

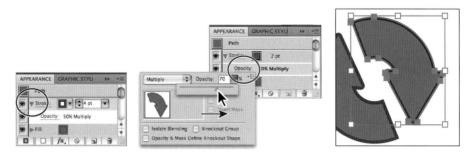

9 Click 2 pt in the Appearance panel to edit the value. Change Stroke Weight to 4 pt. If you want, you can change the stroke color as well.

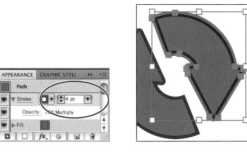

10 Choose File > Save.

Reordering appearance attributes

Now you'll change the appearance of the Multiply blending mode by rearranging the attributes in the Appearance panel.

1 Resize the Appearance panel so that you can view all its contents. Click the triangle (▷) to the left of the word Stroke to hide the stroke properties.

2 Click and drag the Fill attribute above the Stroke attribute. (This technique is similar to dragging layers in the Layers panel to rearrange the stacking order.)

Moving the Fill attribute above the Stroke attribute changes the look of the Multiply blending mode on the stroke. Half the stroke is covered. Blending modes work only on objects that are beneath them in the stacking order.

Adding an additional stroke and fill

You'll now add another stroke to the object using the Appearance panel. Applying another stroke is a way to add interesting design elements to your artwork.

1 With the arrow shape selected, click the Add New Stroke button (■) at the bottom of the Appearance panel. A stroke is added to the top of the list of appearance attributes. It has the same color and stroke weight as the first stroke.

2 For the new stroke, change Stroke Weight to 2 pt in the Appearance panel.

▶ **Tip:** There are many ways to close panels that appear in the Appearance panel, such as the Color panel, including pressing Escape or clicking the Stroke attribute row.

3 Shift-click the Stroke Color to open the Color panel. Choose RGB from the panel menu (▾≡). Change the RGB values to R=76, G=0, and B=121. Press Enter or Return to close the Color panel and return to the Appearance panel.

● **Note:** Clicking Stroke Color in the Appearance panel without the Shift key reveals the Swatches panel.

You are using the RGB color mode because you are working with a web document. Next you will add an effect to change the offset of the stroke by bringing it toward the center of the arrow.

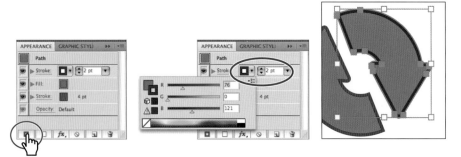

4 With the top Stroke attribute row still selected, click the Add New Effect button (*fx.*) at the bottom of the Appearance panel. Choose Path > Offset Path from the menu that appears.

5 Select Preview in the Offset Path dialog box to see the effect of offsetting as you change the values. Change Offset to −3 px, and click OK.

6 In the Appearance panel, click the arrow to the left of the top Stroke to reveal the Offset Path and Opacity effects. Deselect the eye icon (👁) to the left of Offset Path to hide that effect. Notice that the arrow on the artboard changes. Select the Visibility column to view the Offset Path again.

By clicking the eye icon in the Appearance panel, you disable an attribute without deleting it.

Next you'll rearrange the order of the appearance attributes to prepare for adding live effects.

7 In the Appearance panel, click the triangle to the left of the 2 pt Stroke attribute to collapse the attribute, and then drag the 4 pt Stroke attribute between the Fill attribute and the 2 pt Stroke attribute.

▶ **Tip:** You can view all hidden attributes by choosing Show All Hidden Attributes from the Appearance panel menu.

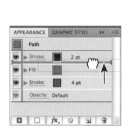

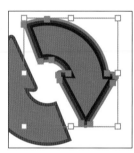

8 Choose File > Save, and keep the arrow selected.

Using graphic styles

A graphic style is a named set of appearance attributes that you can reuse. By applying different graphic styles, you can quickly and globally change the appearance of an object.

For example, if you have a map that uses a symbol to represent a city, you can create a graphic style that paints the symbol green with a drop shadow. You can then use that graphic style to paint all the city symbols on the map. If you decide to use a different color, you can change the fill color of the graphic style to blue. All the symbols painted with that graphic style are then updated to blue.

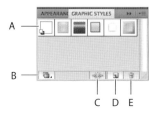

A. Graphic styles

B. Graphic Styles Libraries menu

C. Break Link To Graphic Style

D. New Graphic Style

E. Delete Graphic Style

The Graphic Styles panel lets you create, name, save, and apply various effects and attributes to objects, layers, and groups. Just like attributes and effects, graphic styles are completely reversible. For example, you can apply a style to a circle that contains the Zig Zag effect, turning the circle into a starburst. You can revert the object to its original appearance with the Appearance panel. You can also break the link between that individual object and the graphic style to edit its attributes without affecting other objects painted with the same graphic style.

Graphic styles can also be applied to text. You can preserve the color of type when applying a graphic style by deselecting Override Character Color from the Graphic Styles panel menu.

Creating and saving a graphic style

Now you'll save and name a new graphic style using the appearance attributes you just created for the arrow shape in the Home button. You will then apply the same appearance attributes to the other arrow shape.

1 Click the Graphic Styles tab in the Appearance panel group to bring the panel to the front.

2 Drag the Graphic Styles panel by the panel tab so that it is free-floating in the workspace. Resize the Graphic Styles panel so that all the default styles are visible and there is empty space at the bottom.

3 With the arrow shape on the artboard still selected, in the Appearance panel, drag the Path appearance thumbnail into the Graphic Styles panel.

4 When a small box appears on the inside of the panel, release the mouse button. The box indicates that you are adding a new style to the panel.

   The path thumbnail in the Appearance panel changes to "Path: Graphic Style."

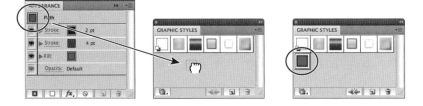

5 In the Graphic Styles panel, double-click the new graphic style thumbnail. In the Graphic Style Options dialog box, name the new style Home button. Click OK.

   Notice in the Appearance panel that Path: Graphic Style has changed to Path: Home button. This indicates that a graphic style called Home button is applied to the selected object.

6 Choose Select > Deselect, and then File > Save.

Applying a graphic style to an object

Graphic styles can be easily applied to other objects. Next you will apply the graphic style of the right arrow shape to the left arrow in the Home button.

1 With the Selection tool (➤), click to select the other arrow.

2 Click the Home button graphic style in the Graphic Styles panel to apply its attributes to the other arrow.

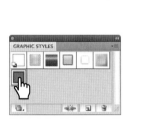

3 Choose Select > Deselect, and then File > Save.

Applying a graphic style to a layer

When a graphic style is applied to a layer, everything added to that layer has that same style applied to it. Now you'll create a new graphic style and apply it to a layer. Then you'll create new shapes on that layer to see the effect of the style.

1 Choose Essentials from the workspace switcher in the Control panel.

2 Open the Appearance panel (◉), and click the Clear Appearance button (⊘) at the bottom of the panel. Select the No Selection appearance name or thumbnail at the top of the panel.

The Clear Appearance button removes all appearance attributes applied to an object, including any stroke or fill. By clicking the Clear Appearance button with nothing selected, you are setting the default appearance for new shapes.

3 In the Appearance panel, click the Add New Effect button (*fx.*) and choose Stylize > Drop Shadow from the Illustrator Effects. Change Opacity to 50%, X Offset to 3 pt, Y Offset to 3 pt, and Blur to 3 pt. Click OK.

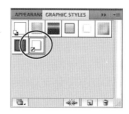

When creating a new style, the Graphic Style panel automatically uses the current appearance attributes displayed in the Appearance panel.

4 In the Graphic Styles panel, Alt-click (Windows) or Option-click (Mac OS) the New Graphic Style button (⬛), and type Drop Shadow as the name of the new style. Click OK.

Now you'll target the Blog button layer to apply a drop shadow to all the shapes on that layer. Targeting selects the path(s) on that layer in the artwork.

5 In the Layers panel, click the triangle (▶) to the left of the Blog button layer to expand the layer. Then click the target icon (○) to the right of the Blog button layer name.

6 In the Graphic Styles panel, click the Drop Shadow style to apply the style to the layer and all its contents. Keep the shapes selected on the artboard.

7 Double-click the Scale tool (⬛) in the Tools panel. Change Uniform Scale to 70%, and then click OK.

8 Choose Select > Deselect, and then File > Save.

Now you'll test the layer effect by adding a shape to the Blog button layer.

9   Select the Zoom tool (🔍) in the Tools panel, and click the blog shapes twice to zoom in.

10 Select the Ellipse tool (⬭) from the same group as the Rectangle tool (▭) in the Tools panel.

11 Make sure that Fill color in the Control panel is set to None (▱), Stroke Color is black, and Stroke Weight is 3 pt.

12 With the Blog button layer still selected, press the Shift key and draw a circle on top of the blog shapes that is about 82 pt in height and width.

13 Choose Object > Arrange > Send To Back to send the ellipse behind the blog shapes. With the Selection tool, position the circle so that it is approximately centered behind the blog shapes. Keep the ellipse selected.

Because the Drop Shadow style contains only an effect, and no stroke or fill, the objects added to the layer retain their original stroke and fill attributes.

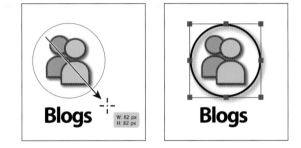

Next you will edit the drop shadow applied to the layer.

In the Appearance panel, notice the name Layer: Drop Shadow at the top of the panel. The Appearance panel shows that the ellipse is on a layer with a drop shadow applied to it.

14 Click the words Layer: Drop Shadow to access the Drop Shadow effect applied to the layer.

Tip: You can also select the Blog button layer target icon, and then edit the effect in the Appearance panel.

15 Click the words Drop Shadow in the Appearance panel and change X Offset to 2 pt, and Y Offset to 2 pt in the Drop Shadow dialog box. Select Preview to see the subtle change. Click OK.

16 Choose View > Fit Artboard In Window.

17 Choose File > Save.

Target icons

The target icon on the Layers panel indicates whether an item in the layer hierarchy has any appearance attributes and whether it is targeted.

- (◎) Indicates that the layer, group, or object is targeted but has no appearance attributes applied to it.

- (○) Indicates that the layer, group, or object is not targeted and has no appearance attributes applied to it.

- (◉) Indicates that the layer, group, or object is not targeted but has appearance attributes applied to it.

- (◉) Indicates that the group is targeted and has appearance attributes applied to it. This icon also designates any targeted object that has appearance attributes more complex than a single fill and stroke applied to it.

—From Illustrator Help

Applying existing graphic styles

> **Tip:** It is a good idea to use the Layers panel to select the objects or layers to which you want to apply styles. Effects and styles vary, depending on whether you're targeting a layer or an object, or a group within a layer.

You can apply graphic styles from libraries that come with Illustrator CS4 to your artwork. Now you'll finish the button designs by adding an existing style to the Chat button layer.

1 In the Layers panel, click the triangle (▶) to left of the Blog button layer to collapse it. Click the triangle (▶) to left of the Chat button layer to expand it.

2 Select the <Path> sublayer to select it. Then click the target icon (○) to the right of the <Path> sublayer.

3 Select the yellow swatch (R=253, G=195, B=17) from the Fill color in the Control panel.

> ● **Note:** If you target a layer or sublayer by mistake, Ctrl-click or Command-click the target icon to deselect it.

Now you'll apply a graphic style to the Chat button. The style contains a color, which you'll apply to the chat object in place of the existing yellow color.

4 In the Layers panel, with the target icon (○) for the <Path> sublayer still selected, click the Style menu in the Control panel. Right-click (Windows) or

Control-click (Mac OS) and hold down on the Chat style in the Graphic Styles panel to preview the graphic style on the chat bubble.

● **Note:** If the Style menu doesn't appear in the Control panel, open the Graphic Styles panel by clicking its icon on the right side of the workspace.

5 Click the Chat graphic style to apply it to the chat bubble.

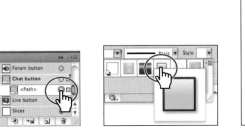

6 Choose File > Save.

Next you'll apply an existing graphic style to some text.

7 Choose Select > Deselect.

8 With the Selection tool (▸), drag a marquee across the button labels (the text below the buttons) to select them.

9 Choose Override Character Color from the Graphic Styles panel menu (▾≡), if it's not already selected. Click the Graphic Styles Libraries menu button (▣₊), and choose the Illuminate Styles library.

▶ **Tip:** The arrows at the bottom of the Illuminate Styles library panel load the previous or next graphic styles library in the panel.

When you apply a graphic style to type, the text fill overrides the fill color of the graphic style. To prevent that, choose Override Character Color.

10 Choose Use Text For Preview from the Illuminate Styles panel menu (▾≡).

11 In the Illuminate Styles library panel, right-click (Windows) or Control-click (Mac OS) and hold down on the Charcoal Highlight graphic style to preview the graphic style on the text. Click the Charcoal Highlight graphic style to apply it. If Override Character Color had been left off, the fill would still be black.

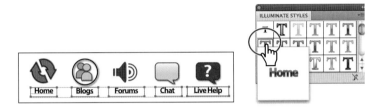

● **Note:** When you click a graphic style from a library, the graphic style is added to the Graphic Styles panel for that document.

12 Close the Illuminate Styles library panel.

13 Choose Select > Deselect, and then File > Save.

Adding to an existing graphic style

You can apply a graphic style to an object that already uses a graphic style applied. This can be useful if you want to add properties to an object from another graphic style. The formatting becomes cumulative.

1 With the Selection tool (▶), click to select the red live help button shape (not the question mark).

Next, you'll make a change to the shape, and then create a new graphic style out of its appearance attributes.

2 Click the Appearance panel tab in the Graphic Styles panel group to open the panel. Select the Fill attribute, and click the Duplicate Selected Item button (▣) at the bottom of the panel. This creates a copy of the fill.

▶ **Tip:** To see larger swatches, choose Large Thumbnail View from the Nature_Animal Skins panel menu.

3 Click the Fill color of the new Fill attribute, which is automatically selected in the Appearance panel, to open the Swatches panel. Click the Swatch Libraries menu button (▣,) at the bottom of the panel. Choose Patterns > Nature > Nature_ Animal Skins. Select the pattern named Tiger to apply it to the fill.

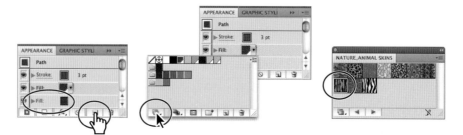

4 Close the Nature_Animal Skins panel.

5 Change Opacity to 30% in the Control panel.

6 Click the Graphic Styles panel tab to show the graphic styles. Alt-click (Windows) or Option-click (Mac OS) the New Graphic Style button (▣). In the Graphic Style Option dialog box, name the style Help. Click OK.

Next you will apply the Bevel Soft Graphic Style to the live help button shape that is still selected.

7 In the Graphic Styles panel, click to apply the Bevel Soft graphic style to the button shape.

Notice that the fills and the stroke are no longer visible. Graphic styles replace the formatting on selected objects by default.

8 Choose Edit > Undo Graphic Styles.

9 Alt-click (Windows) or Option-click (Mac OS) the Bevel Soft graphic style.

Notice that the fills and stroke are preserved and that the bevel is applied as well. Alt-clicking (Windows) or Option-clicking (Mac OS) adds the graphic style formatting to the existing formatting.

10 Open the Appearance panel. Deselect the eye icon (👁) to the left of the Drop Shadow attribute to hide it.

11 Choose Select > Deselect, and then File > Save.

Applying an appearance to a layer

You can also apply simple appearance attributes to layers. For example, to make everything on a layer 50% opaque, target that layer, and change the opacity.

Next you'll target a layer and change its blending mode to soften the effect of the type.

1 In the Layers panel, click the downward triangle next to any open layers to collapse them.

2 Scroll to the Columns layer, and then click its target icon (○).

3 Select the K=50 swatch from the Fill color in the Control panel, and change Opacity to 20%.

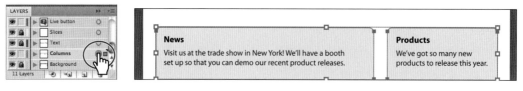

4 Choose File > Save.

Copying, applying, and removing graphic styles

When you create several graphic styles and appearances, you may want to use them on other objects in your artwork. You can use the Graphic Styles panel, the Appearance panel, the Eyedropper tool (✐), or the Paint Bucket tool (⬧) to apply and copy appearance attributes.

Next you'll apply a style to one of the objects using the Appearance panel.

1 Choose Select > Deselect.

2 With the Selection tool (▸), click one of the arrow shapes for the Home button to select it.

⬤ **Note:** Be sure to drag the thumbnail, not the text.

3 In the Appearance panel, drag the appearance thumbnail labeled Path: Home button onto the larger speaker shape of the Forums button to apply those attributes to it.

You can apply styles or attributes by dragging them from the Graphic Styles panel or the Appearance panel onto any object. The object doesn't have to be selected.

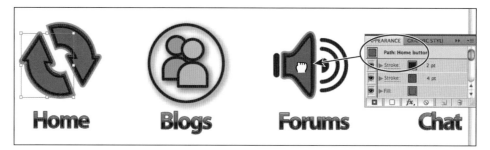

4 Choose Select > Deselect.

Next, you'll apply a style by dragging it directly from the Graphic Styles panel onto an object.

5 With the Selection tool, drag the Charcoal Highlight graphic style thumbnail in the Graphic Styles panel onto the larger speaker shape in the Forums button artwork.

6 Release the mouse button to apply the style to the shape.

7 Drag the same graphic style to the smaller speaker shape to the left in the forums button to apply it.

Now you'll use the Layers panel to copy an attribute from one layer to another.

8 Expand the Layers panel to see all the layers. Click the Blog button layer to select it. Alt-drag (Windows) or Option-drag (Mac OS) the appearance indicator from the Blog button layer onto the appearance indicator of the Header type layer.

Using Alt or Option as you drag copies one layer effect onto another, which is indicated by the hand pointer with the plus sign. To move an appearance or style from one layer or object to another, drag the appearance indicator.

Alt-drag or Option-drag the appearance attributes from one layer to another.

Now you'll remove an appearance from a layer using the Layers panel.

9 In the Layers panel, click the target icon to the right of the Blog button layer.

10 Drag the target icon to the Trash button at the bottom of the Layers panel to remove the appearance attribute.

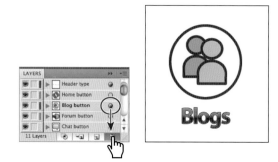

You can also remove attributes of a selected object or layer in the Appearance panel. To do this, select the object and then choose Reduce To Basic Appearance from the panel menu to return the object to its original state (including any stroke or fill) before the appearance attribute or style was applied.

11 Choose File > Save, and then File > Close.

Exploring on your own

Now that you've learned the basic steps to creating and using appearances and graphic styles, you can experiment with different combinations of appearance attributes to fashion interesting special effects. Try combining different styles to produce new ones.

For example, here's how to merge two existing styles to create a brand new style:

1 Choose File > New to create a new file. In the New Document dialog box, make sure that Print is chosen from the New Document Profile menu and click OK.

2 Choose Window > Graphic Styles to open the panel.

3 In the Graphic Styles panel, select the Round Corners 10 pt style.

● **Note:** If the Round Corners 10 pt style does not appear in the Graphic Styles panel, then click the Graphic Styles Library Menu button and choose Image Effects > Yellow Glow.

4 Add another style to the selection by Ctrl-clicking (Windows) or Command-clicking (Mac OS) the style named Arched Green.

● **Note:** If the Arched Green style does not appear in the Graphic Styles panel, then click the Graphic Styles Library Menu button and choose Type Effects > Twine.

5 Choose Merge Graphic Styles from the Graphic Styles panel menu.

6 Name the new style merged style in the Graphic Style Options dialog box, and click OK.

7 On the artboard, draw a shape or create text, and then apply the new style.

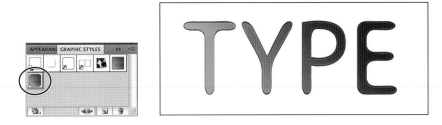

8 Choose File > Close without saving the file.

Review questions

1 Name two types of appearance attributes.

2 How do you add a second stroke to an object?

3 What's the difference between applying a graphic style to a layer versus applying it to an object?

4 How do you add to an existing graphic style?

5 How do you remove an appearance attribute using the Layers panel?

Review answers

1 The Appearance panel contains the following types of editable attributes:

- Fill attributes (fill type, color, transparency, and effects)

- Stroke attributes (stroke type, brush, color transparency, and effects)

- Transparency attributes (opacity and blending mode)

- Effects from the Effect menu

2 Click the Add New Stroke button in the Appearance panel, or choose Add New Stroke from the Appearance panel menu. A stroke is added to the top of the appearance list. It has the same color and stroke weight as the original stroke.

3 After a graphic style is applied to a layer, everything you add to that layer has that style applied to it. For example, if you create a circle on Layer 1 and then move it to Layer 2, which has a Drop Shadow effect applied, the circle adopts that effect. When a style is applied to a single object, other objects on that layer are not affected. For example, if a triangle object has a Roughen effect applied to its path, and you move it to another layer, it retains the Roughen effect.

4 When a graphic style is applied to an object, Alt-click (Windows) or Option-click (Mac OS) a new graphic style in the Graphic Styles panel.

5 In the Layers panel, click the target icon of a layer. Drag the target icon to the Delete Selection button in the Layers panel to remove the appearance attribute. You can also remove the appearance attribute of a selected object or layer using the Appearance panel. Select the object and choose Reduce To Basic Appearance from the Appearance panel menu to return the object to its original state.

13 WORKING WITH SYMBOLS

Lesson overview

In this lesson, you'll learn how to do the following:

- Apply symbol instances.

- Create a symbol.

- Use the symbolism tools.

- Modify and redefine a symbol.

- Store and retrieve artwork in the Symbols panel.

- Discover symbols and Adobe Flash integration.

 This lesson will take approximately an hour to complete. If needed, remove the previous lesson folder from your hard disk and copy the Lesson13 folder onto it.

The Symbols panel lets you apply multiple objects by painting them on the page. Symbols used in combination with the symbolism tools offer options that make creating repetitive shapes, such as grass, easy and fun. You can also use the Symbols panel as a database to store artwork and map symbols to 3D objects. Symbols can also provide excellent support for SWF and SVG export.

Getting started

In this lesson, you'll finish the artwork for a poster. Before you begin, restore the default preferences for Adobe Illustrator. Then open the file containing the finished artwork to see what you are going to create.

1 To ensure that the tools and panels function as described in this lesson, delete or deactivate (by renaming) the Adobe Illustrator CS4 preferences file. See "Restoring default preferences" on page 3.

2 Start Adobe Illustrator CS4.

⬤ **Note:** If you have not already copied the resource files for this lesson onto your hard disk from the Lesson13 folder on the Adobe Illustrator CS4 Classroom in a Book CD, do so now. See "Copying the Classroom in a Book files" on page 2.

3 Choose File > Open, and open the L13end.ai file in the Lesson13 folder in the Lessons folder on your hard disk.

If you want to view the finished poster as you work, choose View > Zoom Out, and adjust the window size. Use the Hand tool (🖐) to move the artwork where you want it in the window. If you don't want to leave the image open, choose File > Close.

4 Choose File > Open to open the L13start.ai file in the Lesson13 folder, located in the Lessons folder on your hard disk.

5 Choose File > Save As. In the Save As dialog box, name the file poster.ai and navigate to the Lesson13 folder. Leave the Save As Type option set to Adobe Illustrator (*.AI) (Windows) or the Format option set to Adobe Illustrator (ai) (Mac OS), and click Save. In the Illustrator Options dialog box, leave the Illustrator options at their default settings, and click OK.

6 Choose Window > Workspace > Essentials.

7 Double-click the Hand tool (🖐) to fit the artboard in the window.

Working with symbols

A symbol is a reusable art object that is stored in the Symbols panel. For example, if you create a symbol from an object in the shape of a blade of grass, you can then quickly add multiple instances of that grass symbol to your artwork, which saves you from having to draw each individual blade of grass. All instances of the grass symbol are linked to the associated symbol in the Symbols panel, so you can easily alter them using symbolism tools. When you edit the original symbol, all instances of the grass that are linked to it are updated. You can turn that grass from brown to green instantly! Not only do symbols save time, but they greatly reduce file size. They can also be used in conjunction with Adobe Flash to create SWF files or artwork for Flash.

Illustrator comes with a series of symbol libraries, which range from tiki icons to hair and fur. You can access the symbol libraries in the Symbols panel or by choosing Window > Symbol Libraries.

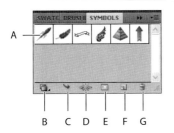

A. Symbols

B. Symbol Libraries menu

C. Place Symbol Instance

D. Break Link To Symbol

E. Symbol Options

F. New Symbol

G. Delete Symbol

Note: The Symbols panel at left is the default Symbols panel for a new Illustrator print document.

Using Illustrator symbol libraries

You will first start by adding some clouds to the artwork from an existing symbol library. Then you will create your own symbol to use as the leaves for the tree.

1   Choose View > Smart Guides to deselect smart guides.

2   If the Symbols panel is not visible, choose Window > Symbols, or click the Symbols panel icon (♣) on the right side of the workspace.

3   In the Symbols panel, click the Symbol Libraries Menu button (▦) at the bottom of the panel, and choose Nature. The Nature library opens as a free-floating panel. This library is external to the file that you are working on, but you can import any of the symbols into the document and use them in the artwork.

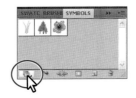

4 Click the Cloud 1 symbol to add it to the Symbols panel. Close the Nature library panel.

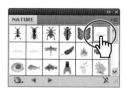

Every document has a default set of symbols in the Symbols panel. When you add symbols to the panel, they are saved with the active document only.

▶ **Tip:** You'll learn how to share symbols between documents later in this lesson.

5 If the Layers panel is not visible, choose Window > Layers. Click the Sky layer to select it.

6 Using the Selection tool (⬉), click and drag the Cloud 1 symbol onto the artboard. Drag a total of four clouds and position them around the sky.

The clouds you dragged onto the artboard are called instances of the Cloud 1 symbol. Next you will resize the symbol instances on the page.

● **Note:** Although you can transform symbol instances in many ways, specific properties of instances cannot be edited. For example, the fill color is locked because it is controlled by the original symbol in the Symbols panel.

7 Using the Selection tool, Shift-drag a corner of one of the cloud instances to make it larger. Make all the clouds varying sizes using the same method.

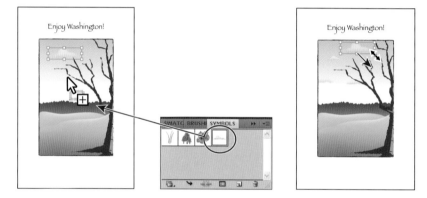

Next you will edit the cloud symbol so that all of the instances are affected.

If there are symbol instances on the page, you can edit the original symbol by double-clicking an instance on the page. When you edit an instance, all other instances of that symbol are updated.

8 With the Selection tool (⬉), double-click one of the clouds on the page. A warning dialog box appears. Click OK to continue. This takes you into isolation mode.

The cloud you double-clicked may appear to change in size. That's because you are looking at the original symbol before you resized it on the page.

9 With the Selection tool, click the cloud. Notice that you can't select any other objects on the page.

10 Make sure that the Fill box is selected in the Tools panel. If the Gradient panel is not visible, choose Window > Gradient, or click its panel icon (▣).

11 In the Gradient panel, click to select the leftmost color stop. Change Opacity to 60%. Collapse the Gradient panel by clicking its tab.

12 With the Selection tool, double-click off the cloud or click the Exit Isolation Mode button (◀) in the upper left corner of the artboard. This exits isolation mode so that you can edit the rest of the content. Notice that all the cloud instances now have the gradient you just edited.

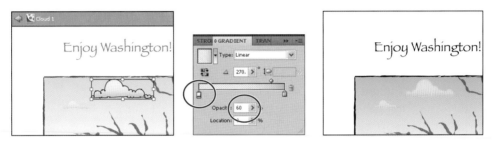

13 Choose File > Save, and leave the document open.

Creating symbols

Illustrator also lets you create your own symbols. You can make symbols from objects, including paths, compound paths, text, raster images, mesh objects, and groups of objects. Symbols can even include active objects, such as brush strokes, blends, effects, or other symbol instances.

● **Note:** You cannot use placed art that is not embedded to create a symbol.

Now you will draw an object and create your own symbol.

1 If the Layers panel is not visible, choose Window > Layers. Click the Leaves layer to select it.

2 Select the Pencil tool (✏) in the Tools panel. Off the right edge of the artboard, on the canvas, click and draw a leaf shape, starting and ending on the same point. When you've drawn all the way around the shape and approach the beginning of the shape, press Alt (Windows) or Option (Mac OS) to close the path automatically.

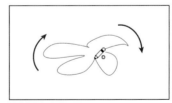

● **Note:** Try to draw the leaf in proportion to the tree. Because this is vector art, if you draw the leaf bigger, you can scale it smaller so that it looks right on the tree.

3 In the Control panel, click the Fill color and select the Dark Green swatch in the Swatches panel. With the Selection tool (➤), Alt-drag (Windows) or Option-drag (Mac OS) two copies of the leaf you drew.

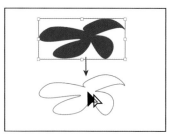

4 If the Color panel is not visible, choose Window > Color. Select the middle copied leaf and change the fill color in the Color panel to a lighter green by typing 75% in the Tint text field. Now select the bottom copied leaf and change the fill color to a light green by typing 50%.

5 If the Symbols panel is not visible, click the Symbols panel icon (♣). With the Selection tool, select the darkest green leaf and drag it into the Symbols panel.

6 In the Symbol Options dialog box, name it leaf1 and select Graphic as the Type. Click OK to create the symbol.

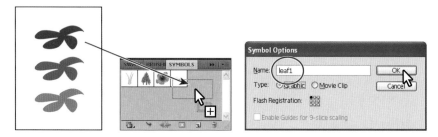

7 Now create symbols for the copied leaves. Name the 75% green leaf, leaf2, and the 50% leaf, leaf3. For both symbols, select Graphic as the Type.

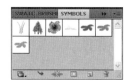

After creating the leaf symbols, the original leaves off the right edge of the artboard are converted to symbol instances. You can leave them where they are or delete them.

8 Choose File > Save.

Spraying symbol instances

Next you will use the Symbol Sprayer tool to apply the leaves to your illustration.

1 Select the Symbol Sprayer tool (![icon]) in the Tools panel.

2 Click the leaf1 symbol in the Symbols panel.

3 Click and drag with the Symbol Sprayer, much like an airbrush or can of spray paint, to create the leaves of the tree. Release the mouse button when a bunch of leaves are on the artboard.

Notice the bounding box around the leaves on the artboard when you release the mouse button. This is referred to as a symbol set. As you spray, the instances are grouped together as a single object. If a symbol set is selected when you begin to spray with the Symbol Sprayer tool, the symbol instances that you are spraying are added to the selected symbol set. You can easily delete an entire symbol set by pressing the Delete key when a set is selected.

4 With the symbol set still selected, click and drag some more with the Symbol Sprayer tool to add more leaves to the tree.

Symbol instances

Keep the following in mind when creating a symbol instance with the Symbol Sprayer:

- All the symbols that appear from each spray become one symbol set that you manipulate and edit as a whole.

- You can enlarge or reduce the spraying radius using the bracket keys. Press [for a smaller spraying radius; press] for a larger spraying radius.

- Pressing Alt (Windows) or Option (Mac OS) while using the Symbol Sprayer deletes instances within a symbol set.

5 Choose Select > Deselect to deselect the leaf1 symbol set on the page.

6 In the Symbols panel, click the leaf2 symbol to select it.

Next you will change the Symbol Sprayer tool options.

Note: A higher intensity value increases the rate of change—the Symbol Sprayer tool sprays more, faster. The higher the symbol set density value, the more tightly packed the symbols are.

7 Double-click the Symbol Sprayer tool ( ) in the Tools panel. In the Symbolism Tools Options dialog box, change Intensity to 5 and Symbol Set Density to 7. Click OK.

▶ **Tip:** Try clicking and releasing without dragging the pointer. This can add a single leaf or a few leaves, depending on the speed of the click.

8 Click and drag again using the Symbol Sprayer tool, as you did in step 3, to create more leaves for the tree with the leaf2 symbol.

The tree now has two colors of leaves, giving it a more realistic appearance. You can try this with leaf3 to give it even more leaves. Just make sure to choose Select > Deselect before selecting the leaf3 symbol.

9 If the Layers panel is not visible, choose Window > Layers. Click the arrow to the left of the Leaves layer to view its content. Note that for every leaf symbol (leaf1, leaf2, and leaf3) that you have sprayed, there is a new symbol set in the Leaves layer. When using the Symbol Sprayer tool, a new symbol set is created each time you spray, as long as no other symbol set is selected.

10 Choose Select > Deselect, and then File > Save.

In this next section, you will use the Symbol Sizer and Spinner tools to alter the look of individual symbol instances.

Editing symbol sets using the symbolism tools

The Symbol Sprayer tool has seven symbolism tools. You can use symbolism tools to change the density, color, location, size, rotation, transparency, or style of symbol sets.

The symbolism tools.

Now you will select the leaf3 symbol set and edit the leaves using the Symbol Sizer and Symbol Spinner tools.

1   In the Layers panel, click the Selection column of the top symbol set (between the target icon and the scroll bar) to select it. Deselect the eye icons (👁) to the left of the other two symbol sets to hide them.

Select the symbol set.

2   In the Tools panel, click and hold down the mouse button on the Symbol Sprayer tool and select the Symbol Sizer tool (🔘). Click and drag over your symbol instances to scale up some of the leaves. Press Alt (Windows) or Option (Mac OS) while you are using the Symbol Sizer tool to reduce the size of the selected instances.

● **Note:** The Symbol Sizer works better when you click and release over symbol instances, rather than holding down the mouse button.

Now you will rotate some of the symbols.

3   Select the Symbol Spinner tool (🌀) from the Symbol Sizer tool group and click and drag over the leaves to rotate.

The more you move the pointer, the more rotation occurs and the more leaves are affected.

▶ **Tip:** If the symbol sizer is working too effectively (sizing too fast), you can double-click the Symbol Sizer tool in the Tools panel to lower the Intensity and Density values in the Symbolism Tools Options dialog box.

● **Note:** Arrows appear as you rotate, indicating the direction of rotation.

4 In the Layers panel, click the Visibility column to the left of the bottom two symbol sets to show them again.

Try selecting another symbol set and edit those instances with the symbolism tools.

5 Choose Select > Deselect.

6 Choose File > Save.

What do the symbolism tools do?

Symbol Shifter tool (⚙)—Moves symbol instances around. It can also change the relative stacking order of symbol instances in a set.

Symbol Scruncher tool (⚙)—Pulls symbol instances together or apart.

Symbol Sizer tool (⚙)—Increases or decreases the size of symbol instances.

Symbol Spinner tool (⚙)—Orients the symbol instances in a set. Symbol instances located near the pointer orient in the direction you move the pointer. As you drag the mouse, an arrow appears above the pointer to show the current orientation of the symbol instances.

Symbol Stainer tool (⚙)—Colorizes symbol instances. Colorizing a symbol instance changes the hue toward the tint color while preserving the original luminosity, so black or white objects don't change at all.

Symbol Screener tool (⚙)—Increases or decreases the transparency of the symbol instances in a set.

Symbol Styler tool (⚙)—Applies the selected style to the symbol instance. You can switch to the Symbol Styler tool when using any other symbolism tool by clicking a style in the Styles panel.

Editing symbols

In the next steps, you will add a symbol for grass, and then edit and update it.

1 If the Layers panel is not visible, choose Window > Layers. Click the Leaves layer to select it if it is not already selected.

2 Using the Selection tool (▶), click Fill color in the Control panel and select None (⬚). Click Stroke color in the Control panel and select grass green in the Swatches panel. Make sure the stroke weight is 1 pt.

3 Using the Zoom tool (🔍), click a few times to zoom into the green area where the grass will go at the base of the tree.

4 Double-click the Pencil tool (✐) . In the Pencil Tool Options dialog box, deselect the Keep Selected option, and click OK.

5 Using the Pencil tool, create several blades of grass. Use at least 10 line segments to make a tuft of grass.

6 Select the Selection tool and drag a marquee to surround the blades of grass.

7 With the blades of grass selected, open the Symbols panel by clicking the Symbols panel icon (♣) on the right side of the workspace. Click the New Symbol button (▣) in the Symbols panel. Name the new symbol grass, and select Graphic as the Type. Click OK. Use the Selection tool to delete the original blades of grass used to create the symbol.

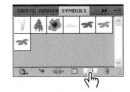

8 In the Tools panel, click and hold down the mouse button on the Symbol Spinner tool and select the Symbol Sprayer tool (▓). Double-click the Symbol Sprayer tool to open the Symbolism Tools Options dialog box. Change Intensity to 9 and the Symbol Set Density to 8, and click OK.

9 In the Symbols panel, click the grass symbol you just added. Click and drag to spray the grass symbol over the base of the tree.

10 In the Control panel, change the Fill color to black.

11 Select the Symbol Stainer tool (▒). Press the right bracket key (]) several times to increase the size of the brush. Click and release over the grass instances, giving them a darker stain. Press Alt (Windows) or Option (Mac OS) to decrease the colorization and reveal more of the original symbol color for some of the instances of grass. Try different color fills (like the light green swatch) to achieve more realistic looking grass.

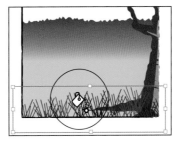

12 Choose File > Save.

Updating a symbol

In this next section, you will edit the grass once, and all instances will be updated.

1 Select the Selection tool (▶) in the Tools panel.

2 In the Symbols panel, double-click the grass symbol to edit it. A temporary instance of the symbol appears in the center of the artboard.

3 Choose Select > All, or drag across the blades of grass with the Selection tool.

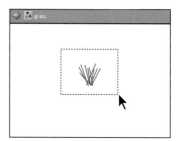

4 Click Stroke Weight in the Control panel and choose 2pt from the menu.

5 Double-click outside of the grass on the artboard, or click the Exit Isolation Mode button (◀) in the upper left corner of the artboard to see all the artwork.

The symbol instances are now using the thicker blades of grass.

6 Choose File > Save.

Breaking a link to a symbol

At times you will need to edit specific instances on the artboard. Because the symbolism tools only let you make certain kinds of changes, you may sometimes need to break the link between a symbol and an instance. This creates a group of unlinked instances (if the object is composed of more than one object) on the artboard. You can then ungroup them and edit the individual objects.

Now you will place several instances of a symbol and break the link to one of the instances.

1 If the Layers panel is not visible, choose Window > Layers. In the Layers panel, click the Flowers layer to select it. Deselect the eye icon (👁) to the left of the Leaves layer to hide it, and click the arrow to the left of the Leaves layer to toggle it closed. Click the Lock column to the left of the Sky layer to lock its contents.

● **Note:** You may need to scroll down in the Layers panel to see the Sky layer.

2 Double-click the Hand tool (✋) in the Tools panel to fit the artboard to the window.

3 In the Symbols panel, select the Hibiscus symbol and drag four copies onto the tree. With the Selection tool (▶), arrange them so that they are spread out.

▶ **Tip:** After you drag one instance from the Symbols panel, you can Alt-drag or Option-drag copies to make more instances.

4 Select one of the symbol instances of the flower on the page. In the Control panel, click the Break Link button.

This object is now a group, as indicated by the word Group on the left side of the Control panel. You should be able to see the points of the shapes within the flower.

5 Select the Zoom tool (🔍) and drag a marquee across the selected flower to zoom in.

6 With the Selection tool, double-click the flower to enter isolation mode. Click the pink flower shape to select it (not the smaller pieces).

● **Note:** To select the center shape, you may need to zoom in further.

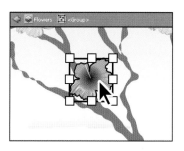

7 Select the Gradient tool (▭) in the Tools panel. Notice the gradient bar that appears when you hover the Gradient tool pointer over the flower shape.

Next you will edit the gradient color of the flower symbol.

8 Double-click the rightmost color stop of the slider bar. In the panel that appears, click the Color button (🎨). Shift-drag the magenta (M) slider to the left until its value is about 14%. Press Enter or Return to accept the color change and close the panel. The flower gradient should be lighter in color on the edge of the flower.

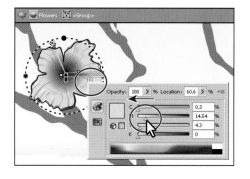

● **Note:** To learn about working with gradients, see Lesson 9, "Blending Shapes and Colors."

9 Select the Selection tool and double-click somewhere outside of the flower to exit isolation mode.

10 Choose File > Save and keep the artwork open.

Replacing symbols

Next you will create a symbol from the modified flower, and then replace a few of the hibiscus instances with the new symbol.

1 Choose View > Fit Artboard In Window.

2 With the Selection tool (▶) click and drag the modified flower into the Symbols panel. In the Symbol Options dialog box, change the name to Hibiscus2 and the Type to Graphic. Click OK.

3 With the Selection tool, select a different hibiscus flower instance on the artboard. In the Control panel, click the arrow to the right of the Replace Instance With Symbol field to open the Symbols panel. Click the Hibiscus2 symbol.

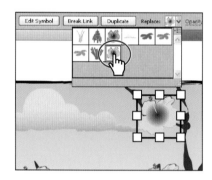

4 Choose Select > Deselect.

5 If the Layers panel is not visible, choose Window > Layers. In the Layers panel, select the Visibility column to the left of the Leaves layer to show it.

6 Choose File > Save. Keep the file open.

Storing and retrieving artwork in the Symbols panel

Saving frequently used logos or other artwork as symbols lets you access them quickly.

In this next lesson, you will take symbols that you've created and save them as a new symbol library that you can share with other documents or users.

● **Note:** Symbol libraries are saved as Adobe Illustrator (.ai) files.

1 In the Symbols panel, click the Symbol Libraries Menu button (▣), and choose Save Symbols.

   ● **Note:** When saving symbols as a separate library, the document that contains the symbols should be open and active in the Document window.

2 In the Save Symbols As Library dialog box, choose a location such as your Desktop to place the symbol library file. Name the library file outdoors.ai. Click Save.

   ● **Note:** When you first open the Save Symbols As Library dialog box, you are taken to a Symbols folder. You can store the libraries that you create in this folder. Illustrator recognizes any libraries stored here and lets you choose them from the Symbol Libraries menu.

   ▶ **Tip:** If you save the library in the default folder, you can make subfolders and create a folder structure that suits you. You can then easily access them using the Symbol Libraries Menu button or by choosing Window > Symbol Libraries.

3 Without closing the poster.ai file, create a new document by choosing File > New. Leave the default settings, and click OK.

4 In the Symbols panel, click the Symbol Libraries Menu button (▣) and choose Other Library at the bottom of the menu. Navigate to the folder where you saved the outdoors.ai library, select it, and click Open.

   The outdoors library appears as a panel in the workspace. You can dock it or leave it where it is. It stays open as long as Illustrator is open. When you close Illustrator, and then relaunch it, this panel does not reopen.

5 Drag any of the Symbols from the outdoors library panel onto the page.

6 Choose File > Close and do not save the new file. Keep the poster.ai file open if you plan on continuing to the Exploring On Your Own section.

Mapping a symbol to 3D artwork

You can apply any 2D artwork stored as a symbol in the Symbols panel to selected surfaces on a 3D object. To learn about mapping symbols to 3D artwork, see Lesson 11, "Applying Effects."

Symbols and Flash integration

Symbols also provide excellent support for SWF and SVG export. When you export to Flash, you can set the symbol type to Movie Clip. In Flash, you can choose another type if necessary. You can also specify 9-slice scaling in Illustrator so that the movie clips scale appropriately when used for user interface components.

You can move Illustrator artwork into the Flash editing environment or directly into Flash Player. You can copy and paste artwork, save files as SWF, or export artwork directly to Flash. In addition, Illustrator provides support for Flash dynamic text and movie clip symbols. A symbol workflow in Illustrator is similar to a symbol workflow in Flash:

- Step 1: Symbol creation

  When you create a symbol in Illustrator, the Symbol Options dialog box lets you name the symbol and set options specific to Flash: movie clip symbol type (which is the default for Flash symbols), Flash registration grid location, and 9-slice scaling guides. In addition, you can use many of the same symbol keyboard shortcuts in Illustrator and Flash, such as F8 to create a symbol.

- Step 2: Isolation mode for symbol editing

- Step 3: Symbol properties and links

- Step 4: Static, dynamic, and input text objects

Next you will create a button, save it as a symbol, and edit the symbol options.

1   Choose File > New.

2   In the New Document dialog box, choose Web from the New Document Profile menu. Keep the rest of the settings at default, and click OK.

3   Choose File > Save As. In the Save As dialog box, name the file buttons.ai and navigate to the Lesson13 folder. Leave the Save As Type option set to Adobe Illustrator (*.AI) (Windows) or the Format option set to Adobe Illustrator (ai) (Mac OS), and click Save. In the Illustrator Options dialog box, leave the Illustrator options at their default settings, and click OK.

4   Open the Symbols panel by clicking the Symbols panel icon (♣).

5   Drag the Bullet - Forward symbol from the Symbols panel onto the artboard.

6   With the Selection tool (▶), Shift-click the upper right corner of the button and drag to make it larger.

▶ **Tip:** As mentioned previously in this chapter, there are a lot more symbols that come with Illustrator. You can find them by clicking the Symbol Libraries Menu button at the bottom of the Symbols panel.

7 With the button still selected, change the Instance Name in the Control panel to Home.

8 With the button selected, drag it to the right, and press Shift+Alt (Windows) or Shift+Option (Mac OS) to create a copy. Release the mouse button first, and then the keys. In the Control panel, type Info in the Instance Name field.

  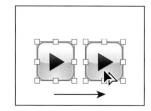

9 With one of the buttons still selected, click the Symbol Options button (⬛) in the Symbols panel. Select Movie Clip, select Enable Guides For 9-slice Scaling, and click OK.

Now you'll adjust the 9-slice scaling guides.

10 With the Selection tool, double-click the leftmost button to enter isolation mode. When the warning dialog box appears, click OK.

11 Click and drag the leftmost guide toward the edge of the button, stopping just before the curve of the rounded corner begins so that the guide starts before the rounded corners. Repeat for the rightmost guide by dragging it to the right. Repeat the same for the horizontal guides.

● **Note:** It may be difficult to drag the guides. You may need to zoom in.

12 With the Selection tool, double-click away from the buttons to exit isolation mode.

13 Choose File > Save.

What is 9-slice scaling?

You can use 9-slice scaling (scale-9) in the Symbol Options dialog box to specify component-style scaling for movie clip symbols destined for export to Flash. This type of scaling lets you create movie clip symbols that scale appropriately for use as user interface components, as opposed to the type of scaling typically applied to graphics and design elements.

—From Illustrator Help

For the next steps, you need to have Adobe Flash CS4 installed on your machine.

14 Open Adobe Flash CS4.

15 Choose File > New. Leave the default settings, and click OK.

16 Choose File > Import > Import To Library in Adobe Flash. Navigate to the buttons.ai file you just saved in Illustrator and click the Import To Library button. The Import "buttons.ai" To Library dialog box appears.

This dialog box lets you select which artboard to import, which layers to import, how to import the content, and more. The Import Unused Symbols option at the bottom of the dialog box brings all the symbols in the Illustrator Symbols panel into the Flash Library panel. This can be very useful if, for instance, you develop a series of buttons for a site.

17 Click OK.

18 Open the Library panel by clicking the Library panel tab on the right side of the workspace. Click the arrow to the left of the folder names to reveal the assets as well as the Bullet - Forward symbol in the Illustrator Symbols folder.

19 Drag the Bullet - Forward symbol onto the stage.

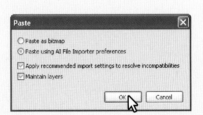

● **Note:** There are several ways to get Illustrator CS4 content into Flash CS4. You can also choose File > Import > Import To Stage. This places the two buttons on the stage, and each instance name appears in the Property panel when they are independently selected. The content is also added to the Library panel.

20 Choose File > Close to close the Flash file, and don't save changes. Close Flash, and return to Illustrator.

Pasting Illustrator artwork into Flash

Another option is to copy and paste content into Flash CS4 from Illustrator CS4. When you paste into Flash CS4, the Paste dialog box appears. You can paste a simple bitmap or paste using the AI File Importer preferences. The latter option works like the File > Import > Import To Stage command, although the Import "buttons.ai" To Stage dialog box does not appear.

When you paste Illustrator artwork into Flash, the following attributes are preserved:

Paths and shapes	Scalability
Stroke weights	Gradient definitions
Text (including OpenType fonts)	Linked images
Symbols	Blending modes

—From Illustrator Help

Exploring on your own

Try to integrate symbols into illustrations with repeated artwork from maps that contain everything from repeated icons and road signs to creative and customized bullets for text. Symbols make it easy to update logos in business cards or name tags, or any artwork created with multiple placements of the same art.

To place multiple symbol instances, do the following:

1 Select the artwork that you want to use as a symbol.

2 Drag the art using the Selection tool into the Symbols panel. Delete the original art when it is in the Symbols panel.

3 To add an instance to the artboard, drag the symbol from the Symbols panel to the artboard.

4 Drag as many instances of the symbol as you like, or Alt-drag (Windows) or Option-drag (Mac OS) the original instance to clone it to other locations.

5 The symbols are now linked to the original symbol in the Symbols panel. If a symbol is updated, all placed instances are updated.

Review questions

1 What are three benefits of using a symbol?

2 Name the symbolism tool that is used for changing tints and shades of a symbol.

3 If you are using a symbolism tool on an area that has two different symbols applied, which one is affected?

4 How do you update an existing symbol?

5 What is something that cannot be used as a symbol?

6 How do you access symbols from other documents?

Review answers

1 Three benefits of using symbols are:

   • Easy application of multiple shapes.

   • You can edit one symbol, and all instances are updated.

   • You can map artwork to 3D objects (covered in depth in Lesson 11, "Applying Effects.")

2 The Symbol Stainer tool changes the tints and shades of a symbol.

3 If you are using a symbolism tool over an area that has two different symbol instances, the symbol active in the Symbols panel is the only instance affected.

4 To update an existing symbol, double-click the symbol icon in the Symbols panel or double-click an instance of the symbol on the artboard. From there, you can make edits in isolation mode.

5 Unembedded images cannot be used as symbols.

6 You can access symbols from saved documents by choosing Window > Symbol Libraries > Other Libraries or from the Symbol Libraries menu.

14

COMBINING ILLUSTRATOR CS4 GRAPHICS WITH OTHER ADOBE APPLICATIONS

Lesson overview

In this lesson, you'll learn how to do the following:

- Differentiate between vector and bitmap graphics.

- Place embedded Adobe Photoshop graphics in an Adobe Illustrator file.

- Create a clipping mask from compound paths.

- Make an opacity mask to display part of an image.

- Sample color in a placed image.

- Replace a placed image with another, and update the document.

- Export a layered file to Adobe Photoshop.

- Place Illustrator files in Adobe InDesign.

- Integrate Illustrator with Adobe Flash.

- Save an Illustrator file for Adobe Flex.

 This lesson takes approximately an hour to complete. If needed, remove the previous lesson folder from your hard disk and copy the Lesson14 folder onto it.

Tech Expo

May 15th - 20th Seattle Expo Center

You can easily add an image created in an image-editing program to an Adobe Illustrator file. This is an effective method for seeing how a photograph looks incorporated in a line drawing, or for trying out Illustrator special effects on bitmap images.

Getting started

Before you begin, you'll need to restore the default preferences for Adobe Illustrator CS4. Then you'll open the finished art file for this lesson to see what you'll create.

1   To ensure that the tools and panels function as described in this lesson, delete or deactivate (by renaming) the Adobe Illustrator CS4 preferences file. See "Restoring default preferences" on page 3.

2   Start Adobe Illustrator CS4.

● **Note:** If you have not already copied the resource files for this lesson onto your hard disk from the Lesson14 folder on the Adobe Illustrator CS4 Classroom in a Book CD, do so now. See "Copying the Classroom in a Book files" on page 2.

3   Choose File > Open. Locate the file named L14end.ai in the Lesson14 folder in the Lessons folder that you copied onto your hard disk. This is a postcard for a technology expo, and you will add and edit graphics in this lesson. Leave it open for reference, or choose File > Close.

Now you'll open the start file from Adobe Bridge CS4.

Working with Adobe Bridge

Adobe Bridge is an application that installs when you install either a Creative Suite 4 component, such as Illustrator, or the entire Creative Suite 4. It allows you to browse content visually, manage metadata, and more.

4   Choose File > Browse In Bridge to open Adobe Bridge.

● **Note:** The first time Adobe Bridge launches, a dialog box may appear asking if you want the Bridge to start at login. Click Yes if you want it to launch at startup; otherwise, click No to manually launch Adobe Bridge when you need it.

● **Note:** For more details on Adobe Bridge, see Illustrator Help.

5   In the Favorites pane on the left, click Desktop and navigate to the L14start.ai file in the Lesson14 folder. Click the file in the Content pane.

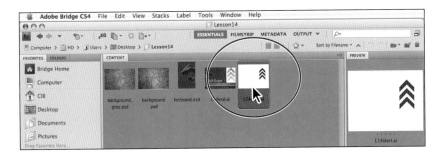

6   At the bottom of the Content pane, drag the slider to the right to increase the size of the thumbnails in the Content pane.

7   In the upper right portion of the Adobe Bridge, click Filmstrip. This changes the appearance of the workspace in Adobe Bridge. This view is a filmstrip view that can give a larger preview of the selected object. Click Essentials to return to the original workspace.

8   With the L14start.ai file still selected in the Content pane, click the Metadata panel tab on the right side of the workspace to see the metadata associated with the selected file. This can be camera data, document swatches, and more. Click the Keywords panel tab to reveal the Keywords panel.

    Keywords can be associated with objects such as images. After associating a keyword, you can later search for content that contains the keyword.

9   In the Keywords panel, click the plus at the bottom to create a keyword. Type techexpo into the keyword field and press Enter or Return. Click the box to the left of the keyword. This associates the keyword with the selected file.

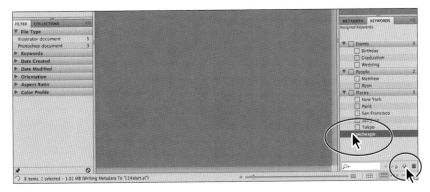

10 Choose Edit > Find. In the Find dialog box, choose Keywords from the first menu in the Criteria section. Type techexpo in the rightmost field of the Criteria options. Leave the middle field set to contains and click Find.

The Find results appear in the Content pane.

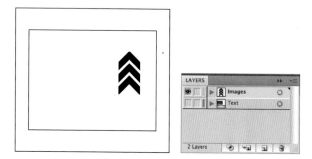

11 Click the x in the upper right corner of the Content pane to close the find results and return to the folder.

12 Double-click the file L14start.ai to open the file in Illustrator. Leave the Adobe Bridge open. Choose View > Fit Artboard In Window.

13 Click the Layers panel icon (🌐) and notice that the file has two layers: Text and Images. You will place images on both. The Images layer also contains objects that you'll make into a mask, which is discussed later in the lesson.

14 Choose File > Save As. In the Save As dialog box, navigate to the Lesson14 folder and open it. Name the file Postcard.ai. Leave the Save As Type option set to Adobe Illustrator (*.AI) (Windows) or the Format option set to Adobe Illustrator (ai) (Mac OS), and click Save. In the Illustrator Options dialog box, leave the Illustrator options at their default settings, and click OK.

Combining artwork

You can combine Illustrator artwork with images from other graphics applications in a variety of ways for a wide range of creative results. Sharing artwork between applications lets you combine continuous-tone paintings and photographs with line art. Even though Illustrator lets you create certain types of raster images, Adobe Photoshop excels at many image-editing tasks. The images can then be placed in Illustrator.

This lesson steps you through the process of creating a composite image, including combining bitmap images with vector art and working between applications. You will add photographic images created in Adobe Photoshop to a postcard created in Adobe Illustrator. Then you'll adjust the color in the photo, mask the photo, and sample color from the photo to use in the Illustrator artwork. You'll update a placed image, and then export your postcard to Photoshop.

Vector versus bitmap graphics

Adobe Illustrator creates vector graphics, also called draw graphics, which contain shapes based on mathematical expressions. Vector graphics consist of clear, smooth lines that retain their crispness when scaled. They are appropriate for illustrations, type, and graphics that need to be scaled to different sizes, such as logos.

Logo is drawn as vector art, and retains its crispness when scaled to a larger size.

Bitmap graphics, also called raster images, are based on a grid of pixels and are created by image editing applications, such as Adobe Photoshop. When working with bitmap images, you edit groups of pixels rather than objects or shapes. Because bitmap graphics can represent subtle gradations of shade and color, they are appropriate for continuous-tone images, such as photographs or artwork created in painting programs. A disadvantage of bitmap graphics is that they lose definition and appear jagged when scaled up.

Logo is rasterized as bitmap art, and loses its definition when enlarged.

In deciding whether to use Illustrator or a bitmap image program such as Photoshop for creating and combining graphics, consider the elements of the image and how the image will be used.

In general, use Illustrator if you need to create art or type with clean lines that looks good at any magnification. In most cases, you also want to use Illustrator for laying out a single-page design, because Illustrator offers more flexibility than Photoshop when working with type, and reselecting, moving, and altering images. You can create raster images in Illustrator, but its pixel-editing tools are limited. Use Photoshop for images that need pixel editing, color correcting, painting, and other special effects. Use Adobe InDesign for laying out anything from a postcard to a multiple chapter book, such as this *Classroom in a Book*.

Editing the artboard

By setting artboard options using the Artboard tool, you can define the size of the artboard and where to crop the artwork. For instance, if you create a postcard that is 9-by-6 inches, you can set the artboard to that size to define the area to crop to.

You can edit or create new artboards using the Artboard tool by either double-clicking it in the Tools panel, or selecting the Artboard tool and editing an artboard. In this next lesson, you will edit the artboard for a postcard.

1 Double-click the Artboard tool (⊞) in the Tools panel. In the Artboard Options dialog box, change the width of the artboard to 9 in and the height to 6 in. Click OK.

2 You now see a gray canvas area, which is the area outside of the artboard. Using the Artboard tool, you can resize or move the crop area manually. When the Artboard tool is selected, the Control panel shows many of the options in the Artboard Options dialog box. Note that you can also create multiple artboards in a single document. To commit the artboard change and exit editing mode, select the Selection tool (▸) in the Tools panel

Next you will set bleed guides for the document.

3 With nothing selected, click the Document Setup button in the Control panel. In the Document Setup dialog box, change Top Bleed to .125 in. All the other bleed options change to match, because the Make All Settings The Same button (⊛) is selected. Click OK.

▶ **Tip:** To learn more about creating and editing multiple artboards, see Lesson 4, "Transforming Objects."

● **Note:** If the Document Setup button doesn't appear in the Control panel, choose File > Document Setup to open the Document Setup dialog box.

4 Choose View > Fit Artboard In Window.

5 Choose Essentials from the workspace switcher in the Control panel to reset the panels.

Placing an Adobe Photoshop file

You can bring artwork from Photoshop into Illustrator using the Open command, the Place command, the Paste command, and drag-and-drop.

Illustrator supports most Photoshop data, including layer comps, layers, editable text, and paths. This means that you can transfer files between Photoshop and Illustrator without losing the ability to edit the artwork. Adjustment layers for which visibility is deselected in Photoshop are imported into Illustrator, although they are inaccessible. When exported back to Photoshop, the layers are restored.

In this lesson, you'll begin by placing a Photoshop file that contains several layer comps in the Illustrator document as an embedded file. Placed files can be embedded or linked. When embedded files are added to the Illustrator file, the Illustrator file size increases to reflect the addition of the placed file. Linked files remain separate external files, and a link to the external file is placed in the Illustrator file. The linked file must always accompany the Illustrator file or the link will break, and the placed file will not appear in the Adobe Illustrator artwork.

● **Note:** Illustrator includes support for Device N rasters. For instance, if you create a Duotone in Photoshop and place that Duotone into Illustrator, it separates properly and prints the spot colors.

About layer comps

Designers often create multiple compositions, or comps, of a page layout to show to clients. Using layer comps, you can create, manage, and view multiple versions of a layout in a single Photoshop file.

A layer comp is a snapshot of a state of the Layers panel in Photoshop. Layer comps record the following information about a layer:

- Visibility—whether a layer is showing or hidden

- Position in the document

- Appearance—whether a layer style is applied to the layer and blending mode

You create a comp by making changes to the layers in your document and updating the comp in the Layer Comps panel in Photoshop. You view comps by applying them in the document. You can export layer comps to separate files, to a single PDF file, or to a web photo gallery. Next you will place a Photoshop file with layer comps.

1 Choose Window > Layers to open the Layers panel.

2 In the Layers panel, select the Images layer if it is not already selected.

   When you place an image, it is added to the selected layer. You'll use the Images layer for the placed image. The layer includes artwork for a mask for the image that you'll create later in the lesson.

3 Choose File > Place.

4 Navigate to the keyboard.psd file in the Lesson14 folder, and select it. Do not double-click the file or click Place yet.

5 Deselect Link in the Place dialog box, if it is selected.

Note: Deselecting the Link option embeds the PSD file in the Illustrator file. The Photoshop Import Options dialog box appears only when you deselect this option.

6 Click Place.

7 In the Photoshop Import Options dialog box, select Black Hands from the Layer Comp menu, and then select Show Preview to preview the artwork

8 Select Convert Layers To Objects and select Import Hidden Layers to import all the document layers from Photoshop. Click OK.

Note: If a color warning dialog box appears, such as Paste Profile Mismatch, click OK.

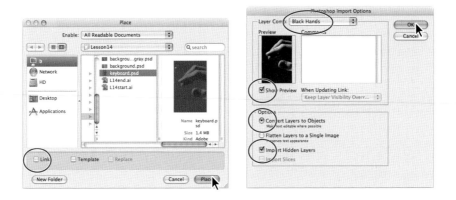

Rather than flatten the file, you want to convert the Photoshop layers to objects, because the keyboard.psd file contains four layers and one layer mask. You will use them later in the lesson.

Now you'll move the placed image.

9 Select the Selection tool (▶) in the Tools panel. Click the center of the image. Don't select a bounding box handle because it resizes the image.

10 In the Control panel, click the word Transform to open the Transform panel. Type 2.375 in for the X value, and 5 in for the Y value. Choose Flip Horizontal from the Transform panel menu (▾≡) to flip the image on its center.

Note: Depending on your screen resolution, the Transform options may appear directly in the Control panel. If they do appear, to access the Flip Horizontal command, click X, Y, W or H in the Control panel to reveal the Transform panel.

11 In the Layers panel, click the arrow (▶) to the left of the Images layer to expand it. Drag the bottom of the panel down so that you can see more of the layers if

necessary. Click the arrow to the left of the keyboard.psd sublayer to expand it. Notice all the sublayers of keyboard.psd.

These sublayers are the result of not flattening the image when it was placed. Deselect the eye icon (👁) to the left of the keyboard.psd sublayer to hide it. The arrows should be the only visible objects on the artboard. In the Layers panel, click the arrow (▼) to the left of the keyboard.psd layer to hide its contents.

12 Choose File > Save

Now you will place an image, edit it, and then duplicate it.

Editing and duplicating a placed image

You can duplicate placed images just as you do other objects in an Illustrator file. You can then modify the copy of the image independently of the original.

Now you'll place the background.psd image and duplicate it in the Layers panel.

1 Choose File > Place and navigate to the background.psd file in the Lesson14 folder, and select it. Do not double-click the file or click Place yet.

2 Make sure that the Link option is deselected, and click Place. The image appears on the artboard.

● **Note:** If a color warning dialog box such as Paste Profile Mismatch appears, click OK.

3 With the Selection tool (▶), click the image to select it. Click the Align To Selection button (⬚) and choose Align To Artboard (⬚) in the Control panel. Click the Horizontal Align Center button (⬚) and the Vertical Align Center button (⬚) in the Control panel to ensure that the image is aligned.

● **Note:** If you don't see the Align To Selection button in the Control panel, you may have a smaller screen resolution. Click the word Align in the Control panel to open the Align panel, then choose Align To Artboard from Align To Selection.

● **Note:** Depending on your screen resolution, the Transform options may appear directly in the Control panel.

4 Click the word Transform in the Control panel to open the Transform panel. Making sure that the Constrain Width And Height Proportions button (🔗) is not selected, change the width to 9.25 in, and the height to 6.25 in. Press Enter or Return to accept the changes.

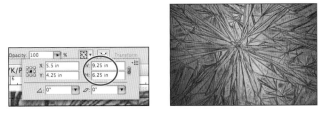

5 In the Layers panel, begin dragging the Background sublayer down the list. While dragging, press Alt (Windows) or Option (Mac OS) to duplicate the sublayer. Drag it to the bottom of the Images layer. Release the mouse button and then the key when the indicator bar appears between the last <Path> sublayer and the Text layer. There are now two background sublayers.

● **Note:** If you press Alt or Option before you begin dragging, it may select objects rather than drag and copy the Background sublayer.

6 Double-click the bottom Background sublayer and rename it Masked Background in the Options dialog box, and then click OK. You will mask this image later in the lesson.

7 Choose File > Save.

Applying color edits to a placed image

You can use color edits in a variety of ways to modify colors in placed images. You can convert to a different color mode (such as RGB, CMYK, or grayscale) or adjust individual color values. You can also saturate (darken) or desaturate (lighten) colors, or invert colors (create a color negative).

Next you'll adjust colors in the Background sublayer. Later in the lesson, you'll apply a mask to this image and then adjust colors in the Masked Background sublayer so that the two layers appear in contrasting colors.

1 In the Layers panel, select the Background sublayer.

2 Deselect the eye icon (◉) to the left of the Masked Background sublayer to hide it.

▶ **Tip:** For information on color modes and modifying colors with color edits, see "About Colors in Digital Graphics" and "Apply an effect" in Illustrator Help.

3 Click the Selection column to the far right of the Background layer to select its contents.

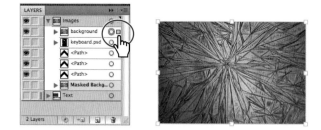

4 Choose Edit > Edit Colors > Adjust Color Balance.

5 In the Adjust Colors dialog box, drag the sliders or enter values for the CMYK percentages to change the colors in the image. You can press Tab to move between the text fields. We used the following values to create more of a blue/purple cast: C=58, M=13, Y=0, and K=0. Feel free to experiment a little. Select Preview so that you can see the color changes.

● **Note:** You may need to select and deselect Preview as you change options in the Adjust Colors dialog box to see the results.

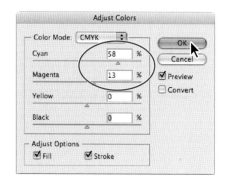

6 When you are satisfied with the color of the image, click OK.

7 Choose File > Save.

Masking an image

Masks crop an image so that only a portion of the image appears through the shape of the mask. You can make a mask from a single path or a compound path. You can also import masks created in Photoshop files.

Applying a clipping mask to an image

In this section, you'll create a clipping mask for the background.psd image and adjust it so that only a small portion of the image is showing.

1   In the Layers panel, select the Visibility column to the left of the Text Layer and the keyboard.psd sublayer. You may need to scroll in the Layers panel to do this.

2   With the Selection tool (↖), and the background.psd image still selected, click the Mask button in the Control panel. This applies a clipping mask to the image in the shape and size of the image. Next you will edit this mask.

● **Note:** You can also apply a clipping mask by choosing Object > Clipping Mask > Make.

3   In the Layers panel, click the arrow to the left (▶) of the <Group> sublayer at the top of the Images layer to reveal its contents. The <Clipping Path> now appears in the Layers panel. This is the mask.

● **Note:** When an object is masked by another shape, you can edit either the mask or the object that is masked.

4   With the Selection tool, click and drag the top bounding point of the selected mask on the artboard to the guide just below the Tech Expo text (see figure below). Click and drag the bottom, middle bounding point to the bottom guide, creating a background image that is masked.

● **Note:** Make sure that you select the mask, not the image.

5 In the Control panel, click the Edit Contents button () to edit the background.psd image, not the mask. With the Selection tool, click the part of the background image that is visible. Drag the image up about an inch, pressing the Shift key as you drag.

6 Choose Object > Hide > Selection to hide the background image.

Creating compound paths and opacity masks

In this section, you'll create a compound path from the arrow pattern on the Images layer and create an opacity mask from the compound path so that the Masked Background layer appears through the mask. You'll also use an opacity mask that was created in Photoshop and saved as a layer mask.

1 Select the Magic Wand tool (✦) in the Tools panel.

The Magic Wand tool selects all objects in a document with the same or similar fill color, stroke weight, stroke color, opacity, or blending mode.

2 Click an arrow in the arrow pattern on the right to select all the arrows. Change the fill color to white in the Control panel.

▶ **Tip:** To learn more about the Magic Wand tool, see "Select objects with the Magic Wand tool" in Illustrator Help.

▶ **Tip:** To make the arrows a compound path, you can also right-click or Control-click and choose Make Compound Path.

3 Choose Object > Compound Path > Make. Notice that all the arrows are placed onto one layer, called <Compound Path> in the Layers panel.

The Compound Path command creates a single compound object from two or more objects. Compound paths act as grouped objects. The Compound Path command lets you create complex objects more easily than if you used the drawing tools or the Pathfinder commands.

4   With the compound path selected, in the Layers panel, select the Visibility column to the left of the Masked Background sublayer to show its contents. You may need to scroll down to see the Masked Background sublayer.

5   With the Selection tool (➤), Shift-click the Selection column to the far right of the Masked Background layer. The Selection indicator (■) appears, and the Masked Background layer is added to the current selection.

Note: To create a mask, you need to select the masking object and the object to be masked. The masking object also needs to be above the masked object in the Layers panel.

Next you'll mask the Masked Background layer with the arrows used as an opacity mask. This allows you to use the change in luminosity in the overlying arrow pattern to affect the background. Similar to a clipping mask, an opacity mask lets you make color and other fine adjustments that you can't make with a clipping mask.

6   Click the word Opacity in the Control panel to open the Transparency panel. If the word Opacity isn't visible, choose Window > Transparency.

7   In the Transparency panel menu, choose Make Opacity Mask. Make sure that the Clip option is selected in the Transparency panel.

The Masked Background layer is now masked with the arrow pattern, as indicated by the dashed underline beneath the layer name in the Layers panel.

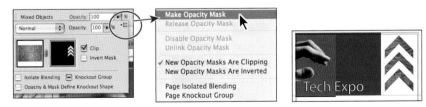

Next you'll adjust the opacity mask that you just created.

Tip: To disable and enable an opacity mask, you can also choose Disable Opacity Mask or Enable Opacity Mask from the Transparency panel menu.

8 Click the Transparency panel icon (🖲) on the right side of the workspace to open the Transparency panel. Shift-click the mask (as indicated by the white arrows on the black background) to disable the mask. Notice that a red x appears in the mask and that the entire Masked Background image reappears in the Document window.

Note: You are opening the Transparency panel on the right side of the workspace because the Transparency panel in the Control panel will close when you interact with the artwork.

9 In the Transparency panel, Shift-click the mask again to enable the opacity mask again. Make sure the arrows are still selected.

10 Click to select the mask in the Transparency panel.

11 In the Layers panel, notice that Layers (Opacity Mask) appears. Click the toggle arrow (▶) to the left of the <Opacity Mask> layer to expand it.

12 With the mask selected, in the Control panel, click the fill color and select a black to white linear gradient, called Linear Gradient 1.

Note: In Illustrator, as in Photoshop, masks follow this general rule: white shows, black hides. A gradient mask lets you gradually show an image or other object. Try changing the direction and length of the gradient. Also, try adjusting the opacity in the Transparency panel to achieve different effects.

13 Select the Gradient tool (▭) in the Tools panel. While pressing the Shift key, start at the top edge of the arrows and drag down. Release the mouse button, and then the Shift key.

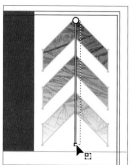

Apply a gradient fill, and drag with the Gradient tool to change the gradient direction. Notice how the mask changes in the Transparency panel.

14 In the Transparency panel, click the Masked
Background image to edit content rather than
the mask.

● **Note:** If you forget to stop the opacity mask editing, you can't
do much to the other artwork.

15 Choose File > Save.

Editing an imported mask

You've made an opacity mask from artwork created in Illustrator. Now you'll use a
mask that was created in Photoshop and imported when you placed the
keyboard.psd file. You'll experiment with changing the color of the image and then
adjusting the transparency of the opacity mask to tone down the effect.

1 In the Layers panel, select the Visibility column to
the left of the <Group> sublayer at the top of the
Images layer to make the masked blue image visible.
Click the arrow to the left of the keyboard.psd
sublayer to reveal its contents. Click the Selection
column to the right of the Hands sublayer to select
its contents.

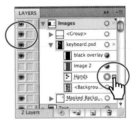

The dashed line under the layer name indicates that
the Hands layer has an opacity mask applied to it.

2 Click the word Opacity in the Control panel, and change the blending mode to
Multiply in the Transparency panel.

3 In the Layers panel, deselect the eye icon to the left of the Black Overlay sublayer.

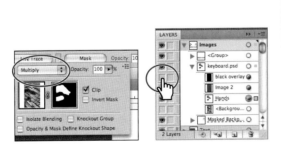

4 Choose Effect > Sketch > Halftone Pattern to open the Effect Gallery. In the Halftone Pattern options, set Size to 2 and Contrast to 5. Click OK.

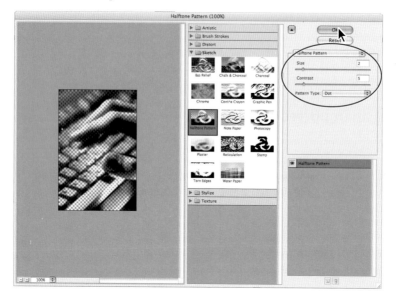

5 Choose File > Save.

Sampling colors in placed images

You can sample, or copy, the colors in placed images to apply the colors to other objects in the artwork. Sampling colors enables you to easily make colors consistent in a file that combines Photoshop images and Illustrator artwork.

In this section, you'll use the Eyedropper tool to sample colors from the placed image, and apply the colors to selected type on the Text layer.

1 In the Layers panel, click the arrow (▶) to the left of the Text layer to expand it, and then deselect the lock icon (🔒) to the left of the first <Group> below the guides to unlock the sublayer. Click the Selection column to the right of the same <Group> to select the text that has been converted to paths.

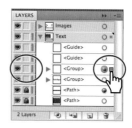

2 Select the Eyedropper tool (🖋) in the Tools panel, and Shift-click in the image anywhere to sample a color to be applied to the selected text. (We chose a light blue color right above the text in background.psd.) You can try as many times as you like.

● **Note:** You may need to choose Select > Deselect to see the color change.

The color you sample is applied to the selected text.

▶ **Tip:** Hold down Shift and then Alt or Option while clicking to add the appearance attributes of an object to the selected object's appearance attributes. Alternatively, click first, and then hold down Shift and then Alt or Option.

3 Choose File > Save.

Replacing a placed image

You can easily replace a placed image with another image to update a document. The replacement image is positioned exactly where the original image was, so you don't have to align the replacement image. If you scaled the original image, you may have to resize the replacement image to match the original image.

Now you'll replace the background.psd image with the background_gray.psd image to create a new version of the postcard.

1 Choose File > Save As. In the Save As dialog box, navigate to the Lesson14 folder and open it. Name the file Postcard2.ai. Leave the Save As Type option set to Adobe Illustrator (*.AI) (Windows) or the Format option set to Adobe Illustrator (ai) (Mac OS), and click Save. In the Illustrator Options dialog box, leave the Illustrator options at their default settings, and click OK.

2 Choose Window > Links.

3 Click the top link in the Links panel—the blue background image—to select it. If the first link is not the blue background image, scroll until you see it. These links don't have names in the Links panel because they are embedded instead of linked.

4 Click the Go To Link button (→ 🔳) at the bottom of the Links panel to see the linked image on the artboard. Click the link in the Links panel again, and then click the Relink button (🔳~🔳) at the bottom of the panel.

5 In the Place dialog box, navigate to the background_gray.psd image in the Lesson14 folder and select it. Make sure that the Link option is selected. Click Place to replace the background image with the new one.

The replacement image appears in the Images layer as the background_gray.psd sublayer with no color adjustments applied. When you replace an image, the color adjustments that you made to the original image are not applied to the replacement. However, masks applied to the original image are preserved. Any layer modes and transparency adjustments that you've made to other layers also may affect the image's appearance.

6 Choose File > Save.

If you want to learn how to open and manipulate a layered Illustrator file in Photoshop, continue to the next section. If not, skip to "Exploring on your own."

Exporting a layered file to Adobe Photoshop

Not only can you open layered Photoshop files in Illustrator, but you can also save layered Illustrator files and then open them in Photoshop. Working with layered files between Illustrator and Photoshop is helpful when creating and editing web graphics. You can preserve the hierarchical relationship of the layers by selecting the Write Layers option when saving your file. You can also open and edit type objects.

► **Tip:** In the Export dialog box, the Use Artboards selection allows you to export the artboards as separate Photoshop PSD files.

1 Choose File > Export.

2 Navigate to the folder where you'll save the file, and name the file Postcard2.psd. Changing the file name preserves your original Illustrator file.

3 Choose Photoshop (PSD) from the Save As Type (Windows) or Format (Mac OS) menu, and click Save (Windows) or Export (Mac OS).

4 In the Photoshop Export Options dialog box, make sure that CMYK is the Color Model, select High (300 ppi) for the resolution, and make sure that Write Layers is selected. Leave the rest of the settings at their defaults. Preserve Text Editability is grayed out because all the text was already converted to outlines. Click OK.

The Anti-alias option removes jagged edges in the artwork. The Write Layers option lets you export each Illustrator top-level layer as a separate Photoshop layer.

▶ **Tip:** You can also copy and paste or drag and drop between Illustrator and Photoshop. When you copy and paste, a dialog box appears asking what type of object you'd like to place the content from Illustrator as: Smart Object, Pixels, Path, or Shape Layer. To learn more about bringing Illustrator content into Photoshop, search for "Duplicate selections using drag and drop" in Illustrator Help.

5 Start Adobe Photoshop CS4.

● **Note:** You can open Illustrator files in previous versions of Adobe Photoshop, but for this lesson, it's assumed that you are using Adobe Photoshop CS4.

6 Open the Postcard2.psd file that you exported in step 4.

7 Click the Layers tab to view the Layers panel. Notice all the layers. Choose File > Close, and don't save the changes.

8 Close Photoshop CS4.

Placing Illustrator files in Adobe InDesign

You can place Illustrator (AI) files and PDF files in Adobe InDesign. You can also copy and paste content from Illustrator, and drag and drop from Illustrator into InDesign. How you save and import Illustrator graphics depends on how you want to edit the art once you place it in InDesign. Next you will place an Illustrator file into InDesign CS4.

● **Note:** Although you can place Illustrator files in earlier versions of InDesign, you need to install Adobe InDesign CS4 to follow the steps in this section exactly.

1 Open Adobe InDesign CS4.

2 Choose File > New > Document, and leave the defaults set in the New Document dialog box. Click OK.

3 Choose File > Place. In the Place dialog box, locate the logos.ai file in the Lesson14 folder. Select Show Import Options, and then click Open.

4 In the Place PDF dialog box, select Range and type 2 to import the second artboard (there are two). Click the Layers tab.

5 In the Show Layers section, deselect the eye icon to the left of the Logo Tagline layer to hide that content when the file is placed. Notice the preview on the left side of the dialog box. Click OK.

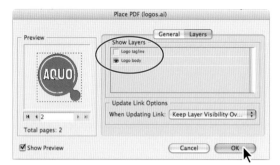

6 A loaded image cursor appears. Click in the center of the page to place the Illustrator file.

Note: Double-click the logos.ai:2 name if the file information does not appear in the bottom of the Links panel. Notice that the Layer Overrides indicate that the visibility of the layers was changed when the file was placed.

7 Click the Links panel tab on the right side of the workspace. The logos.ai:2 graphic is listed in the panel. The :2 after the filename indicates that the second artboard was imported. More information about the linked file appears at the bottom of the Links panel.

Note: To change the layer overrides, select the image with the Selection tool, and then choose Object > Object Layer Options.

8 Click the Edit Original button (✐) in the Links panel to open the logo in Illustrator.

The InDesign Links panel

9 In the orange logo in Illustrator, change the color fill of the Aquo text. Choose File > Save, and leave the file open in Illustrator. When the file is done saving in Illustrator, return to InDesign to see the changes reflected on the page.

Note: The logo file does not have to be closed in Illustrator, only saved, for the change to be applied in InDesign.

10 Return to Illustrator. With the Selection tool (▶), drag a marquee around the red logo to select it. Choose Edit > Copy.

11 Return to InDesign, and choose Edit > Paste.

When you paste from Illustrator, there is no link to the original graphic. The content you paste is typically the objects that make up the logo. They are grouped together and editable in InDesign.

12 Close InDesign without saving, and return to Illustrator. Choose File > Close to close the logos.ai file without saving it.

Getting Illustrator content to Adobe InDesign

- **If you plan to edit a graphic only in Illustrator:** Save the graphic in native Illustrator format (AI). Some graphics require the extensive drawing tools available in Illustrator or are in their final form and shouldn't be edited. In InDesign, you can place a native Illustrator graphic and transform it as a single object (you can resize or rotate it, for example). Use the Edit > Edit Original command to open the graphic in Illustrator and edit it there.

- **If you want to adjust layer visibility in InDesign:** Save the Illustrator CS4 file as a layered PDF file or in native Illustrator format (AI). For some documents, you want to control the visibility of the layers of a graphic depending on the context. For example, for a multiple language publication, you can create a single illustration that includes one text layer for each language. Using a layered PDF file or native Illustrator format (AI), you can transform the illustration as a single object in InDesign, but you cannot edit the paths, objects, or text within the illustration.

- **If you want to edit objects and paths in InDesign:** Copy the artwork from Illustrator and paste it into an InDesign document. For some graphics, you might want to edit them after they're placed in the InDesign document. For example, in a magazine, you might use the same design element in each issue, but want to change its color every month. If you paste a graphic into InDesign and edit it there, you cannot set layer transparency or edit the text.

Integrating Illustrator and Adobe Flash

Illustrator CS4 lets you use Illustrator content in Adobe Flash or export in the Flash file format (SWF). The SWF file format is a vector-based graphics format for interactive, animated web graphics. Next you will export a simple Illustrator file to a SWF file.

1   Switch to Adobe Bridge and double-click the animation.ai file in the Lesson14 folder. This is a simple animation of a snowboarder that opens in Illustrator.

2   In Illustrator, click the Layers panel icon (🌐) to view the layers in the file if not already open. Notice that the mountain layer, which contains the background for the animation, is locked. Each frame in the animation will be made from other layers.

▶ **Tip:** For a document with multiple artboards, select Use Artboards at the bottom of the Export dialog box. This lets you specify how the artboards are exported in the SWF Options dialog box.

3   Choose File > Export. In the Export dialog box, navigate to the Lesson14 folder and open it. In the Save As Type menu, choose Flash (*.SWF) (Windows) or in the Format menu, choose Flash (swf) (Mac OS). Click Save (Windows) or Export (Mac OS).

4   In the SWF Options dialog box, choose AI Layers To SWF Frames from the
    Export As menu to convert each layer into a separate frame in the Flash movie.
    Select Clip To Artboard Size so that the movie dimensions match the Illustrator
    document dimensions. Select Compress File to make the file size smaller (if
    possible). Click the Advanced button.

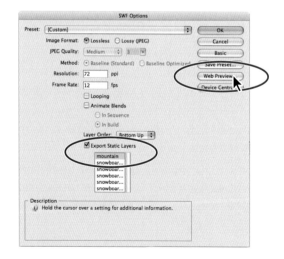

5   In the advanced settings of the SWF Options dialog box, select Export Static
    Layers and make sure that Mountain layer is chosen in the list of Illustrator
    layers. This ensures that the content of the Mountain layer appears in every
    frame as the movie background. Click the Web Preview button to preview the
    animation in a browser.

6   Close the browser and return to Illustrator.

7 Click OK to export the SWF file.

8 Close the animation.ai file without saving changes.

▶ **Tip:** To learn about bringing Illustrator symbols into Adobe Flash, see Lesson 13, "Working with Symbols."

Bring Illustrator artwork into Adobe Flash

If your goal is to bring Illustrator artwork into a Flash document, you can simply paste it in. All paths, strokes, gradients, text (specify Flash Text), masks, effects (such as drop shadow on text), and symbols are maintained. In addition, you can specify how layers are imported when pasting: as Flash layers, frames, or graphic symbols.

—From Illustrator Help

Creating Illustrator files for Adobe Flex

In Illustrator CS4, you can save an Illustrator file in the FXG format to use in Adobe Flex. This is an efficient way to deliver more editable, workable content to developers for projects in Adobe Flex.

1 Switch to Adobe Bridge and double-click the L14start2.ai file in the Lesson14 folder. This is a mockup for a Flex interface. You'll save the file as an FXG file for use in Adobe Flex.

The interface to be saved for use in Adobe Flex

2 In Illustrator, with the file open, choose File > Save As. In the Save As dialog box, navigate to the Lesson14 folder and open it. Rename the file mockup. In the Save As Type menu, choose FXG (*.FXG) (Windows) or in the Format menu, choose FXG (fxg) (Mac OS). Click Save. In the FXG Options dialog box, leave the default settings and click Show Preview.

▶ **Tip:** For more Flex content, choose File > Scripts > Flex Skins to create a new document that contains Flex Components, such as buttons, accordions, and more, that you can use in your artwork.

The file appears in the FXG Preview window.

3   Click OK after previewing to return to the FXG Options dialog box.

Note: On Windows, the Show Code button may not preview the code.

4   Click Show Code to see the XML code that will be generated. This opens a text file in a text editor. Close the file and return to Illustrator.

5   Click OK in the FXG Options dialog box. When the FXG Save Warnings dialog box opens, review the changes and click OK.

Note: The FXG file format is editable in Illustrator, because Preserve Illustrator Editing Capabilities was selected in the FXG Options dialog box. The FXG file is currently open in Illustrator.

6   Choose File > Close.

7   Switch to the Adobe Bridge and choose File > Exit (Windows) or Adobe Bridge CS4 > Quit Adobe Bridge CS4 (Mac OS) to close it, returning to Illustrator.

Exploring on your own

Now that you know how to place and mask an image in an Illustrator file, you can place other images and apply a variety of modifications to the images. You can also create masks for images from objects that you create in Illustrator. For more practice, try the following.

1   In addition to adjusting color in images, apply transformation effects (such as shearing or rotating), filters, or effects (such as one of the Artistic or Distort filters/effects) to create contrast between the two images in the arrow pattern.

2   Use the basic shape tools or the drawing tools to draw objects to create a compound path to use as a mask. Then place the background.psd image into the file with the compound path, and apply the compound path as a mask.

3   Create large type and use the type as a mask to mask a placed object.

Review questions

1 Describe the difference between linking and embedding in Illustrator.

2 How do you create an opacity mask for a placed image?

3 What kinds of objects can be used as masks?

4 What color modifications can you apply to a selected object using effects?

5 Describe how to replace a placed image with another image in a document.

6 Name two ways that you can bring content from Illustrator into Adobe InDesign.

Review answers

1 A linked file is a separate, external file connected to the Illustrator file by an electronic link. A linked file does not add significantly to the size of the Illustrator file. The linked file must accompany the Illustrator file to preserve the link and ensure that the placed file appears when you open the Illustrator file. An embedded file is included in the Illustrator file. The Illustrator file size reflects the addition of the embedded file. Because the embedded file is part of the Illustrator file, no link can be broken. You can update linked and embedded files using the Replace Link button in the Links panel.

2 You create an opacity mask by placing the object to be used as a mask on top of the object to be masked. Then you select the mask and the objects to be masked, and choose Make Opacity Mask from the Transparency panel menu.

3 A mask can be a simple or compound path. You can use type as a mask. You can import opacity masks with placed Photoshop files. You can also create layer clipping masks with any shape that is the topmost object of a group or layer.

4 You can use effects to change the color mode (RGB, CMYK, or grayscale) or adjust individual colors in a selected object. You can also saturate or desaturate colors or invert colors in a selected object. You can apply color modifications to placed images, as well as to artwork created in Illustrator.

5 To replace a placed image, select the image in the Links panel. Then click the Replace Link button, and locate and select the replacement image. Click Place.

6 Choose File > Place in InDesign to place a graphic and create a link to the original, or choose Edit > Paste after copying content from Illustrator. Pasting content does not create a link.

15 OUTPUT

Lesson overview

In this lesson, you'll learn the following:

- Understand different types of printing requirements and printing devices.

- Know different printing concepts and printing terminology.

- Apply basic color principles.

- Separate color artwork for output to print.

- Use spot colors for two-color printing.

- Consider special issues when printing.

- Save and print files with transparency effects.

- Create files in PDF, EPS, and more.

 This first part of this lesson takes approximately 45 minutes to complete and the second part takes approximately 20 minutes. If needed, remove the previous lesson folder from your hard disk and copy the Lesson15 folder onto it.

The quality and color of your final printed output are determined by the process you follow to prepare an image for print. Whether you're printing a draft of your work on a desktop printer or outputting color separations to a commercial press, learning fundamental printing concepts helps ensure that your print work meets your expectations.

Getting started

Before you begin, you must restore the default preferences for Adobe Illustrator CS4. Then you'll open the art file for this lesson.

1   To ensure that the tools and panels function as described in this lesson, delete or deactivate (by renaming) the Adobe Illustrator CS4 preferences file. See "Restoring default preferences" on page 3.

2   Start Adobe Illustrator CS4.

● **Note:** If you have not already copied the resource files for this lesson onto your hard disk from the Lesson15 folder on the Adobe Illustrator CS4 Classroom in a Book CD, do so now. See "Copying the Classroom in a Book files" on page 2.

3   Choose File > Open, and open the L15start.ai file in the Lesson15 folder, located in the Lessons folder on your hard disk.

4   Choose File > Save As, name the file party_invite. ai, and select the Lesson15 folder. Leave the Save As Type option set to Adobe Illustrator (*.AI) (Windows) or the Format option set to Adobe Illustrator (ai) (Mac OS), and click Save. In the Illustrator Options dialog box, leave the Illustrator options at their default settings, and click OK.

● **Note:** If a warning dialog box appears about using spot colors with transparency, click Continue.

5   Choose View > Fit Artboard In Window.

Understanding the printing process

When you print from a computer, data is sent from the document to the printing device, either to be printed on paper or converted to a positive or negative image on film. For black-and-white, grayscale, or small quantities of color artwork, you can use a desktop printer. If you need large quantities of the printed output, such as for a brochure or magazine ad, you'll need to prepare your artwork for a commercial printing press. Printing on a commercial press is an art that requires time and experience to perfect. In addition to communicating with a printing professional throughout the process, you need to learn basic printing concepts and terminology.

● **Note:** This lesson assumes that you have a desktop printer for use with the exercises. If you don't have a desktop printer available, you can read the sections and skip the step-by-step instructions.

Different printing requirements involve different printing processes. To determine your requirements, consider the following:

- What effect do you want the printed piece to have on your audience?

- Will your artwork be printed in black and white or color?

- Does it require special paper?

- How many printed copies do you need?

- If you're printing in color, is precise color matching necessary, or is approximate color matching adequate?

Take a moment to consider several types of printing jobs:

- Black-and-white interoffice newsletter, requiring a small quantity of printed copies—You can generally use a 300-600 dots per inch (dpi) desktop laser printer to output the original, and then use a copy machine to reproduce the quantity needed.

- Business card using black and one other color—The term two-color printing typically refers to printing with black and one other color, although it may also refer to printing with two colors that are not black. Two-color printing is less expensive than four-color printing and lets you select exact color matches, called spot colors, which can be important for logos. For precise color matching, two-color printing is done on a printing press. If only an approximate color match is required, you can use a desktop color printer.

- Party invitation using two colors and tints of those colors—In addition to printing two solid colors, you can print tints of the colors to add depth to your artwork. Two-color printing is often done on colored paper that complements the ink colors. Whether to use a desktop color printer or a printing press depends on the quantity and degree of color matching required.

- Newspaper—Newspapers are typically printed on a printing press, because they are time-sensitive publications printed in large quantities. Newspapers are generally printed on large rolls of newsprint, which are then trimmed and folded to the correct size.

- Magazine or catalog requiring accurate color reproduction—In four-color printing, the four process ink colors (cyan, magenta, yellow, and black, or CMYK) are mixed. When accurate color reproduction is required, printing is done on a printing press using CMYK inks. CMYK inks can reproduce a good amount of the visible color spectrum, with the exception of neon or metallic colors.

You'll learn more about color models in the next section.

Understanding printing devices

Now that you are familiar with different ways to reproduce several types of publications, you'll begin learning basic printing concepts and printing terminology.

Halftone screens

To reproduce any type of artwork, a printing device typically breaks down the artwork into a halftone screen, which is a series of dots of varying sizes. Black dots are used to print black-and-white or grayscale artwork. For color artwork, a halftone screen is created for each ink color (cyan, magenta, yellow, and black). These inks then overlay one another at different angles to produce the full range of printed color. For a good example of how individual halftone screens overlay each other at different angles on a printed page, look at a page in a color comic book through a magnifying glass.

The size of the dots in a halftone screen determines how light or dark colors appear in print. The smaller the dot, the lighter the color appears; the larger the dot, the darker the color appears.

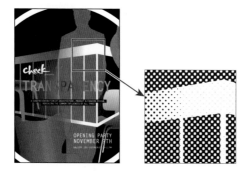

Enlarged detail shows the dots in the halftone screen.

Screen frequency

Screen frequency, also called line screen, screen ruling, or halftone frequency, refers to the number of rows or lines of dots used to render an image on film or paper. The rows of dots are broken down into individual squares, called halftone cells. Screen frequency is measured in lines per inch (lpi) and is a fixed value you can set for your printing device.

As a general rule, higher screen frequencies produce finer detail in printed output because the higher the screen frequency, the smaller the halftone cells, and subsequently, the smaller the halftone dot in the cell.

A high screen frequency alone does not guarantee high-quality output. The screen frequency must be appropriate to the paper, the inks, and the printer or printing press used to output the artwork. Your printing professional can help you select the appropriate line screen value for your artwork and output device.

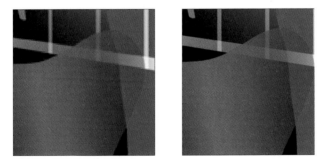

Low-screen ruling (65 lpi), shown at left, is often used to print newsletters.
High-screen ruling (150–200 lpi), shown at right, is used for high-quality books.

Output device resolution

The resolution of a printing device describes the number of dots the printing device has available to render, or create, a halftone dot. The higher the output device resolution, the higher the quality of the printed output. For example, the printed quality of an image output at 2400 dpi is higher than the printed quality of an image output at 300 dpi. Adobe Illustrator is resolution-independent and always prints at the printing device's highest resolution capability.

The quality of printed output depends on the relationship between the resolution of the output device (dpi) and the screen frequency (lpi). As a general rule, high-resolution output devices use higher screen frequency values to produce the highest quality images. For example, an imagesetter with a resolution of 2400 dpi and a screen frequency of 177 lpi produces a higher quality image than a desktop printer with a resolution of 300 to 600 dpi and a screen frequency of 85 lpi.

About color

The human eye perceives color according to the wavelength of the light it receives. Light containing the full color spectrum is perceived as white. In the absence of light, the eye perceives black.

Computer monitors and printing devices use two different color models to produce color. A color model is a method for displaying and measuring color. Each color model has a range of colors that can be displayed or printed, called a color gamut. The largest color gamut is that viewed in nature; all other color gamuts are a subset of nature's color gamut. The two most common color models are red, green, and blue (RGB), and cyan, magenta, yellow, and black (CMYK). Monitors use RGB to display color, and printing devices typically use CMYK to produce color.

RGB color model

A large percentage of the visible spectrum of color can be represented by mixing three basic components of colored light—red, green, and blue— in various proportions. These components are known as the additive colors. The RGB color model is called the additive color model because various percentages of each colored light are added to create color. Monitors display color using the RGB color model.

CMYK color model

If 100% of red, green, or blue is subtracted from white light, the resulting color is cyan, magenta, or yellow. For example, if an object absorbs (subtracts) 100% red light and reflects green and blue, cyan is the perceived color. Cyan, magenta, and yellow are called the subtractive primaries, and they form the basis for printed colors. In addition to cyan, magenta, and yellow, black ink is used to generate true black and to deepen the shadows in images. These four inks—CMYK—are called process colors because they are the four standard inks used in the printing process.

Spot colors

Spot colors are premixed inks used in place of, or in addition to, CMYK colors. Spot colors can be selected from color-matching systems, such as the PANTONE® or TOYO™ color libraries.

Many spot colors can be converted to their process color equivalents when printed. However, some spot colors, such as metallic or iridescent colors, require their own plate on a printing press.

Use spot color in the following situations:

- To save money on one-color and two-color print jobs. When your printing budget doesn't allow for four-color printing, you can still print relatively inexpensively using one or two colors.

- To print logos or other graphic elements that require precise color matching. You want the printer in San Diego to use the same color of red as the printer in New York.

- To print special inks, such as metallic, fluorescent, or pearlescent colors.

What is color management?

Color-matching problems result from various devices and software using different color spaces. One solution is to have a system that interprets and translates color accurately between devices. A color management system (CMS) compares the color space in which a color was created to the color space in which the same color can be output, and makes the necessary adjustments to represent the color as consistently as possible on different devices.

A color management system translates colors with the help of color profiles. A profile is a mathematical description of a device's color gamut, also called a color space. Because some devices are capable of producing more color (or have a larger color gamut) than others, Adobe applications use ICC profiles, a format defined by the International Color Consortium as a cross-platform standard to keep color within a printing device's gamut.

In this lesson, you will learn how to use color settings to prepare an Illustrator CS4 file for print output.

Basic steps for producing consistent color

1. **Consult with your production partners (if you have any) to ensure that all aspects of your color management workflow integrate seamlessly with theirs.** Discuss how the color workflow will be integrated with your workgroups and service providers, how software and hardware will be configured for integration into the color management system, and at what level color management will be implemented.

2. **Calibrate and profile your monitor.** A monitor profile is the first profile you should create. Seeing accurate color is essential if you are making creative decisions involving the color you specify in your document.

3. **Add color profiles to your system for any input and output devices you plan to use, such as scanners and printers.** The color management system uses profiles to know how a device produces color and what the actual colors in a document are. Device profiles are often installed when a device is added to your system. You can also use third-party software and hardware to create more accurate profiles for specific devices and conditions. If your document will be commercially printed, contact your service provider to determine the profile for the printing device or press condition.

4. **Set up color management in Adobe applications.** The default color settings are sufficient for most users. However, you can change the color settings by doing one of the following:

   - If you use multiple Adobe applications, use Adobe® Bridge CS4 to choose a standard color management configuration and synchronize color settings across applications before working with documents. (See Synchronize color settings across Adobe applications.)

   - If you use only one Adobe application, or if you want to customize advanced color management options, you can change color settings for a specific application. (See Set up color management.)

5. **(Optional) Preview colors using a soft proof.** After you create a document, you can use a soft proof to preview how colors will look when printed or viewed on a specific device. (See Soft-proofing colors.)

6. **Use color management when printing and saving files.** Keeping the appearance of colors consistent across all of the devices in your workflow is the goal of color management. Leave color management options enabled when printing documents, saving files, and preparing files for online viewing. (See Printing with color management and Color-managing documents for online viewing.)

—From Illustrator Help

Setting up color management in Illustrator

When you select the appropriate color profile, you can expect a more realistic on-screen view of how the printed artwork will appear. Color management enables the RGB monitor to represent consistent color as it appears when printed in CMYK.

The default color settings are sufficient for most users. However, you may want to change color settings for a specific application, or customize the color management settings. For this example, you will choose North America Prepress 2.

1 Choose Edit > Color Settings.

2 Select North America Prepress 2 from the Settings menu, and click OK.

● **Note:** The settings in Adobe Bridge may become unsynchronized, which is OK.

● **Note:** Talk to your service provider or printer for more specifications to help you create more accurate color.

Synchronizing color using Adobe Bridge

If you installed the entire Creative Suite 4 and frequently use multiple Adobe applications, you can use Adobe Bridge to choose a standard color management configuration and synchronize color settings across applications before working with documents.

When you set up color management in Adobe Bridge, color settings are automatically synchronized across applications.

1   Choose File > Browse In Bridge.

● **Note:** To open Adobe Bridge directly, either choose Adobe Bridge from the Start menu, or double-click the Adobe Bridge icon.

2   In Adobe Bridge, choose Edit > Creative Suite Color Settings.

3   Select North America Prepress 2 from the list, and click Apply.

● **Note:** If the default settings do not meet your requirements, you can select Show Expanded List Of Color Settings Files to view additional settings. To install a custom settings file, such as a file you received from a print service provider, click Show Saved Color Settings Files.

Soft-proofing colors

In a color-managed workflow, you can use the precision of color profiles to soft-proof your document directly on the monitor. Soft-proofing lets you preview on-screen how the colors in your document would look when reproduced on a particular output device, such as a commercial press.

The reliability of soft-proofing depends on the quality of your monitor, monitor profile, and the ambient lighting conditions of your workstation area. In other words, if you are working in an inconsistent environment with varying light throughout the day, you might not get reliable results. For information on creating a monitor profile, see "To calibrate and profile your monitor" in Illustrator Help.

1   In Illustrator, choose View > Proof Setup > Customize. The profile for the party_invite.ai file is set to U.S. Web Coated (SWOP) v2. Leave it set to this profile, and click OK.

The Proof Colors option is selected by default (indicated by a check mark) so that you can view the artwork as it would look when printed to the selected standard, U.S. Web Coated (SWOP) v2.

Next, you'll change the profile to see what the image would look like on a different output device.

2 Choose View > Proof Setup > Customize.

3 In the Proof Setup dialog box, choose Euroscale Uncoated v2 from the Device To Simulate menu, and select Preview. Click OK. Because the view is still set to Proof Colors, the image preview automatically shifts colors to display what it would look like using the Euroscale Uncoated v2 profile.

Now you'll return the settings to the SWOP settings.

4 Choose View > Proof Setup > Customize. Set the profile to U.S. Web Coated (SWOP) v2, and click OK.

5 Choose View > Proof Colors to deselect the soft-proofing preview.

Next you'll work with printing color artwork.

Color separations

To print color artwork on a printing press, you must first separate the composite art into its component colors: cyan, magenta, yellow, and black, and any spot colors, if applicable. The process of breaking composite artwork into its component colors is called color separation.

Before setting separation options, it's important that you discuss the specific requirements of your print job with your printing professional. You cannot separate colors with a non-PostScript® printer.

Previewing color separations

Next you'll set separation options in the Print dialog box, and preview them in the Separations Preview panel.

1 In the Party_invite.ai file, choose Window > Separations Preview.

2 In the Separations Preview panel, select Overprint Preview.

3 Click the Next button (▶) in the status bar to navigate to artboard 2.

● **Note:** You may need to drag the bottom of the Separations Preview panel down or scroll down to reveal all inks.

4 In the Separations Preview panel, deselect the eye icon (👁) to the left of CMYK.

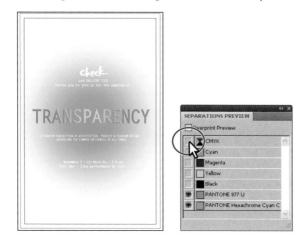

5 To return to normal view, deselect Overprint Preview in the Separations Preview panel.

6 Close the Separations Preview panel.

▶ **Tip:** To hide all separations except one, Alt-click or Option-click the eye icon for that separation. Alt-click or Option-click the eye icon again to view all separations again.

Printing color separations

Next you will print the separations for the Party_invite.ai file.

● **Note:** To continue with this section, your computer must be connected to a PostScript printer. If you are connected to an inkjet printer or not connected to a printer, the separation options are dimmed in the Print dialog window.

1 Choose File > Print.

2 If you are connected to a PostScript printer, choose that printer from the Printer menu, then proceed to the next step. If you are not connected to a printer, choose the Adobe PostScript® File printer.

3 Select a PPD.

PostScript Printer Description (PPD) files contain information about the output device, including available page sizes, resolution, available line screen (frequency) values, and the angles of the halftone screens.

● **Note:** The Lesson15 folder contains a PPD file with limited selections. When you install Adobe Illustrator, two PPDs are automatically installed in the Utilities folder in the Adobe Illustrator folder, and additional PPDs are provided on the Adobe Illustrator DVD.

4 Choose Other from the PPD menu.

5 Navigate to the General.ppd file, located in the Lesson15 folder in the Lessons folder on your hard disk. Select it, and click Open.

The Print dialog box is updated with general printer parameters, and a preview of your artwork is displayed in the lower left side of the dialog box. The preview of your artwork depends on the page size selected in the Size menu. Each output device has a variety of page sizes available.

Print multiple artboards

When you create a document with multiple artboards, you can print the document in a variety of ways. You can ignore the artboards and print everything on one page (tiling may be required if your artboards expand the page boundaries). Or you can print each artboard as an individual page. When you print artboards as individual pages, you can choose to print all artboards, or a range of artboards.

1 Choose File > Print.

2 Do one of the following:

- To print all artboards as separate pages, select All. You can see all the pages listed in the preview area in the lower left corner of the Print dialog box.

- To print a subset of artboards as separate pages, select Range, and specify the artboards to print.

- To print the artwork on all the artboards together on a single page, select Ignore Artboards. If the artwork extends past the boundaries of the page, you can scale or tile it.

3 Specify other print options as desired, and click Print.

—From Illustrator Help

6 Choose US Letter for the paper size in the Media section.

7 Click Marks And Bleed in the options on the left.

In the Print dialog box, you can choose which printer's marks are visible. Printer's marks help the printer align color separations on the press, and check the color and density of the inks being used.

A. Registration mark
B. Page information
C. Trim marks
D. Color bar

8 Select All Printer's Marks.

The preview shows the crop and other marks in the preview.

9 Leave the Print dialog box open for the next section.

Specifying the bleed area

Bleed is the amount of artwork that falls outside the printing bounding box or outside the crop marks and trim marks. You can include the bleed area in your artwork as a margin of error to ensure that the ink is still printed to the edge of the page after the page is trimmed or that an image can be stripped into a keyline in a document. For artwork that extends into the bleed area, you can specify the size of the bleed.

Changing the bleed area makes Illustrator print more or less of the artwork beyond the crop marks; however, the crop marks still define the same size printing bounding box. By default, Illustrator uses the bleed set in the file. You can set the bleed in the Document Setup dialog box. You can also override the bleed for a document in the Print dialog box.

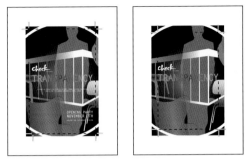

A small bleed is shown at left; a large bleed is shown at right.

10 In the Print dialog box, leave Use Document Bleed Settings selected, which is the default.

By leaving Use Document Bleed Settings selected, you are accepting the bleed size previously set for this document, which is to extend the artwork 9 points beyond the crop marks. The maximum bleed you can set is 72 points; the minimum bleed is 0 points.

The size of the bleed depends on its purpose. A press bleed (an image that bleeds off the edge of the printed sheet) should be at least 18 points. If the bleed needs to ensure that an image fits a keyline, it can be 2 or 3 points. Your print shop can advise you on the size of the bleed necessary for your particular job.

11 Leave the Print dialog box open.

Separating colors

12 Click Output on the left side of the Print dialog box. Choose Separations (Host Based) from the Mode menu.

The invitation artwork is composed of process colors and two spot colors, which are displayed in the Document Ink Options.

To the left of the color names, a printer icon (🖶) indicates that a separation will be generated for each color. To the left of the spot color names, the spot color icon (◉) indicates that the spot color will be printed as separate color. The color of the icon matches that of the spot color. To the left of the process color names a process color icon (▨) is displayed.

Illustrator CS4 output mode options

Illustrator CS4 provides the following output mode options:

- **Composite**—Sends all the color information in your file to your output device. This is the typical setting for everyday printing to a desktop color printer or a color copier.

- **Separations (Host Based)**—Produces the separations on your computer and sends the separated data to your output device.

- **In-RIP Separations**—Performs color separations at the RIP (Raster Image Processor), leaving the host computer free to perform other tasks. When using this mode, the output device receiving the data must support In-RIP separations.

If you print color separations at this point, all the colors, including the spot color in the artwork, would be printed into six separations. This is referred to as a six-color job, which requires a specialized press capable of printing six colors. On a four-color press, the paper would have to be sent back through the press to print the fifth and sixth color.

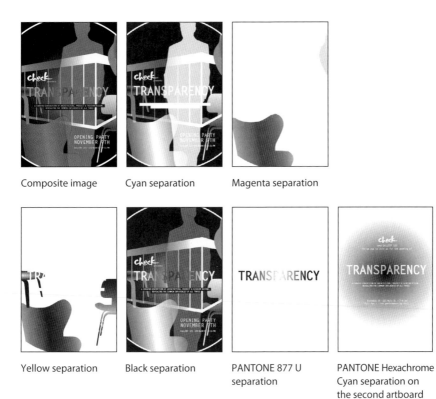

Composite image   Cyan separation   Magenta separation

Yellow separation   Black separation   PANTONE 877 U separation   PANTONE Hexachrome Cyan separation on the second artboard

13 Select Convert All Spot Colors To Process. With this option selected, the spot colors will be broken down into the CMYK builds, and printed with four separations.

14 Deselect Convert All Spot Colors To Process. Notice that the spot colors are no longer dimmed, and the process icon to the left of the spot colors returns to spot icons, indicating that they will print.

As you learned earlier, you can print separations using process colors or spot colors, or you can use a combination of both. Now you'll convert only the spot color (PANTONE 877 U) to a process color, because a precise color match isn't necessary.

15 To convert PANTONE 877 U to a process color, click the spot color icon to the left of its name in the list of colors.

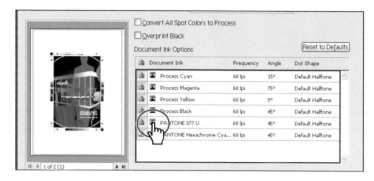

If you printed at this point, five separations would be generated: one each for the cyan, magenta, yellow, and black plates (including the spot color converted to a process color), and the PANTONE Hexachrome Cyan C spot color.

Composite image   Cyan separation   Magenta separation

Yellow separation   Black separation   Spot separation

Specifying the screen frequency

At the beginning of this lesson, you learned that the relationship between the output device resolution and the screen frequency determines the quality of the printed output. Depending on the output device you select, more than one screen frequency value may be available.

16 In the Printer Resolution menu, make sure 60 lpi/300 dpi is chosen. The first value, 60, represents the screen frequency (lpi), and the second value, 300, represents the output device resolution (dpi).

Discuss additional separation options, such as Emulsion Up/Down, and Positive or Negative film, with your printing professional, who can help you determine how to set these options for your particular job.

Before printing your separations to a high-resolution output device, you may want to print a set of separations, called proofs, on your black-and-white desktop printer. You'll save time and money by making any needed corrections to your files after reviewing the black-and-white proofs.

17 Click the Save Preset button (💾) in the Print dialog box, and name the preset Invite. In the future, you can choose it from the Preset menu. Click OK.

18 If you have chosen a PostScript printer in the Print dialog box, click Print to print separations. Five pages are printed—one each for cyan, magenta, yellow, black, and the spot color. If you chose the PostScript print driver, click Done.

⬤ **Note:** Depending on the printer you choose, you may get a warning dialog box saying that your PPD doesn't match the current printer. Click Continue to print the proofs.

19 Choose File > Save, and close the Party_invite.ai file.

Working with two-color illustrations

Two-color printing generally refers to printing with black and one spot color, but can also refer to two spot colors. In addition to printing two solid colors, you can print tints, or screens, of the colors. Two-color printing is much less expensive than four-color printing. You can create a rich range of depth and color with two colors, when used effectively.

Separating spot colors

For a two-color illustration, separating spot colors into their process color equivalents is less cost-effective than outputting the spot color to its own separation (converting to four CMYK plates versus one plate for each individual spot color).

1 Choose File > Open, and open the L15start2.ai file in the Lesson15 folder.

2 Choose View > Fit Artboard In Window.

Composite image　　　Separation 1: Black　　　Separation 2: Spot color

3 Choose File > Print.

4 Make sure that you have a printer selected in the Printer menu. If not, select the Adobe Postscript® File printer.

5 Choose Other from the PPD menu.

6 Navigate to the General.ppd file, located in the Lesson15 folder. Select it and click Open.

7 Select the center of the Placement Reference Point (▦) to center the content on the media.

8 Click Output on the left side of the Print dialog box.

9 Choose Separations (Host-Based) from the Mode menu.

10 You may notice printer icons (🖨) to the left of multiple colors. Because this is a two-color job, make sure that only Process Black and PANTONE Hexachrome Cyan are selected. Deselect the printer icon of all unnecessary colors.

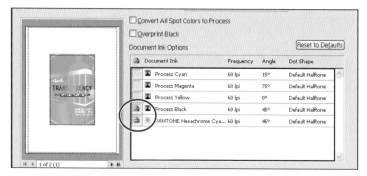

The printer icon indicates that the color will print.

11 Click the Save Preset button (💾) at the bottom of the Print dialog box. Name the preset Invite 2-color, and click OK.

12 Click Done to save the settings, but do not print at this time.

13 Save and close the L15start2.ai file.

Understanding trapping

Trapping is used to compensate for any gaps or color shifts that may occur between adjoining or overlapping objects when printing. These gaps or color shifts occur from misregistration, which is the result of the paper or the printing plates becoming misaligned during printing. Trapping is a technique developed by commercial print shops to slightly overprint the colors along common edges.

Gap created by misregistration

Gap removed by trapping

Although trapping sounds simple, it requires a thorough knowledge of color and design, and an eye for determining where it is needed. You can use the Trap effect to create a trap for simple artwork whose parts can be selected and trapped individually or by setting a Stroke value for individual objects you want to trap.

About trapping

There are two types of traps:

A **spread**, in which a lighter object overlaps a darker background and seems to expand into the background;

A **choke**, in which a lighter background overlaps a darker object that falls within the background and seems to squeeze or reduce the object.

Spread: Object overlaps object.

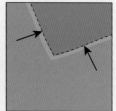
Choke: Background overlaps background.

When overlapping painted objects share a common color, trapping may be unnecessary if the color that is common to both objects creates an automatic trap. For example, if two overlapping objects contain cyan as part of their CMYK values, any gap between them is covered by the cyan content of the object underneath.

Trapping type can present special problems. Avoid applying mixed process colors or tints of process colors to type at small point sizes, because any misregistration can make the text difficult to read. Likewise, trapping type at small point sizes can result in hard-to-read type. As with tint reduction, check with your print shop before trapping such type. For example, if you are printing black type on a colored background, simply overprinting the type onto the background may be enough.

—From Illustrator Help

Overprinting objects

When preparing an image for color separation, you can define how you want overlapping objects of different colors to print. By default, the top object in the artwork knocks out, or removes the color of, underlying artwork on the other separations and prints with the color of the top object only. Misregistration may occur when you knock out colors.

Composite image

First plate

Second plate

You can also specify objects to overprint, or print on top of, any artwork under them. Overprinting is the simplest way to prevent misregistration on press. The overprinted color automatically traps into the background color.

Composite image

First plate

Second plate

Next you'll select an object in the invitation and apply an overprint. Then you will preview the overprint on-screen.

1 Choose File > Open. Locate and open the L15start3.ai file in the Lesson15 folder, and click Open.

2 In the Missing Profile dialog box, select Assign Current Working Space: US Web Coated (SWOP) v2, and click OK.

> **Tip:** To learn more about missing or mismatched color profiles, search for "About missing and mismatched color profiles" in Illustrator Help.

3 With the Selection tool (▶), click the yellow chair to select it.

4 Choose View > Overprint Preview if there is no check mark next to this command.

5 Choose Window > Attributes.

Now you'll see an approximation of how overprinting and blending appear in the color-separated output.

6 In the Attributes panel, select Overprint Fill.

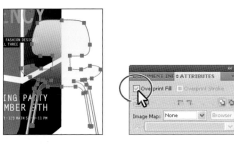

7 With the yellow chair still selected, deselect Overprint Fill in the Attributes panel.

If an object has a stroke, you can also select the Overprint Stroke option to make sure that the stroke overprints on the object below it as well. Next you'll add a stroke to an object to create a trap.

8 With the yellow chair selected, select the CMYK Yellow swatch from the Stroke color in the Control panel. Make sure the stroke weight is set to 1 pt in the Control panel.

9 In the Attributes panel, select Overprint Stroke.

Depending on what you have discussed with your printing professional, you may want to change the amount of trap specified. You'll try changing the specified trap now.

10 With the chair shape still selected, change the Stroke Weight to 6pt in the Control panel. Because Overprint Preview is selected, you can see the results on the artboard.

No Overprint preview   Overprint Stroke preview

Strokes are centered over the object's path. This means that if an object is stroked with the same color as its fill, only half the stroke weight actually overprints. For example, if your printing professional wants a 0.5-point trap added to the yellow chair, you would use a 1-point stroke weight to achieve the trap. Half of the stroke appears inside the fill area, and the other half appears outside the fill area.

11 Choose File > Save, and keep the file open.

You've finished this part of the lesson. In an ordinary workflow situation, you would now be ready to send your artwork to a commercial press to be printed. When you send your electronic file to a printer, include proofs of color separation setups. In addition, tell your printer about any traps that you created in the artwork. Keep in mind that you must remain in close communication with your printing professional for each print job. Each print job has unique requirements that you must consider before you begin the process of color separation.

Saving and exporting artwork

You can save Illustrator files in several different native file formats including—AI, PDF, EPS, and SVG—which preserve all data, including multiple artboards. You can also export files in a variety of non-native file formats, including BMP and PNG, which you can use in other applications. If you save files in non-native file formats, Illustrator cannot retrieve all the data when you reopen them in Illustrator. For this reason, it is recommended that you save artwork in the native AI format until you are finished creating it, and then export the artwork to the desired file format.

● **Note:** For PDF and SVG formats, you must select the Preserve Illustrator Editing Capabilities option to preserve Illustrator data. EPS can save individual artboards as separate files.

Using the Document Info panel

The Document Info panel displays information about the objects, linked and placed files, colors, gradients, patterns, and fonts in your document. Before you take your color artwork to a prepress professional or begin the process of creating color separations, use the Document Info panel to generate and save a list of information about all the elements in your artwork file. If you're working with prepress professionals, they can help you determine what you'll need to include with your artwork. For example, if your artwork uses a font that the prepress house does not have, you'll need to supply a copy of the font with your artwork.

1   With the L15start3.ai file open, choose Window > Document Info to open the Document Info panel.

2   In the Document Info panel, select different options for the document in the panel menu (▾≣). The panel displays information about each option that you select.

3   Select an object on the artboard, and make sure Selection Only is selected (has a checkmark to the left) in the Document Info panel menu to display information for that object only. Select Objects from the same menu and notice the information change in the Document Info panel.

You can also view or print the entire contents of the Document Info panel by saving it and then opening it in a text editor.

4   Choose Save from the panel menu, name the Document Info file, and then click Save.

5 When you have looked through the document information file, leave the Document Info panel open for reference, or close it.

6 Leave the file open.

Saving a file with transparency

If you are saving a file for use in other Adobe applications, such as InDesign or Photoshop, keep the transparency live by saving the artwork in the native Adobe Illustrator format. Transparency for this file format is supported in these other applications.

Next, you will save your shape file in two different formats so that you can place it in an InDesign document.

1 Choose File > Open, and open the shapes.ai file in the Lesson15 folder, located in the Lessons folder on your hard disk.

2 Choose File > Save As, name the file shapes2.ai, select the Lesson15 folder, and click Save. In the Illustrator Options dialog box, click OK.

● **Note:** If a warning dialog box appears, click Continue.

● **Note:** To follow the rest of the steps in this section, you need to have Adobe InDesign CS4 installed.

3 Launch Adobe InDesign CS4, and choose File > New. Create a letter-sized document.

▶ **Tip:** For more information on placing files in InDesign, see Lesson 14, "Combining Illustrator CS4 Graphics with other Adobe Applications."

4 Choose File > Place. Locate the shapes2.ai file you saved in the Lesson15 folder, and click Place.

5 Return to Illustrator, keeping the file open in InDesign. Leave the shapes2.ai file open.

Using Place to import your file maintains transparency in the artwork.

● **Note:** When you drag and drop artwork from one Adobe application to another, transparency is not supported.

Saving in the EPS format

You can save a file as an Encapsulated Postscript (EPS) file for use in non-Adobe applications or if you do not need to maintain transparency. The EPS format preserves many graphic elements that you can create with Adobe Illustrator, which means that EPS files can be reopened and edited in other Adobe applications as Illustrator files. EPS files can contain both vector and bitmap graphics, as well as multiple artboards.

1   Choose File > Save As, name the file shapes3.eps, and select the Lesson15 folder. Choose Illustrator EPS (*.EPS) from the Save as Type menu (Windows) or choose Illustrator EPS (eps) from the Format menu (Mac OS), and click Save.

●**Note:** Click Continue if a warning dialog box appears.

2   In the EPS Options dialog box, choose a transparency preset from the Preset menu in the Transparency section. Click OK.

3   Return to the InDesign document.

4   Choose File > Place, select the shapes3.eps file that you just saved, and click Place.

Notice that transparency is not supported. The transparent areas of the artwork do not interact with the rest of the document.

Adobe Illustrator format

EPS format

●**Note:** A yellow filled frame was placed behind the placed Illustrator and EPS file in the figure above to see the effect better.

5   Return to Illustrator, and choose File > Close, or leave the file open to experiment with other flattening options.

Printing transparent artwork

If your computer is connected to a printer, you can experiment with different flattening settings in the Print dialog box.

1   Choose File > Open Recent Files and choose shapes2.ai.

2   Choose File > Print.

3   Click Advanced in the options window on the left side of the Print dialog box.

4   In the Preset menu, choose a transparency preset or click the Custom button to create your own.

●**Note:** For more information about printing artwork with transparency, see the PDF file, Print_transparency.pdf, on the Classroom In A Book CD.

5   Click Print to print the file if you are connected to a printer and it is chosen.

6   Close the shapes2.ai file.

Saving as Adobe PDF

Adobe Portable Document Format (PDF) is a universal file format that preserves the fonts, images, and layout of source documents created on a wide range of applications and platforms. PDF is the standard for the secure, reliable distribution and exchange of electronic documents and forms around the world. Adobe PDF files are compact and complete, and can be shared, viewed, and printed by anyone with free Adobe Reader® software. In addition, Adobe PDF can preserve all Illustrator data, which means that you can reopen the file in Illustrator with everything intact.

Adobe PDF is effective in print publishing workflows, and is an efficient way to convey ideas to someone who doesn't have Adobe Illustrator. By saving a composite of your artwork as an Adobe PDF file, you create a compact, reliable file that you or your service provider can view, edit, organize, and proof. Your service provider can then output the Adobe PDF file directly, or process it using tools from various sources for post-processing tasks like preflight checks, trapping, imposition, and color separation.

1   With the L15start3.ai file open, choose File > Save As, name the file shapes1.ai, and select the Lesson15 folder. Change Save As Type to Adobe PDF (*.PDF) (Windows), or Format to Adobe PDF (pdf) (Mac OS), and click Save.

2   In the Save Adobe PDF dialog box, leave the Adobe PDF Preset at [Illustrator Default].

The Illustrator Default command does not compress raster artwork, but does compress text and line art.

3   With the General options selected on the left side of the dialog box, deselect Create Acrobat Layers From Top-Level Layers. By default, Acrobat layers that are editable in Acrobat and Reader are created from the top-level layers in your Illustrator document.

4   Deselect Embed Page Thumbnails to make the file size smaller.

5   Click Save Preset, and name it invites in the Save Adobe PDF Settings As dialog box. Click OK. Next time you create a PDF document, you can select invites from the Adobe PDF Preset menu.

▶ **Tip:** To delete a preset, choose Edit > Adobe PDF Presets. In the Adobe PDF Presets dialog box, select the preset, and click Delete.

6   Click Save PDF. Open the PDF file in Acrobat or Reader.

7   Choose File > Close to close the PDF file and return to Illustrator.

8   Choose File > Close without saving the changes.

9   Choose Edit > Color Settings.

10 Select North America General Purpose 2 from the Settings menu to set the color settings back to default, and click OK.

PDF presets

When creating PDFs from Illustrator there are many presets to choose from.

High Quality Print Creates a PDF file for quality printing on desktop printers and proofers. It downsamples color and grayscale images with resolutions above 450 ppi to 300 ppi and prints to a higher image resolution. PDF files created with this settings file can be opened in Acrobat 5.0 and Adobe Reader 5.0 and later.

Illustrator Default Creates a PDF file in which all Illustrator data is preserved. PDF files created with this preset can be reopened in Illustrator without any loss of data.

PDF/X-1a:2001, PDF/X-3:2002, PDF/X-4:2007, PDF/X-4:2008: Use these settings to create Adobe PDF documents that are to be checked or must conform to either the PDF/X-1a:2001, PDF/X-3:2002, PDF/X-4:2007, or PDF/X-4:2008 ISO standards for graphic content exchange. If the file fails compliance checks, a warning message appears that lets you cancel saving the file or continue by saving a file that is not marked as PDF/X-compliant. PDF files created with PDF/X-1a:2001 or PDF/X-3:2002 settings files can be opened in Acrobat 4.0 and Adobe Reader 4.0 and later. Created PDF documents created with PDF/X-4:2007 or PDF/X-4:2008 can be opened with Acrobat and Adobe Reader 5.0 and later.

Press Quality Creates PDF files for high-quality print production (for example, for digital printing or for separations to an imagesetter or platesetter), but does not create files that are PDF/X-compliant. In this case, the quality of the content is the highest consideration. The objective is to maintain all the information in a PDF file that a commercial printer or prepress service provider needs in order to print the document correctly. This set of options downsamples color and grayscale images with resolutions above 450 ppi to 300 ppi and monochrome images with resolutions above 1800 ppi to 1200 ppi, embeds subsets of fonts used in the document (if allowed), and creates a higher image resolution than the Standard settings. These PDF files can be opened in Acrobat 5.0 and Adobe Reader 5.0 and later.

Smallest File Size Creates PDF files for displaying on the web, on an intranet, for distribution through an email system for on-screen viewing, or for display on smaller more portable devices (such as handhelds). This set of options uses compression, downsampling, and a relatively low image resolution. It converts all colors to sRGB, and does not embed fonts unless absolutely necessary. These PDF files can be opened in Acrobat 5.0 and Adobe Reader 5.0 and later.

—From Illustrator Help

Review questions

1 How do the RGB and CMYK color gamuts affect the relationship between on-screen colors and printed colors?

2 How can you create a closer match between your on-screen colors and printed colors?

3 What is the benefit of printing interim drafts of your artwork on a black-and-white desktop printer?

4 What does the term color separation mean?

5 What are two ways to output spot colors?

6 What are the advantages of one-color or two-color printing?

7 What is trapping?

8 What is a simple method to create a trap?

9 Describe what rasterization is.

10 Why would you save a file as a PDF document?

Review answers

1 Each color model has a gamut of color that overlaps, but does not precisely match, the others. Because monitors display color using the RGB color gamut, and printed artwork uses the smaller CMYK color gamut, there may be times when a printed color cannot precisely match an on-screen color.

2 You can select one of Illustrator's built-in color management profiles to better simulate the relationship between on-screen colors and printed colors. You can choose View > Proof Setup and select an output device profile. Then choose View > Proof Colors to get an on-screen version of how the artwork will look when printed to the selected device.

3 You may want to print black-and-white drafts of your artwork on a desktop printer to check the layout and the accuracy of text and graphics before incurring the expense of printing to a color printer or imagesetter to check separations.

4 Color separation breaks down composite artwork into its component colors—for example, using the four process colors (cyan, magenta, yellow, and black) to reproduce a large portion of the visible color spectrum.

5 You can convert a spot color to its process color equivalent if a precise color match is not required, or you can output a spot color to its own separation.

6 One-color and two-color printing are less expensive than four-color printing, and you can use spot colors for precise color matching.

7 Trapping is a technique developed by commercial print shops to slightly overprint the colors along common edges. Trapping is used to compensate for any gaps or color shifts that may occur between adjoining or overlapping objects when printed.

8 You can specify objects to overprint, or print on top of, any artwork under them. Overprinting is the simplest way to create a trap, which compensates for misregistration on press.

9 Rasterization is the process of changing vector graphics, vector fonts, gradients, and gradient meshes into bitmap images for display and printing, essentially turning vector artwork into pixels. Bitmap images that have higher ppi (pixels per inch) typically result in higher quality output. The amount of ppi or dpi is referred to as the resolution of the artwork.

10 Adobe PDF is effective in print publishing workflows, and is an efficient way to convey ideas to someone who doesn't have Adobe Illustrator.

INDEX

SYMBOLS

^ (caret) symbol
  direction point indicator, 141, 142
  indicating direction line for curve, 145
] (left bracket key), 289
– (minus sign)
  Zoom tool's, 44
+ (plus sign)
  indicating style override, 221
  red, 210, 218
  when dragging content between tiled
    Windows documents, 48
  Zoom tool's, 44
[(right bracket key), 289

A

activating
  artboards, 115
  smart guides, 86
Add Anchor Point tool, 155
Add Arrowheads dialog box, 146
Add New Effect option (Appearance panel),
  345
Adjust Colors dialog box, 402
Adobe applications. *See* combining Adobe
    graphics; *and specific application*
Adobe Bridge
  synchronizing color with, 426, 428
  working in, 392–394
Adobe Certified program, 5
Adobe Flash
  exporting Illustrator content for, 413–415
  moving symbols into, 384–387
  using symbols with SWF files, 369, 371
Adobe Flex, 415–416
Adobe Illustrator CS4. *See also* quick tour
  additional resources for, 4–5
  configuring color management in, 427
  copying and pasting from Photoshop,
    400–401, 411
  creating Flex files from, 415–416
  default preferences for, 3–4

editing Photoshop images, 400–402
exporting content as SWF files, 413–415
installing, 2
layered files exported to Photoshop,
  410–411
masks in, 406
new features of, 6–9
output mode options in, 434
pasting image in Flash from, 387
placing files in InDesign, 411–413
placing Photoshop artwork in, 17, 397–398
Adobe Illustrator CS4 Community Help, 4
Adobe Illustrator CS4 Support Center, 4
Adobe InDesign
  linking content from Illustrator to, 417
  placing Illustrator files in, 411–413
Adobe Photoshop, 397–411
  copying and pasting from Illustrator, 411
  editing images in Illustrator, 400–402
  importing Illustrator layered files to,
    410–411
  layer comps, 398–399
  mapping image from, 341–342
  placing images in Illustrator, 17, 397–398
  replacing placed images from, 409–410,
    417
  sampling color in images from, 408–409
  working with masked images from,
    402–408
Adobe TV, 5
AI files
  exporting as SWF frames, 413–415
  using in InDesign, 413
Align panel. *See also* aligning
  Distribute Spacing options on, 74
  options of, 76
aligning
  blends to page or path, 275
  content to artboard, 75, 76
  exploring, 76
  images with key objects, 73–74, 76
  lesson files for, 62
  objects, 73
  points, 74

reviewing, 77
smart guides and, 14–16
strokes, 92
text from Paragraph panel, 220
using Align panel options, 76
anchor points. *See also* direction
    handles
    aligning, 74
    appearance and types of, 138
    changing appearance of, 64
    converting curved to corner,
        140–143
    converting smooth to corner,
        150–151
    deleting and adding, 155–156
    direction handles for multiple
        selected, 154
    dragging to adjust curves, 153,
        154
    measurement label for, 64
    selecting/deselecting, 135
    smooth paths and distance
        between, 157
    undoing, 139
    warnings when converting, 141
appearance attributes. *See also*
        Appearance panel
    about, 247
    adding effect to object's, 322
    clearing all, 355–356
    defined, 349
    editing and adding, 349–351
    exploring, 364–365
    layers using, 361–362
    lesson files for, 348
    reordering, 351
    reviewing, 366
    saving as graphic style, 21–22, 354
    stroke and fill, 352
    using, 349
    viewing all hidden, 353
Appearance panel
    adding drop shadow effect in, 331
    adjusting stroke color in, 330
    applying appearance attributes
        from, 349
    editing from, 9, 327
    features of, 20–21, 349, 366
    Fill and Stroke attributes of, 168
    illustrated, 349
    opening and closing other panels
        from, 352
    removing effect in, 324
    viewing hidden attributes, 353

Application bar, 31
area type
    creating, 206
    creating area type object for
        imported text, 207, 208
    defined, 205
    options for, 209
    point vs., 207
Area Type Options dialog box, 208,
    209
Area Type tool, 210
Arrange Documents button, 49–50
Arrange Documents window, 6, 47
arrows
    adding arrowheads to, 146
    drawing straight line for, 144–145
    using in apple illustration, 161
Art brushes
    about, 292–293, 318
    colorizing, 300
Artboard Options dialog box, 397
artboards
    activating, 115
    adding and removing document,
        111
    aligning content to, 75, 76
    creating document with multiple,
        80–82
    deleting, 112, 113
    duplicating, 112
    editing, 112–114, 396–397
    elements of, 30
    keyboard shortcuts for View
        commands, 43
    navigating multiple, 14–16, 45–46
    navigation buttons for, 69
    number you can use, 30
    preset sizes for, 114
    printing multiple, 431
    tiling multiple, 82
    using multiple, 7, 12–14
artwork. *See also* images; mapping
    adding reflection with gradient,
        273–274
    applying as symbol on 3D object,
        336–337
    assigning colors to, 184–188
    bleeds, 30, 82, 113
    combining images from other
        software, 395
    erasing, 96–97
    halftone screens for, 422
    importing text into, 207–208
    mapping symbol to 3D, 384
    matching color of existing, 170

merging layers of, 248–249
moving symbols into Flash,
    384–387
placing Photoshop art in
    Illustrator, 397–398
printing transparent, 445
saving and exporting, 443–447
screen frequency and, 422,
    436–437
selected-art indicator, 240, 256
storing and retrieving in Symbols
    panel, 383
viewing, 42–43
aspect ratios for gradient, 267
Assign tab (Recolor Artwork dialog
    box), 184–187
attributes. *See also* appearance
        attributes
    applying to layers, 250–252
    changing for text in Character
        panel, 217–219
    copying color, 175
    fill and stroke, 168
    formatting paragraph, 219–220
    preserving when pasting in Flash,
        387
    sampling type, 223–224
Attributes panel, 442
axes
    reflecting objects across, 118–119
    shearing objects along, 123
    used with 3D effects, 333, 345

B

Backspace key, 156
banners
    creating type for, 329
    stylizing drop shadow for,
        330–333
Bezier curves, 137–143
bitmap graphics
    rasterizing vector graphics, 449
    vector vs., 104, 395–396
bleeds
    area for artboard, 30, 113
    defined, 82
    specifying for color separations,
        432–433
Blend Options dialog box
    illustrated, 276
    reshaping spine, 277–279
    smoothing color, 275, 279–280
Blend Steps, 341
Blend tool, 275, 276, 277

blending shapes and colors. *See also* blends; gradient fills
    adding and adjusting gradient color, 261, 266–267, 268, 269
    applying linear gradients, 261–263
    direction and angle of gradient blend, 264–265
    expanding blend, 278–279
    exploring gradients and blends, 281
    reviewing, 282–283
    specifying steps for blended objects, 275, 276, 277
    starting lesson for, 260
    transparency added to gradients, 273–274
    working with Blend too, 275
blends
    creating with specified steps, 276
    expanding, 278–279
    exploring further, 281
    gradient fill vs., 282
    modifying, 277–279
    releasing from object, 279
    reviewing, 282–283
    smoothing color for, 275, 279–280
    working with, 275
Blob Brush tool
    about, 8
    drawing with, 287–288
    editing with, 288–289
    exploring, 316
    merging paths with, 290–291
    options for, 291
    quick tour of, 16
    using Eraser with, 289
Bold character styles, 222–223
bounding boxes
    aligning objects relative to, 76
    effect of object transformation on, 122
    hiding, 144
    scaling objects with, 130
    using, 62–63
bracket keys ([ ]), 289
brackets for type on path, 229–230
Bridge. *See* Adobe Bridge
Brush Options dialog box
    colorizing with, 300, 319
    Hue Shift colorization method for, 300, 301–302
    Key Color box, 301–302
    modifying options, 297–298

Tints colorization method for, 300, 302–303
brushes. *See also* Blob Brush tool; Paintbrush tool; Pattern brushes; Scatter brushes
    applying, 292, 293–295, 316, 318
    Art, 292–293, 300, 318
    Blob Brush, 287–291
    Calligraphic, 300, 305–306, 318
    changing color attributes of, 300–303
    creating swatches for Pattern, 310–311
    customizing, 316–317
    editing paths with Paintbrush tool, 295–297, 319
    exploring, 316–317
    found on Brushes panel, 292
    making from swatches, 311–312
    modifying options for, 297–298
    Pattern, 307–309, 311–314, 318
    reviewing, 318–319
    saving to brush library, 312
    Scatter, 297–299, 318
    starting lesson on, 286
    using color fill with, 304–305
    using Scribble effect with, 314–315
    visible on Brushes panel, 293
Brushes panel. *See also* brushes
    Art brushes, 292–293, 300, 318
    Calligraphic brushes, 305–306
    features of, 292
    Scatter brushes, 297–299
    showing brushes on, 293
    viewing new brushes in current document's, 312
business cards
    Free Distort effects on artwork, 127–128
    making multiple copies for print, 128–129
    printing, 129, 421
    resizing artboard for, 113
    scaling objects on, 116–118
    working with, 110
buttons
    Arrange Documents, 49–50
    Cap on/Cap off, 334
    Close Gaps With Paths, 194
    Document Setup, 82
    found in Edit Colors dialog box, 181
    importing to library, 386
    Make Envelope, 224, 225
    navigating artboards with, 69

C

Calligraphic Brush Options dialog box, 306
Calligraphic brushes
    about, 305–306, 318
    changing color of, 300
Cap on/Cap off buttons (3D Extrude & Bevel Options dialog box), 334
caret (^) symbol
    direction point indicator, 141, 142
    indicating direction line for curve, 145
CD-ROM, copying lesson files from, 2
Character panel
    changing text attributes in, 217–219
    opening, 215, 218
Character Styles Options dialog box, 223
characters. *See also* Character panel
    adding styles for, 221, 222–223, 233
    special, 218–219
    superscript, 219
choke, 440
Clear key, 156
clipping masks
    about, 25
    applying, 403–404
    showing map on wall clock with, 247–248
cloning selected objects, 71
Close Gaps With Paths button (Gap Options dialog box), 194
closing
    panels, 39, 352
    paths, 152–153, 194
CMYK color mode. *See also* spot colors
    about, 167, 424
    converting PANTONE color to, 188
    libraries in, 172
    process color, 172
color. *See also* color management; color modes; gradient fills; swatches
    adjusting placed image, 401–402
    applying fill color to brushes, 304–305
    assigned to layers, 239, 256
    assigning to artwork, 184–188
    brush colorization methods, 300–303, 319

building and saving custom, 170–171

changing gradient, 266–269

color groups, 176–181

Color Guide panel, 169, 177–178

controls for applying, 168–169

converting to CYMK, 188

copying attributes of, 175

editing swatch of, 171

exploring use of, 198

global, 171, 173

graphic styles and text, 354, 359

harmonizing, 177–178, 180, 182

Kuler panel themed colors, 182–184

lesson files for, 166

matching artwork, 170

painting with Live Paint, 194–197

producing consistent, 426

recoloring artwork, 181–182

review questions and answers for, 199–200

revolved object's, 339

selecting from Color Picker, 170, 174–175

separating, 434–436

smart guide, 87

soft-proofing, 426, 428–429

spot vs. process, 172

synchronizing with Bridge, 426, 428

tints, 175

trapping, 439–440, 449

color groups

editing, 178–181

hiding, 185

working with, 19

Color Guide panel, 169, 177–178

color management. *See also* color separations

about, 424–425, 448

color separations, 429–442

configuring Illustrator, 427

producing consistent color, 426

soft-proofing colors, 428–429

synchronizing color with Bridge, 426, 428

using profiles, 448

color matching, 424–425

color model. *See* color modes

color modes. *See also* spot colors

about, 167, 448

converting PANTONE color to CMYK, 188

libraries in CMYK, 172

printing and, 423–424

process color, 172, 424

using effects to change, 417

Color panel, 168, 170–171

Color Picker

using, 170, 174–175

viewing color swatches from, 186, 332

color separations, 429–442

about, 448

overprinting objects, 440–442, 449

previewing, 429–430

printing, 430–432

saving presets for, 437

screen frequency for, 436–437

separating colors, 434–436

specifying bleed area, 432–433

spot colors, 437–438

Color Settings dialog box, 427

Color Spectrum bar (Color panel), 168–169

color stops

about, 261

adding, 268

adjusting, 266–267, 282

reordering, 269

repositioning white dot between, 268

columns of text, 208–209

combining Adobe graphics. *See also* Adobe Photoshop; *and specific Adobe applications*

color management in Adobe applications, 426

creating Illustrator files for Flex, 415–416

editing artboard, 396–397

exploring, 416

integrating Illustrator and Flash, 413–415

lesson files, 392

overview, 395

placing Illustrator files in InDesign, 411–413

reviewing, 417

using Photoshop images, 397–411

vector vs. bitmap graphics, 104, 395–396

working with Bridge, 392–394, 426, 428

commands

Fit All In Window, 46

Paste In Front, 245

Pathfinder, 98

typographic conventions for, 1

Undo, 140

View, 43

composites, 434

compound paths, 100, 404–405

constraining

objects with Shift-drag, 116

Pen tool paths, 136

shape proportions, 88

context sensitivity

Control panel and, 35

displaying context-sensitive menus, 41

Control panel

Align options in, 73

Document Setup button, 82

formatting type in, 214–220

illustrated, 31

Swatches panel available in, 170

Transform options on, 117, 125

using, 35–36

Convert Anchor Point tool, 150

copying

Classroom in a Book files, 2

color attributes, 175

color in placed Photoshop images, 408–409

graphic styles between layers, 363

objects while reflecting, 118–119

and pasting between Photoshop and Illustrator, 411

text formatting lost when, 207

corner points. *See also* anchor points

converting curved to, 140–143

dragging to create, 149

illustrated, 138

turning smooth into, 150–151

crosshair icon, 134

curves. *See also* direction handles

controlling with direction handles, 139–140

creating for leaf shape, 147–148

drawing different kinds of, 148–149

editing object's, 153–154

selecting, 147

customizing

brushes, 316–317

color swatches, 170–171

document views, 42

grids, 83

Magic Wand tool, 66

patterns, 191

cylinders using 3D effects, 333–335

D

default settings
  returning leading to, 218
  returning workspace to, 41–42
Delete key, 156
deleting
  all appearance attributes, 355–356
  anchor points, 155–156
  artboards, 112, 113
  color in gradient, 271
  Illustrator preferences, 3–4
  presets, 446
  saved workspaces, 42
deselecting smart guides, 63, 136, 147
Direct Selection tool. *See also* selections
  changing shape of curves with, 147
  exercises using, 70
  resizing type objects with, 213
  using, 63–64
  working with Live Paint selections, 197
direction handles
  about, 137
  appearance of, 138
  changing curve's shape, 147
  controlling curves with, 139–140
  dragging to adjust curves, 153
  showing for multiple selected anchor points, 154
direction of gradient blend, 264–265
distorting objects, 120–122
Distribute Spacing options (Align panel), 74
distributing objects, 74–75
docking
  adding/removing panel groups from dock, 39–40
  conserving space by, 41
  Control panel, 36
  Tools panel, 34
document groups, 50–51
Document Info panel, 443–444
document profiles. *See* profiles
Document Setup button (Control panel), 82
Document Setup dialog box, Top Bleed option in, 114
document tabs, about, 47
Document window
  arranging documents in, 47–50
  dragging content between, 48–49
  illustrated, 31

documents
  adding and removing artboards in, 111
  adjusting bleed in, 113
  arranging, 47–50
  creating with multiple artboards, 80–82
  loading swatches from other, 170
  number of artboards for, 30
  reverting to last version of, 63
  scrolling with Hand tool, 45
  scrolling with Navigator panel, 51–52, 57
  tiling, 48
  viewing options for, 42–43
  working with document groups, 50–51
dots per inch (dpi), 423, 449
dpi (dots per inch), 423, 449
dragging
  anchor point adjustments by, 153, 154
  appearance attributes between layers, 362–363
  content between Document windows, 48–49
  creating corner points by, 149
drawing. *See also* apple illustration; Pen tool; Pencil tool
  assembling parts of apple, 160–161
  curves of apple, 147–149
  ellipses, 88
  lines, 93–94
  polygons, 89, 90, 107
  practicing with Pen tool, 134–136
  rectangles, 85
  rounded rectangles, 86–87
  with smart guides displayed, 85
  spirals, 90
  stars, 90, 96, 100–103
  straight lines with Pen, 136–137
  using Blob Brush for, 287–288
  using template layers, 144
  veins for leaf with Pencil, 156–157
Drop Shadow dialog box, 252, 326, 332
Drop Shadow effect
  adding from Appearance panel, 331
  applying, 326
  editing, 327–328
  merging paths if applied, 290
drop shadows. *See also* Drop Shadow effect
  adding to layer, 250–252, 356, 357

  drawing with Blob Brush tool, 287–288
  stylizing for banner, 330–333
duplicating
  artboards, 112
  Photoshop images, 400–401
duplicating objects, 87–88

E

Edit Color/Recolor Artwork dialog box, using, 19, 187
Edit Colors dialog box
  illustrated, 179
  options and buttons on, 181
  similarity to Recolor Artwork dialog box, 179
  using, 178–180
editing
  appearance attributes, 349–351
  artboard, 396–397
  artboards, 112–114
  artwork color with Recolor Artwork dialog box, 181–182
  brush paths with Paintbrush tool, 295–297
  color groups, 178–181
  curves of apple, 153–154
  and duplicating Photoshop images, 400–401
  effects, 327–328
  Eraser tool for, 289
  imported masks, 407–408
  lines and shapes with Pencil tool, 158
  Live Paint regions, 196–197
  patterns, 192–193
  placed image color, 401–402
  shapes independently from Effect menu, 324
  swatches, 171
  symbols, 377–378
  unlinked harmonizing colors, 180
  using Blob Brush, 288–289
  warped text, 225
Effect Gallery, 325
effects
  applying, 323–327, 345
  creating banner logo with Warp, 329–333
  cylinders using 3D, 333–335
  Drop Shadow, 326
  editing, 327–328
  exploring, 343–344

Pathfinder, 98, 99–100
removing, 324, 327, 328
reviewing, 345
Rotate, 333, 345
rotating objects with 3D, 343
Scribble, 314–315, 319
starting lesson for, 322
Subtract, 324
3D Extrude & Bevel, 333, 334–335, 345
3D Revolve, 333, 338–341, 345
uses for, 321
using live, 321, 322
ellipses, drawing, 88
enabling/disabling, opacity masks, 406
envelope warp, using with text, 224–226
envelopes
precisely positioning logo on, 124–125
working with, 110
EPS files, 444–445
Eraser tool
editing with, 289
using, 96–97
expanding, panels, 37, 39
expanding blend, 278–279
exploring
appearance attributes and graphic styles, 364–365
brushes, 316–317
color use and tools, 198
combining Adobe graphics, 416
effects, 343–344
features of navigation and organization, 56
gradients and blends, 281
layers, 254
selections and aligning, 76
shapes, 106
symbols, 388
transforming objects, 129
type features, 232
ways to recreate graphic with Pen tool, 162
exporting
artwork, 443–447
Illustrator content as SWF files, 413–415
layered file to Photoshop, 410–411
Extrude & Bevel effects, 333, 334–335, 345
eye icon, 236, 242, 255

Eyedropper tool
applying sampled type attributes to text, 223–224
copying color attributes with, 170, 175
sampling color in placed images, 408–409
sampling gradient color with, 271
using Key Color, 301–302

F

Fidelity settings
Blob Brush too, 291
Pencil tool, 157, 159
fields, typing values in, 80
files. *See also* lesson files
AI, 413–415
copying *Classroom in a Book*, 2
embedding Photoshop artwork in Illustrator, 397–398
EPS format for, 444–445
exporting layered, 410–411
formats for imported text, 207
formats for saving, 443
importing plain text, 207–208
linked, 417
native Illustrator format, 413
pasting layers files into other, 244–246, 256
PDF, 446–447, 449
placing Illustrator files in InDesign, 411–413
PPD, 431
saving, 29
saving in FXG format, 415–416
saving with transparency, 444
SWF, 369, 371, 413–415
fill. *See also* gradient fills
adding to apple illustration, 161
applying fill color to brushes, 304–305
defined, 84
selecting for pencil strokes, 159
Fill attributes (Appearance panel), 168
Fill box (Tool panel), illustrated, 168
filters, using Pucker & Bloat distort, 122
Finder, 45
Fit All In Window command, effect of, 46
Flash. *See* Adobe Flash
flattening layers, 249, 253
Flex, 415–416
flipping type on path, 230

floating Tools panel, 33, 34
Font Size menu, 216
fonts
adjusting size of, 216
changing style, 214–215
installed on Illustrator CS4 DVD, 2, 215
OpenType, 216, 233
formatting
keeping in imported Word text, 210
lost when copying/pasting text, 207
overriding styles, 221
paragraph attributes, 219–220
type, 214–220
Free Distort effect, using, 127–128
Free Transform tool, 125–126, 131
FXG files, 415–416

G

Gap Options dialog box, 194
getting started, 1–5. *See also* lesson files
installing Illustrator software, 2
other resources for Illustrator CS4, 4–5
prerequisites for, 1
restoring Illustrator completing lesson, 4
global color, 171, 173
Glyphs panel, 218–219
Gradient box (Tools panel), 261
gradient fills. *See also* color stops
applying linear, 261–263
blends vs., 282
changing color and adjusting, 266–269
creating and editing, 22–24
defined, 261, 282
direction and angle of, 264–265
exploring further, 281
filling text outlines with, 232, 269–272
making layer containing visible, 189
radial, 193, 265–266
repositioning origin of, 268
reviewing, 282–283
sampling color of, 271
transparency for, 8, 273–274
using for multiple objects, 269–272
working with, 261

Gradient panel
  illustrated, 261
  rotating angle of gradient, 265
Gradient tool
  about, 264
  adjusting gradient with, 266–269
  enhancements to, 8
graphic styles
  about, 247
  applying, 355, 358–360, 366
  character color with, 354, 359
  copying, applying, or removing,
    362–364
  defined, 353
  exploring, 364–365
  layers with, 355–357, 366
  lesson files for, 348
  reviewing, 366
  saving appearance attributes as,
    21–22, 354
  using multiple, 360–361
Graphic Styles panel, 9. *See also*
    graphic styles
  about, 353–354
  applying appearance attributes
    from, 349
graphics. *See* artwork; bitmap
    graphics; vector graphics
grids
  showing and customizing, 83
  snapping to, 84–85
Group Selection tool, 67
groups
  adding/removing panel groups
    from dock, 39–40
  applying appearance attributes
    to, 250
  color, 176–181
  consolidating, 249
  converting blend to individual
    objects from, 278–279
  document, 50–51
  editing content within, 130
  isolating for selection, 68
  making object, 66–67
guides. *See also* smart guides
  aligning objects with, 14–16
  using, 115

H

halftone screens, 422
Hand tool
  repositioning artwork with, 139
  scrolling document with, 45
  using, 43

harmonizing colors
  linking, 182
  unlinking, 180
  using, 177–178
height values, 86
Help, 54
highlighting anchor points, 64
host-based separations, 434
Hue Shift colorization method, 300,
    301–302

I

ICC profiles, 425
icons
  collapsing panel to, 37
  effect of Caps Lock on tool, 134
  eye, 236, 242, 255
  global color, 171
  loaded text, 211
  spot color, 173
  target, 250, 251, 256, 358, 366
  triangle, 171, 173, 238
Illuminate Styles library panel, 359
Illustrator. *See* Adobe Illustrator CS4
Illustrator CS4 DVD, 2, 215
Illustrator Help, 54
images. *See also* placed images
  masking Photoshop, 402–408
  placing in Illustrator from
    Photoshop, 17
  raster vs. vector, 104, 395–396
  symbols can't be made from
    unembedded, 373, 389
  working with in Bridge, 392–394,
    426, 428
Import To Library dialog box, 386
importing
  buttons to library, 386
  Illustrator artwork into Flash, 387
  Illustrator layered files to
    Photoshop, 410–411
  text into artwork, 207–208
InDesign, 411–413, 417
in-RIP separations, 434
installing Adobe Illustrator software, 2
interactive demonstration. *See* quick
    tour
Internet access for Kuler themes, 183
invitation printing, 421
isolation mode
  editing content in groups with,
    125, 130
  entering, 100, 225
  using, 68, 69
  working with layers in, 252–253

J

Join dialog box, 95
joining paths, 94–96

K

kerning, 219
Key Color box (Brush Options dialog
    box), 301–302
key objects
  aligning to, 73–74, 76
  defined, 73
keyboard
  Caps Lock and tool icons, 134
  deleting points with Delete,
    Backspace, and Clear keys,
    156
keyboard shortcuts
  adjusting font size with, 216
  Hand tool, 45
  Mac Zoom shortcuts open
    Spotlight or Finder, 45
  opening tools with, 33
  View command, 43
Kuler panel
  about, 182
  using, 182–184
  viewing theme online, 184

L

layer comps, 398–399
Layer Options dialog box, 238
layers. *See also* template layers
  about, 237
  advantages of, 235
  appearance attributes for,
    361–362
  applying appearance attributes to,
    250–252
  clipping masks with, 247–248
  color assigned to, 239, 256
  converting Photoshop layers to
    objects, 399
  creating, 237–239
  exploring, 254
  eye icon and visibility of, 189,
    236, 242
  flattening, 249, 253
  graphic styles applied to, 355–
    357, 366
  hiding, 240, 255
  isolating, 252–253
  lesson files for, 236–237
  locking, 241–242, 255

merging, 248–249

moving objects with selected-art indicator to other, 240, 256

pasting, 244–246, 256

reordering objects by moving, 239–241

reviewing, 255–256

selecting, 240

target icon on, 250, 251, 256

triangle on, 238

using Photoshop layer comps, 398–399

viewing, 242–244, 255

Layers panel

color assigned to layers in, 239

displaying, 238

expanding and collapsing layer view on, 247, 248

graphic styles applied from, 358

illustrated, 236

target icons of, 358

leading, 218

learning resources for Illustrator, 4–5

left bracket key ([ ), 289

lesson files

appearance attributes and graphic styles, 348

blending shapes and colors, 260

brushes, 286

color and painting, 166

combining Adobe graphics, 392

effects, 322

fonts for, 2

installing, 2

layers, 236–237

output, 420

Pen and Pencil tool, 134, 143–144

resources for selecting and aligning, 62

restoring preferences after completing, 4

shapes, 80

symbols, 370

transforming objects, 110

type, 204

workspace, 28–29

libraries

adding symbols from, 371–373

applying graphic styles from, 358–360

Illuminate Styles library panel, 359

importing buttons to, 386

PANTONE and TOYO, 172

saving brushes to, 312

saving symbols as, 383

selecting Pattern brush from, 307

swatch, 170, 172

web symbol, 384

Library panel, 387

lighting 3D objects, 340–341, 342–343

linear gradients, 261–263

lines

drawing, 93–94, 136–137, 144–145

editing, 158

joining paths for, 94–96

making curved paths, 137–143

paths and, 138

splitting path for, 145–146

lines per inch (lpi), 422, 423

Link option (Place dialog box), 17

linked files, 417

links

breaking with symbol instances, 380–382

to harmonized colors, 180, 182

live effects, 321, 322

Live Paint, 18–19, 194–197

Live Trace, 17–18, 103–106, 107

loaded text icon, 211

locking

guides, 115

layers, 241–242, 255

selected objects, 73

logo label

applying effects to, 323–327

creating banner logo with Warp effects, 329–333

designing 3D cylinders, 333–335

stylizing drop shadow for type, 330–333

lpi (lines per inch), 422, 423

M

Mac computers

convention for commands on, 1

free-floating Tools panel for, 33

menu items above application bar in, 31, 49

Zoom tool shortcuts open Spotlight or Finder, 45

magazine/catalog printing, 421

Magic Wand tool selections, 66

Make Envelope button, 224, 225

Map Art dialog box, 336, 342

mapping

applying symbols as mapped artwork, 336–337, 345

artwork to 3D objects, 338

Photoshop image, 341–342

symbol to 3D artwork, 384

marquee selections, 65

masks

about, 402, 417

clipping, 25, 247–248, 403–404

editing imported, 407–408

opacity, 405–407, 417

pattern, 190

measurement labels

anchor point, 64

negative values for, 124

viewing when zooming, 111

menus

displaying context-sensitive, 41

Effect, 324

Font Size, 216

Presets, 114

using panel, 40–41

merging

layers, 248–249

panel groups, 40

paths with Blob Brush tool, 290–291

Microsoft Word

keeping text formatting in imported text, 210

placing document in shape, 209–210

minus sign (−)

Zoom tool's, 44

Missing Profile dialog box, 28, 441

monitor profiles, 426

multiple artboards

creating document with, 80–82

number you can use, 30

tiling, 82

using, 7, 12–14

multiple transformations of objects, 128–129

N

names

giving selections, 72

viewing Swatches by, 192

native Illustrator file format, 413

navigating

artboards with buttons, 69

exploring on your own, 56

multiple artboards, 14–16, 45–46

scrolling documents, 45, 51–52

Navigator panel, 51–52, 57

nesting objects, 66–67

New Brush dialog box, 311

New Color Group dialog box, 176

New Document dialog box
illustrated, 12
selecting color modes from, 167
setting up profiles for, 81
new features, 6–9
Appearance panel editing, 9
Blob Brush tool, 8
enhancements to Gradient tool, 8
Graphic Styles panel, 9
multiple artboards, 7
smart guides, 7
transparency in gradients, 8
workspace improvements, 6
New Paragraph Style dialog box, 221
New Swatch dialog box, 170
newsletter printing, 421
newspaper printing, 421
9-slice scaling, 385
nonprintable area of artboard, 30

O

objects. *See also* symbols; 3D objects;
transforming objects
adding stroke and fill, 352, 366
aligning, 14–16, 73–74, 75
appearance attributes applied to,
250, 362–363
applying artwork as symbol to
3D, 336
changing perspective of, 125–126
cloning selected, 71
combining to create shapes,
99–103
consolidating, 249
constraining, 116
converting Photoshop layers to,
399
distorting, 120–122
distributing, 74–75
duplicating, 87–88
editing curves of apple, 153–154
editing Illustrator objects in
InDesign, 413
filmstrip view of, 393
gradients for multiple, 269–272
graphic styles applied to, 355,
360–361
grouping and nesting, 66–67
importing text to area type, 207,
208
lighting 3D, 340–341, 342–343
locking selected, 73
overprinting, 440–442, 449
pasting from different layers, 256
precisely positioning, 124–125

reference point for scaled, 117,
130, 131
reflecting, 118–119
releasing blend from, 279
reordering by moving layers,
239–241
resizing type, 212–213
revolved, 333, 338–341
rotating, 119–120, 343
scaling, 116–118
selecting, 63, 65, 68
sending to back, 85
shearing, 123
smart guides for aligning, 14–16
threading text between, 211
3D, 333, 334–335, 345
transforming, 128–129
unable to merge, 248
ungrouping, 67
wrapping text around, 227
Offset Path dialog box, 331, 352
offsetting
previewing stroke, 352–353
stroke around text, 330–331
opacity
adjusting text, 228, 231
editing mask, 406
modifying stroke's, 350
opacity masks
creating, 417
enabling/disabling, 406
using, 405–407
opening
Character panel, 218
items from Welcome Screen,
28–29
panels from Appearance panel,
352
OpenType fonts, 216, 233
outline mode
about, 87
viewing text in, 117
Outline view
about, 42, 43
adjusting type paths in, 213
outlining
color gradient fill for outlined
text, 269–272
strokes, 91–93
text, 230–232, 233
output. *See also* color management;
color separations; printing
color matching for, 424–425
color models and, 423–424
color separations, 429–432

concepts and terms for printing,
422–423
Illustrator options for, 434
lesson files for, 420
overprinting objects, 440–442,
449
overview of printing process,
420–421
PDF files, 446–447, 449
printing multiple artboards, 431
producing consistent color, 426
reviewing, 448
saving and exporting artwork,
443–447
separating spot colors, 437–438
soft-proofing colors, 426,
428–429
specifying bleed area, 432–433
trapping, 439–440, 449
output device resolution, 423, 437
overflow text
adjusting, 210–211
resizing, 212–213
threading between objects, 211
tracking for, 218
Overprint preview, 42–43

P

Paintbrush tool
applying brushes with, 292,
293–295, 318
drawing with, 293–295
editing paths with, 295–297, 319
Paintbrush Tool Options dialog box,
294
painting. *See also* color; Paintbrush
tool
apple illustration, 161
lesson files for, 166
objects with fill color, 304–305
with Pattern brushes, 312–314
types of controls used for,
168–169
using Live Paint, 194–197
panel menus, 40–41
panels. *See also specific panels*
accessing from Appearance panel,
352
adding or removing groups from
dock, 39–40
closing, 39, 352
collapsing, 37
expanding, 37, 39
illustrated, 31
resizing and reorganizing, 38–39

selecting items from Tools, 33–34

showing/hiding, 37, 69

using menu on, 40–41

working with, 36–40

PANTONE colors

appearance of swatches for, 173

changing to CYMK mode, 188

converting to process color, 436

using library of, 172

paragraphs

adding styles to, 221, 233

attributes for formatting, 219–220

Paste In Front command, 245

Paste Profile Mismatch dialog box, 399, 400

Paste Remembers Layers option, 245, 256

pasting

images between Photoshop and Illustrator, 411

layers, 244–246, 256

preserving attributes when pasting in Flash, 387

text formatting lost when copying and, 207

path

adjusting curved, 150–151

aligning blends to, 275

reshaping spine of blend, 277–279

Pathfinder panel

types of commands for, 98

using effects on, 98, 99–100

working with shape modes on, 98, 100–103

paths. See also anchor points

adjusting type, 213

applying Scatter brush to, 299

closing with Pen tool, 152–153

components of, 138

compound, 100, 404–405

constraining Pen tool, 136

creating type on, 205, 227–230

distance between points and smoothness of, 157

drawing closed, 156, 157

editing brush, 295–297

editing Illustrator paths in InDesign, 413

flipping type on, 230

formatting text on, 228

gaps in Live Paint, 194

joining, 94–96

Live Paint's effect on modified, 196–197

making curved, 137–143

merging with Blob Brush tool, 290–291

selecting, 95, 135

splitting for straight line, 145–146

using Pencil tool for, 156–157, 159

Pattern Brush Options dialog box, 308, 312, 313

Pattern brushes

colorizing, 300

creating swatches for, 310–311

making new brush from swatches, 311–312

painting with, 312–314

using, 307–309, 318

patterns

applying, 192

creating custom, 191

editing, 192–193

using preset, 189–190

PDF files, 446–447, 449

Pen tool

advantages of, 133, 134

creating paths without fill, 144

curved paths with, 137–143

drawing different kinds of curves, 148–149

exploring features of, 162

lesson files for, 134, 143–144

making straight lines with, 136–137

practicing on blank artboard, 134–136

reviewing, 163

undoing points with, 139

Pencil tool

advantages of, 133, 156

editing with, 158

Fidelity settings for, 157, 159

lesson files for, 134, 143–144

modifying settings for, 159, 163

reviewing, 163

setting Smoothness for, 157, 159

Pencil Tool Options dialog box, 159

perspective, 125–126, 131

Photoshop. See Adobe Photoshop

Pixel preview, 42–43

Place dialog box, Link option in, 17

Place PDF dialog box, 411–412

placed images

applying color edits to, 401–402

editing and duplicating, 400–401

moving into Illustrator, 398–400

placing Illustrator files in InDesign, 411–413

replacing, 409–410, 417

sampling color in, 408–409

platforms. See also Mac computers

conventions used for commands, 1

plus sign (+)

indicating style with override, 221

red, 210

when dragging content between tiled Windows documents, 48

Zoom tool's, 44

point type

area vs., 207

creating, 205–206

defined, 205

points. See anchor points; corner points; direction handles

Polygon dialog box, 99

polygons, 89, 90, 107

ports for threading text, 207, 210

positioning objects precisely, 124–125

PostScript

EPS file format, 444–445

printers using, 429, 430

PPD (PostScript Printer Description) files, 431

preferences

changing point and selection options, 64

saving, deleting, and restoring Illustrator, 3–4

prerequisites for this book, 1

presets

artboard size, 114

deleting, 446

pattern, 189–190

PDF file, 447

saving color separation, 437

Presets menu, 114

Preview view, 42, 43

previewing

color separations, 429–430

color with soft proofs, 426, 428–429

lighting for 3D objects, 340

Print dialog box, 430, 431

printable area of artboard, 30

printer's marks, 432

printing. See also color separations

business cards, 129, 421

color models and, 423–424

color separations, 430–432

printing *(continued)*
   concepts and terms for, 422–423
   managing color during, 426
   multiple artboards, 431
   overprinting objects, 440–442, 449
   preparing multiple images for, 128–129
   preventing banding with blend steps, 341
   transparent artwork, 445
   trapping, 439–440, 449
   two-color, 421, 437–438, 449
   understanding, 420–421
process colors
   converting spot color to, 435, 449
   creating tint from, 175
profiles
   about, 12
   configuring document, 81
   ICC, 425
   missing, 28, 441
   monitor, 426
   using, 448
Proof Setup dialog box, 429
proxy view area, about, 52
Pucker & Bloat dialog box, 122

Q

quick tour, 10–25
   aligning objects with smart guides, 14–16
   Appearance panel, 20–21
   applying warp to text, 22
   Blob Brush tool, 16
   clipping masks, 25
   creating and editing gradients, 22–24
   Live Paint, 18–19
   Live Trace feature, 17–18
   placing Photoshop images in Illustrator, 17
   saving appearance as graphic style, 21–22
   symbols, 24–25
   using multiple artboards, 12–14
   using type, 20
   working with color groups, 19

R

radial gradients
   adjusting, 193
   creating, 265–266

radius of gradient, 268
raster effects, 322, 325
raster graphics, 104, 395–396
rasterizing
   3D objects, 335
   vector graphics, 449
Recolor Art option
   Edit Colors dialog box, 179
   Recolor Artwork dialog box, 185
Recolor Artwork dialog box
   assigning colors with, 184–187
   editing color in, 181–182
   Recolor Art option, 185
   similarity to Edit Colors dialog box, 179
   using, 19
Rectangle dialog box
   adjusting width in, 99
   entering values in inches, 13
   using, 107
Rectangle tool, 107
rectangles
   adjusting width of, 99
   drawing, 85
   entering values in inches, 13
red plus sign (+), 210, 218
reference point for scaled objects, 117, 130, 131
reflecting objects, 118–119
removing
   document artboards, 111
   effects, 324, 327, 328
   graphic styles, 364
   groups from panels, 39–40
reordering appearance attributes, 351
reorganizing panels, 38–39
replacement images, 409–410, 417
replacing symbols, 382
resizing
   artboards, 112–113
   panel group, 38
   type objects, 212–213
resolution
   bitmap image, 449
   output device, 423, 437
restoring default preferences, 4
reverting to last version of document, 63
reviewing
   appearance attributes and graphic styles, 366
   brushes, 318–319
   color and painting, 199–200
   combining Adobe graphics, 417
   effects, 345

gradients and blended objects, 282–283
   output, 448
   Pen and Pencil tools, 163
   selections and aligning, 77
   shapes, 107
   symbols, 389
   transforming objects, 130–131
   type, 233
   workspaces, 57–58
revolved objects, 333, 338–341, 345
RGB color mode, 167, 424
right bracket key ( ]), 289
Rotate dialog box, 89, 119, 126
Rotate effects, 333, 345
rotating
   angle of gradient, 265
   leaf illustration, 160–161
   objects with 3D effects, 343
   Scatter Brush objects, 298
   2D objects, 119–120
Roughen dialog box, 325
rounded rectangles, 86–87
Roundness settings (Blob Brush tool), 291
rows of text, 208–209
rulers
   changing units for, 83
   resetting origin point for, 115

S

sampling
   color in placed Photoshop images, 408–409
   gradient color, 271
   type attributes, 223–224
Save Proof dialog box, 437
Save Workspace dialog box, 41
saving
   appearance attributes as graphic style, 21–22, 354
   brushes to brush library, 312
   color management options when, 426
   colors in color groups, 176–177
   data in EPS format, 444–445
   file with transparency, 444
   files, 29
   gradient swatch, 263
   Illustrator files in FXG format, 415–416
   Illustrator preferences, 3
   PDF files, 446–447
   selections, 72
   symbols as libraries, 383

tints, 175
workspaces, 41–42
Scale dialog box, 126, 190, 229
scaling
leaf illustration, 160–161
9-slice, 385
objects, 116–118
objects with bounding box, 130
Pattern brush, 307–308
point type, 206
reference point for object, 117, 130, 131
Scatter Brush Options dialog box
Hue Shift colorization method for, 300, 301–302
modifying, 297–298
Tints colorization method for, 300, 302–303
Scatter brushes. *See also* Scatter Brush Options dialog box
about, 297, 318
applying to paths, 299
colorizing, 300
modifying options for, 297–298
Scissors tool, 145
screen frequency, 422, 436–437
Scribble effect, 314–315, 319
scrolling
documents with Hand tool, 45
with Navigator panel, 51–52, 57
selected-art indicator, 240, 256
Selection tool
exercises using, 70–71
using, 62–63
selections. *See also* Direct Selection tool; Selection tool
based on similar objects, 68
Blob Brush merges affected by artwork, 291
changing preferences for, 64
cloning, 71
creating with marquee, 65
exercises in making, 69–72
exploring, 76
hiding, 77
isolating groups for, 68
layer, 240
lesson files for, 62
Live Paint group, 197
locking selected objects, 73
Magic Wand tool for, 66
making from panel, 33–34
making path, 95
reassigning colors to artwork, 188
reviewing, 77

saving and naming, 72
selecting anchor points, 135
sending objects to back, 85
shape modes
Pathfinder, 98, 100–103
working with, 100–103
shapes
accessing tools for, 83
constraining proportion of, 88
creating text on, 227–230
drawing, 84–90, 288
editing, 158, 324
erasing, 96–97
experimenting with, 106
lesson files for, 80
outlining strokes of, 91–93
placing text in, 209–210
review questions and answers for, 107
tracing existing artwork, 103–106, 107
using Pathfinder effects and shape modes for, 98, 99–103
working with blends, 275
zooming while working with, 93
shearing objects, 123
showing/hiding
appearance attributes, 353
bounding boxes, 144
color groups, 185
layers, 240, 255
panels, 37, 69
template layers, 153
Transform options in Control panel, 117, 125
smart guides
about, 7
activating and using, 86
changing color of, 87
deselecting, 63, 136, 147
drawing with, 85
sampling text formatting with, 224
using, 14–16, 62
smooth points. *See also* anchor points
converting corner to, 150–151
illustrated, 138
smoothing blend color, 275, 279–280
Smoothness settings
Blob Brush tool, 291
Pencil tool, 157, 159
Snap To Grid, 84–85
soft-proofing
black-and-white artwork, 448
colors, 426, 428–429

spacing
between artboards, 81
Scatter Brush objects, 298
spirals, 90
spot colors
about, 424
converting to process, 435, 449
creating, 172–173
icon for, 173
making tint from, 175
process vs., 172
separating, 437–438
Spotlight, 45
spread, 440
Star dialog box, 323
stars
drawing, 90, 96, 100–103
transforming flower into, 120–121
Status Bar, 31
Stroke attributes (Appearance panel), 168
Stroke box (Tool panel), 168
Stroke Options (Art Brush) dialog box, 303
Stroke panel, 330–331
strokes
adding to object, 352, 366
aligning, 92
Blob Brush's effect on, 287
color of revolve object set by color of, 339
colorizing brush, 302, 319
cutting path by clicking closed shape's, 145
defined, 84
modifying opacity of, 350
outlining, 91–93
overprinting, 442
selecting item using, 63
styles. *See also* graphic styles
changing font, 214–215
characters, 221, 222–223, 233
overriding, 221
paragraph, 221, 233
saving graphic, 21–22
sublayers. *See also* layers
creating, 238
merging, 248
target icon on, 250
Subtract effect, 324
superscript characters, 219
suppressing Welcome Screen, 28
swatch libraries, 170, 172
Swatch Options dialog box, 171, 176, 191

swatches. *See also* Swatches panel
  creating for Pattern brush, 310–311
  editing, 171
  icon for spot color on, 173
  loading from other document, 170
  making new Pattern brush from, 311–312
  saving gradient, 263
  viewing by name in Swatches panel, 192
  viewing from Color Picker, 186
Swatches panel
  about, 169
  finding also in Control panel, 170
  gradient swatches in, 189, 263
  showing swatches by name in, 192
  using preset patterns in, 189–190
  viewing color group for Live Color selection, 195
SWF files
  exporting Illustrator content as, 413–415
  using symbols with, 369, 371
SWF Options dialog box, 414
symbol instances
  about, 371, 372, 375
  breaking link to, 380–382
  spraying, 375–376
Symbol Options dialog box, 24, 333, 374, 385
Symbol Sprayer tool, 375–378
Symbol Stainer tool, 378, 389
symbolism tools, 377–378
Symbolism Tools Options dialog box, 376
symbols. *See also* Symbols panel
  about, 359
  adding from Illustrator libraries, 371–373
  applying as mapped artwork, 336–337, 345
  breaking link to instance, 380–382
  creating, 373–374
  defined, 24
  editing with symbolism tools, 377–378
  exploring, 388
  inserting with Glyphs panel, 218–219
  lesson files for, 370
  mapping to 3D artwork, 384
  moving into Flash, 384–387
  quick tour of, 24–25

replacing, 382
resizing in preview area, 337
reviewing, 389
saving as libraries, 383
spraying instances of, 375–376
unembedded images unavailable for, 373, 389
updating, 380, 389
working with, 371
Symbols panel
  accessing web symbol libraries from, 384
  illustrated, 371
  storing and retrieving artwork in, 383
  working with, 369
synchronizing color in Bridge, 426, 428

T

target icon, 250, 251, 256, 358, 366
template layers
  characteristics of, 254
  hiding, 153
  tracing with apple illustration with, 139, 147, 149
  using, 144
text. *See also* characters; styles; type
  adding sampled type attributes to, 223–224
  adjusting type paths, 213
  applying Bold character style, 222–223
  changing attributes of, 217–219
  columns and rows of, 208–209
  converting to vector graphic, 232
  creating type on path, 205, 227–230
  editing font style, 214–215
  exploring other features of, 232
  filling with gradient color, 232, 269–272
  font size adjustments, 216
  graphic styles and color of, 354, 359
  importing into artwork, 207–208
  keeping formatting of imported Word, 210
  kerning, 219
  kinds of type, 205
  offsetting stroke around, 330–331
  outlines of, 230–232, 233
  overflow, 210–211
  perspective of, 125–126
  placing in shape, 209–210

point vs. area type, 207
reshaping with envelope warp, 224–226
resizing type objects, 212–213
returning leading to default, 218
setting paragraph attributes, 219–220
special characters in, 218–219
styling paragraphs and characters, 221–223
threading, 211
tracking overflow, 218
viewing in outline mode, 117
warping, 22
wrapping, 206, 227
Text Import Options dialog box, 208
Text Wrap Options dialog box, 227
threading
  ports for, 207, 210
  text between objects, 211
3D Extrude & Bevel effect, 333, 334–335, 345
3D objects, 333–335
  light sources for, 340–341, 342–343
  mapping artwork to, 338
  Revolve, 333, 338–341
  Rotate, 333, 345
  ways to create, 333
3D Revolve effects, 333, 338–341, 345
3D Rotate effects, 333, 345
tiles for Pattern brushes, 307
tiling
  documents, 48
  multiple artboards, 82
tints, 175
Tints colorization method, 300, 302–303
tool tips, 33
tools. *See also* Tools panel; *and specific tools*
  accessing for shapes, 83
  effect of Caps Lock on icons for, 134
  found on Tools panel, 32
  opening with keyboard shortcuts, 33
  symbolism, 377–378
  turning on/off tool tips, 33
  used for color, 198
Tools panel
  accessing shape tools, 83
  defined, 31
  Direct Selection tool, 63–64
  Fill and Stroke boxes on, 168
  Gradient box on, 261–262

illustrated, 31, 32
selecting items from, 33–34
Selection tool, 62–63
TOYO color library, 172
tracing
deselecting smart guide for, 147
existing artwork, 103–106, 107
using template layer for, 139, 147, 149
tracking overflow text, 218
Transform Each dialog box, 128–129, 273
Transform panel
adjusting units in, 84
positioning objects precisely from, 124–125
uses for, 131
transforming objects
about, 115
changing perspective with Free Transform, 125–126
distorting objects, 120–122
exploring further, 129
lesson files for, 110
making multiple transformations, 128–129
precision positioning of objects, 124–125
reflecting objects, 118–119
reviewing, 130–131
rotating objects, 119–120
scaling objects, 116–118
setting up ruler and guides for, 115
shearing objects, 123
using Free Distort effect, 127–128
transparency
adding to gradient, 8, 273–274
modifying stroke opacity, 350
printing a, 445
saving file with, 444
Transparency panel, 228
trapping, 439–440, 449
triangle icon
found on layer, 238
indicating global color, 171, 173
twisting objects, 121
2D artwork
applying as symbol to 3D object, 336
rotating 2D objects, 119–120
two-color illustrations, 421, 437–438, 449
type. *See also* styles; text; Type tool
adjusting type paths, 213
along paths, 205, 227–230

exploring other features, 232
flipping on path, 230
formatting, 214–220
importing text into artwork, 207–208
kinds of, 205
point, 205–206
point vs. area, 207
reshaping with envelope warp, 224–226
resizing objects, 212–213
reviewing, 233
special characters, 218–219
trapping, 440
using, 20
Type On A Path Options dialog box, 230
Type tool
creating point type with, 205
reaching Area Type tool via, 210
selecting, 205

U

undoing
points with Pen tool, 139
series of actions, 140
ungrouping objects, 67
units
adjusting in Transform panel, 84
changing ruler's, 83
entering inches in Rectangle dialog box, 13
unlinking harmonizing colors, 180
updating symbols, 380, 389
user interface. *See* artboards; workspaces

V

vector effects, 322
vector graphics
bitmap vs., 104, 395–396
converting text to, 232
painting with Live Paint, 194–197
rasterizing, 449
viewing
artwork, 42–43
hidden appearance attributes, 353
Kuler themes, 184
layers, 242–244, 255
measurement labels when zooming, 111
text in outline mode, 117

views
commands for, 43
creating custom, 42
options for displaying documents, 42–43
visibility
adjusting Illustrator layers in InDesign for, 413
eye icon and layer, 236, 242
turning on for layers, 189

W

Warp Options dialog box, 121, 225, 329
warping
banner logo with Warp effect, 329–333
text, 22
type with envelope warp, 224–226
Welcome Screen, 28–29
width values, 86
Windows commands in text, 1
Word. *See* Microsoft Word
workspaces
about, 27
Control panel elements, 35–36
deleting saved, 42
elements of, 31
exploring, 56
improvements to, 6
lesson files, 28–29
resetting and saving, 41–42
reviewing, 57–58
Tools panel and, 31–34
working with panels in, 36–40
wrapping text, 206, 227

X

X axis, 333

Y

Y axis, 333, 345

Z

Z axis, 333, 345
zero point for ruler, 115
Zoom tool, 43, 44–45
zooming
controlling size of shape by, 93
viewing measurement labels when, 111

Production Notes

The *Adobe Illustrator CS4 Classroom in a Book* was created electronically using Adobe InDesign CS3. Art was produced using Adobe InDesign, Adobe Illustrator, and Adobe Photoshop. The Myriad Pro and Warnock Pro OpenType families of typefaces were used throughout this book.

References to company names in the lessons are for demonstration purposes only and are not intended to refer to any actual organization or person.

Images

Photographic images and illustrations are intended for use with the tutorials.
Images provided by istockphoto.com: Lesson 6.
Images provided by Comstock: Lesson 14.
Image provided by Clipart.com: Lesson 2 (French fries).

Typefaces used

Adobe Myriad Pro and Adobe Warnock Pro are used throughout the lessons. For more information about OpenType and Adobe fonts, visit www.adobe.com/type/opentype/.

Team credits

The following individuals contributed to the development of this edition of the *Adobe Illustrator CS4 Classroom in a Book*:

Project Manager: Wyndham Wood
Developmental Editor: Brian Wood
Production Editor: Brian Wood
Technical Editor: Jeff Hannibal
Compositor: Brian Wood
Copyeditor: Techprose
Proofreader: Techprose
Indexer: Rebecca Plunkett
Cover design: Eddie Yuen
Interior design: Mimi Heft

Contributors

Brian Wood   An Adobe Certified Instructor in Illustrator, Brian is the author of Illustrator and InDesign training books, as well as Acrobat, InDesign, and Illustrator online video training titles. As Co-Owner and Director of Training at eVolve Computer Graphics Training Inc., an Adobe Authorized Training Center, he has provided in-person and online training to dozens of companies in a variety of industries. Brian speaks regularly at national conferences, including The Creative Suite Conference, The InDesign Conference, The Web Design Conference, and other industry events. He is also the featured speaker of the "Getting Started with Dreamweaver and CSS" national seminar tour, as well as the "CSS Master Class" tour. To learn more, visit www.evolvelive.com

Wyndham Wood   In 2002, Wyndham joined Brian to use her 10+ years of marketing and business experience to launch eVolve Computer Graphics Training Inc., an Adobe Authorized Training Center that began as a freelance consulting/training venture. The business has grown exponentially since those early days, and now provides in-person as well as custom online training to clients nationwide. In addition to helping to write and edit training books, Wyndham has written articles and white papers that have appeared in various industry magazines and publications.

Many thanks to sibyl.com for their creative lesson designs, Jeff Hannibal of Coherent Interactive for his well-honed eye as an editor and tester, TechProse for their editing services, and Rebecca Plunkett for her indexing prowess.